'HAMLET' AND WORLD CINEMA

'Hamlet' and World Cinema reveals a rich history of cinematic production extending around the globe. Making a case for *Hamlet* as the world's most frequently filmed text, and using specially commissioned interviews with cast, directors and screenwriters, it discusses films from Africa, Asia, Europe, Latin America and the Middle East. The book argues that the play has been taken up by filmmakers worldwide to allegorize the energies, instabilities, traumas and expectations that have defined the twentieth and twenty-first centuries. In so doing, it rejects the Anglophone focus which has dominated criticism up to now and explores instead the multiple constituencies that have claimed Shakespeare's most celebrated work as their own. *'Hamlet' and World Cinema* uncovers a vital part of the adaptation story. This book facilitates a fresh understanding of Shakespeare's cinematic significance and newly highlights *Hamlet*'s political and aesthetic instrumentality in a vast range of local and global contexts.

MARK THORNTON BURNETT is Professor of Renaissance Studies at Queen's University Belfast and Director of the Sir Kenneth Branagh Archive. He is the author of *Masters and Servants in English Renaissance Drama and Culture* (1997), *Constructing 'Monsters' in Shakespearean Drama and Early Modern Culture* (2002), *Filming Shakespeare in the Global Marketplace* (2007; 2nd edn 2012) and *Shakespeare and World Cinema* (Cambridge University Press, 2013). His co-edited publications include *Shakespeare, Film, Fin de Siècle* (2000), *Screening Shakespeare in the Twenty-First Century* (2006) and *Filming and Performing Renaissance History* (2011).

'HAMLET' AND WORLD CINEMA

MARK THORNTON BURNETT

Queen's University Belfast

 CAMBRIDGE
UNIVERSITY PRESS

CAMBRIDGE
UNIVERSITY PRESS

University Printing House, Cambridge CB2 8BS, United Kingdom

One Liberty Plaza, 20th Floor, New York, NY 10006, USA

477 Williamstown Road, Port Melbourne, VIC 3207, Australia

314–321, 3rd Floor, Plot 3, Splendor Forum, Jasola District Centre,
New Delhi – 110025, India

79 Anson Road, #06–04/06, Singapore 079906

Cambridge University Press is part of the University of Cambridge.

It furthers the University's mission by disseminating knowledge in the pursuit of
education, learning, and research at the highest international levels of excellence.

www.cambridge.org
Information on this title: www.cambridge.org/9781107135505
DOI: 10.1017/9781316471708

First published 2019

Printed in the United Kingdom by TJ International Ltd. Padstow Cornwall

A catalogue record for this publication is available from the British Library.

Library of Congress Cataloging-in-Publication Data
NAMES: Burnett, Mark Thornton, author.
TITLE: 'Hamlet' and world cinema / Mark Thornton Burnett.
DESCRIPTION: Cambridge, United Kingdom ; New York, NY : Cambridge University Press,
2019. | Includes bibliographical references, filmography, and index.
IDENTIFIERS: LCCN 2019005970 | ISBN 9781107135505 (hardback : alk. paper)
SUBJECTS: LCSH: Shakespeare, William, 1564–1616. Hamlet – Film adaptations. | English
drama (Tragedy) – Film adaptations. | Film adaptations – History and criticism.
CLASSIFICATION: LCC PR2807 .B87 2019 | DDC 822.3/3–dc23
LC record available at https://lccn.loc.gov/2019005970

ISBN 978-1-107-13550-5 Hardback

To Henry John Burnett and Louis Thornton Burnett

Contents

Figures

Acknowledgements

I owe primary thanks to the institutions that have funded this research. The Folger Shakespeare Library awarded me a short-term fellowship during which this project was developed, and Queen's University Belfast granted me a semester of study leave which enabled its completion. Queen's University has been equally enabling in the form of grants from the Publications Fund and the Research and Travel Fund. The British Academy, the Arts and Humanities Research Council and the University of London funded me to organize a *Hamlet* screening/interview event, 'Figuring Commonality', that formed part of the national 'Being Human' festival of the humanities, and the British Council and the Royal Irish Academy funded public engagement events, talks and workshops connected with this book.

At Queen's, I have been tremendously fortunate in having three Shakespearean colleagues, Edel Lamb, Richard Schoch and, as World Leading Researcher, Richard Dutton. They have each been generous in friendship, support and insight. I am also fortunate to have working with me Rosa María García Periago and Thea Buckley on their respective funded projects, 'Shakespeare and Indian Cinematic Traditions' (EC/ Marie Curie) and 'South Indian Shakespeares' (Leverhulme Early Career). The Renaissance-Shakespeare community at Queen's has made the university an invigorating place to work, and here I thank Claude Fretz, Ilana Gilovich, Mia Hewitt, Sonja Kleij, Samantha Lin, Cynthia Martin, Romano Mullin, Kevin Murray and Matt Williamson. Other colleagues at Queen's have supported this project with conversation, good cheer and advice: they include Sian Barber, Muhammed Basheer, Maaz Bilal, Fran Brearton, Marilina Cesario, Xiwu Han, Debbie Lisle, Des O'Rawe, Andrew Pepper, Daniel Sanjiv Roberts, Deepthi Sebastian, Yo Tomita, Isabel Torres and Ian Woodfield.

Further afield, Shakespeareans and non-Shakespeareans far and wide have been encouraging, resourceful and lent a kindly ear, so thank you to:

Salar Abdolmohamadian, Susan Anderson, David Baker, Martin Banham, Shani Bans, Simon Russell Beale, Marilese Rezende Bertin, Birgit Beumers, Victoria Bladen, Jerry Brotton, Richard Burt, Maurizio Calbi, Clara Calvo, Tom Cartelli, Sheila Cavanagh, Paromita Chakravarti, Koel Chatterjee, Danielle Clarke, Louisa Costelloe, Katharine Craik, Melissa Croteau, Susan Crowl, Manishita Daas, Esha Niyogi De, Jerome de Groot, Andrew Dickson, José A. Pérez Díez, Michael Dobson, Maura Dutton, Paul Edmondson, Jacek Fabiszak, Ewan Fernie, Alison Findlay, Michael Friedman, Rajmohan Gandhi, Annosheh Ghaderi, Stephen Greenblatt, Jane Grogan, Anthony Guneratne, Andrew Hadfield, Nigel Harkness, Diana Henderson, Katherine Hennessey, Jean Howard, Russell Jackson, Randall Johnson, Alexa Alice Joubin, Dennis Kennedy, Diarmuid Kennedy, Bill Kerwin, Peter Kirwan, Tina Krontiris, Doug Lanier, Carola Lentz, Jill L. Levenson, Ruru Li, Patrick Lonergan, Naomi McAreavey, Laura McCaughan, Liz McBain, Emer McHugh, Gordon McMullan, Pauline McNamara, Maryam Moosavi Majd, Silke Meyer, Alfredo Michel Modenessi, Taarini Mookherjee, Lucy Munro, Andy Murphy, Dan North, Robert Ormsby, Laurie E. Osborne, Shekufeh Owlia, Shormishtha Panja, Jesús Tronch Pérez, Elizabeth Ramos, Deana Rankin, Anne Sophie Refskou, Tom Rice, Katherine Rowe, Minami Ryuta, Lorrie Santos, David Schalkwyk, Edel Semple, Marcel Vieira Barreto Silva, Surjit Singh, Peter Smith, Robert Stam, Adrian Streete, Ayanna Thompson, C. Claire Thomson, Poonam Trivedi, Rajiva Verma, Elsie Walker, Ana Laura Magis Weinberg, R. S. White, Deirdre Wildy, Claire Withers and Marion Wynne-Davies. For extraordinarily helpful and stimulating conversations and courtesies, I would like to mention Pascale Aebischer, N. P. Ashley, Samuel Crowl, James Gibbs, Peter Holland, Courtney Lehmann, Aimara da Cunha Resende, Stan Semerdjiev, Jyotsna Singh, the late Mariangela Tempera, and Ann Thompson.

My interest in *Hamlet* and world cinema has been nurtured and refined on the conference, festival and public engagement circuit. Different versions of some of these chapters have been delivered as discussions, papers or plenaries in Alexandria ('Shakespeare 400: Forever and a Day', Bibliotheca Alexandrina), Atlanta ('Shakespeare and Film Form', Shakespeare Association of America), Belfast ('Foreign Shakespeare: Twenty-Five Years On', British Shakespeare Association Conference, Queen's University Belfast, and 'Shakespeare: Here and Elsewhere', Linen Hall Library), Belgrade ('BELLS 90', International Conference of the English Department, Faculty of Philology, University of Belgrade), Dún Laoghaire ('Shakespeare: Here and Elsewhere', dlr LexIcon), Ferrara ('Shakespeare in Tatters: Referencing his Works on Film and Television'), Le Havre ('*Hamlet*: Shakespeare à l'Écran'), Leicester ('Shakespeare and Japan: A One-Day Conference'), London ('Indian Shakespeares on Screen', Asia House, and 'Shakespeare in Europe and the Americas', British Library), Manila ('Shakespeare, Traffics, Tropics', Asian Shakespeare Association), Maynooth ('Shakespeare 400 in Ireland Symposium'), Munich ('Money and Power: Shakespeare's Balance Sheets', Deutsche Shakespeare-Gesellschaft Conference), New Delhi (St Stephen's College), Princeton ('Ireland and Shakespeare Symposium'), Salvador ('*Festival Cinefuturo: IX Seminário Internacional de Cinema e Audiovisual*'), Tehran ('First International Conference in Iran on Shakespeare Studies') and Washington, DC (Folger Shakespeare Library). I am indebted to the audiences on those occasions for their informed attention, the organizers of the events at which I spoke, and the colleagues who invited me to address their staff and students. Notably, I am greatly obliged to N. P. Ashley, Maryam Beyad, Thea Buckley, Koel Chatterjee, Deborah Cartmell, Tobias Döring, Deborah Douglas, Heba El-Rafey, Charles Forsdick, Sarah Hatchuel, Katharine Hennessey, Judy Celine Ick, Marian Keyes, Courtney Lehmann, Beatrice Bi-qi Lei, Pauline McNamara, Stephen O'Neill, Varsha Panjwani, Gail Kern Paster, Ismail Salami, Sabine Schülting, Ismail Serageldin, Natasha Sofranac, Preti Taneja, Poonam Trivedi, the late Mariangela Tempera, Luciana Vasconcelos, Nathalie Vienne-Guerrin and Clair Wills. For the opportunity to speak in a different format ('Shakespeare and World Cinema', the Folger Shakespeare Library's 'Shakespeare Unlimited' podcast series), I would like to thank Gail Kern Paster.

This book has benefited hugely from the formative input of the world film community. The following cast members, directors and screenwriters were invaluable in that they both facilitated my research and agreed to be interviewed, offering wonderful insight into the filmmaking process: Ernest Abbequaye, Daniel Beretta, Vishal Bhardwaj, Herbert Fritsch, Sherwood Hu, Varuzh Karim-Masihi, Aki Kaurismäki, Mário Kuperman, Hugues Serge Limbvani, Kaf Malère, the late Kofi Middleton-Mends, Martin Owusu, V. K. Prakash, Mário Prata, Aleksandar Rajković, Mireia Ros, Martin Šulík, Angelos Theodoropoulos and Chenaktshang Dorje Tsering or Jangbu. Whether as administrators, archivists, creatives, custodians, festival organizers, journalists, lawyers, librarians, performers, producers and writers, related film industry professionals were accommodating in multiple ways, and they are: Tetteh Abbequaye, Devansh Agarwal, Ashwin B., Adrian Barci, Ulrika Bengts, Vanessa Berman, Jennifer Bertani, George Bolanis, Stephen Cavanagh, Liz Cooper, Cobbie de Graft, Kweku de Graft, Arijit Dutta, Tharik Faia, Lígia Farias, Minnie Ferrara, Marta Figueras, Lila Foster, Arun Francis, Jake Garriock, Katerina Georgiou, Manu Gomez, Jerry Hatfield, Lianne Hu, Eevi Kareinenn, Nicolas Klotz, Dimitris Koliodimos, Tatiana Korobeinik, Joe Kreczak, Claudio Leal, Ellénore Loehr, Dave McCall, Tom Magill, Aalaap Majgavkar, Tatevik Manoukyan, Nikhil Mehta, Alexandre Miyazato, Andrea Montgomery, Thomas Ostermeier, Lucie Pardubová, Mimi Plauché, Eugenio Poppo, Mila Rozanova, Hugo Salas, Hugo Santander, Kenneth Scicluna, Naoki Shinozaki, Zoran Sinobad, Matheus Sundfeld, Haije Tulokas, Miroslav Ulman and Peter Woditsch. As well as the Language Centre, Queen's University Belfast, colleagues, subtitlers and translators gave crucial assistance: Elisangela Franco, Mania Karim Masihi Gregorian, Viju Kurian, Noelle McCavana, Serena Parisi and Patricia Schiaffini. Inessa Adler provided me with expert translations of (and commentaries on) contemporary Russian materials, while Ivan Ewart oversaw some super-lative photography.

Early versions of parts of Chapter Seven appeared as 'Capital, Commodities, Cinema: Shakespeare and the Eastern European "Gypsy" Aesthetic', *Shakespeare Jahrbuch*, 150 (2014), pp. 146–60, a dry-run for parts of Chapter Four appeared as 'Re-reading Akira Kurosawa's *The Bad Sleep Well*, a Japanese Film Adaptation of *Hamlet*: Content, Genre and Context', *Shakespeare*, 9.4 (2013), pp. 404–17, and iterations of parts of Chapters Four and Six appeared in 'New Directions: *Hamlet*, Cinema, the World', in Ann Thompson, ed., *'Hamlet': A Critical Reader* (London and New York: Bloomsbury, 2016), pp. 135–60. I am grateful to Bloomsbury Publishing, the Deutsche Shakespeare-Gesellschaft and Routledge for permission to reproduce some of that material.

At Cambridge University Press, I am indebted to Sarah Stanton, who originally contracted this project, and commissioning editor Emily Hockley and editorial assistants Tim Mason and Carrie Parkinson who have been patient, facilitative and supportive. I am also obliged to three anonymous readers who provided extremely insightful recommendations, observations and suggestions.

Last, but by no means least, I thank Louis Thornton Burnett and Henry John Burnett who have generously forgone football time and metalwork time to help Daddy get his book done. Their love for life has reminded me of what is properly important. For Ramona Wray there are the most heartfelt thanks: she provided illuminating reflections on, and understanding of, how the manuscript might be improved: without her, this book would never have seen the light of day.

A Note on Texts and Titles

The edition of the play used for quotation is the Arden *Hamlet*, revised edition, edited by Ann Thompson and Neil Taylor (London and New York: Bloomsbury, 2016). The play exists, of course, in three versions (Q1, Q2 and F), and, where appropriate, I have distinguished between them.

How film titles are referred to is a notoriously inconsistent business. For first citations, I have tended to use the non-English title followed by the English translation provided for international distribution. In subsequent references, I use the non-English title alone. There are some world cinema *Hamlet* titles that are better known by their English-language title; in these instances, there is no necessity for translation. Other films, possibly because they never received international distribution, are referred to by a title in the original language. There is inevitably a certain amount of titular variation in response to local contexts and conventions.

Introduction

In *Tardid/Doubt* (dir. Varuzh Karim-Masihi, 2009), a stylish and innovative Iranian film adaptation of *Hamlet*, 'To be, or not to be' is allusively referenced. In an archivist's cluttered and grimy basement office, the camera zooms in on a framed quotation in Farsi hanging on the walls, but, rather than the words of the Qur'an, as might be expected, it is the opening lines of Shakespeare's most famous soliloquy that are visualized. The power and reach of the lines were brought home to me on a blustery autumnal day in 2014 as I made plans to interview *Tardid*'s director and speak at the inaugural 'First International Conference on Shakespeare in Iran'. In search of an elusive visa, and in the context of the closure of the Iranian Embassy in London, I presented myself at the Iranian Embassy in Dublin. Once beyond the forbidding gates, the official in charge leaned in towards the glass separating us and inquired rather fiercely as to the purpose of my visit. Eager to ingratiate myself, I explained that I was keen to speak at the first Shakespeare conference in Iran. The official seemed uncomprehending, and a barrage of unpromising questions followed. At no point did I mention *Hamlet*. But, after ten minutes back and forth, he beckoned me closer and, with a half-smile playing around his lips, whispered, 'To be, or not to be', before whipping away my passport for approval. Left alone, I wondered if he knew of the Qur'an-like soliloquy in *Tardid* or perhaps was aware of the long-standing traditions of translation and performance of Shakespeare in the Middle East. Whichever way, the brief moment of connection was typical of the often humbling encounters that have informed my thinking about *Hamlet*'s cinematic kudos and power in the world.

This book makes a case for *Hamlet* as the world's most frequently filmed text and reveals a rich and diverse history of cinematic production reaching across the globe. It explores adaptations of Shakespeare's most celebrated play outside of the UK/US screen axis, moving between a range of periods from the 1930s to the present day. Case-studies are angled towards illuminating some of the earliest German and Italian adaptations and extend to the most recent explosion of Indian screen interpretations. This means that the book addresses cinema produced in a multiplicity of languages, including Danish, Greek, Japanese, Malayalam, Romani, Tibetan and Turkish. In terms of numbers, *'Hamlet' and World Cinema* introduces thirty adaptations not generally recognized in order to identify the extent to which Shakespeare's play functions as a creative hub and transnational touchstone. Focusing on non-Anglophone registers, the approach prioritizes several genres of adaptation, including crime drama, urban thriller, corporate parody, comic fantasy and martial arts epic. In this way, works generated from the film industries of Africa, Asia, Central, Eastern and Western Europe, Latin America and the Middle East are uncovered and the relationship between creative appropriation and economic-industrial praxis is contextualized. With such a wide canvas, a gamut of categories and classifications comes quickly into view – state-sponsored product, commemorative contribution, censor-sensitive grass-roots intervention, big-budget cinematic statement, commercial and non-commercial creation, low-budget art-work, community initiative, professional undertaking, *avant-garde* reflection and amateur experiment. Among the multifarious *Hamlet* cinematic adaptations there are degrees of visibility (most of the examples in this book have not been critically examined previously) and accessibility (several films discussed are no longer extant). Investigating the place of the play in the cinemas of over twenty nation-states, I argue that world cinema adaptations of *Hamlet* are consistently characterized by the ingenious identification of alternative habitats for Shakespeare's work. Wherever it is transposed – to a working *favela* or a village of mud huts, a western ranch or a ruined Islamic cinema, a gypsy encampment or the Himalayan mountains, a samurai residence or a South Asian temple complex, a luxurious French *chateau* or a fantasy Italianate court – *Hamlet* is made to speak in and to a variety of locales. Exposed to *Hamlet* in world cinema, audiences find ratified the play's manoeuvrability – its capacity for commenting on local situations and ideologies that run along asymmetrical lines. If there is huge generic and regional scope in the sample, there are also marked differences in meaning and import, with adaptations taking up sometimes conflictual positions in terms of political vision and responsiveness. Where there is consistency is in the ways in which *Hamlet* has been taken up by filmmakers worldwide in order to allegorize the energies, instabilities, traumas and expectations that have defined the twentieth and twenty-first centuries. By refusing the unidirectional flow that invariably travels from the 'west' and to the 'rest', this study reveals the multiple constituencies that have claimed the play as their own, reinstating a vital and as yet unexplored part of the *Hamlet* story.

The book emerges from a critical context that has consistently prioritized *Hamlet* as an object of scrutiny. The play is among the small number of Shakespeare's works that merit a monograph in their own right. Some recent examples include Stephen Greenblatt, *Hamlet in Purgatory* (2001), Margreta de Grazia, *'Hamlet' Without Hamlet* (2007), Andrew Cutrofello, *All for Nothing: Hamlet's Negativity* (2014), William F. Zak, *Hamlet's Problematic Revenge: Forging a Royal Mandate* (2015), András Kiséry, *Hamlet's Moment: Drama and Political Knowledge in Early Modern England* (2016), Gabriel Josipovici, *Hamlet: Fold on Fold* (2016) and Rhodri Lewis, *Hamlet and the Vision of Darkness* (2017).[1] Insightful and sophisticating, these studies elucidate the play by returning it to its early modern contexts but, via such a critical focus, bypass the play's afterlives or its cinematic manifestations. The emphasis on, variously, the play's religious intertexts, its investment in humanist traditions of learning, its structural felicities, its use of political knowledge as cultural capital, its tragic design, its concern with property and territory, its absorption in the workings of government, and its philosophical disenchantment means that *Hamlet* is situated firmly inside European contexts, with its being taken up to affirm particular linguistic and cultural circuits of interpretation. In an alternative camp, several works have solely addressed *Hamlet*'s posthumous histories. Important investigations into *Hamlet* on film and in performance include Anthony B. Dawson, *Shakespeare in Performance: 'Hamlet'* (1995), Mary Z. Maher, *Modern Hamlets and Their Soliloquies* (2003), Tony Howard, *Women as Hamlet: Performance and Interpretation in Theatre, Film and Fiction* (2007) and David Bevington, *'Murder Most Foul': 'Hamlet' Through the Ages* (2011), stimulating and influential works that position the play in relation to a number of later reception contexts.[2] But the difficulty with these studies is that *Hamlet*'s screen appearances outside of the UK/US axis receive scant mention, an omission which inevitably compromises the books' conclusions about *Hamlet*'s circulation and its wider significances. Apart from isolated analyses of the Japanese *The Bad Sleep Well* (dir. Akira Kurosawa, 1960) and the Russian *Gamlet* (dir. Grigori Kozintsev, 1964), and, to a lesser extent, the Chinese *The Banquet* (dir. Xiaogang Feng, 2006) and the Indian *Haider* (dir. Vishal Bhardwaj, 2014), little attempt has been made to address how pervasively the play has been taken up by filmmakers worldwide. Instead, much ink has been spilled on variations on a familiar quartet of directors

(Laurence Olivier, Franco Zeffirelli, Kenneth Branagh and Michael Almereyda) and their English language *Hamlet* adaptations, as a clutch of older and recent studies attest.[3] Despite the fact that, as Samuel Crowl acknowledges, 'the world of *Hamlet* on film' is 'the richest for any of Shakespeare's plays', non-Anglophone traditions of film interpretation tend to be represented by Kozintsev and/or Kurosawa only, with these two directors standing in for a plethora of other examples.[4] The result is not only a skewed cinematic canon but, more fundamentally, a failure to grasp the crucial importance accorded Shakespeare's most celebrated hero in the international imaginary. By charting the play's presence in more extensive cultural and linguistic registers, the majority of which are non-Anglophone, this book adjusts conventional axes of argument and provides new materials for discussion and debate. Where David Bevington has argued that the play is a paradigm for 'the English-speaking world', *'Hamlet' and World Cinema* argues for a fresh awareness of Shakespeare's play's global malleability and transformative energies.[5]

In so doing, *'Hamlet' and World Cinema* chimes with current orientations in Shakespeare studies. In recent years, 'global Shakespeares' have assumed a prominent place, with attention increasingly focused on Shakespeare's global afterlives. Conference programming, academic posts and book series are signs of the health of a more internationally angled playwright, while college and university courses are featuring in greater numbers illustrations of the ways in which Shakespeare's works are translated across different nations, cultures and media. Over the course of 2012, the Olympic year, a host of festivals, exhibitions and events centred on Shakespeare as a dramatist newly alive in different languages and contexts, as the 'Globe to Globe' season and the 'World Shakespeare Festival' abundantly demonstrated. When, in 2016, attention again turned to Shakespeare to celebrate the four-hundredth anniversary of his death, an even greater volume of world-facing activities was launched. Emphasis lay firmly on the extent to which Shakespeare was a vital and relevant instrument, speaking to a range of constituencies (to women in Arabic and Indian contexts, for instance, as in the British Council 'Shakespeare Lives' initiative) and resonating with shifts in convention, ideology and viewpoint; as Sonia Massai writes, reflecting on that celebratory year, 'Shakespeare is no longer anchored to ideals of Englishness understood as a combination of blood, land and language'.[6] The academic expression of this change in perspective is reflected in essay collections and volumes that push at existing boundaries of knowledge and entertain new performance and representational scenarios. Hence, studies of the 2012 'Globe to Globe' season demonstrate the appeal of a globally inflected Shakespeare while, at the same time, exploring cultural programming practices and officially sanctioned expressions of national identity.[7] The 2016 festivities were similarly generative, evidencing the historical global reach of adaptations of Shakespeare and the place of the plays in Africa, China, India and elsewhere. Inasmuch as these studies examine potential areas of common understanding, and promote intercultural dialogue for the purposes of the commemorative occasion, they also shine a light on distinctive constructions of Shakespeare in different parts of the world, contested legacies of engagement and particularized reception modalities.[8] Such has been their effect that the conjunction of 'Shakespeare' and 'world' is now a familiar one: Shakespeare is becoming indivisible from his 'world' manifestations, these two terms being bracketed together in recent discussions as an indication of a paradigm shift.[9] While the focus in this methodological development has generally been on theatrical performance, cinema is also being looked at anew. Critic Greg Colón Semenza describes 'world cinema' as 'the next, if not the final, frontier for Shakespeare on film scholarship', and, in my own work, I have attempted to push parameters, and interrogate canons, by reimagining the field.[10]

Inside cultural practices centred on Shakespeare as a global icon, and against the backdrop of worldwide celebrations and commemorative events, the pre-eminence accorded *Hamlet* is striking. Over the course of 2014–2016, a Shakespeare's Globe *Hamlet* production toured the world, each country finding in the production local resonances.[11] Meantime, *Hamlet*, as it signifies in particular regions and nation-states, and as a play that carries with it distinctive traditions of appropriation, has continued to establish itself as a key object of investigation.[12] And, slowly but surely, the cinematic landscape is following suit, a smaller number of salutary and invigorating studies testifying to a recognition that the play's global screen manifestations are all-important.[13] To be sure, the global complexions of Shakespearean film and theatrical performance are more widely accessible than ever before. And a resource such as the 'Global Shakespeares' website, which features extracts of key examples, continues to change thinking, teaching and interpretation.[14]

'Hamlet' and World Cinema is a contribution to this ongoing discussion as well as to *Hamlet* studies. Crucially, 'adaptation' is understood throughout this study as a film which either translates *Hamlet* directly or models its narrative closely, meaning that the works examined here are characterized by intricate, allusive and energizing relations between cinematic idiom and 'source'. Fredric Jameson sees the process as inherently competitive,

suggesting that 'individual works, either as external adaptations or as internal echo chambers of the various media, be grasped as allegories of . . . never-ending and unresolvable struggles for primacy'.[15] It is as a two-way struggle, with points of contestation and complementarity in between, that I seek to explain how the play and a film adaptation reinforce and enlighten each other. As part of that push-and-pull, additional interpretive communities are created and new texts forged out of old. The emergence of new works of art has been a focus for several commentators. Julie Sanders, for example, defines adaptation as a 'transposition' that 'take[s] a text . . . and deliver[s] it' to 'new . . . audiences', while Colin MacCabe contends that the films that emerge from the multiple transactions that inform the adaptive process are of 'real value'.[16] Adaptations, of course, are not free-floating. Further informing this book's understanding of adaptation is the notion that any engagement with the ways in which *Hamlet* signifies in world cinematic cultures must be historically situated. 'Media shift and change over time', writes Daniel Fischlin, adding, 'adaptation . . . shapeshift[s] across a wide continuum [of] . . . contexts, voicings, histories'.[17] Absorbing this caveat into the book's approach, I situate each adaptation in terms of a nexus of factors, including material crises, population shifts, regime change, regional self-assertion, political protest and the status of national film industries.

The method whereby each adaptation is appreciated is therefore multi-layered. Approaching examples on their own terms, *'Hamlet' and World Cinema* closely situates the work of art at a micro-level, using local traditions (such as translation, music, religious mythology and theatrical performance) to point up the films' indigenous creativity. In this, there is often aesthetic delight, and it is for this reason that individual chapters are oriented towards unpacking the adaptations' formal features, finding in *mise-en-scène*, sound and style a key with which to unlock location-specific visions and constructions. Such an approach does not necessarily prioritize the 'original'; as Maurizio Calbi notes, adaptations 'need to be judged . . . as . . . critical response[s] to Shakespeare's play, and not on the basis of . . . faithfulness to the language of the "original"'.[18] Indeed, as the majority of the examples discussed in this book suggest, it is the ways in which *Hamlet* is transposed into other languages, or non-Anglophone languages are utilized, that becomes the focal point. For example, in *Hamlet* (dir. Stephen Cavanagh, 2005), Irish is reserved for the 'To be, or not to be' soliloquy, a potent choice given the film's Londonderry/Derry setting and interrogative engagement with Northern Irish politics. *Hamlet* (dir. Alexander Fodor, 2007) also makes an arresting language decision.

The '"travelling troupe"' comprises 'classically trained, fierce-looking, German-speaking actors', the idea being that audiences will be liberated from an '"addiction" to standardized versions of Shakespeare' and so stimulated by '"foreign Shakespeare"' that the '"original"' appears less powerful and spellbinding.[19] The notion of how language figures, and what role language plays, are central to definitions of 'world cinema'. Definitions tend to circulate around the question – if not problem – of the English language, with most discussions of 'world cinema' arguing for the need, in Shekhar Deshpande and Meta Mazaj's words, to 'displace . . . Hollywood as a dominant player': 'Hollywood cannot be equated to world cinema despite its own claims', they observe.[20] This study enlists a working application of 'world cinema', arguing that, in the context of the general neglect of non-Anglophone *Hamlet* adaptations, an account that eschews the domination of Hollywood – and the English language – is a political obligation. This is not to suggest that the terminology of world cinema is always unproblematic, or that a geographical template is sufficient in itself. Any spatial understanding of *Hamlet* afterlives must recognize the fact that its subjects (i.e. the film adaptations) do not uniformly emerge across the globe. Rather, the numbers of adaptations discovered in any one geographical site are intricately linked to historical processes of education, colonialism and empire. In this sense, this book works with an additional definition of 'world cinema' – what has recently been termed the 'latitudinal' approach. According to Rob Stone, Paul Cooke, Stephanie Dennison and Alex Marlow-Mann, as much as it is incumbent on us to take full account of national and regional diversity, we also need to recognize and integrate 'theoretical, industrial, thematic, aesthetic, technological and commercial imperatives and parameters'.[21] Accordingly, *'Hamlet' and World Cinema* pursues a mixed methodology, combining close readings of the films' adaptive procedures with an informed sense of issues around audience, reception and distribution as well as reflections on production praxes.

Satirist Max Beerbohm famously remarked that 'Hamlet is a hoop through which every very eminent actor must, sooner or later, jump'.[22] A final aspect of the book's approach is its use of interviews with directors, screenwriters and cast attracted to the play's aura as a measure of quality and achievement. The acknowledgements to this book spell out the detail, but suffice it to say here that the method integrates actors such as Kofi Middleton-Mends (Hamlet in the Ghanaian *Hamile: The Tongo 'Hamlet'* [dir. Terry Bishop, 1965]), directors such as Martin Šulík (the Slovakian and shantytown-set *Cigán/Gypsy* [2011]) and screenwriters such as

Chenaktshang Dorje Tsering or Jangbu (a Tibetan poet who collaborated on the screenplay for a 2006 Chinese adaptation, *Prince of the Himalayas*). These interviews have been conducted face-to-face and *in situ* where possible, the priority being to highlight original voices as an essential part of the warp and the weft of the imaginative undertaking. The deployment of witnesses allows us to identify not only the local but also the often personal circumstances surrounding the fascination of the play, permits a more nuanced sense of how *Hamlet* operates as a text associated with 'high culture' and imported values, provides us with content that illuminates films as processes rather than as finished products, and reminds us of the ways in which Shakespeare's drama possesses a critical and cultural currency. In the light of the interviews, one also gains a fuller appreciation of the cinematic opportunities the play presents to artists and practitioners. Several directors emerge as auteur figures: they include, for example, the Greek Angelos Theodoropoulos, who, in *Ithele Na Ginei Vasilias/He Wanted to Become King* (1967), starred, directed and wrote music, financing through his own production company, and the Italian Carmelo Bene, who, in *Un Amleto di Meno/One Hamlet Less* (1973), assumed an even greater number of roles, directing, writing, acting, designing, selecting music and creating costumes. Yet, however much auteurship enables, it simultaneously limits, illuminating gaps, fissures and constraints. Most obviously, where world Shakespearean cinematic direction is concerned, auteurship tends to be a male preserve. In interview, Mireia Ros, the only female director to have helmed a long feature world cinema *Hamlet* (the Spanish adaptation, *El Triunfo/The Triumph* [2006]), speaks of the challenge – as well as directing, writing and contributing to the score – of adapting a male-authored play that has already been mediated in a male-authored novel. 'I did try to introduce a woman's point of view', she notes, 'by changing the method of narration, inventing new situations, writing some of the songs and playing up the emotive rather than the physical'.[23] Here Ros registers, via her flagging of a purposeful rewriting of source and script, the difficulties involved in confronting gendered accretions and constructions of Shakespearean authority, perhaps finding in representations of historical subjects and places options for thinking through her own position – and exceptionalism – as a cinematic creative. As the example of *El Triunfo* may suggest, adapting *Hamlet* gives access to an eloquence not always permitted to practitioners as speaking subjects and, in conditions of seeming impossibility, allows for representational possibility. Cinematic *Hamlet* adaptations matter globally because pertinent conversations cannot always be held publicly, and, as a result, many of the film examples discussed in this book refract the extent to which in particular nation-states and communities the play is mediated in the belief that the word and the image can serve an interventionist, transformative purpose. Chapters attend, therefore, to how cultures of censorship impact on the production of a *Hamlet* film and explore the workings of individual modalities of dissemination inside often repressive state machines. The Brazilian *O Jogo da Vida e da Morte/A Game of Life and Death* (dir. Mário Kuperman, 1971) is a singular instance of an adaptation that exploits the classic mandate of *Hamlet* to skirt the restricting dictates of a military government. Placing *Hamlet* on screen in some parts of the world, then, is to subscribe to a self-protecting semiotics; it is to recognize a vulnerability to institutional operations while taking advantage of the opportunity, through Shakespeare, to pass critical contemporary judgement; and it is to endorse the affective functions of adaptation in the same moment as expressing a civic need for questioning, comment and argument.

Hamlet, in the case-studies that this book presents, is consistently differently inflected: if, for one filmmaker, the play intrigues because of its association with past history, for another it is the drama's present purchase that appeals. Often, individual interpretations clash and conflict – if one group of representations approves *Hamlet*'s free-floating cultural pedigree, an alternative group responds to the play's association with capital and the market. What is more, differences in emphasis and orientation slip and slide according to location. Taking on board a further definition of world cinema (the 'longitudinal' approach that embraces the determining role of 'geographical, national, regional, transnational and global' factors), *'Hamlet' and World Cinema* organizes its material inside seven regional and/or national configurations – Western Europe, Africa, Brazil, Asia (China and Japan), India, the Middle East (Iran and Turkey), Russia and Central and Eastern Europe.[24] This arrangement allows for a conceptual focus on the key domains of filmic activity, crucially without privileging rigid notions of 'the regional' or 'the national'. At the core of the book's 'longitudinal' approach is a recognition of the provisional and constructed nature of location identifiers: 'Middle East', for example, is a western term discursively created in the crucible of colonialism and imperialism.[25] As several commentators have argued, however, notwithstanding their histories, some identifiers are interpretively enabling. Pertinent is Shohini Chaudhuri's observation that 'Middle East' helps to designate territories that possess 'historical and cultural commonalities that validate cross-cultural comparisons'.[26]

If there is elasticity in how regional and/or national categories are conceptualized, there is flexibility in terms of content. Some chapter case-studies consider four to eleven primary examples (invariably indicative of well-established Shakespearean traditions), while others concentrate on just two isolated examples (suggestive of contingency and discontinuity). Different foci are reflective of the fact that, in some parts of the world (such as Western Europe), *Hamlet* is reproduced across a longer historical era and in substantial numbers; in contradistinction, in other environments (such as in Brazil), it is possible to identify the phenomenon of a small number of films released within a single year. By letting extant material dictate its shape, *'Hamlet' and World Cinema* allows for a series of creative and open encounters. The culminating effect of the study is to underscore the shifting nature of borders, nations and even regions across time. For example, in the discussion of *Hamile*, the 1965 African adaptation, the assertion of Ghana's national identity in the wake of independence is read as part of the film's *zeitgeist*; similarly, *Karmayogi* (dir. V. K. Prakash, 2012), a South Indian adaptation, summons a long-standing dialogue about the extent of Kerala's influence and possessions within the larger Indian land-mass. *Hamlet*, in these instances, becomes a reflection of territorial instabil-ity *and* a means to intervene in territorial dispute. In the absence of definitive boundaries, I have opted for a self-conscious approach. Mirroring the play's own location in history, chapters are organized so as to mime a typically Renaissance trajectory, a circumnavigation beginning and ending with Europe. The book, then, imitates a journey that brought the world into view in an unprecedented way, inaugurating, for better and worse, processes of globalization that persist into the present day. There is a disciplinary dimension, too. As film scholars have argued, assessing world cinema involves mapping of various kinds. Writing on the need for an 'atlas of world cinema', Dudley Andrew proposes understanding the field not only in terms of topographies but also demographics, orientation and language. Such a method necessitates identifying 'specific "cinema sites"' and applying to them a mixture of methods – in Andrew's reading, 'co-ordinates for navigating'.[27] Or, to put the point in another way, as does Fredric Jameson in a study of cinema and space in the world system, 'cognitive mapping', as much as it involves locations, is a 'retrospective and analytical instrument' that brings 'critical and historical' methods into play so as to spotlight 'new geotopical cartographies'.[28] Working with distinctive places enables a consideration of politics and histories, and deploying the map allows for the local conditions underpinning a particular film product to move into visibility. Contextualized within a world atlas, cinematic *Hamlet* adaptations allow for national-regional readings at the same time as they invite us to take up theoretical challenges and possibilities.

Beginning with Western Europe, Chapter 1, '*Hamlet*, Cinema and the Histories of Western Europe', contends that cinematic adaptations of *Hamlet* testify to the historicized ways in which Western Europe has represented and continues to represent itself. The play is first deployed both as a means of democratization and as a conduit for unease. In the immediate post-war period, the challenge facing many European nations was how to deal with the legacies of conflict, with Italian and German adaptations, *Io, Amleto/I, Hamlet* (dir. Georgio Simonelli, 1952) and *Der Rest ist Schweigen/The Rest Is Silence* (dir. Helmut Käutner, 1959), working as crucial contributors to larger reckoning processes. A later grouping of Finnish, French, Greek and Italian adaptations – *Ophélia* (dir. Claude Chabrol, 1963), *Ithele Na Ginei Vasilias/He Wanted to Become King* (dir. Angelos Theodoropoulos, 1967), *Quella Sporca Storia nel West/Johnny Hamlet* (dir. Enzo G. Castellari, 1968), *Dans la Poussière de la Soleil/In the Dust of the Sun* (dir. Richard Balducci, 1971), *Un Amleto di Meno/One Hamlet Less* (dir. Carmelo Bene, 1973) and *Hamlet liikemaailmassa/Hamlet Goes Business* (dir. Aki Kaurismäki, 1987) – demonstrates anxieties about the nation-state in relation to its global neighbours. A final film grouping – the Danish *Festen/Celebration* (dir. Thomas Vinterberg, 1998), the Spanish *El Triunfo/The Triumph* (dir. Mireia Ros, 2006) and the German *Elf Onkel/Eleven Uncles* (dir. Herbert Fritsch, 2010) – clarifies how the post--war project of European integration collides with new developments arising from immigration, demographic realignment and increasingly networked European organizations. Cinematic *Hamlet* adaptations, then, take up ambivalent positions in relation to a European system that espouses unification and co-operation, and notable here is the prominence accorded a series of ambiguously coded Fortinbras figures.

Where Western Europe exhibits a substantial volume of Hamlet adaptations, Africa yields a smaller sample. Chapter 2, 'Thematizing Place: *Hamlet*, Cinema and Africa', reads *Hamile: The Tongo 'Hamlet'* (dir. Terry Bishop, 1965), from Ghana, and the Boyokani Company's *Hamlet* (dir. Hugues Serge Limbvani, 2007), from the Republic of Congo, as expressions of what has been termed 'Africanity', a repository of shared discourses, experiences and inheritances. As such, these two films thematize 'Africanity' through images either of a walled compound in which the action takes place or of a royal palace, a sepia-saturated elongated building whose steps, porch and yard become the arena on which *Hamlet*'s post-colonial significances are played out. A text stamped with colonial meanings and legacies, *Hamlet* is written over in films that affirm, in the first instance, the *élan* of a newly formed nation-state and, in the latter, ventilate African-centred questions about woman and the supernatural. Developing alternating concerns and ambitions, these adaptations intersect with the circumstances of their making: *Hamile* refracts the artistic and cultural development programme of the then Ghanaian president, while the Boyokani *Hamlet* suggests a pan-national ideology. Interestingly, both films use the languages of the colonial pasts (English and French), combining these with terms and expressions in, for example, *Dyula, Twi* and *Wolof* that bleed into, complement and contest the associations that gather about *Hamlet* as an educational and institutional import.

A single Shakespearean year – 1971 – anchors the discussion of Chapter 3 and the shift to Brazil's cinematic engagement with the play. '*Hamlet* and the Moment of Brazilian Cinema' focuses on two adaptations, *A Herança* (dir. Ozualdo Candeias, 1971) and *O Jogo da Vida e da Morte* (dir. Mário Kuperman, 1971), addressing, in particular, the ways in which the films deploy peripheral locales (the *favela* or slum and the *sertão* or northeastern rural region) so as to highlight a series of intricate relationships between land, property and poverty. At a time of military rule, and in the midst of censorship, these films make a virtue of focusing on occluded communities via a concentration on particular types of setting characterized by scarcity and lack. *O Jogo da Vida e da Morte* and *A Herança*, the chapter maintains, are preoccupied with communities that fail or are unable to provide for their own, thereby introducing images of Brazil that run counter to populist conceptions. For example, the black Ophelia figure in *O Jogo da Vida e da Morte* and *A Herança* is utilized as a significant vehicle through which Brazil's troubled racial histories are made visible, while the films' Hamlet figures are arresting for the extent to which they point up differing reactions to the straitened conditions of Brazil in the 1970s. Where one film endorses an ideal of socialist utopia, the other underlines a more nihilistic attitude, suggesting how *Hamlet* can be pulled in contrary directions, occupying simultaneously recuperative and defeatist positions.

Moving to Asia, Chapter 4, 'Pairing the Cinematic Prince: *Hamlet*, China and Japan', juxtaposes *Hamlet* adaptations inside a doubled structure which highlights the fascination exercised by the play in Asian contexts. Attention focuses on the critical value of placing what have become better known examples in conversation with their less valued siblings – adaptations of the same text, produced within the same timeframe, but to considerably less acclaim. Hence, reading *The Bad Sleep Well* (dir. Akira

Kurosawa, 1960) alongside *Castle of Flames* (dir. Katô Tai, 1960), the chapter explores the ways in which two Japanese adaptations align themselves with anti-governmental agitations of the late 1950s and the early 1960s, subscribing to a politically rebarbative stance. In the second part of the chapter, a later pairing of Chinese productions, *Prince of the Himalayas* (dir. Sherwood Hu, 2006) and *The Banquet* (dir. Xiaogang Feng, 2006), invite comparison in that they enlist the dysfunctional family as an underlying premise. Specifically, these adaptations address the significances of the Gertrude figure via a narrative emphasis on mobility, sexuality and space. In this way, they demonstrate how the profiling of China's global power and the recasting of *Hamlet* are inter-related – a changing nation-state is shadowed in a new-found confidence in the adaptive process. Overall, I suggest, the pairing methodology insists upon the need to think not so much in terms of the individual output but always in terms of a holistic sense of the depth and diversity of a spectrum of Shakespearean responses.

Contesting the ways in which the 'Bollywood' label serves as a catch-all category, Chapter 5, '*Hamlet* and Indian Cinemas: Regional Paradigms', argues that, fully to capture the diversity of *Hamlet* adaptations in India, we need to take much greater account of regional distinctiveness. Accordingly, the chapter initiates a dialogue between *Karmayogi* (dir. V. K. Prakash, 2012), set in Kerala's northern border parts, *Haider* (dir. Vishal Bhardwaj, 2014), set in Jammu/Kashmir, and *Hemanta* (dir. Anjan Dutt, 2016), set in Kolkata, West Bengal. Each film's representational strategy affirms its regional agenda. For example, *Karmayogi* centres on a *kalarippayattu* (martial arts) community and privileges Keralan folkways so as to promote an ideal of Malayali manhood; *Haider* intertextually interrogates 'Bollywood' via insets and a sustained deployment of the Kashmiri memoir, *Curfewed Night* (2011); and *Hemanta* consistently privileges the cultural status of Kolkata though echoes of the city's cinematic past, affirming nostalgic constructions of a lost world. The inventive indigeneity of these three adaptations is reflected in the use of native parlance, classical poetry, set design and mythological allusion. *Karmayogi*, *Haider* and *Hemanta* inject into 'To be, or not to be' and *The Mousetrap* strategic vernacular idioms and marshal music and dance to celebrate the vitality of networks of poetry, literature and citation that hinge on precise local and regional signifiers. Pursuing a regional methodology allows us to situate Shakespeare's utility and to contextualize *Hamlet* inside a fresh constellation of Indianized habitations.

Tracing Hamlet's journey across regional categories, such as the Middle East, can help to pinpoint areas of representational contact. Hence, Chapter 6, 'Gendering Borders: *Hamlet* and the Cinemas of Turkey and Iran', contends that *Hamlet* adaptations *İntikam Meleği/Kadin Hamlet* (dir. Metin Erksan, 1976), from Turkey, and *Tardid/Doubt* (dir. Varuzh Karim-Masihi, 2009), from Iran, are distinguished by elaborating different constructions of the Old Hamlet/Ghost figure, which is foregrounded in such a way as to address ideas about the execution of justice, the mission of the Hamletian protagonist and the status of the image. Purposefully reworking key debates sparked by the play, the films show themselves as acutely self-conscious, whether this reveals itself in *Tardid*'s concern with *Hamlet* as a drama from the past whose action recurs in the present (Siavash/Hamlet is a photojournalist haunted by the return of the play in 'real life') or in *İntikam Meleği*'s surrealist recreations of famous Shakespearean moments (this latter film's Hamlet is a woman who has trained as a performer and dramaturge). In their engagement with *Hamlet*, then, *İntikam Meleği* and *Tardid* subject expectations about the play to scrutiny and reversal. This is nowhere more obvious than in both films' privileging, via casting or rewriting, of women's roles: *İntikam Meleği*'s dynamic female Hamlet, for example, is matched by an equivalently pro-active Mahtab/Ophelia in *Tardid*, who is granted an agency beyond the constrictions of her Shakespearean equivalent. And, even as women's roles are being extended or invented, the Hamlet figure at the centre of both films is reconceived. Forestalling the deaths of the protagonists, *İntikam Meleği* and *Tardid* reify their respective Hamlets as wounded icons, thereby voicing mixed hopes for future reconstitution and reform.

Bringing to a close the Renaissance trajectory with which we began, Chapter 7, 'Materializing *Hamlet* in the Cinemas of Russia, Central and Eastern Europe', opens with what is perhaps the best known of world cinema *Hamlet* adaptations, the Russian *Gamlet* (dir. Grigori Kozintsev, 1964). The chapter approaches this 'Soviet Bloc' *Hamlet* not so much as an end-point of Russian engagements with the play as a beginning, arguing that this adaptation establishes a template for interpretation that has shaped the thinking of subsequent filmmakers. *Gamlet*'s positive protagonist, and material and elemental features, are adumbrated in the ways in which the play is referenced in a parodic process that is itself determined by the erosion of ideologies, and social and economic challenges, that accompanied the break-up of the Soviet Union. The Russian black comedy *Hamlet* adaptation, *Playing the Victim* (dir. Kirill Serebrennikov, 2006), coloured by domestic angst, gutter vocables and a depressed aesthetic, is a salient example here. It is against the backdrop of huge material challenges, themselves exacerbated by the budgetary crises that went hand-in-hand with the collapse of Central and Eastern European communist systems, that the chapter goes on to discuss *Hamlet, Ciganski Princ* (dir. Aleksandar Rajković, 2007) and *Cigán/Gypsy* (dir. Martin Šulík, 2011), respectively Serbian and Slovakian adaptations. Cleaving to *Hamlet*, and constituting a neglected genre of 'gypsy' Shakespearean cinema, these two works represent the plight of the Roma peoples at a time of rapid political and social change. Reacting against the high cultural status of an adaptation such as *Gamlet*, they depict despoiled worlds, prioritizing motifs of displacement and modes of existence that function at impoverished extremes. In this way, *Hamlet, Ciganski Princ* and *Gypsy* are the distant inheritors of Kozintsev's sense of *Hamlet*, continuing in the vein of interpreting the play in a materialist fashion but simultaneously problematizing the Russian film's radical portrayal of the protagonist. Consorting with the gloomy outlook of *Playing the Victim*, they offer irredeemably bleak visions that admit of no different prospects for their subjects.

In a recent discussion, Dennis Kennedy notes the numerous benefits of Shakespeare 'without his language'.[29] The gains of translation, he writes, 'include a more easily achievable social and political topicality, often leading to radical appropriation in acting or setting, and the replacement of the original cultural context with sometimes remarkable inventions, often visual in nature'.[30] Something similar can be claimed for *Hamlet* in world cinema manifestations which prompt us to think about the play in different terms. Looking at *Hamlet* through a global lens means that we reach beyond our own cultural perimeters and recognize a plurality of expressions of Shakespeare's work. We become sensitized to an alternative atlas of enterprise and, to adopt the arguments of Shekhar Deshpande and Meta Mazaj, positively cognizant of 'multiple loci' that share 'relationships of meaning' and 'interconnectedness'.[31] Equipped with mostly lesser known film materials, we are able to pursue non-mainstream routes to creativity and to appreciate manifold realms of Shakespearean interaction. Such a critical experience shifts a sense of the balance of authority. For instance, in the light of a continuing trajectory of cinematic adaptations, power can be seen to articulate itself across a range of sites, each of which enjoys a degree of autonomy. Mediated in world cinema, *Hamlet* encourages changes of vision and perspective. So transformed, the play asks us to grasp the significance of uncustomary positions and, on more than one occasion, to spectate from the point of view of the periphery. These processes generate *Hamlet*s innovated in complexion and outlook.

Germane here are adaptations such as *İntikam Meleği* and *Tardid* which apprehend the play as primarily concerned with the artist's responsibilities and the responsibilities of art inside Middle Eastern histories, past, present and yet in the making. Douglas M. Lanier writes that, in cinematic history, *Hamlet* is conceptualized in one of two ways, as a 'tragedy of character' or as a 'tragedy of society'.[32] Several examples explored in this book, however, run against the grain of this tendency and occupy a third conceptual domain. Illuminatingly, in Indian and African films, we see prioritized a thematics of place, whether this is demonstrated, as in the case of *Karmayogi*, in an ideal of Keralan integrity or, as in the case of the Boyokani *Hamlet*, with the ways in which a Shakespearean play travels to several locations, taking energy from fresh habitations and reflecting back upon them in turn. The Boyokani *Hamlet* also alerts us to intersections between race and tradition in the play's performance history. Ian Smith writes that 'Hamlet is ... white – his iconic black clothing serving to contrast with his pale northern European complexion'.[33] These distinctions are subject to revision in adaptations as diverse as *Gypsy, Hamile, Hemanta* and *Prince of the Himalayas* in which the protagonist is racially other not once but several times over, alternatively visualized in contravention of western expectations. Indeed, taken as a whole, world cinema *Hamlet* adaptations take the embeddedness of stereotypical western conventions to task. Hence, Ophelia figures are more assertively limned and wider family affiliations are concomitantly foregrounded. These are, of course, generalizations, but they are nevertheless of significance in helping us to acknowledge how a western canonical *Hamlet* is consistently flipped, augmented and re-envisioned. What this suggests is that the raw material of Shakespeare's *Hamlet* – its textual specifics as well as its interpretive legacies – are prompts to thinking anew. Inside this new narrative, the few world cinema *Hamlet* adaptations that have attracted comment appear in another guise. Establishing a larger and more variegated background for world cinema *Hamlet* production allows us to internalize the fact that Kozintsev, Kurosawa and their ilk are not exceptional in their treatment of the play but, rather, belong to a more extensive network of adaptive tendencies. In the world and of the world, *Hamlet* is an integral part of the rich and voluminous fabric of the global screen.

How have the *Hamlet* adaptations introduced in this study been received? Individual chapters provide the necessary grist and point up how particular examples are nationally and internationally celebrated. But it is certainly the case that recognition is rarely uniform even for films that achieve global exposure. For example, while *Haider* was favourably screened to cinema audiences in the UK, the USA and elsewhere, it was banned in Pakistan, censors stating that the film runs counter to the country's 'ideology'.[34] Other adaptations are limited to plaudits at film festivals, rarely straying beyond distribution within their own national borders. World cinema *Hamlet* adaptations demonstrate, in fact, the contingencies and contradictions tied to Shakespeare's status as a commodity and brand-name power and point up, in their mixed fortunes, the discontinuous nature of his mobilization on the international stage. As a result, as much as this book is concerned with the rehabilitation of occluded content, it is also concerned with use. The bibliography and tabulated filmography, it is hoped, will stimulate not simply additional investigation but also the further integration of 'global Shakespeares' into the classroom. A reorientation of our pedagogical co-ordinates, in turn, might spark interdisciplinary dialogue. For the most part, Shakespeare scholars eschew film studies; film studies scholars, for their part, tend not to look to Shakespearean examples. Mould-breaking and agenda-shaping as it is, the recently published *The Routledge Companion to World Cinema* mentions only three Shakespeare film examples, suggesting the way is clear for denser cross-pollination and a pooling of knowledges. The meshing of educational and disciplinary initiatives could begin to explain the 'why' – that is, 'why' *Hamlet* adaptations have proved so fixed a feature of the global film industries. Particular chapters address specifics, but as a general rule it might be argued that the *Hamlet* story, in discrete instantiations and at precise historical junctures, enables social and political critique to the extent that the play that emerges from these pages appears more barbed, weaponized and interrogative than previously perceived. The number of occasions in which, through cinema, *Hamlet* is identified as the work to turn to during periods of regime change is both illuminating and suggestive. In this process, it is not always the play's vengeful emphasis that is approved. Rather, it is interesting to note the frequency with which world cinema *Hamlet*s have visited upon them ameliorative endings that aspire to better things and institutional repair. The cinemas of the world showcase the play's timely instrumentality; at the same time, they place on display a willingness and readiness to revolutionize its generic imprint.

Many manifestations of *Hamlet* and/in world cinema – those which exceed the book's definition – are not explored for reasons of time and space. But such manifestations are undoubtedly ripe for critique and, alongside the adaptations which make up the content here, testify to the play's sedimented place on the global scene and exchanges that renew belief in its cultural *cachet*. As a staple of world cinema, *Hamlet* is continually referenced at the level of character echoes, familiar motifs, quotations from soliloquies and parodies of cinematic tradition. These types of engagement run the gamut of film types and point up how amenable Shakespeare's work is to continuing global play.[35] As performative inset, *Hamlet* is active in reappearing. Whether through stories involving fictional stage productions, or via plotlines centred on a Shakespeare company, the play is mobilized in the cinematic idiom variously to affirm or upturn ideas about psychic reformation and the recovery of a community ethos.[36] Linked to the genre, documentaries – some centring on a 'real-life' theatrical enterprise – enshrine an ongoing practice whereby *Hamlet* is taken to different parts of the world to undergird rehabilitative projects, facilitating investigation into the interstices of conflict zones and canvassing the virtues of intercultural collaboration.[37] Interestingly, several documentaries which suggest *Hamlet* can operate in this fashion are directed by women, stressing an alternative tradition to the film feature adaptation and the gender-specific ways in which amateur and professional constituencies come together in pursuit of artistic experiment.[38] Nor does the notorious length of the play pre-empt energetic and creative applications of its utility. In fact, *Hamlet*, perhaps alone among Shakespeare's works, is the play that is most often realized as a cinematic 'short', its seeming monolithic and impregnable stature offering an invitation to amputation, reduction and fragmentation.[39] In a recent collection, Sonya Freeman Loftis, Allison Kellar and Lisa Ulevich write that 'audiences and directors increasingly feel that there are no more *Hamlet*s left to make'.[40] We have, they suggest, 'exhausted the interpretive possibilities of Shakespeare's most popular tragedy' and are approaching its 'imagined death', a Shakespearean 'apocalypse'.[41] While writing this book, I became all the more aware of an opposite scenario – that is, cognizant of the multiplicity of other screen forms through which *Hamlet* moves and of further lines of representational enquiry. Future work will surely be directed towards unpacking and extrapolating *Hamlet* in more networked and horizon-challenging iterations. This, in turn, will involve us in a process whereby categories of adaptation and the Shakespearean are tested, making available, in Daniel Fischlin's words, 'marginal or exploratory sites where non-traditional interpretations of non-traditional forms of the Shakespeare effect are in evidence'.[42] Like the clouds to which Polonius is directed, the play through cinema belies closure or ending and persists in the process of assuming unpredictable, unforeseen forms. We are not approaching the end of *Hamlet*; rather, we are embarking on a more inclusive and variegated stage in its journey.

Notes

1. Stephen Greenblatt, *Hamlet in Purgatory* (Princeton and Oxford: Princeton University Press, 2001); Margreta de Grazia, *'Hamlet' Without Hamlet* (Cambridge: Cambridge University Press, 2007); Andrew Cutrofello, *All for Nothing: Hamlet's Negativity* (Cambridge, Mass.: MIT Press, 2014); William F. Zak, *Hamlet's Problematic Revenge: Forging a Royal Mandate* (Lanham and Boulder: Lexington Books, 2015); András Kiséry, *Hamlet's Moment: Drama and Political Knowledge in Early Modern England* (Oxford: Oxford University Press, 2016); Gabriel Josipovici, *Hamlet: Fold on Fold* (New Haven and London: Yale University Press, 2016); Rhodri Lewis, *Hamlet and the Vision of Darkness* (Princeton and Oxford: Princeton University Press, 2017).
2. Anthony B. Dawson, *Shakespeare in Performance: 'Hamlet'* (Manchester: Manchester University Press, 1995); Mary Z. Maher, *Modern Hamlets and Their Soliloquies* (Iowa City: University of Iowa Press, 2003); Tony Howard, *Women as Hamlet: Performance and Interpretation in Theatre, Film and Fiction* (Cambridge: Cambridge University Press, 2007); David Bevington, *'Murder Most Foul': 'Hamlet' Through the Ages* (Oxford: Oxford University Press, 2011).
3. See, for example, Patrick J. Cook, *Cinematic 'Hamlet': The Films of Olivier, Zeffirelli, Branagh, and Almereyda* (Athens: Ohio University Press, 2011); Nives Sanura, *Immer Wieder 'Hamlet': Shakespeares Tragödie im Film – Immer Wieder Anders* (Trier: WVT, 2004).
4. Samuel Crowl, *Screen Adaptations: Shakespeare's 'Hamlet'* (London and New York: Bloomsbury, 2014), p. xii; Bernice W. Kliman, *'Hamlet': Film, Television, and Audio Performance* (Madison and Teaneck: Fairleigh Dickinson University Press, 1988), pp. 87–113; Kenneth S. Rothwell, *A History of Shakespeare on Screen: A Century of Film and Television*, 2nd ed. (Cambridge: Cambridge University Press, 2004), pp. 182–85; Philippa Sheppard, *Devouring Time: Nostalgia in Contemporary Shakespearean Screen Adaptations* (Montreal and Kingston: McGill-Queen's University Press, 2017), pp. 180–81, 183–84.
5. Bevington, *'Murder'*, p. 183.
6. Kalki Koechlin, *A Document in Madness: Do Indian Women Mirror Ophelia?* (London: British Council, 2016); Sonia Massai, '"The Wide World": Shakespeare Across the Globe', in Gordon McMullan and Zoë Wilcox, eds, *Shakespeare in Ten Acts* (London: The British Library, 2016), p. 79; Ahlem Mosteghanemi, *When Shakespeare Thought I Was Cleopatra* (London: British Council, 2016).
7. Susan Bennett and Christie Carson, eds, *Shakespeare Beyond English: A Global Experiment* (Cambridge: Cambridge University Press, 2013); Paul Edmondson, Paul Prescott and Erin Sullivan, eds, *A Year of Shakespeare: Reliving the World Shakespeare Festival* (London and New York: Bloomsbury, 2013); Paul Prescott and Erin Sullivan, eds, *Shakespeare and the Global Stage: Performance and Festivity in the Olympic Year* (London and New York: Bloomsbury, 2015).

8. Jane Plastow, 'Introduction', in Jane Plastow, ed., *Shakespeare in and out of Africa* (London: James Currey, 2013), pp. x–xiv; Edward Wilson-Lee, *Shakespeare in Swahililand* (London: HarperCollins, 2016); Tian Yuan Tan, Paul Edmondson and Shih Pe Wang, eds, *1616: Shakespeare and Tang Xianzu's China* (London and New York: Bloomsbury, 2016).

9. See Andrew Dickson, *Worlds Elsewhere: Journeys around Shakespeare's Globe* (London: Bodley Head, 2015); Jill L. Levenson and Robert Ormsby, eds, *The Shakespearean World* (London and New York: Routledge, 2017); Bruce R. Smith, ed., *The Cambridge Guide to the Worlds of Shakespeare*, 2 vols (Cambridge: Cambridge University Press, 2016).

10. Greg Colón Semenza, 'Introduction', *Shakespeare Studies*, 38 (2010), p. 23; Mark Thornton Burnett, *Shakespeare and World Cinema* (Cambridge: Cambridge University Press, 2013).

11. See Dominic Dromgoole, *Hamlet: Globe to Globe* (Edinburgh: Canongate, 2017).

12. Andreas Höfele, *No Hamlets: German Shakespeare from Nietzsche to Carl Schmitt* (Oxford: Oxford University Press, 2016); Peter W. Marx, ed., *Hamlet-Handbuch: Stoffe, Aneignungen, Deutungen* (Stuttgart and Weimar: Verlag J. B. Meltzler, 2014); Ruth J. Owen, ed., *The Hamlet Zone: Reworking 'Hamlet' for European Cultures* (Newcastle-upon-Tyne: Cambridge Scholars, 2012).

13. Ailsa Grant Ferguson, *Shakespeare, Cinema, Counter-Culture: Appropriation and Inversion* (London and New York: Routledge, 2016), pp. 87–158; Sarah Hatchuel and Nathalie Vienne-Guerrin, eds, *Shakespeare on Screen: 'Hamlet'* (Mont-Saint-Aignam: Publications de l'Université de Rouen et du Havre, 2011); R. S. White, *Avant-Garde Hamlet: Text, Stage, Screen* (Madison and Teaneck: Fairleigh Dickinson University Press, 2015).

14. See 'Global Shakespeares', globalshakespeares.mit.edu (accessed 8 August 2018).

15. Fredric Jameson, 'Afterword: Adaptation as a Philosophical Problem', in Colin MacCabe, Kathleen Murray and Rick Warner, eds, *True to the Spirit: Film Adaptation and the Question of Fidelity* (Oxford: Oxford University Press, 2011), p. 232.

16. Julie Sanders, *Adaptation and Appropriation*, 2nd ed. (London and New York: Routledge, 2016), pp. 22, 25; Colin MacCabe, 'Introduction: Bazinian Adaptation', in MacCabe, Murray and Warner, eds, *True*, p. 8.

17. Daniel Fischlin, 'Outerspeares: Shakespeare, Intermedia, and the Limits of Adaptation', in Daniel Fischlin, ed., *OuterSpeares: Shakespeare, Intermedia, and the Limits of Adaptation* (Toronto, Buffalo and London: University of Toronto Press, 2014), pp. 27, 29.

18. Maurizio Calbi, *Spectral Shakespeares: Media Adaptations in the Twenty-First Century* (New York: Palgrave, 2013), p. 142.

19. Calbi, *Spectral*, pp. 110, 112.

20. Shekhar Deshpande and Meta Mazaj, *World Cinema: A Critical Introduction* (London and New York: Routledge, 2018), pp. 22, 23.

21. Rob Stone, Paul Cooke, Stephanie Dennison and Alex Marlow-Mann, 'Introduction: The Longitude and Latitude of World Cinema', in Rob Stone, Paul Cooke, Stephanie Dennison and Alex Marlow-Mann, eds, *The Routledge Companion to World Cinema* (London and New York: Routledge, 2018), p. 2.

22. Stanley Wells, 'Hamlet the Hoop', *Times Literary Supplement*, 7 February (2014), p. 6.

23. Interviews between Mireia Ros and Mark Thornton Burnett (1 and 8 December 2017).

24. Rob Stone, Paul Cooke, Stephanie Dennison and Alex Marlow-Mann, 'Introduction: The longitude and latitude of World Cinema', in Stone, Cooke, Dennison and Marlow-Mann, eds, *Companion*, p. 2.

25. Karima Laachir and Saeed Talajooy, 'Introduction', in Karima Laachir and Saeed Talajooy, eds, *Resistance in Contemporary Middle Eastern Cultures: Literature, Cinema and Music* (London and New York: Routledge, 2013), p. 2.

26. Shohini Chaudhuri, *Contemporary World Cinema: Europe, the Middle East, East Asia and South Asia* (Edinburgh: Edinburgh University Press, 2005), p. 54.

27. Dudley Andrew, 'An Atlas of World Cinema', in Stephanie Dennison and Song Hwee Lim, eds, *Remapping World Cinema: Identity, Culture and Politics in Film* (London and New York: Wallflower Press, 2006), p. 19.

28. Fredric Jameson, *The Geopolitical Aesthetic: Cinema and Space in the World System* (Bloomington and Indianapolis: Indiana University Press, 1992), pp. 188–89.

29. Dennis Kennedy, 'Found in Translation', *Around the Globe*, 50, Spring (2012), p. 2.

30. Kennedy, 'Translation', p. 2.

31. Deshpande and Mazaj, *World*, p. 23.

32. Douglas M. Lanier, '*Hamlet*: Tragedy and Film Adaptation', in Michael Neill and David Schalkwyk, eds, *The Oxford Handbook of Shakespearean Tragedy* (Oxford: Oxford University Press, 2016), pp. 572–73.

33. Ian Smith, 'We Are Othello: Speaking of Race in Early Modern Studies', *Shakespeare Quarterly*, 67.1 (2016), p. 107.

34. Mark Thornton Burnett, 'Global Shakespeare and the Censor: Adaptation, Context, and *Shakespeare Must Die*, a Thai Film Adaptation of *Macbeth*', *Shakespeare Survey*, 71 (2018), p. 276.

35. See, for example, the Argentine, French, German, Iranian and Italian films, *In Nome del Popolo Italiano* (dir. Dino Risi, 1971), *Hitler, Ein Film aus Deutschland* (dir. Hans Jürgen Syberberg, 1978), *La Nube/The Cloud* (dir. Fernando E. Solanas, 1998), *Pola X* (dir. Leos Carax, 1999) and *Persepolis* (dir. Vincent Paronnaud and Marjane Satrapi, 2007). For fascinating overviews, see Douglas M. Lanier, 'Film Spin-Offs and Citations', in Richard Burt, ed., *Shakespeares After Shakespeare: An Encyclopedia of the Bard in Mass Media and Popular Culture*, 2 vols (Westport and London: Greenwood, 2007), I, pp. 132–365; Mariangela Tempera, '"Not to Be": Referencing the Rest of

Hamlet on Screen', in Hatchuel and Vienne-Guerrin, eds, *'Hamlet'*, pp. 345–68.

36. Examples from Egypt, France, Germany, Japan and South Korea include *Yabure Daiko/The Broken Drum* (dir. Keisuke Kinoshita, 1949), *The Alexandria Trilogy* (dir. Youssef Chahine, 1979, 1982, 1989), *Le Champignon des Carpathes* (dir. Jean-Claude Biette, 1990), *Guns and Talks* (dir. Jang Jin, 2001) and *Barrière* (dir. Andreas Kleinert, 2010). For an energizing exploration, see Sarah Hatchuel, 'Plays-within-the-Film', in Smith, ed., *Worlds*, II, pp. 1946–53.

37. See *Amleto . . . Frammenti* (dir. Bruno Bignoni, 1997), *The Hamlet Adventure* (dir. Greg Roach and Ivaylo Dikanski, 2008) and *Hamlet en Palestine* (dir. Nicolas Klotz and Thomas Ostermeier, 2017), respectively Italian, Bulgarian and French-German productions. See also the book-length discussion, Katia Ippaso, *Amleto a Gerusalemme* (Roma: Editoria & Spettacolo, 2009).

38. See *Nu är du Hamlet* (dir. Ulrika Bengts, 2002), *Opération Shakespeare à la Vallée de Joux* (dir. Anne Cuneo, 2006) and *Il Était une Fois Hamlet et Ophélie à Shanghai* (dir. Ellénore Loehr, 2016), Finnish-Swedish, Swiss and French examples.

39. See the Danish, Dutch and Maltese examples, *Ofelia's Bloomster* (dir. Jørgen Leth, 1968), *To Be or Not to Be* (dir. Peter Woditsch, 1999) and *Plangent Rain* (dir. Kenneth Scicluna, 2010).

40. Sonya Freeman Loftis, Allison Kellar and Lisa Ulevich, 'Introduction: Post-*Hamlet*', in Sonya Freeman Loftis, Allison Kellar and Lisa Ulevich, eds, *Shakespeare's 'Hamlet' in an Era of Textual Exhaustion* (London and New York: Routledge, 2018), p. 1.

41. Loftis, Kellar and Ulevich, 'Introduction', p. 2.

42. Fischlin, 'Introduction', p. 4.

CHAPTER ONE

Hamlet, *Cinema and the Histories of Western Europe*

Hamlet, in filmic form, crops up across most of the nation-states that have come to constitute Western Europe, including Denmark, Finland, France, Germany, Greece, Italy and Spain, with adaptations found in each of the post-war decades. Most of the eleven films explored in this chapter have their origins in a screenplay derived from the play, and two originate in a stage production and/or novel. Clearly, the consistency and creativity with which *Hamlet* features in Western European cinemas can be tied to well-established Shakespearean traditions. In France, Italy and the Nordic countries, for instance, Shakespeare was a cultural reference-point from the eighteenth and nineteenth centuries onwards – as translated text, critical commentary, political polemic or theatrical spectacle.[1] Several nation-states are distinguished by long associations with the play, as the examples of Spain and Germany testify. In Spain, *Hamlet* was the first of Shakespeare's works to be translated in 1772, while, in Germany, the notion that 'Germany is Hamlet' has been widely discussed since the Ferdinand Freiligrath poem of 1844.[2] Such contexts of knowledge and translation are cinematically mobilized in interlocking ways. *Un Amleto di Meno/One Hamlet Less* (dir. Carmelo Bene, 1973) realizes *Hamlet* in a classically inflected and decorous Italian; by contrast, other adaptations vernacularize, pointing up a more general tendency to transliterate the language of the play in contemporary expression and aphorisms. A final group of adaptations registers the play's language via citation and extract. Direct quotations from *Hamlet* – 'To be, or not to be' and Hamlet's riposte about Polonius, 'At supper' (4.3.17) – in the French adaptation, *Ophélia* (dir. Claude Chabrol, 1963), are so deployed as to highlight Yvan/Hamlet's (misplaced) conviction that he resembles a modern-day Shakespearean protagonist. Similarly, at the start of the Italian production, *Quella Sporca Storia nel West/Johnny Hamlet* (dir. Enzo G. Castellari, 1968), one of the visiting players rehearses 'To be, or not to be' as a prelude to Johnny/Hamlet's recognition of his predicament as a battle-torn combatant in the

American Civil War. However the films refract their investment in *Hamlet*, they draw on a range of linguistic understandings and demonstrate how pervasively and pointedly the Shakespearean story answers to changing imperatives.

Exploring *Hamlet* adaptations inside a chronological arrangement reveals multiple Western European histories. This chapter argues that cinematic adaptations of *Hamlet* illuminate the cross-fertilizing ways in which Western Europe has continued to define and represent itself. The play is enlisted firstly as a means of assurance and democratization and as a channel for unease. In the immediate post-war period, the urgent challenge facing many European nations was how to deal with the legacies of conflict. For those associated with the Axis powers, the problem was particularly acute, involving questions about complicity, accountability and violence on an unprecedented scale. Given that *Hamlet* unfolds a scenario of military defeat, it is perhaps not surprising that the play should lend itself so readily to reckoning initiatives. As the first section of this chapter argues, two remarkable but little studied adaptations from the 1950s, the Italian *Io, Amleto/I, Hamlet* (dir. Georgio Simonelli, 1952) and the German *Der Rest ist Schweigen/ The Rest Is Silence* (dir. Helmut Käutner, 1959), are crucial interventions in this post-war debate.

Discussing the art cinema of Italy and France from the late 1950s to the 1970s onwards, Mark Betz writes that 'anxieties in Europe about economic and cultural co-operation on the one hand and nationalism and national identity on the other are present and readable' throughout, and the thesis is eloquently illustrated in the adaptations discussed in section two.[3] A singular grouping of French, Greek and Italian films – namely, *Ophélia* (dir. Claude Chabrol, 1963), *Ithele Na Ginei Vasilias/He Wanted to Become King* (dir. Angelos Theodoropoulos, 1967), *Quella Sporca Storia nel West/Johnny Hamlet* (dir. Enzo G. Castellari, 1968), *Dans la Poussière de la Soleil/In the Dust of the Sun* (dir. Richard Balducci, 1971) and *Un Amleto di Meno/One Hamlet Less* (dir. Carmelo Bene, 1973) – voices conflicting national preoccupations in contexts of industrial discontent, youth culture and mass movement protest. In so doing, these films shape, and are shaped by, related considerations around women's roles and class interrelations. A Finish addendum to this grouping – *Hamlet liikemaailmassa/Hamlet Goes Business* (dir. Aki Kaurismäki, 1987) – begins to push the thematics characterizing Western Europe into a global arena. Central to this chapter's thesis is, in Tony Judt's words, the ways in which the period between 1945 and 1989 functioned as an 'interim age: a post-war parenthesis, the unfinished business of a conflict that ended in 1945 but whose epilogue had lasted for another half a century'.[4]

The final section of the chapter examines the *Hamlet* films produced since 1990. *Festen/Celebration* (dir. Thomas Vinterberg, 1998), *E! Triunfo/ The Triumph* (dir. Mireia Ros, 2006) and *Elf Onkel/Eleven Uncles* (dir. Herbert Fritsch, 2010) – adaptations from Denmark, Spain and Germany respectively – demonstrate how the post-war project of European integration comes into conflict with new developments arising from mass immigration, demographic realignment and the pressures involved in increasingly networked European organizations. Notably, all three films rework Fortinbras as an outsider and/or *émigré*, suggesting uncertain attitudes towards transitional processes. *Festen, El Triunfo* and *Elf Onkel* figure Fortinbras as a power from elsewhere while going on to situate what he represents multifariously – as invasion, as alliance, as unknown quantity. All three films, in fact, adopt mixed and ambivalent positions in relation to the prospects of a European system that espouses unification and co-operation, pointing up as they do so the structural and demographic determinants shaping the work of Shakespearean adaptation.

Post-War Legacies

Two modern language adaptations – the Italian *Io, Amleto/I, Hamlet* (dir. Georgio Simonelli, 1952) and the German *Der Rest ist Schweigen/The Rest Is Silence* (dir. Helmut Käutner, 1959) – take generically distinct approaches to some of the challenges of post-war Western Europe. Set in a fantasy Renaissance court, *Io, Amleto*, a parodic adaptation of *Hamlet*, sees popular comedian, Erminio Macario, playing the Danish prince, and accordingly foregrounds his diminutive frame, simpleton persona, high-voiced delivery and flat-footed gait, with the *commedia all'italiana* the perfect showcase for the star's own production company and his performative versatility.[5] (The film's title might more aptly be rendered in English as 'It's me, the one-and-only Macario, playing Hamlet!') A parodic strain is evident in the reorientation of soliloquies (as referee, Amleto/Hamlet addresses a football, intoning, 'Penalty, or not penalty, that is the question', as a life-or-death debate is comically turned in a sporting environment) and in the representation of a risk averse, petrified protagonist. (Fearing a parental reprimand, Amleto/Hamlet tries to avoid meeting the Queen in her 'closet', saying, 'mummy's . . . going to tell me off because I spent the night out!') Adding to the parodic mixture are characters such as Rosadorno (Silvio Noto), a 'wicked servant' whose function is to accentuate the black-and-

Figure 1: Poster for *Io, Amleto/I, Hamlet* (dir. Georgio Simonelli, 1952).
Courtesy of Macario Film/Author Collection.

white dynamics of the action, and Yorick (Guido Riccioli), a 'jester' who, 'forced to retire', works to emphasize the humourless cast of the new monarchical order. Like the *zanni* figure, Amleto/Hamlet speaks more wisely than he realizes, his dilemma ('Revengeness or forgivenge?') suggesting the ethical push-and-pull of post-war Italy. Giving voice to a conflicted course of action, Amleto/Hamlet articulates the preoccupations of a nation-state recovering from the struggle of an internal civil war and torn between retribution and reconciliation demands.

Conversely, *Der Rest ist Schweigen* is set in the modern day and is the first adaptation to transfer the action of *Hamlet* to the 'corporate *noir*' world of business (the Claudius family runs a steelworks empire).[6] The film is set in the Ruhrgebiet, the industrial heartland of West Germany, and revolves around the identity crisis of John H. Claudius (Hardy Krüger) who returns home after twenty years in exile as a Harvard University academic. John/ Hamlet is a philosophy professor with research specialisms in Heidegger and Sartre, a plot update consonant with his involvement in questions of being and existentialism. Much of the action of *Der Rest ist Schweigen* takes place in and around a sumptuous family residence. Wood-panelled, bay-windowed and comprised of a series of spacious reception rooms, it brings into focus tense interconnections between the Claudius family's past and present fortunes. Adjusted figures from the *dramatis personae* of *Hamlet* include Johannes Claudius/Old Hamlet (Siegfried Schürenberg), an industrialist who died, it is claimed, in an air-raid, Stanley Goulden/ Guildenstern (Richard Allan) and Mike Krantz/Rosencrantz (Boy Gobert), gay *emigré* ballet company directors called back to Germany to work as informants, and Horace/Horatio (Rainer Penkert), a demobbed British 'secret service' and 'military government' agent. Such character shifts illuminate deaths and displacements in the wake of war. For instance, Stanley Goulden/Guildenstern and Mike Krantz/Rosencrantz, as much as they are spies, simultaneously bring to mind anti-gay legislation and persecution under the Nazi regime. Similarly, Horace/Horatio signifies a historical 'enemy' on German soil: in line with the balance of power that obtains in Western Europe in the 1950s, however, he is here reimagined as a force of ideological good and insight.

It is generally recognized that, in the wake of the separation of Germany into two states, cinema proved a responsive instrument to working through issues of guilt and atrocity. (The neorealist tradition in Italian cinema, with its documentary-style emphasis on scenes of physical destruction and human despair, played a not dissimilar role.)[7] Wreckage and rubble provided the backdrop to films that allowed Germany to initiate reckoning processes, not least, according to Thomas Elsaesser, as this was expressed in *vergangenheitsbewältigung* – 'coming to terms with the past' or 'mastering the past'.[8] As Sabine Hake writes in a discussion of national cinemas, German consciousness was 'haunted by the experience of war and defeat and the loss of nation and homeland'.[9] Marked by sharply angled camera work, *chiaroscuro* effects and an expressionistic style, *Der Rest ist Schweigen* is a late entry to this reckoning genre, alternating between images of ruin (shots of bombed-out factories) and a return to economic vitality (lorries accelerating on freshly opened arteries and new buildings rising). Relevant here are John/Hamlet's suspicions about the circumstances surrounding his father's death and his discovery of collusion and war crimes. 'Leave the past … Forget the whole thing', advises Horace/Horatio, his comment registering an abnegation of his former investigative role and the difficulties involved in John/Hamlet's task. Envisioning Johannes Claudius/Old Hamlet via retrospective insets, and through the 'photos … tapes [and] recordings from radio and meetings' assembled as evidence, *Der Rest ist Schweigen* is unprecedented in lending the supernatural a technological presence. The film is also distinctive in the ways in which it gradually unveils Johannes Claudius/Old Hamlet as having been 'pushed' by his scheming brother, Paul/Claudius (Peter van Eyck), into manufacturing armaments for the Nazi cause, unwittingly becoming, in John/Hamlet's estimation, a 'mass murderer'. The film is structurally arranged so as to highlight a pervasive collective guilt, with rebuffs and forgetfulness continually forestalling John/Hamlet in his mission to reveal the hidden national and political narratives that shaped his family's involvement in the war.

In this sense, John/Hamlet is what Ewa Mazierska has termed the 'possessor of post-memory' who has an 'unfilled identity' and carries 'a multiple burden'.[10] The type, particular to contemporary European cinema's preoccupation with traumatic discourses and fissured or missing legacies, suggests how purposefully *Der Rest ist Schweigen* inflects its Shakespearean source. If Shakespeare's *Hamlet* delineates a protagonist wedded to the idealized 'combination and . . . form' of his father (3.4.58), *Der Rest ist Schweigen* presents us with a compromised paternal figure – a successful capitalist *vater* who, notwithstanding fraternal machinations, is still culpable. The film goes on to trace how the sins of the father are visited on the son, with John/Hamlet's physiologically vulnerable, dissatisfied and appalled state being linked to his dawning realizations. For all his professional philosophical expertise, he is incapable of resolving questions of 'essence' and 'motive'. In this sense, his situation is emblematic, all of the characters being dented and diminished by their experience. War has made Herbert/Laertes (Heinz Drache), an ex-Nazi, embittered at his inability to 'reconcile' himself to his past; similarly, Von Pohl/Polonius (Rudolf Forster), a doctor and former Nazi sympathizer, has become inured to corrupt misdiagnoses. They, too, labour under the weight of earlier existences. Further unifying threads are conditions of exhaustion, metaphors for the rottenness at the heart of the play. Statements such as 'I'm very tired' and 'I took a nap' index both the film's title and the idea of a 'rest-cure', a fate (equivalent to imprisonment or exile) with which several characters are threatened. In this way, *Der Rest ist Schweigen* pushes at the meanings of Hamlet's final pronunciation, 'The rest is silence' (5.2.342), pointing up aftermath, rejection and expulsion, a thematic cluster with a specific resonance in post-war German contexts.

In most discussions, Helmut Käutner, the director, is deemed a politically 'neutral' artist who subscribed to 'conciliatory and defeatist' positions.[11] Drill down into *Der Rest ist Schweigen*, however, and a more oppositional perspective emerges. Producers of armaments, the Claudius family may be read as analogous to the disgraced Krupp manufacturing

Figure 2: John/Hamlet (Hardy Krüger) dances with Fee/Ophelia (Ingrid Andree) in *Der Rest ist Schweigen/The Rest Is Silence* (dir. Helmut Käutner, 1959). Courtesy of Getty Images.

dynasty, also based in the Ruhr; found guilty during the Nuremberg trials of 'murder, pillage and enslavement', the Krupps during the 1950s, in a not dissimilar way to their filmic equivalents, were engaged in restitution, reparation and rehabilitation.[12] The parallel is made manifest in the cast-metal statue of a crucible-bearing industrial worker that dominates the family residence entrance hall. Bare-chested and downtrodden, the figure recalls the use in Krupp factories of 'slave labour' from occupied countries, a war crime that the film briefly references in Johannes/Old Hamlet's cryptic diary entry ('Minus ten degrees ... two raids ... had to call ... about the foreign workers' suggests a dehumanized working situation, resistance and unrest).[13] With these contexts in mind, the reverberations of the film's title multiply. In particular, 'silence' conjures the voiceless predicament of the workers, unmentionable things (conversations about what exactly the factories produce either tail off or are interrupted) and cover-ups, extending and complicating the play's concern with silence and mortality. There is an echo of this Shakespearean meaning in the opening credits. As the title comes into view, splashes of crimson – in what is an otherwise monochrome filmic palette – wash over the lettering, suggesting participation, victimization, accountability and violence. Beginning with the words of the play's end, *Der Rest ist Schweigen* contemplates Germany's end, worlds after defeat and what is entailed in speaking to and about repressed histories. Working in this capacity, the film alerts us to what John/Hamlet represents – and how he can be – in environs that underline the uneasy relation between the war's legacies and rehabilitative initiatives.

Io, Amleto emerged during the period immediately after military occupation when Italy was beginning a process of re-identification and re-adjustment under a Christian Democrat government.[14] Crucially, of course, *Io, Amleto* is a comedy or, more specifically, a species of Italian parody that, as several critics have noted, allows for 'recollection', 'social criticism' and a questioning of the 'rule of inept governing elites and institutions', constituting a 'response to historical trauma'.[15] More broadly, parody, as Linda Hutcheon notes, often offers a route through which 'modern artists . . . come to terms with the past'.[16] Central to the operations of the genre in *Io, Amleto* is the way in which a clownish Hamlet is represented as an anti-military type, bypassing physical conflict, relying on the cheek of wit rather than the collision of fists ('Cleverness wins over strength, 3-0', he opines) and being imbricated in revolution without actively seeking it out. Amleto/Hamlet's misunderstandings and malapropisms propel an entertainment in which he succeeds in outwitting the murderers sent against him through serendipity and his abilities as a clever clown. The fact that he floats above catastrophe, or avoids it through good luck, establishes his alternative comic credentials and accidental alignment with the forces of right. For example, when Amleto/Hamlet ducks the cannon ball aimed at him by Claudio/Claudius (Luigi Pavese), the projectile bounces back at his assailant, meaning that the 'treacherous villain' is vanquished, 'Hoist[ed] with his own petard' (3.4.205). True to the Macario persona, Amleto (and here the comic's previous role as clumsy, uncomprehending soldier in *Come Persi La Guerra/How I Lost the War* [dir. Carlo Borghesio, 1947] is alluded to) appears as an *inetto* (or bungler), a creation poised purposefully against recently compromised ideals of muscled Italian *machismo* and constructions of fascist aggressivity.[17] As such, and in this Amleto/Macario's slight form is vital, the character proves inseparable from the film's simultaneous canvassing and qualifying of what were, in the early 1950s, still raw and recent images and memories. Hence, at those points where a stereotypical phallocentric male body is realized, comic demythologization is the accompaniment.

Claudio/Claudius, pompous, vainglorious and festooned in padded, extravagant costumes, brings Benito Mussolini to mind and, in particular, the Italian leader's fondness for sartorial excess and fist-clenched gestures.

In much the same way that Italy's demagogic leader was termed *Il Duce*, the dialogue of *Io, Amleto* invariably identifies Claudio/Claudius in depersonalized and symbolic terms as *Il Tiranno* ('Tyrant'), imagining him and Amleto/Hamlet as physical antitheses. Other reminders of an Italy at war are quick to suggest themselves. The internal divisions that led to Italy's downfall are suggested in the film's references to 'Gottinga', a fictive 'province' which, following 'revolt' and the overthrow of the 'governor', ends up in the 'rebels' hands', while Mussolini's use of the Press Office as a censorship mechanism is hinted at in Ofelia/Ophelia (Rossana Podestà) and Amleto/Hamlet's humorous discussion about letters and the 'law' that 'punishes the uttering and publishing of false notes'.[18] During these and similar episodes, Amleto/Hamlet precipitates, or focalizes, comedic confusion. Dressed in striped and flowery jerkins, he scandalizes the 'dignitaries' during a mock-trial (echoing how Hamlet 'offend[s]' [3.4.8] at the play-within-the-play), makes an unconvincing 'plebeian' when he inadvertently bumps into the 'republican ... rebels', versions of Fortinbras, at the aptly named 'Red Salmon' tavern, and mistakes passwords for restaurant orders: 'Bread and freedom for me too', he announces, with suitably disorderly consequences (the 'method' [2.2.203] in Hamlet's 'madness' [2.2.202] is here parodically repurposed). Part of the fun is how *Io, Amleto* selectively prioritizes key episodes from *Hamlet* to deflate constructions of authority all too familiar to post-war Italian audiences. So angled, the film stages an exorcism, ridding itself of the ghosts of power in favour of a parodic landscape premised on fantasy concoctions of mayhem.

Film historian Ruth Ben-Ghiat notes that, when 'German and Allied troops flooded the peninsula' in the final years of World War II, 'Italian officers and soldiers' were forced to choose between either 'loyalty to the King and his Royal Army' or 'loyalty to Mussolini ... [and] the troops of the Republic of Salò'.[19] After defeat, and the referendum of 1946, of course, Italy instituted a democratic government, the last representative of the Savoy monarchy abdicating and entering exile. Interestingly, *Io, Amleto* knits together its various narrative strands by having the victorious Amleto/Hamlet proclaimed 'President of the Republic' only to have him state, 'That's not possible, I am the King now'. As his response indicates, confronted with a choice between very different socialist republic and autocratic monarchical systems, the film opts for the latter. However, faced with continuing 'revolution' by the rebels, Amleto/Hamlet goes on to fudge the issue, declaring he will be 'King of the Republic for you, and the President of the Kingdom for the others', a purposeful swapping of titles and discourses – and a blurring of modes of government – that is greeted with general hilarity. On the one hand, the mix-up rhymes with contemporary shifts in Italian politics. On the other hand, Amleto/Hamlet's answer suggests a comic cynicism about all forms of leadership. Fittingly, he is interested less in securing this fantasy Denmark's political dispensation than in finally winning Ofelia/Ophelia; as he states, 'Won't you give me a kiss, now?', pushing aside questions about fealty and loyalty so as to prioritize romance and desire.

Io, Amleto and *Der Rest ist Schweigen* depart from each in the ways in which they address the need to initiate and embrace post-war progress. Common to both films, however, is an eventual problematization or rejection of revenge as praxis and ideology. In *Io, Amleto*, for instance, once it is clear that, as the final tableau reveals, the Ghost of Amleto/Hamlet's father (Luigi Pavese) and the new ghost of Claudio/Claudius have made up (as the comic *inetto* reflects on his glimpse of their heavenly after-life, 'they are getting along up there'), reconciliation can be affirmed. The play's representations of purgatory and a political takeover are here neatly left aside. A general burying of differences are the preconditions for a joyous finale centred on, in the voice-over words of the English Ambassador (Manlio Busoni), 'the reign of love', pointing up how the conclusion accepts if not celebrates reparation and moving on. *Io, Amleto*'s generically determined tableau is complemented by *Der Rest ist Schweigen* in which, in contradistinction to their Shakespearean fates, John/Hamlet and Fee/Ophelia (Ingrid Andree) survive. The complicities of the past having finally been spoken about (Gertrud/Gertrude [Adelheid Seeck] owns up to family truths in a series of staggered confessions) means that the prevailing and distorting silence is finally broken. Thus, when Paul/Claudius is shot by a newly awakened – and linguistically liberated – Gertrud/Gertrude, speech is affirmed as the route to restitution and reform. As a result, and in the wake of the lifting of verbal restriction, phantoms evaporate (Johannes/Old Hamlet is last 'present' in the form of a nagging telephone in the domestic shoot-out) and vision is no longer occluded: significantly, John/Hamlet is represented taking off his spectacles for the first time. (The film consistently privileges glass surfaces as mediums that suggest transparency but, instead, insist on opacity.) Yet, bringing back into the frame ideas of 'rest', the ending also reinforces the idea that recovery is complex. 'All my flowers have died … Death is nothing special to me', the infantilized Fee/Ophelia states in an observation that foregrounds her Shakespearean counterpart's lament ('my . . . violets . . . withered . . . [4.5. 177]), her own future (now that she has 'lost all contact with the outside world', she is whisked off to a sanatorium) and an environment comprised of disaffiliated subjects. For John/Hamlet, adrift outside the Claudius family residence and ringed by smoking industrial chimneys, reckonings have proved only partially disencumbering. As he walks off into a snowy scene, it is clear that he remains divided between his 'New England' philosophical existence and a 'homeland' not yet at ease with its burdens and remembrances.

Consolidation, Integration, Resistance

As the 1950s faded, the pressures to restore and rehabilitate took on fresh forms. Crucially, as adaptations of *Hamlet* from the early 1960s to the late 1980s suggest, attention became increasingly focused on the situation of the worker, registering a concern with a rapidly changing industrial landscape, and on sexuality as a marker of either emancipation or a repressive *status quo*. The 'economic boom' experienced by many Western European nation-states, itself facilitated by post-war initiatives, was the precondition for a more integrated sense of Europe, as the founding of the EC in 1967 suggests, as well as for an escalation in global trade.[20] At the same time, as *Hamlet* adaptations across this thirty-year period indicate, there were simultaneous efforts to shore up the singularity of national identities. Alongside came generational urgencies, as expressed in the worldwide impact of youth movements, which in turn took energy from, and served to further, experimentation in the arts and broader debate about political organization and social *mores*. In cinema, *Hamlet* was inflected accordingly, with adaptations absorbing and conveying a new interrogative energy.

Two Hamlet adaptations – the French *Ophélia* (dir. Claude Chabrol, 1963) and the Greek *Ithele Na Ginei Vasilias/He Wanted to Become King* (dir. Angelos Theodoropoulos, 1967) – take the conceit of the factory/industry setting first explored in *Der Rest ist Schweigen*, pushing it into terrain that allowed for reflection on emergent relations between class affiliation, national identity and aspiration. Uniquely in Western European *Hamlet* adaptations, this signalled a sustained attempt to mould Shakespeare's play into a meditation on the social complexions and implications of the developing European world. Critical tradition has tended to see *Ophélia* in psychological terms as highlighting 'the

Figure 3: Lucie/Ophelia (Juliette Mayniel) in autumnal mood in *Ophélia* (dir. Claude Chabrol, 1963). Courtesy of the British Film Institute.

compulsion to repeat fictions', not least as this is manifested in Yvan/ Hamlet's obsessiveness, but, in fact, it reads more forcefully as an intervention in an ongoing discussion about employee-employer relations, France's problematic post-war dissolving colonial landscape and the country's place in a shifting European order.[21] The adaptation takes a French symbolist construction of the hero – 'haunted by the spectre of the absolute [and] harassed by cosmic doubt' – and plays up its ironic resonances.[22] Yvan/Hamlet (André Jocelyn) is the spoilt scion of a wealthy *haut bourgeois* family living in a sumptuous *chateau* in the countryside. He sulks, wanders the fields and fancies he is exceptional. As Douglas M. Lanier writes, as a 'moral … crusader … reciting poetry', Yvan/Hamlet is neither engaging nor attractive.[23] The film takes strands from French cinematic and theatrical cultures, gesturing to *Orphée* (dir. Jean Cocteau, 1950) and comedy of manners traditions in its elaboration of an Yvan/Hamlet who is universally abrasive, most often at the dinner table, the archetypal French locus for familial interaction. Hearing a snatch of dubbed dialogue (1.2.68–92) from

Laurence Olivier's *Hamlet* (1948), he persuades himself that his situation, and that of Shakespeare's Dane, are one and the same (as intertext, the film surrogates for the Ghost). *Ophélia* is the first *Hamlet* adaptation to realize the play-within-the play as a cinematic intervention – with the working-class Lucie/Ophelia (Juliette Mayniel) part of Yvan/Hamlet's cineaste role-play – although here it indexes his snobbery rather than his counter-cultural integrity.

As a film immersed in, and adjusting to, the post-war economy, *Ophélia* illuminates the respective positions of the intellectual and the worker. Within the *chateau* grounds, armed guards (the film's version of the sentinels) fearfully control the perimeter; beyond the *chateau*, Adrien/Claudius' (Claude Cerval) factory workers are threatening to strike. The film's industrial take on Laertes' revolting supporters – the 'rabble' (4.5.102) with a 'riotous head' (4.5.101) – has a contextual specificity. In the early 1960s, the trade union, the *Confédération Générale du Travail*, was one of the most powerful of French blue-collar organizations.[24] Despite Charles de Gaulle's resounding election victory in 1962, deep grievances, exacerbated by processes of modernization, remained. As Gordon Wright argues, 'government policies' worsened the lot of the 'marginal and the weak' and 'opposition on the left' concomitantly gained ground.[25] The strike in *Ophélia* does not materialize, but its threat is felt nonetheless, and, revealingly, Adrien/Claudius – innocent of his brother's death – takes his own life because of the deteriorating industrial situation. Further afield in the film, France struggles with turbulent territories: 'Stop the Massacre!' a headline to a newspaper announces. The reference is to the massacres during the Algerian War, and, when *Ophélia* was completed in late 1962, soon after the country had gained independence, the representation of a Hamlet seemingly uninterested in a world outside of his own interiority must have reverberated negatively.[26] But, paving the way for Yvan/Hamlet's reformation, *Ophélia* goes on to underscore the hero's growing empathy. 'Trees bear strange fruit these days', Yvan/Hamlet observes on coming across André/Polonius (Robert Burnier), the plebeian family factotum, who has accidentally hanged himself from a tree. A parallel suggests itself between Yvan/Hamlet's feeling response (he rushes for help and thinks immediately of 'Poor Lucie') and the attitudes arraigned in the Billie Holiday protest song, 'Strange Fruit', full of melancholic choler at the lynching of African Americans. The French working class and the condemned black American make a brief metaphorical alliance, refracting Algeria's postcolonial trials and affirming Yvan/Hamlet's change of heart.

At almost the same time as France was negotiating internal class arrangements and a shrinking empire, Greece was facing up to anti-communist
backlashes and the rise of militant conservatism. Given that *Ithele Na Ginei
Vasilias* is lost (the original negative disappeared when Angelo Films went
out of business), discussion can only ever be partial. Nevertheless, enough
exists in the form of image, score, interviews and synopses to insert the film
into a trajectory of *Hamlet* adaptations that chime with the concerns of
their times.[27] Released on 22 September 1967, five months after the Greek
coup d'état of 21 April 1967, *Ithele Na Ginei Vasilias* – through a title that
identifies an equation between ambition and monarchy – implicitly reflects
on the takeover by the 'Regime of Colonels' which was characterized by
hyper-Hellenic nationalism, the abolition of a democratic constitution and
the flight and exile of King Constantine II.[28] In interview, the director
plays down the connection, stating that the 'title indicates the aspirations
of the Claudius character', yet the film's specifically anti-authoritarian
interests are everywhere apparent.[29] For example, *Ithele Na Ginei
Vasilias*' social commitment is realized in the ways in which Alekos/
Hamlet (Angelos Theodoropoulos) learns of his father's murder *only*
through the gardeners 'who have spoken' to the ghost. This plot modification amplifies the role of the gardeners (or sentinels), tones down the
importance of the supernatural and emphasizes inter-class relations as
a constituent dynamic. In addition, when it emerges that Chrysanthou/
Old Hamlet drowned during a fishing trip with his business colleague,
Yerolimos/Claudius (Lykourgos Kallergis), the fact that they share
a business (rather than familial) bond is underscored as significant.
The desire for control of the factory is what motivates Yerolimos/
Claudius, with his envy of his partner's lifestyle, and social resentment,
propelling him into murderous action. Director Angelos Theodoropoulos
confirms *Ithele Na Ginei Vasilias* is to be read as a 'social drama',
a recognizably Greek genre defined by its exploration of class rivalry and
its realist aesthetic.[30]

It is possible to speculate that the form, mediated through *Hamlet*,
allowed for critique of Greece's ideological turn to conservatism via
a purposeful privileging of youth culture. Franco Zeffirelli's *Romeo and
Juliet*, a film adaptation that brought youth and Shakespeare to the forefront, was, of course, only a year away, and, in *Ithele Na Ginei Vasilias* we
see a not dissimilar emphasis on youthful characters as ciphers of ideological currency. For example, before he returns to Athens, Alekos/Hamlet is
a student in London, seat of fashion and popular culture; similarly, the
film's detailing of desirable accessories and interiors suggests how

Figure 4: Cover sleeve for the record accompanying the release of *Ithele Na Ginei Vasilias/He Wanted to Become King* (dir. Angelos Theodoropoulos, 1967). Courtesy of Angelos Theodoropoulos.

concentratedly it plays to a youth demographic and market. An association with London is also shadowed in the film's score – the dominant melody is played with contemporary (British-style) pop electric keyboards and guitars. The suggestion, at a time of ideological retrenchment, is not only that, as Lydia Papadimitriou notes, 'Greece can accommodate foreign lifestyles' but also that it is willing to enter 'the western sphere of influence'.[31] Revealingly, matching a contemporary middle-class commodification of the tradition, the melody is also played in the film as classic Greek – *bouzouki* – music, suggesting how seamlessly the film aligns the old and the new. The *mise-en-scène* assists in this endeavour, continually juxtaposing establishing shots of the new Athens (such as shopping districts) and its ancient monuments. On the cover sleeve for the single distributed at the same time as *Ithele Na Ginei Vasilias*, the strategy is self-evident. A medieval-style castle glowers in the background, symbol of Shakespearean association, while, in the foreground, against restless skies, the affluent-looking but anguished Alekos/Hamlet is comforted by a stylishly dressed Filitsa/Ophelia (Anna Iasonidou). The 'Regime of Colonels', Tony Judt writes, was 'anti-modern to the point of parody . . . [they] censored the press, outlawed strikes and banned modern music along with mini-skirts [and] long hair'.[32] At release, then, *Ithele Na Ginei Vasilias* sounded a critical note. Occupying the maternal position, Filitsa/Ophelia assumes the dominant role, demonstrating, as the director reflects, 'willpower' and refusing to be 'led by the nose'. Her carefully messed bee hive, sparkling dress, handbag, jewellery and earrings mark her out as a youth culture icon, her chic appearance indivisible from her empowered status.

In complementary ways, *Ophélia* and *Ithele Na Ginei Vasilias* stress women's roles. The 'women' in *Ophélia*, notes Anthony Guneratne, 'are eminently sane', and, thanks to Lucie/Ophelia, Yvan/Hamlet gradually abandons contempt and affectation and divests himself of fantasy.[33] 'You're Yvan, and I'm not Ophelia but Lucy', she tells him in the final scene. As she cradles him in her arms in a composition that looks forward to the cover sleeve from *Ithele Na Ginei Vasilias*, her import is highlighted. *Ophélia* subscribes ultimately, then, to a romantic *rapprochement* that cuts across classes and is premised on human-political sensitivities. Like *Ophélia*, *Ithele Na Ginei Vasilias* decentres the Hamlet character as revenger, playing up instead his role as lover. The marriage between Alekos/Hamlet and Filitsa/Ophelia, a cross-class union that recalls *Ophélia*, enables the factory foreman/Polonius (Giorgos Velentzas), rough-voiced and wearing overalls, to retain his job. Via 'social drama', then, working- and middle-class groups are combined and a more egalitarian and inclusive notion of the employer and employee contract is proposed. Importing the worker from the margins so as to situate women more openly, *Ophélia* and *Ithele Na Ginei Vasilias* take to *Hamlet* and away from it a revisionist gender and class agenda.

In 1968, the year after *Ithnele na Ginei Vasilias*' release, Europe was rocked by local expressions of disorder. Protests often associated with France (such as the 'May '68' agitations in which students and workers joined forces) assumed other manifestations elsewhere in Europe – in Italy, for example, where the aptly named 'Sessantotto' movement brought together students and artists in the occupation of buildings and

institutions.[34] Comprising a series of linked events around political free-
doms, working conditions, the position of women, civil rights and nuclear
disarmament, the unrest of 1968 furnishes a background to the contemporary genre of the 'Euro-Western', the co-produced European filmic
phenomenon that subjected the ideals of the American Western to scrutiny. *Quella Sporca Storia nel West/Johnny Hamlet* (dir. Enzo G. Castellari,
1968) and *Dans la Poussière de la Soleil/In the Dust of the Sun* (dir. Richard
Balducci, 1971) were released with different titles between 1968 and 1973.
And the discontent and demons of contemporary protests are shadowed in
each film's Hamlet figure – Johnny/Hamlet (Andrea Giordana), youthful,
unshaven and beautiful, and Hawk/Hamlet (Daniel Beretta), long-haired,
blonde-bearded and sporting a cross that signifies western-hippie identifications. At base an Italian production with an all-European cast, *Johnny
Hamlet* namechecks the constituent features of the genre – fist-fights,
gunplay and a disillusioned hero. Johnny Hamilton/Hamlet returns
from the Civil War to discover that his father been killed and that
$300,000 in Confederate gold has disappeared: the silky Claude/
Claudius (Horst Frank) is suspected. Utilizing the genre's conflicted
types (as set out by Flavia Brizio-Skov, the 'capitalist individual' and the
'revolutionary'), *Johnny Hamlet* shines a light on the state of contemporary
Italy, with the 'revolutionary' (Johnny/Hamlet) and the 'capitalist
individual' (Claude/Claudius) mirroring what were at the time easily
recognizable ideological rifts.[35] A mainly French production with a pan-
European cast, *In the Dust of the Sun* was filmed in the rugged, inhospitable terrain of Almeria, Spain, and is similarly made up of generically
recognizable features (a border town, a score, heavy on percussion and
strings, and a Hawk/Hamlet shot against the natural glare), although the
play is more obviously instanced in credits ('Inspired by William
Shakespeare's *Hamlet*') and casting. Key episodes offer correlatives for
Joe Bradford/Claudius (Bob Cunningham), a landowner who kills with
impunity, Maria/Ophelia (Karin Meier), a sheriff's daughter suitably
drawn to desert waterholes, and Hawk/Hamlet, who takes refuge in the
scorched mountainside before a culminating gun-battle/duel. *Johnny
Hamlet* exploits Spanish landscapes even further. Almeria and La
Ciudad Encantada, Cuenca (populated by monumental, mushroom-
shaped rocks sculpted by erosion), are so lensed as to emphasize the
fungal excrescences radiating from the 'El Señor' ranch. The 'whole . . .
of Denmark / Is . . . Rankly abused' (1.5.36, 38), states the Ghost; similarly, in *Johnny Hamlet* and *In the Dust of the Sun*, the entirety of the
hero's world appears corrupted.

If both films are indebted to the discourses and praxes of protest, then this shows itself in their striking amalgam of pornography and pacifism. *In the Dust of the Sun* presents a hero who remains silent except for his promise to Maria/Ophelia that, his duty done, they will leave the border town to farm orange groves in California ('California, it won't be long', he states). At one level, a taciturn *pistolero* is akin to the Shakespearean Hamlet, purposefully performing 'strange or odd' (1.5.168) behaviour.[36] At another level, the type answers to a need in the 'Euro-western', in which the voice-track was multiply dubbed, to favour action in the place of dialogue. Or, to put the point more graphically, this is a film in which 'soft core' sex scenes and nudity are given far greater emphasis than language, salient examples including the 'closet' episode in which Hawk/Hamlet overly comforts a grieving Gertie/Gertrude (Maria Schell) and the equivalent moment at which Joe/Claudius assaults her, his previously having accosted and stripped one of the 'saloon girls'. Richard Burt writes that 'porn adaptations of classics are caught within … a paradoxical dynamic; on the one hand, the classic sublimes the porn, creates a critical distance on the sex; on the other, the classic makes porn even sexier by deferring desire'.[37] Certainly, *In the Dust of the Sun* offers interpretive challenges. At first blush, the film is consonant with the ways in which the so-called 'liberated "Sixties"' did not actually arrive in Europe until the Seventies'.[38] More fundamentally, Hawk/Hamlet's silence realigns the spaces of gender and desire demarcated by *Hamlet*. 'Sex' is coded as either 'good' or 'bad', the effect of which is to make the body a self-evident site of Oedipal conflict, to demonize Joe/Claudius and to position Gertie/Gertrude as traumatized sexual victim.

Taking advantage of a new permissiveness, *In the Dust of the Sun* opens out the sexual sub-texts with which *Hamlet* is underpinned and demonstrates how it, along with *Johnny Hamlet*, subscribes to different forms of trauma as interpretive rationales. So, in *Johnny Hamlet*, in the scene in the 'Danark' cemetery where the cowboy-hero reflects on his filial obligations, a camera attached to a wheel captures his face revolving in appalled close-up, indicating psychic damage. Like the soldier exposed to extended conflict, he suffers from war fatigue. The theme of suffering is extended via the spectacle of Johnny/Hamlet's crucifixion, which places in unsettling juxtaposition bodily mortification, Catholic iconography and ideas of sacrifice. Contemporary Europe-wide protests against the Vietnam War provide a context for the representation and situate, too, this film's anti-militaristic stances. At the close, for instance, Johnny/Hamlet casts his pistol into a well in a renunciation of violence, a choreographed gesture

Figure 5: Poster for *Dans la Poussière de la Soleil/In the Dust of the Sun* (dir. Richard Balducci, 1971). Courtesy of Univers-Galaxie-Films/Author Collection.

that both reminds us of the Chief Player's (John Bartha) philosophically fatalistic statement ('War only harms') and looks forward to *Dust in the Sun* and to Hawk/Hamlet's pacifist persona (intertextually consolidated and popularized when Daniel Beretta went on to play Jesus in the French production of *Jesus Christ Superstar*). More broadly, Hawk/Hamlet is charitably disposed (rescuing drunks and families hounded by Joe/Claudius) and in search of an alternative lifestyle (his farming fantasy aligns him with the 'back-to-the-land'/commune initiative). In France, 1968 was a watershed moment, one that saw virtues centred on patriotism and religion superseded by the energies of secularism and revolution. Shakespeare was comparably affected, and, according to Nicole Fayard, the dramatist by the 1960s was established in French intellectual circles as a spokesperson for 'experiences of . . . disillusionment' and 'the incoherence and uncertainty of modernity'.[39] *In the Dust of the Sun* is intimately bound up with this reconceptualization of Shakespeare, and it accommodates the spirit of youth and rebellion to engage *Hamlet* as a viable means of contemporary commentary.

Also vigorously engaged in the intellectual circles of the 1960s and beyond, Carmelo Bene, the critically acclaimed Italian actor, director and artist, experimented with *Hamlet* in stage productions, television adaptations, radio recordings and other media.[40] His *avant-garde* film adaptation, *Un Amleto di Meno/One Hamlet Less* (1973), can be seen as the culmination of that continuing experimental process. Notably, alongside *Hamlet*, the film includes revised and repurposed extracts from the short story parody by Jules Laforgue, the French symbolist writer, 'Hamlet or the Consequences of Filial Piety', first published in 1887.[41] From Laforgue Bene derives, in particular, the dialogue of a protagonist marked by isolation ('I have not a friend to tell my sad story') and reluctance to assume the burdens of royalty ('I don't give a damn about my throne').[42] Part of the effect *Un Amleto di Meno*, indeed, can be traced to the way in which the film strategically melds Shakespeare's *Hamlet* with other European poetry and *Hamlet* adaptations. Exhibiting a restless and innovative approach to Shakespeare, *Un Amleto di Meno* anticipates the 'counter-cinematic work' of Derek Jarman, which, as Pascale Aebischer notes, stages 'transgressive desires and dissident identities'.[43] And, because it demonstrates, in the words of Gilles Deleuze, artistry that proceeds 'by substitution, by amputation', the film gives birth to 'the unexpected'.[44] The playing up of a perverse eroticism is one 'unexpected' by-product of Bene's representational protocols. For example, Polonio/Polonius (Pippo Tuminelli) is discovered as a bearded psychologist whispering to a naked Gertrude (Luciana Cante) sections from Freud's landmark discussion of Hamlet and the Oedipus complex.[45] At other points, in an otherwise white (studio) set, scenes of lust/rape – Old Amleto/the Ghost assaults Gertrude – disturb Amleto/Hamlet's (Carmelo Bene) filial remembrances. Both episodes push at the play's sexual back-stories, and place graphic emphasis on the readings to which *Hamlet* has been subjected, in the process heightening sexuality and pressing issues around trauma and memory referenced, but not always visualized, in previous adaptations. Jumbled effects and images add to the sense of the 'unexpected' by creating disorientation. Germane here is the phantasmagoria of zooms and dollies that identifies a headless Fortinbras, lips purposefully non-synched to dialogue, Egyptian and Japanese décor and outlandish costumes suggestive of playing cards and board game pieces. Matching the jumbled visuals, reallocated extracted lines destabilize assumptions about characters and their ownership of particular sentiments, as when the 'rogue and peasant slave' (2.2.485) soliloquy is shown being torn from an ancient volume and given to Orazio/Horatio (2.2.533–39), played by Franco Leo, who then reads it out. Similarly, when Gertrude delivers the plan for the play-within-the-play (2.2.523–540), a dovetailing of speech and character is unmoored, the result of which is to suggest a purposeful splintering of the Hamletian

Figure 6: Amleto/Hamlet (Carmelo Bene), with suitcase, agitates to escape in *Un Amleto di Meno/One Hamlet Less* (dir. Carmelo Bene, 1973). Courtesy of Ermanno Dannutelli/Author Collection.

protagonist. It is as the film wants to dispense with any association between play and book, and between word and speaker, in the interests of forging a hybrid Shakespeare that has the power to surprise, distract and scandalize.

David Martin-Jones notes that a 'jumbled, fragmented, multiplied or reversed film narrative . . . can [often] be interpreted as an expression of the difficulty of narrating national identity at a time of historical crisis or transformation'.[46] His comment chimes with the ways in which, in the early 1970s, Italy was struggling to deal with new labour demands, grass-roots discontent and acts of terrorism at each end of the political spectrum.[47] Because, as Giles Deleuze states, forces in Bene's work are 'always in disequilibrium', what matters in this 'subtraction of stable components' is the 'potentiality' and 'the becoming'.[48] Becoming, for Bene, translates as frustrated creativity. Chafing at the disapproval of the black-suited Orazio/Horatio, Amleto/Hamlet is realized as aspiring to artistic liberation, striving for a new identity (he twice cites the Guido Gozzano poem, 'Felicity', with its reverberating line, 'And I don't want to be me anymore!') and ultimately lamenting talents unfulfilled (his last lines are Nero's: '*Qualis ... artifex ... pereo!*' [With my death, what a great artist is lost!']).[49] The film thus ends by situating Amleto/Hamlet as the latest in a long line of flawed, failed and fated creatives. In this sense, and clarifying the extent to which it consistently gives birth to the 'unexpected', *Un Amleto di Meno* overturns long-standing constructions of the protagonist's symbolic applications. The film takes its title from the final lines of the Laforgue short story ('One Hamlet less does not mean the end of the human race'), elaborating its parodic dismantlement of the idea that only Shakespeare's hero can represent or speak to humanity.[50] The world continues, *Un Amleto di Meno* agitates to suggest, as Bene subjects the myths that sustain Shakespeare to pointedly demythologizing treatment. And, as Amleto/Hamlet dies in the graveyard next to the ocean, the 'disequilibrium' of the adaptation comes into its own. *Un Amleto di Meno* takes its cue from the effects of marshalling a range of Western European texts and cultures and placing them in juxtaposition; at one and the same time, it echoes the troubles of its location in history, illuminating Italy's ongoing negotiations with itself.

Post-*Un Amleto di Meno*, no film feature *Hamlet* adaptations would follow in Western Europe for a decade: Bene, arguably, had temporarily pushed the play as far as it was possible to go. However, in the late 1980s, there came a return to the factory/industry model of interpretation with the Finnish *Hamlet liikemaailmassa/Hamlet Goes Business* (dir. Aki Kaurismäki, 1987), which returns to and significantly develops the concept first deployed in earlier French, Greek and German cinematic outings.[51] Hamlet (Pirkka-Pekka Petellus), heir to the 'Group', a shipbuilding and sawmills business, is imagined as a greedy loser-loafer who disdains his inferiors and is interested only in comic books and his next dinner appointment. In the final reel, Simo/Horatio (Hannu Valtonen), chauffeur to the 'Group', poisons him. Melissa Croteau notes that *Hamlet Goes Business* presents a 'triumph of the proletariat over the bourgeoisie', or, in the words of the director, 'a working-class victory . . . that brings out the romantic'.[52] Affirming the 'romantic' dimension, Simo/Horatio is represented as a union official who not only sacrifices personal relations for the sake 'of the shipyard' but also murders his new boss to prevent local industries being sold off to global partners, tearing up the deal Hamlet has just signed. In this sense, the film puts into play national *and* global pressures, refracting in parodic fashion the 'wave of economic and social challenges' brought upon late twentieth-century Western European nations by 'open competition within and across borders'.[53]

The film's global interstices are easily apparent, not least because the 'Group' is represented as comically pincered between competition from Japan and a takeover bid from Norway, all in the context of a joint investment in a 'Caribbean Sea Cruisers' initiative. These, a downbeat Klaus/Claudius (Esko Salminen) informs us, are the pressures that push the 'international market'. The scenario mirrors the 'casino-economics' policies that overtook Finnish businesses in the late 1980s while simultaneously suggesting 'key' national 'issues' – Finland's 'relation to Russia . . . Sweden . . . Europe [and] the Nordic countries' and its position within the 'political . . . outskirts of Western Europe'.[54] Symptomatic of its impatient camerawork, *Hamlet Goes Business* frequently focuses in on global brand-name products, such as advertisements for Levi's or shots of bottles of Ballantine's whiskey and Smirnoff vodka, juxtaposing Finnish environs with the insignia of capitalist transnationalism. When a well-known folk song (*Muuttuvat Laulut*) is heard over the closing images of a sawmill, therefore, the film's tensions come full circle. On the one hand, sound and visuals would seem to affirm Finnocentrism; on the other hand, the parodic thrust problematizes any straightforward endorsement of nationalist sentiment. *Hamlet Goes Business* is a revealing coda to the strains and tendencies that *Hamlet* adaptations from the 1960s to the 1980s exhibit, for it takes the models that have defined interpretation of the play in the postwar cinematic consciousness and subjects them to revision and comic exaggeration. It plays with the worker figure, upturns its generic investments, broadens and debunks analogies, and echoes in another key an alternative mindset. But it does so by simultaneously acknowledging the invitation to join an increasingly integrated European arena and resisting its premises and significations.

Others/Ideologies

Since the reunification of Germany in 1990 and the foundation of the EU in 1993, the continuing development of a Europe premised on the efficient and productive co-existence of communal economies and cultures has been complicated by the ways in which large-scale population shifts in the form of mass immigration have disrupted the smooth flow from one order to another. A symptom of disruption has been the extent to which, as Tom Buchanan writes, Europe's 'professed liberal and humanitarian values' have crashed against 'the rise of a powerful and destabilizing xenophobia', detaching in the process long-established 'political philosophies' from 'specific geographical or historical moorings'.[55] A grouping of three recent Western European *Hamlet* adaptations – the Danish *Festen/Celebration* (dir. Thomas Vinterberg, 1998), the Spanish *El Triunfo/The Triumph* (dir. Mireia Ros, 2006) and the German *Elf Onkel/Eleven Uncles* (dir. Herbert Fritsch, 2010) – leaves behind the factory/industry model, prioritizing instead a more nebulous sense of the ways in which forms of symbolic capital are bound up with anxieties about migration and ethnic adulteration. In a climate of disenchantment, it might be suggested, cinematic *Hamlet* adaptations have provided a conduit, ventilating concerns around regionally determined assertions of distinctiveness and giving expression to the perceived demands and compromises involved in belonging to a European community.

As several critics have noted, *Hamlet* can be detected in *Festen* in 'reconstructions that variably divide or conflate Shakespeare's characters', the film operating 'at the level of inference'.[56] Accordingly, the plot centres on restaurateur Christian/Hamlet (Ulrich Thomsen) who attends Helge/Claudius' (Henning Moritzen) extravagantly appointed sixtieth birthday party at the magnificent family-run hotel, using the occasion to reveal his father's hidden past as a serial sex abuser. The splendid neoclassical Skjoldenæsholm Castle, near Ringsted, hosts the scenes of 'heavy-headed revel' (1.4.17). A product of the Dogme 95 movement, which insists on a pared-down, 'natural' digital shooting-style, *Festen* is characterized by a grainy if not degraded texture indicative of moral degeneration.[57] *Hamlet* is adumbrated in allusions to incest, concealment ('The main course is a secret'), ghosts ('There have always been ghosts in this house', Helene [Paprika Steen], Christian/Hamlet's sister, announces), drowning (Linda [Lene Laub Oksen], Christian/Hamlet's other sister, who has been abused by her father, dies in her bathtub), suicide and dirt (hands are soiled and grimy). Madness is instanced as explanation (Christian/Hamlet is 'mad . . .

sick'). Similarly, the dream, that Shakespearean staple, surfaces when Christian/Hamlet sees Linda in a hallucinatory vignette. Integral to the film's preoccupation with an unspeakable family history is a structure based on rhythms of accusation and retraction. In a series of five toasts that operate as plays-within-the-play and that divide the action into acts, Helge/Claudius is held to account ('Here's to the man who killed my sister', Christian/Hamlet exclaims), and eventually his crimes are publicly uncovered. But, in ways not dissimilar to *Der Rest ist Schweigen*, the film also highlights the cost involved in the telling – Christian/Hamlet's toasts are stuttering, imperfect and self-contradictory statements that point up crisis and compromise.

Festen contemplates how *Hamlet* figures in a contemporary narrative about trauma. By contrast, *Elf Onkel* goes backwards to a *Hamlet* before *Hamlet* to hypothesize about what remains. In fact, *Elf Onkel* exhibits contrary tendencies; on the one hand, the film relinquishes Shakespeare to simulacra and spectacle, but, on the other, works to reinstate his critical valency. Asserting Saxo Grammaticus' *The History of the Danes* as part of an unbroken line to *Hamlet, Elf Onkel* extends director Herbert Fritsch's fascination with the play as this has shown itself in the multi-media, experimental art project, *hamlet-x*. Distinctively, *hamlet-x* aims to dismantle the texts of *Hamlet*, even as it also affirms them, via a series of gallery installations, television programmes, lectures, print works and gaming platforms.[58] For its part, *Elf Onkel* both rehearses the Grammaticus narrative and places upon it a peculiarly postmodern exuberance (as suggested in baroque visuals, split screens, acoustic exaggeration and flipped shots): it is as if, to get to *Hamlet*, Fritsch must make cinematically hyperbolic the pre-*Hamlet* literary and cultural landscape.[59] Hence, the film concentrates in grotesque close-up on biting, snapping brothers, discovers a dirty protagonist (Alexander Khuon) who, in speeded-up motion, escapes from a web of cords to feed a duplicitous secretary to the pigs, and, comically invoking Da Vinci's 'The Last Supper', lends a climactic importance to a banquet at which the eleven uncle figures are roped and strangled. 'To be, or not to be' is realized in terms of an assembly of body parts which, in a bloody miasma, give voice to fragments that recall the soliloquy: 'The end, death, the end . . . Escape. Where? Into nothingness . . . Eternal crossing of worlds'. More self-conscious than *Hamlet Goes Business* in its brand-name satire, *Elf Onkel* trades in images and logos that stand in for the commodity and imitations that surrogate for originals, ensnaring Shakespeare, too, in an ironic logic of cultural capital. Architectural echoes of German ascendancy – filming unfolds in a nineteenth-century mansion (Guthaus Streckenthin, Pritzwalk) – suggest

Figure 7: Nen/Hamlet (Antonio Fernández Montoya) and Palito/Horatio (Cheto),
to the right, are denizens of Barcelona's *El Raval* neighbourhood in *El Triunfo/The
Triumph* (dir. Mireia Ros, 2006). Courtesy of Marta Figueras/Mireia Ros.

how the film draws on heritage so as to offset its hyperbolic register and recall
its own antecedents. At the same time, because establishing shots of the
mansion's exterior collide with discontinuous episodes, we are alerted to
the implications of bringing together a spectrum of *Hamlet* iterations and to
the histories out of which the film emerged.

The eruption of the past into the present is the pretext for *El Triunfo*. Set
in the Barcelona neighbourhood of *El Raval* in the 1980s, the film centres
on Gandhi/Claudius (Juan Diego), a local crime boss and ex-legionnaire,
and his nostalgia for the wars in Spanish Morocco. The Hamlet figure,
Nen (Antonio Fernández Montoya), a young 'gypsy' *rumba catalana*
singer, aspires to escape and make his mark in music: the 'triumph' in
the title refers to his ambitions for a better life. *El Raval* is emphasized (in
the director's estimation, it functions as a 'character in its own right') as
a space that encodes memories of empire and the cultural and political
heritage of Francoist Spain.[60] In post-Francoist Spain, Tom Buchanan
argues, 'membership of the European Community' has come into conflict
with 'nationalist traditions' and the corresponding diminution of Madrid

as the political centre.[61] Some of this ideological friction is captured in visuals – green-filtered glimpses of narrow alleyways and puddled gutters – and a soundscape made up of breaking glass and the wail of cats. Similarly, the figuration of *El Raval* gains in depth and density when we consider how the film's dissemination answers to the requirements of multiple funding bodies and several national-cultural agendas. *El Triunfo* was released in Catalan- and Spanish-language versions and, as a politically charged accompaniment, features Catalan-language music, indicative of a resurgence of Catalan cinema spearheaded by women practitioners and of a growing attention to secessionist initiatives.[62] For Ros, the only female director to have adapted *Hamlet* in world cinema, the aim was to marry a regional perspective with revisions to her main source, a novel itself indebted to *Hamlet*, to create an adaptation of the play in its own right.[63] *Hamlet* is most obviously referenced in the young protagonist's meeting with his dying, exiled father, El Guacho/Old Hamlet (Jesús Cabrero), in a derelict, barred house (a type of 'prison-house' [1.5.14]), in inset clips from old movies that (as in *Ophélia*) suggest the Ghost's speeches, in Nen/Hamlet's encounter with Chata/Gertrude (Ángela Molina) at the morgue, a type of 'closet', in his own subsequent flight from the neighbourhood, and in the retrospective mode of narration (Palito's [Cheto] summary that 'what caused this misfortune was a series of mean actions and misunderstandings' resembling Horatio's observations about 'accidental judgements, casual slaughters . . . And . . . purposes mistook' [5.2.366, 368]). The play's subscription to remembrance is conjured in the scene in which Nen inherits his father's notebook of songs (making visible Hamlet's 'table of . . . memory' [1.5.98]) and in the ways in which, mourning-garbed, he uses a song to condemn his enemies. This much is indicative of the film's Shakespearean undercurrent, but, in interview, Ros confesses to interpolating one line of dialogue, '*un barrio que aprieta y asfixia, que no te deja vivir en paz*' ('a neighbourhood that pressures and suffocates you, that prevents you from living in peace'), to register her own take on 'To be, or not to be'. The expression's alternation between states of being, concentration on an afflicted state of mind and contemplation of mortality succinctly rehearse some of the thematic threads of the Shakespearean soliloquy. In this film of remembering a former Barcelona, Ros flags the forces at play in the shift to democracy: in the same moment, her adaptation of *Hamlet* illuminates the multiple roles she is obliged to undertake as a creative – woman, Catalonian, Shakespearean interpreter.

Recent world cinema adaptations of *Romeo and Juliet* have understood the play in relation to deterritorialization, demographic mobility and local realignments of race. Typically, Romeo and Juliet are imagined as belonging not to different classes as different ethnic groups, pointing up what Arjun Appadurai terms the '*ethnoscape* . . . the landscape of persons who constitute the shifting world in which we live' and emphasizing imperfectly acclimatized societies.[64] *Festen, El Triunfo* and *Elf Onkel* inhabit a not dissimilar ideological hinterland to these adaptations – the '*ethnoscape*', however, is expressed through Fortinbras or some version of the Norwegian prince rather than a pairing of lovers. Whether as African American (*Festen*), Arab/North African (*El Triunfo*) or African (*Elf Onkel*), the Fortinbras figure is so realized as to focalize racial alterity. *Elf Onkel*, for example, is cut across by insets in which a dreadlocked, red-cloaked and yellow-robed '*Afrikaner*' (his title in the credits), played by Mizrayim Komi Togbonou, is seen rowing towards the mansion in a dinghy singing to himself: his tattoos and bangles declare his difference from the all-white cast. His refrain, 'I'm coming!', signals both a mission and an inverted colonial narrative. On arrival, the '*Afrikaner*' kisses the ground in a sigh of relief. 'Europe!', he exclaims, his announcement clarifying that he has reached his destination. Significantly, this is one of the departures from the Grammaticus plot, a reversion to *Hamlet*'s envisioning of a journey from Norway to Denmark that facilitates the film's confrontation with what the '*ethnoscape*' signifies.[65] Similar insets punctuate *El Triunfo*, although more violently oriented. 'Blacks and Arabs were arriving', Palito/Horatio reflects, adding, 'they started busting people's balls'. To illustrate the complaint, the film privileges scenes in which black characters are involved in violence or hatch drug deals and interludes of gang mayhem. Ahmed/Fortinbras (Ahmed Krim), scarred, speaking haltingly and only ever glimpsed in the shadows, is the new kingpin threatening Gandhi/Claudius' neighbourhood rule, out-of-focus cinematography accentuating racialized dissimulation. After Spain had joined the EC in 1986, the country attracted large numbers of *émigrés* from 'the Maghreb and sub-Saharan Africa', testing, in the process, 'collective' attitudes towards 'racism [and] . . . social welfare'.[66] Via contextually suggestive sequences, *El Triunfo* joins forces with related Spanish-language films that, as, Maria Van Liew writes, demonstrate an 'ability to exhibit new cultural formations and alliances that are at a crossroads with Spanish/European policy'.[67] Introducing a Fortinbras, the film captures the post-EU membership tensions of a metropolis such as Barcelona and, ironically, equates through the nostalgia of the older generation the ways in which warfare between gangs (or between Denmark and Norway) re-instates earlier conflicts (the Rif and Ifni wars) between the Spanish military and Moroccan insurgents.

In *Festen*, Fortinbras is the black American, Gbatokai (Gbatokai Dakinah), boyfriend to Christian/Hamlet's sister. Although he is subject to mockery – he is labelled a 'monkey' and, amidst immaculate dinner jackets and mirrored, designer interiors, made the butt of a children's racist song, '*Jeg Har Set en Rigtig Negermand*' ('I have seen a real black man') – he persists through offers of empathy and gestures of friendship in assisting Christian/Hamlet in his unravelling of his family's tangled history (the connection between them is ratified in the ways in which both are stigmatized, one via racism and the other via sexual abuse). In the mid- to late 1990s, writes C. Claire Thomson, Denmark was renegotiating 'what it meant to be Danish in the face of globalization, European economic and political integration, and increasingly visible integration'.[68] It is against this backdrop that the representation of Gbatokai assumes an importance greater than the role itself – he stands as a counter-force to nationalist and far-right discourses, and in this he evokes a 'voice of ethics or of moral conscience'.[69] By contrast with a type such as Ahmed/Fortinbras in *El Triunfo*, Gbatokai/Fortinbras in *Festen* is a reassuring presence in the *mise-en-scène* – a properly joyous agency (celebratory, advisory, influential) and an indivisible part of Christian/Hamlet's decision not to 'move back [to Denmark] for good'.

Endings and readings of Fortinbras are critically intertwined. How we judge Shakespeare's Fortinbras steers how we interpret the endings of Western European cinematic adaptations of *Hamlet*. Once Christian/Hamlet has absorbed Gbatokai/Fortinbras' counsel in *Festen*, he elects to return to Paris and his restaurant business with Pia (Trine Dyrholm), the waitress with whom, thanks to the banishment of his ghosts, he has rekindled a relationship. With this decision, Christian/Hamlet is represented as rejecting the family and its poetic significances as a national metaphor; rather, it is only by breaking with the past that accommodation can be reached. But endings are not always affirmatively angled. At the close of *El Triunfo*, Nen/Hamlet, having 'vanished and taken with him' the neighbourhood's 'hopes', his friends are bundled into a police van while Ahmed/Fortinbras looks on. 'Divide and conquer', he intones, his use of the classical maxim associating him with a host of previous empire builders and altering the implications of the film's triumphalist title. This, then, is an ending that speaks of a takeover of a traditional Spanish dispensation: Gandhi/Claudius' order, and the imperial memories it entailed, is superseded and in its place is a Fortinbras-like 'conquest' (5.2.334), a 'sight' (5.2.346) over which Ahmed presides. Although, as Thea D. Boldt notes, the contemporary 'German European identity project' favours 'pluralistic interpretations of belonging, based on reiterated demarcation lines', some material and political tendencies have veered in opposite directions: immigration has tested the liberal quality of German polity and populist right-wing groups have grown in support.[70] A work that mirrors, in Wilhelm Hortmann's words, 'interculturalism' and the task of 'de-Teutonizing the Bard', *Elf Onkel* encodes the '*Afrikaner*' as uncertain in status.[71] At its Grammaticus-inspired ending, as Hamlet and Gertrud (Gitta Schweighöfer) bundle the bodies of the eleven uncles into carpets and set them alight, the '*Afrikaner*'/Fortinbras is seen through the smoke contemplating the conflagration. Imaged on the other side of the fire, he smiles enigmatically: his ritualistic leaps across the blaze indicate either possession of territory or communal celebration, while his accompanying dance suggests hostility and friendship at one and the same time. *Elf Onkel* wants to embrace the 'other' in the spirit of a Western Europe premised on welcome and good relations; simultaneously, it remains locked in an either-or dialectic. Ideological praxes, and filmic *Hamlet* adaptations, are mediated through continuing conditions of volatility and unpredictability, disrupting any neat conclusions and highlighting the partial narratives of a holistic Western Europe.

Conclusions

Although Western European *Hamlet* adaptations are differently inflected according to their specific moment, they consistently take on the complexions of a changing European landmass. Clustering together thematically even as they announce themselves as distinctive, there are moments of obvious generic consanguinity (e.g. the 'Euro-Western'), with *noir* cropping up repeatedly if not uniformly, an indication of how variously the form can be made to function (as psychic reckoning or as parodic reflection). In films such as *Ophélia* and *Ithele Na Ginei Vasilias*, the focus is on a socially attuned perspective that touches on the ways in which adaptations of *Hamlet* are drawn to exploring minority positions and experiences. And in related adaptations, such as *Un Amleto di Meno*, the pressures of social and economic transformation take energy from while also shaping the methods and practices of a radical artistry.

Traceable across these eleven adaptations is an increased attention to the nation-state *in relation to* global neighbours and concerns. For instance, *Io, Amleto* and *Der Rest ist Schweigen* are centred on the identities of Italy and Germany respectively as they emerge from the post-war twilight into visibility. By contrast, as a more recent film such as *Hamlet Goes Business* suggests, the nation-state is apprehended in terms of extra-national networks (even if these are parodied in the distinctively downbeat manner that Kaurismäki has made his own). More critically, as *Hamlet* is rewritten and written over, categories of the national are forced into confrontation with the non-national as this is embodied in an outsider figure, an 'other' who traverses borders and does not easily or evenly belong. On the eve of continuing negotiations about the futures of the EU and its members, this most recent development in the Western European *Hamlet* film is singularly expressive. Spottily present in early cinematic adaptations, the Fortinbras type comes into its own at the end of the twentieth century and the beginning of the twenty-first, a sign of continuing assertions of nationalism and a turn to xenophobia: while physical walls have been disassembled, ideological walls are once again beginning to be erected. Ensnared in such processes is the disappearance in the Western European *Hamlet* imaginary of the factory/industry analogy. As *Hamlet Goes Business* illustrates, the factory is conceptually laid off in the late 1980s; thereafter, business inheres in less well-defined circuits of capital that have no obvious basis or context. *Hamlet*, of course, is thought of archetypally as a tragedy. Yet, in all but three of these adaptations (*Un Amleto di Meno, In the Dust of the Sun* and *Hamlet Goes Business*), the protagonist lives on. These are works that want to keep open the possibility for other lives and narratives not predicated on despair or disenchantment. Western European *Hamlet* films aspire to change the play's tragic imprimatur, seeing in the story possibilities for an individual's recuperation and repair. Atsuko Ichijo considers Western Europe 'a story of continual constitution and reconstitution of a multiplicity of political and cultural programmes'.[72] The same might be said for *Hamlet* which, infinitely hospitable to cinematic reinvention, enables the continuing European project to be questioned, debated, forwarded and remade.

Notes

1. Shaul Bassi, 'The Tragedies in Italy', in Michael Neill and David Schalkwyk, eds, *The Oxford Handbook of Shakespearean Tragedy* (Oxford: Oxford University Press, 2016), pp. 692, 694; Pascale Drouet and Nathalie Rivère de Carles, 'French Receptions of Shakespearean Tragedy: Between Liberty and Memory', in Neill and Schalkwyk, eds, *Handbook*, p. 727; Kristian Smidt, 'The Discovery of Shakespeare in Scandinavia', in Dirk Delabastita and Lieven D'Hulst, eds, *European Shakespeares: Translating Shakespeare in the Romantic Age* (Amsterdam and Philadelphia: John Benjamins, 1993), p. 92.

2. Keith Gregor, *Shakespeare in the Spanish Theatre: 1772 to the Present* (London and New York: Continuum, 2010), p. 3; Heiner O. Zimmermann, 'Is Hamlet Germany? On the Political Reception of *Hamlet*', in Mark Thornton Burnett and John Manning, eds, *New Essays on 'Hamlet'* (New York: AMS, 1994), p. 300.

3. Mark Betz, *Beyond the Subtitle: Remapping European Art Cinema* (Minneapolis and London: University of Minnesota Press, 2009), p. 57.

4. Tony Judt, *Postwar: A History of Europe Since 1945* (London: Vintage, 2010), p. 2.

5. See Maurizio Ternavasio, *Macario: Vita di un Comico* (Turin: Lindau, 1998), p. 115.

6. See Douglas M. Lanier, 'Shakescorp *Noir*', *Shakespeare Quarterly*, 53.2 (2002), p. 170.

7. Pierre Sorlin, *Italian National Cinema* (London and New York: Routledge, 1996), pp. 89, 94, 103.

8. Thomas Elsaesser, *German Cinema – Terror and Trauma: Cultural Memory Since 1945* (London and New York: Routledge, 2014), p. 4.

9. Sabine Hake, *German National Cinema* (London and New York: Routledge, 2002), p. 92.

10. Ewa Mazierska, *European Cinema and Intertextuality: History, Memory and Politics* (Basingstoke: Palgrave, 2011), pp. 23, 30.

11. Hake, *German*, p. 92.

12. William Manchester, *The Arms of Krupp, 1587–1968: The Rise and Fall of the Industrial Dynasty that Armed Germany at War* (New York and Boston: Little Brown, 2003), p. 686; 'Obituaries: Berthold Beitz', *The Times*, 2 August (2013), p. 49.

13. Manchester, *Arms*, p. 608.

14. Louis Bayman, 'Neorealism', in Louis Bayman, ed., *Directory of World Cinema: Italy* (Bristol and Chicago: Intellect, 2011), p. 55.

15. Peter Bondanella, 'From Italian Neorealism to the Golden Age of Cinecittà', in Elizabeth Ezra, ed., *European Cinema* (Oxford: Oxford University Press, 2004), p. 127; Marcia Landy, *Italian Film* (Cambridge: Cambridge University Press, 2000), p. 98; Mazierska, *European*, p. 21.

16. Linda Hutcheon, *A Theory of Parody: The Teachings of Twentieth-Century Art Forms* (Urbana and Chicago: University of Illinois Press, 2000), p. 101.

17. See Ruth Ben-Ghiat, 'Unmaking the Fascist Man: Masculinity, Film and the Transition from Dictatorship', *Journal of Modern Italian Studies*, 10.3 (2005), pp. 336–37.

18. Guido Bonsaver, 'Mussolini's Fascism, Literary Censorship, and the Vatican', *Primerjalna Književnost*, 31 (2008), pp. 201–212.

19. Ben-Ghiat, 'Unmaking', p. 348.

20. Judt, *Postwar*, pp. 326, 736.

21. Karen Newman, *Essaying Shakespeare* (Minneapolis and London: University of Minnesota Press, 2009), p. 83.

22. See Helen Phelps Bailey, *Hamlet in France: From Voltaire to Laforgue* (Geneva: Librairie Droz, 1964), p. 137.

23. Douglas M. Lanier, '*Nouveau Noir*: Claude Chabrol's *Ophélia*, Shakespeare's *Hamlet*, and the *Nouvelle Vague*', in Sarah Hatchuel and Nathalie Vienne-Guerrin, eds, *Shakespeare on Screen: 'Hamlet'* (Mont-Saint-Aignam: Publications de l'Université de Rouen et du Havre, 2011), p. 243.

24. See Judt, *Postwar*, p. 362.

25. Gordon Wright, *France in Modern Times*, 5th ed. (New York and London: Norton, 1995), pp. 415–16.

26. See Tom Buchanan, *Europe's Troubled Peace: 1945 to the Present*, 2nd ed. (Oxford: Wiley-Blackwell, 2012), pp. 92, 94.

27. See Peter Cowie, ed., *World Filmography 1967* (London: Tantivy, 1977), p. 229; Dimitris Koliodimos, *The Greek Filmography, 1914 Through 1996* (Jefferson and London: McFarland, 1999), p. 893; Rena, '*Ithele Na Ginei Vasilias/He Wanted to Become King*', *Variety*, 25 October (1967), n.p.

28. Richard Clogg, *A Concise History of Greece*, 3rd ed. (Cambridge: Cambridge University Press, 2013), p. 160; Emmi Mikedakis, 'Manipulating Language: Metaphors in the Political Discourse of Georgios Papadoulos (1967–1973)', in Elizabeth Close, Michael Tsianikas and George Frazis, eds, *Greek Studies in Australia: Research Perspectives* (Adelaide: Flinders University Press, 2003), pp. 83, 84.

29. Interviews between Angelos Theodoropoulos and Mark Thornton Burnett (14 April 2011 and 9 February 2012). Unless otherwise stated, all Theodoropoulos quotations are from these interviews and appear in the text or notes.

30. Koliodimos, *Filmography*, p. 16.

31. Lydia Papadimitriou, 'Music, Dance and Cultural Identity in the Greek Film Musical', in Lydia Papadimitriou and Yannis Tzioumakis, eds, *Greek Cinema: Texts, Histories, Ideologies* (Bristol and Chicago: Intellect, 2012), pp. 149, 162.

32. Judt, *Postwar*, p. 507.

33. Anthony Guneratne, *Shakespeare, Film Studies, and the Visual Cultures of Modernity* (New York: Palgrave, 2008), p. 208.

34. Angelique Chrisafis, 'Myths of 68?', *The Guardian*, 15 January (2018), p. 37; Mark Kurlansky, *1968: The Year That Rocked the World* (New York: Random House, 2004), pp. 82, 222, 230, 370.

35. Flavia Brizio-Skov, 'Spaghetti Westerns and Their Audiences', in Peter Bondanella, ed., *The Italian Cinema Book* (London: BFI, 2014), pp. 185, 186.

36. Hawk, reflects Daniel Beretta, 'has to appear foolish and mute, and never speak, the better to try to avenge himself' (interview between Daniel Beretta and Mark Thornton Burnett [12 December 2017]).

37. Richard Burt, *Unspeakable ShaXXXspeares: Queer Theory and American Kiddie Culture* (Basingstoke: Macmillan, 1998), p. 84.

38. Judt, *Postwar*, p. 377.

39. Nicole Fayard, 'France', in Peter W. Marx, ed., *Hamlet-Handbuch: Stoffe, Aneignungen, Deutungen* (Stuttgart and Weimar: Verlag J. B. Meltzler, 2014), p. 286.

40. Carmelo Bene, *Opere: Con l'autographia di un ritratto* (Milan: Bompiani, 2008), p. 1351; Armando Petrini, *'Amleto' da Shakespeare a Laforgue per Carmelo Bene* (Pisa: Edizioni ETS, 2004), pp. 9–11.
41. The story imagines Hamlet as a 'dandy ... repelled by the *aurea mediocritas*' who, agitating to escape Elsinore with Kate, one of the players, and write plays in Paris is waylaid and killed at the graveyard. See Bailey, *Hamlet*, pp. 147, 149.
42. See Jules Laforgue, *Moral Tales*, tr. William Jay Smith (London: Picador, 1985), pp. 17, 36. See also Bene's use of the poem, 'Complainte de l'époux outragé', in J. A. Hiddleston, ed., Poems of Jules Laforgue (Oxford: Blackwell, 1975), pp. 120–22.
43. Pascale Aebischer, *Screening Early Modern Drama: Beyond Shakespeare* (Cambridge: Cambridge University Press, 2013), p. 2.
44. Gilles Deleuze, *The Deleuze Reader*, ed. Constantin V. Boundas (New York: Columbia University Press, 1993), pp. 204, 205.
45. See Sigmund Freud, *The Interpretation of Dreams*, tr. A. A. Brill (Ware: Wordsworth, 1997), pp. 155–60.
46. David Martin-Jones, *Deleuze, Cinema and National Identity: Narrative Time in National Contexts* (Edinburgh: Edinburgh University Press, 2006), p. 1.
47. See Roy Palmer Domenico, *Remaking Italy in the Twentieth Century* (Lanham and Boulder: Rowman and Littlefield, 2002), pp. 126–27. Some historians go further in their analysis of Italy's crisis, arguing for a continuation of the discontent of 1968 that manifested itself in riots, militancy, a fluctuating economy and a protest culture that extended to schools, public services, the army and the police. See Martin Clark, *Modern Italy, 1871–1995*, 2nd ed. (London and New York: Longman, 1996), p. 374.
48. Deleuze, *Reader*, p. 207.
49. Guido Gozzano, *The Man I Pretend to Be*, tr. Michael Palma (Princeton: Princeton University Press, 1981), p. 89; Laforgue, *Moral*, p. 40.
50. Laforgue, *Moral*, p. 42.
51. Aki Kaurismäki notes that *Hamlet Goes Business* had its origins in a drunken bar conversation with Finnish director, Pauli Pentti: 'Suddenly he announces that he wanted to direct *Macbeth* and that I have to produce it. I replied, "O.K., but that means that I will have to make a *Hamlet* adaptation". Both films were made' (interview between Aki Kaurismäki and Mark Thornton Burnett [1 March 2018]). Unless otherwise stated, all Kaurismäki quotations are from this interview and appear in the text or notes.
52. Melissa M. Croteau, 'Aki Kaurismäki's *Hamlet Goes Business*: A Socialist Shakespearean Film Noir Comedy', in Richard Fotheringham, Christa Jansohn and R. S. White, eds, *Shakespeare's World/World Shakespeares* (Newark: University of Delaware Press, 2008), pp. 194–95.
53. Judt, *Postwar*, p. 736.
54. See Pietari Kääpä, *The National and Beyond: The Globalization of Finnish Cinema in the Films of Aki and Mika Kaurismäki* (Oxford and Bern: Peter Lang, 2010), p. 104; Marjo Eskola, Tiina Räisä and Henrik Stenius, 'Identity

Construction and Modernity in Finland: Borders, Ruptures and Significant Others', in Atsuko Ichijo, ed., *Europe, Nations and Modernity* (Basingstoke: Palgrave, 2011), pp. 186, 193.

55. Buchanan, *Peace*, pp. 228, 230.

56. Alisa Grant Ferguson, *Shakespeare, Cinema, Counter-Culture: Appropriation and Inversion* (London and New York: Routledge, 2016), p. 107; Yvonne Griggs, 'Dogmatic Shakespeare: A "Recognition of Ghostly Presences" in Thomas Vinterberg's *Festen* and Kristian Levring's *The King Is Alive*', *Journal of Adaptation in Film and Performance*, 2.2 (2009), p. 110.

57. See 'Dogme 95 – The Vow of Chastity', in Catherine Fowler, ed., *The European Cinema Reader* (London and New York: Routledge, 2002), pp. 83–84.

58. See Conny Loder, 'Siting *Hamlet* for the Online Generation: The *Hamlet_X* Project', in Ruth J. Owen, ed., *The Hamlet Zone: Reworking 'Hamlet' for European Cultures* (Newcastle-upon-Tyne: Cambridge Scholars, 2012), pp. 85–90; Birgit Wiens, 'Hamlet and the Virtual Stage: Herbert Fritsch's Project, *hamlet_x*', in Freda Chapple and Chiel Kattenbelt, eds, *Intermediality in Theatre and Performance* (Amsterdam and New York: Rodopi, 2006), pp. 223–236. Fritsch is infamous for an approach to Shakespeare that plays up outrageousness and excess. In the cartoon book manifestation of the *hamlet-x* project, for example, pseudo-autobiographical expostulations are highlighted ('My dad is dead!') in the same moment as abusive scatology ('*Und der rest sind schweine!* ['And the rest are pigs!']). See Herbert Fritsch and Sabrina Zwach, *Hamlet_X: Interpolierte Fressen* (Berlin: Theater der Zeit, 2006), n.p.

59. See Saxo Grammaticus, *The History of the Danes*, ed. Hilda Ellis Davidson, 2 vols (Cambridge: D. S. Brewer, 1979), I, pp. 83–90.

60. Interviews between Mireia Ros and Mark Thornton Burnett (1 and 8 December 2017). Unless otherwise stated, all Ros quotations are from these interviews and appear in the text or notes.

61. Buchanan, *Peace*, pp. 186, 232; Marvin D'Lugo, 'Catalan Cinema: Historical Experience and Cinematic Practice', in Fowler, ed., *European*, pp. 171–2; Gregor, *Spanish*, p. 123.

62. See Stephen Burgen, 'Court Remands Catalan Leader', *The Guardian*, 27 March (2018), p. 19; María Camí-Vela, 'Contemporary Barcelona Through the Female Eye', in Helio San Miguel and Lorenzo J. Torres Hortelano, eds, *World Film Locations: Barcelona* (Bristol and Chicago: Intellect, 2013), pp. 106–7; Paolo Dardanelli, *Restructuring the European State: European Integration and State Reform* (Montreal and Kingston: McGill-Queen's University Press, 2017), pp. 219, 224, 234.

63. Francisco Casavella's 1990 novel contains several quotations from the play. See, for example, the epitaph, referencing 1.5.91, 'Adiós, adiós, Hamlet, recuérdame' (*El triunfo* [Barcelona: Editorial Anagrama, 2017], p. 13). The back-cover blurb characterizes Nen as 'a Hamlet of the street who only wants to bring those who brought down his father to account'.

64. Arjun Appadurai, *Modernity at Large: Cultural Dimensions of Globalization* (Minneapolis: University of Minnesota Press, 1996), p. 33; Mark Thornton Burnett, *Shakespeare and World Cinema* (Cambridge: Cambridge University Press, 2013), pp. 195–231.

65. In interview, Herbert Fritsch speculates: 'I always try to change something. What would happen if Fortinbras was African? There is the desire to come to Europe. Old Hamlet fought with Old Fortinbras. Perhaps it was in the colonies. Now that history comes back' (interview between Herbert Fritsch and Mark Thornton Burnett [7 August 2018]).

66. Tatjana Pavlović, Inmaculada Álvarez, Rosana Blanco-Cano, Anitra Grisales, Alejandra Osorio and Alejandra Sánchez, *100 Years of Spanish Cinema* (Oxford: Wiley-Blackwell, 2009), pp. 183–84.

67. Maria Van Liew, 'Immigration Films: Communicating Conventions of (In) visibility in Contemporary Spain', in Jay Beck and Vicente Rodríguez Ortega, eds, *Contemporary Spanish Cinema and Genre* (Manchester and New York: Manchester University Press, 2008), p. 260.

68. C. Claire Thomson, *Thomas Vinterberg's 'Festen' ('The Celebration')* (Seattle: University of Washington Press, 2013), p. 32.

69. See Ferguson, *Shakespeare*, p. 114.

70. Thea D. Boldt, 'European Identities Made in Germany', in Ichijo, ed., *Europe*, p. 78; Buchanan, *Peace*, pp. 251, 265.

71. Wilhelm Hortmann, *Shakespeare on the German Stage: The Twentieth Century* (Cambridge: Cambridge University Press, 1988), p. 475.

72. Atsuko Ichijo, 'Introduction: Europe as Modernity', in Ichijo, ed., *Europe*, p. 3.

CHAPTER TWO

Thematizing Place: Hamlet, *Cinema and Africa*

Across Africa, cultural engagement with Shakespeare, as Jane Plastow observes, foregrounds questions of 'language, reception, understandings, Africanisation [and] patronage'.[1] This particularity is due in no small part to Shakespeare's status as an Anglophone colonial import, and his association with education, government and administration belongs with an order that many nations wished to reject. Professor of English, Ime Ikiddeh, spoke for various West African constituencies when he remarked in a 1975 conference paper that 'Shakespeare has come to constitute a real danger . . . to students and writers of drama in this part of the world . . . its manifestation is the distortion of our native sensibilities and values including our very image of ourselves'.[2] Something similar might be said for Francophone traditions and African nations formerly under French dominion; here, too, there was a backlash against 'European' writers in favour of an indigenous culture and mindset.

Perhaps not surprisingly, then, Shakespeare in Africa has an irregular and uneven history. Notable translations include a translation of *Julius Caesar* into Swahili by Julius Nyerere, first President of Tanzania, of *Othello* into Amharic by Tsegaye Gebre-Medhin, the Ethiopian playwright, and of *The Comedy of Errors* into Setswana by Solomon Plaatje, South African linguist and activist.[3] Important stage productions include a production of *Macbeth* (*A'are Akogun*) in Ibadan, Nigeria, in 1968 and a further *Macbeth* (*Macbet*) in 1993 by the Ivory Coast company, Bin Kadi-So.[4] But these manifestations of Shakespeare are neither widespread nor continuous; there are, for example, only a handful of translations of *Hamlet* into the major African languages and few stage productions of note. Touring productions have made something of a mark, as evidenced in *uMabatha*, the isiZulu language adaptation of *Macbeth* by Welcome Msomi that toured Italy, the UK and the USA, and those African productions that came to Shakespeare's Globe as part of the 2012 Cultural Olympiad. (In both cases, debate raged around the productions' 'authenticity'.)⁵ Cinematic adaptations are scarcer still and not well-known outside of their countries of origin. *Thunderbolt* (dir. Tunde Kelani, 2000), a Nigerian adaptation of *Othello, uGugu no Andile* (dir. Minky Schlesinger, 2008), a South African adaptation of *Romeo and Juliet, Dezdemona* (dir. Manyazewai Endeshaw, 2010), an Ethiopian adaptation of *Othello*, and *Julie et Roméo* (dir. Boubakar Diallo, 2011), a Burkinabé adaptation of *Romeo and Juliet*, essentially comprise the canon. Compared with other parts of the world and time periods, therefore, the sample is circumscribed and bears out John Akomfrah's argument about the illusory nature of 'African cinema'. Even inside a limited Shakespearean cinematic canon, we need to speak of 'African cinemas' and of a variety of 'Africas' represented in a range of nation-specific industries.⁶

Given such scattered patterns of engagement, the existence of two African *Hamlet* films is all the more striking. This chapter discusses *Hamile: The Tongo 'Hamlet'* (dir. Terry Bishop, 1965), from Ghana, with an all-black cast, and the Boyokani Company's *Hamlet* (dir. Hugues Serge Limbvani, 2007), from the Republic of Congo, which, with the exception of one white actor, also deploys a black cast. *Hamile* is significant as the first African Shakespeare film, the first, and last, Ghanaian Shakespeare film, and the first black *Hamlet*. For its part, the Boyokani *Hamlet* shows how the play was radically reimagined for film, and written over, in an African setting. Both films bear the weight of their linguistic and colonial inheritances, and, significantly, neither elects to translate the play into an African language, underscoring the ways in which English, French and Portuguese continue to feature, sometimes in combination with indigenous languages, in the work of Shakespearean adaptation. For example, *Hamile*, reflecting the fact that Ghana is a predominantly English-speaking nation, other languages having been subordinated during the colonial period, is made in English, although with occasional local references to cities, foods and drinks intervening in the dialogue.⁷ Putting the script together was a collaborative and improvisational exercise ('There was no script', recalls Martin Owusu, who played Karim/Horatio, 'just ... copies of [Shakespeare's] *Hamlet* ... we changed the names and went through and cut and cut'), African dialect being substituted as part of that process.⁸ In the Boyokani *Hamlet*, Jean-Michel Déprats' French language translation of *Hamlet* is used, with snippets of other African languages entering throughout.⁹ Anna Cetera describes the Déprats translation as one of 'controlled literariness', combining 'euphony ... impetus [and] *gestus*' in an approximation of the 'physicality of Shakespeare's language', but the Boyakani *Hamlet* shepherds these formal qualities in different directions.¹⁰

Stirring in reordered scenes, speeded up soliloquies and a variety of African songs and vocabularies, the film repurposes *Hamlet*, placing on the French translation a vernacular gloss. Hence, '*Les trahisons finissent par surgir, / Même si la terre entière les dissimule aux yeux des hommes*', Déprats' translation of 'foul deeds will rise / Though all the world o'erwhelm them to men's eyes' (1.2.255–56), becomes, in the hands of the Boyokani *Hamlet*, '*on ne peux pas dissimuler; ces actes finissent toujours par remontir à la surface*' ('you can't deny it; these things always end up rising to the surface'), a simplification that purposefully loses rhetorical flourish in the same moment as it privileges modern idiom.[11] Simplification is also at work in geography. 'Wittenberg' appears as a 'foreign land', while 'England' figures as 'Europe', the effect of which is to map Africa's dialogic relations with the rest of the world in general terms and to insist on the play's accessibility.

Further characterizing the films is the fact that both originated in stage productions. *Hamile* traces its genesis to a stage production first performed by students at the School of Music and Drama, the University of Ghana (Legon).[12] No documentation of the production is extant; however, it is referenced on the film credits ('based on the production by Joe de Graft'), confirming a direct influence as well as a landmark moment in Ghana-Shakespeare relations.[13] In the pre-independence period, the Gold Coast Film Unit, established by Sean Graham, a British producer and director, had spearheaded educational films to support the local colonial administration. Following independence in 1957, the new President of Ghana, Kwame Nkrumah, nationalized the Unit, turning it into a state-of-the-art production facility in Accra, renamed, with nationalist enthusiasm, the Ghana Film Industry Corporation, and it was this organization that put the *Hamile* stage production on celluloid.[14] The Ghana Film Industry corporation (GFIC), in fact, was a key part of Nkrumah's programme of artistic and cultural development.[15] For a political leader committed to disseminating what he termed the 'African personality', a *Hamlet* film made and produced in Ghana in such a way as to connect the nation-state to the rest of the continent must have proved an exciting prospect.[16] At material and practical levels, the GFIC offered infrastructural training for fledgling local talent to back its mission of propagating 'traditional values' and a 'unifying national consciousness', yet, in the event, produced only a handful of films; in the wake of Nkrumah's overthrow in 1966, the corporation was disbanded.[17] During its brief heyday, the GFIC drew on British and Ghanaian expertise. For example, *Hamile*'s film director – brought in to replace the original theatre director – was Terry Bishop, a British national who had helmed a raft of 'B'-film comedies and thrillers and who was recruited through Sean Graham of the Gold Coast Film Unit.[18] Previously, Bishop had directed the Oscar-winning documentary, *Daybreak in Udi* (1949), about the founding of a maternity hospital in Enugu, Nigeria, and it is possible that his experience of shooting scenes involving masks and dances for the documentary was seen as having equipped him for the later directorial task.[19] Traces of documentary realism persist into *Hamile*, too, suggesting the extent to which, even as its vision, like other films of the time, is rooted in Ghanaian traditions, its possibility grew out of the conventions and practices of an earlier educational remit. Reflecting on his own experience of playing Hamile in the film, Kofi Middleton-Mends describes Bishop as barking out 'directorial commands in bursts – very quick', but, in contrast to a reading that would see this recollection as an example of colonialism writ large, he simultaneously draws attention to how the interpretive sensitivity of the original theatre production was carried forward into the film proper. The film can be seen, then, as a synergistic interplay between British and African creative practitioners (the directors in fact liaised with each other), as an example of two sensibilities coming together on a shared Shakespearean endeavour.[20]

The Boyokani *Hamlet*, released in 2007, is based on a stage production that took place at the Musée Honmé (King Toffa's Palace), Porto-Novo, Benin, in 2004. The film is informed by the bifurcated identity of its creator, Hugues Serge Limbvani, the director, comedian and stage actor. Typical of many Francophone-African creatives, Limbvani is based in Paris while rooted culturally in Brazzaville, the Republic of Congo, his homeland, and hence is equipped to exploit what Magali Compan terms the 'creative friction' emerging from many Francophone-African artists' relocations.[21] Such 'friction' is enabled by particular funding arrangements. Marketed as part of the 'Collection Théâtre Africain' series, the film was backed by the African division of a French broadcasting channel and, in common with similar examples, distributed as a niche cultural product. The film typifies how, through continued access to European-based finance networks and production facilities, filmmakers in Francophone parts of Africa have been able to establish themselves in the creative industries, and here such schemes as *Fonds Sud*, part of a French national initiative, have proved invaluable.[22] But, as Nwachukwu Frank Ukadike notes, 'French aid for the production of African films . . . is . . . paternalistic at best and imperialistic at worst'.[23] The emphasis on civilization and cultural identity in the funding agenda has undoubtedly discouraged postcolonial critique, one effect of which is the emergence of what Roy

Armes terms a 'neutered cinema' which can be circumscribed in 'social and political terms'.[24] The Boyokani *Hamlet* mediates the conditions of its making by stressing ideas of union and agreement (in *Lingala*, a language spoken in many parts of Central Africa, including the Democratic Republic of Congo and the Republic of Congo, 'Boyokani' translates as accord). Indeed, pan-national casting is a central part of the film's conceit, not least because this highlights in a visual form the company ethos. Thus, so as to replicate original theatre production casting, the film features performers from France, the Ivory Coast, Mali, the Republic of Congo and Senegal, foregrounding in the bodily presence of the performers both the colonial intertexts at work in this reimagining of *Hamlet* and a range of African responses to the play. A hybridized Shakespeare, the Boyokani *Hamlet* is part documentary (recording the views of director and cast), part cinema (camera angles and daytime and night-time shooting suggest a cinematographic conception of the whole) and part television; it is shaped by the circumstances of its first manifestation, its filmed moment and its subsequent distribution histories. In view of its origins, the Boyokani *Hamlet* is additionally inflected by the numerous places to which the stage version toured. Various African nations featured in the itinerary as well as Canada, Europe, Latin America and the USA.[25] As is argued here, the film adaptation can be seen at one level as a species of 'travelling' Shakespeare, an interpretation which absorbs into itself the meanings and resonances of the particular sites with which it is associated.[26]

Perhaps because of their site-specific origins, *Hamile* and the Boyokani *Hamlet* are preoccupied with a thematics of place, whether this shows itself, in the former case, in the will to affirm the *élan* of a newly formed nation-state or, in the latter case, in the ventilating of African-centred questions about woman and the supernatural. Developing such thematics, both films assert varieties of what has been termed 'Africanity', a repository of shared discourses, experiences and inheritances, and find that a British/European play can indeed be made to work in an African *milieu*.[27] In *Hamile*, for instance, northern-facing expressions and images serve to undergird a construction of magic and mysticism, while the prioritization of a compound as the main playing area assists in the film's espousal of a national imaginary. Distinctive clothing materials, and reference to royal motifs, are additionally instrumental in suggesting structures of power articulated in strategically Ghanaian terms. At one and the same time, the attention granted to music and ceremonial takes on a charged, if not anticipatory importance, mirroring the escalating political tensions of the film's historical moment. In its addressing of 'Africanity', the Boyokani *Hamlet* supplements the Shakespearean text, combining story-telling traditions with a narrative prioritization of the Gertrude and Ghost figures. Inside these revisions, the film shows itself responsive to African thinking and conceptions, imaginatively situating its representations according to the opportunities afforded by the Musée Honmé performance space. This inventiveness extends to the film's investment in costumes and props which, as well as suggesting fractured relations between characters, illuminates its absorption in issues of translation and identity. *Hamlet* is honoured in these transformations; it is also pushed, debunked and written anew, demonstrating how widely its African thematics reverberate.

Disappointingly, the reception history of the films does not register their interpretive ingenuity. In Ghana, following an Accra screening, *Hamile* was dismissively branded 'a bit high-browed', while, following a showing at the Commonwealth Arts Festival, London, one reviewer wrote that 'it is ... tepid ... [the] director ... has no camera sense ... [recording] in a dull and stilted way. There is no rhythm ... no feeling for the drama'.[28] For one reviewer, then, the film is too elevated; for another, it fails to reach necessary standards of artistic achievement. More complicatedly, although the stage production attracted plaudits, the Boyokani *Hamlet* film generated no critical visibility other than the occasional reference; once festival exposure had failed to materialize, it was broadcast on French television, for any filmmaker a less attractive dissemination option. The limited attention accorded the Boyokani *Hamlet* brings the comparable reception of *Hamile* to mind and forcefully bears out the ways in which, to cite Emmanuel Sama, 'African films are foreigners in their own countries'.[29] This chapter maintains that the extant traces of reception blind us to the films' particular contributions: inside a thematics of place, *Hamile* and the Boyokani *Hamlet* are cinematically inviting and aesthetically remarkable. Moving beyond the binaries of essentialist judgements, the argument assesses the films on their own terms to reveal their value and shift the terms of debate. In so doing, the chapter establishes the significance of *Hamile* and the Boyokani *Hamlet* inside a still unfolding relationship between Shakespeare and Africa.

Ghana: 1965

An on-screen announcement at the start of *Hamile* establishes that the 'action of the play takes place in Tongo ... the home of the Fra-Fra

people … in the far north of Ghana'. Both town and region in the
Upper East Region, this surrogate for Denmark is continually referenced, as titles such as 'King of Tongo' or exclamations such as 'This is
I, Hamlet of Tongo!' make clear. Such substitutions point up how
important this altered setting is to the interpretation of the film as
a whole. For contemporary audiences, 'Tongo', still a primarily agri-
cultural economy, signified a less adulterated Africa, a part of Ghana
constituted through its connections with history and traditionalism.[30]
Importantly, the cult of Tongnaab (or 'Lord of the Earth'), a Talensi
deity associated with 'fertility, security and stability', originated in these
parts before spreading southwards to be taken up in anti-witchcraft
practices. In addition, even in the early 1960s, the Tong shrines, fetish
caves and whistling rocks celebrated in local folklore as places of
pilgrimage were generally recognized as indicators of ritual power.[31]
Certainly, images of the hills – rising precipitously from the sandy
flats, slabs of pink granite are jumbled imposingly, strewn about as if
by a giant, unearthly hand – circulated in popular print as part of
a fledging Ghanaian tourist industry that prioritized the spiritual energy
of local attractions.[32] For Ernest Abbeyquaye, who played Ibrahim/
Polonius, Tongo evoked 'a magical *pot pourri* full of strange elements'.
Invocations of spiritual and cultic forces sit easily with the film's
elaboration of a northern geography. Hamile/Hamlet's own name
recalls a place name and northern border village in the Upper West
Region of Ghana; identifiers from each side of the northern territories,
therefore, highlight the film's conceptual provenance.[33] Of further
interest here is the term 'Fra-Fra' – a divisive term which stems from
early missionaries' approximation of indigenous expressions of greeting
and thanks, this colonial descriptor works to conjure distant terrains
and long-standing affiliations.[34] An umbrella identifier which gathers
into itself a number of different ethnic and linguistic groups, 'Fra-Fra' is
used in the film in a thematically suggestive rather than culturally
nuanced sense. The term reappears in a second on-screen announcement which informs us that 'the text is unaltered, except where it would
not make sense in a Fra-Fra community, or when an archaic word
obscures the meaning'. Accordingly, nouns and properties are altered:
the 'Nemean lion' (1.4.83) is replaced by a 'desert lion' (drier, *sahel*-like
regions are here invoked), and the King, instead of devising a 'chalice
for the nonce' (4.7.158), seizes upon the idea of a 'poisoned calabash of
pito' (a fermented corn-based drink common in northern areas).
The priority is to emphasize the vernacular utility of Shakespeare and

to see in his work a transferable language in recognition of his fit with African and specifically Ghanaian imperatives and ambitions.

Tongo is also represented relationally so as to distinguish it from other African nations. City references are a case in point. The play-within-the-play, for example, is 'the image of a murder done in ... Timbuktu' and Hamile/Hamlet is sent to 'Sokoto' to collect the tribute payment. Via such references, *Hamile* gestures to cities – in Mali and Nigeria respectively – geographically north of Ghana and suggests a will to situate Ghana at the imaginative centre of an increasingly networked African universe.[35] The idea that Ghana could play so central a situating role finds an echo in the spirit of pride and exuberance that accompanied independence.[36] The same excitement animated Joe de Graft, director of the stage production, when he noted that, in Ghana in the early 1960s, 'there was an outburst of enthusiasm for our own way of doing things'.[37] To put *Hamlet* on a Ghanaian screen was, then, a culturally and nationally assertive and ambitious endeavour.

Ambition is writ large in the set, which, built to purpose in Kwabenya, an area of dry savannah not far from the University of Ghana, was clearly intended to differentiate the film from the stage production in scale and design. Specifically, the compound, which was constructed for the film to include arches, squat towers, individual chambers and steps in a ringed arrangement, resembles a type of amphitheatre in the round, providing a grand and majestic playing space within which the action unfolds. Unique in cinematic adaptations, the roofless compound means that *Hamile* is almost completely envisaged in terms of exteriors. Making full use of natural effects and light (The ''Tis now the very witching time of night' [3.2.378] soliloquy is filmed outside in natural darkness, with pin-pointed eyes staring in the dark to eerie effect) allows for the action to be at one with its natural environment. Hence, this approximation of Elsinore is lensed against a backdrop of trees tossed by the winds, open skies and a dust-strewn landscape, with speech and reference often intriguingly paired (the protagonist's references to 'this most excellent canopy the air' [2.2.265–6] or 'the winds of heaven' [1.2.141] are precisely captured in the material realities of his location). Against this backdrop, much of the suggestiveness of *Hamile* inheres in objects and dress. Eschewing black, Hamile is represented wearing a white striped smock – or *fugu* – a clothing item that, in the early 1960s in Ghana, had lost its royal associations and become a popular mode of dress. So presented, Hamile/Hamlet appears more as commoner than prince, discontent showing itself in angrily crossed arms and a downward gaze (his 'vailed lids' seek his 'father in the dust' [1.2.70–71]). In comparison to Hamile/Hamlet, the King (Joe Akonor) is splendidly attired and accoutred with a staff of office (a ceremonial property used to stress the importance of his speeches) and a buffalo tail flywhisk (a marker of monarchy used to brush aside evil influences), which he wields aggressively.[38] His toga-like robes – a *batakari* – with striped and chequered patterns are layered (one length of cloth is draped over one shoulder), ornate and sumptuous; the visual complexity of the fabric mirrors the intricacy of the decorations on the buildings, involving the audience in a constant matching exercise. In the case of the King, this mirroring suggests ownership and connection, in contrast to Hamile/Hamlet whose costuming suggests disaffection and alienation.

In keeping with a Ghana-inflected focus, the King's costume is purposefully made up of *kente*-style textiles. Woven historically for Ashanti and Ewe royalty in Ghana, these strip-woven cloths constituted, as Peter Adler and Nicholas Barnard write, both a 'luxury consumable' that met court demands and a 'vocabulary that conveys information to the owner and the viewer'.[39] Crucially, *kente* textiles during this period were evolving into a Ghanaian form of dress that was distinguished from the earlier colonial suit. To cite clothing historian, Kofi Anyidoho, 'much of the credit [for] … the emergence of *kente* as the national dress … goes to … Nkrumah … and members of his cabinet and government'.[40] Foregrounded in the political *milieu* of *Hamile*, rich textiles declare the resurgence of Africa and the newly liberated status of Ghana.[41] Interestingly, specific *kente* textiles appear in the few interior chamber scenes, used here as wall coverings or room dividers; these furnish a link between public and private spaces and show how the King's patterned appearance finds a visual correlative across inside and outside locales. In particular, royalty is reinforced in the wall coverings decorated with drum motifs which signify praise; in these apartment scenes (2.2 and 4.1), the pressure on servants and underlings, such as Ibrahim/Polonius and Abdulai/Rosencrantz and Guildenstern (Gad Gadugan), to honour their royal masters is made abundantly evident.[42] The drum motif appears again on background tapestries in the closing duel/wrestling scene, functioning at this point, as the King's authority begins to crumble, in a more contentious and critical capacity. Fabrics and patterns chart thematic rhythms and involve intricate exercises of reading and decipherment.

When not dwelling on costume in *Hamile*, the viewer is invited to contemplate the buildings' rectilinear and triangular decorations which evoke some styles of northern architecture.[43] Elsinore is nativized via the

Figure 8: Hamile/Hamlet (Kofi Middleton-Mends) is lensed against patterned buildings in *Hamile: The Tongo 'Hamlet'* (dir. Terry Bishop, 1965). Courtesy of the British Film Institute.

transformation, with the horizontal lines of the compound's walls contrasting with the vertical lines of the trees beyond. Inspired by Adinkra symbolism originally associated with Ashanti royalty, these interlinked motifs betoken the achievements and moral attributes of the buildings' owner; their purpose in Ghanaian cultural life is to endorse links between the living and the dead as well as to promote wisdom, prudence, humility, learning and munificence.[44] The camera lingers most often on a cross-hatched pattern (signifying an ability to cross divisions), on concentric circles (suggesting royalty and greatness) and a sharply angled V-shape (betokening seriousness, diligence and perseverance). Intertextually, the proverbial lore embedded in the film's symbolism intersects with the proverbs of *Hamlet*; more importantly, however, as the action progresses, the buildings' visual messages – or *ukra* – come to offer an ironic counterpoint to the King's behaviour. This is in contradistinction to the representation of Hamile/Hamlet, who, at his return from Sokoto, is represented dressed in a traditional *batakari* whose design affirms his imbrication in his environment, neatly reversing his earlier disconnected status.

In general, Hamile/Hamlet is rendered understatedly. Although a figure of mobility when he enters the action on horseback, riding across the savannah to broach the compound, he is a figure of stasis, leaning disconsolately on an arch, walking listlessly, mounting stairs slowly, sitting down in dejection. In speech, he is measured and careful, and his pared down soliloquies are characterized by long pauses. 'To be, or not to be', while stripped of its central examples of injustice (3.1.67–74) and cut across by the chirrup of birdsong, is delivered with deliberation and presented, via alternating close-ups, as a performative set-piece. Throughout, Hamile/Hamlet's body is choreographed in relation to the compound's architecture. Typical are the ways in which his lurking in the shadows of an entrance, or looking wistfully over the walls, signal a distressed relation to kin and condition. His isolation sets him off from the business surrounding the King, environed, as the latter is, by admiring onlookers (ambassadors bow down to him, underlings take off their footwear in his presence, and conical-hatted guards brandishing spears accompany his appearances). A salient feature of *Hamile*, indeed, is the interleaving of political and domestic activity: the *mise-en-scène* is animated by the simultaneous to-and-fro of mounted messengers and the labour of community. Habiba/Ophelia (Mary Yirenkyi) may be a political pawn, but she is represented carrying a gourd as a prop rather than a book: the textual change underplays ideas about illiteracy, alerting us, instead, to her material participation in a local economy. More generally, deep focus photography shows millet being ground and animal skins being laid out to dry, the effect of which is to suggest rural rhythms. Meanwhile, a passing shot of scattering goats and tethered horses indicates the proximity of royal preoccupations and village practicalities. *Hamile* foregrounds, in fact, how smoothly a Shakespearean tragic drama can be accommodated to a workaday world.

Crucial to the workings of this northerly society is music. Music features notably as an aural bridge between scenes, in which instances it is clearly non-diegetic, but it also operates diegetically in the form of two court musicians: one plays a *kologo*, a lute with base and treble strings made out of a *calabash* gourd; the other picks out a beat on an hourglass *donno* drum, thereby highlighting the participatory role of music in assisting expressions of rule.[45] On occasions, the distinctive sounds of Ghanaian instrumentation accentuate mood and tone, as when minor plucked notes are heard descending before 'To be, or not to be'. At other moments, such as the departure of the King and his train (1.2) or his corresponding entrance before the duel/wrestling match (5.2), the court musicians, even as they mime the beat of the iambic pentameter, mark phases in the exercise of royal power, signature harmonies registering interlinked narratives within the larger frame. Elsewhere, musicians function as announcers, as at the start of 5.1, the burial of Habiba/Ophelia, offering commentary and alternative perspectives (songs are delivered in *Twi*, a dialect form of the *Akan* language, and overlay Shakespearean language with folkloric allusions). The prioritization of the music in *Hamile* is both authenticating (the chief *axatse* or rattle player, Amua Frafra, hailed from the northern regions and was enlisted to add local flavour) and contextually suggestive. Adopting the practices of Ghanaian chiefdoms, Nkrumah insisted that praise songs be delivered on formal occasions. Music and drums legitimated rule, as historically it had done in the Ashanti royal courts, supporting, as Paul Schauert argues, Nkrumah's 'performance of power' and his claims to embrace a 'multi-ethnic identity'.[46] *Hamile*, too, plays with political-musical relations. During the play-within-the play, the musicians are clearly conspiratorially involved and form an allegiance with the players: their jangling acoustics sound over the prologue and rise to a provocative and discordant frenzy as the King storms out. Types of commentator, they assist in the revelation of villainy. Indeed, music is at its most energetically percussive at pivotal action points, as when, immediately after the 'How all occasions do inform against me' (4.4.31) soliloquy, Hamile/Hamlet rides off, the thwack of his whip on the horse being picked up in a rattle-heavy *mise-en-bande*. In many ways, musicians populate vacated space; in the gap created by the removal of Rosencrantz and Guildenstern, as at 3.2 and 4.2, and their compression into one character, Abdulai, opportunities are afforded for alternative activity. And it is at such moments that the musicians are prominent – leading processions, participating in choric capacities, registering emotional measure and, where language is lacking, filling the soundscape.

The film also amputates, not least in its vision of an animist society. *Hamile* prioritizes a pre-Christian moment, arguably as a way of taking the country back to, or away from, the religious impositions that legitimized colonialism. Purging *Hamlet* of Christianity becomes an ideological act of cultural and national reclamation. Almost all Christian references are excised, then: 'heaven [and] . . . hell' (1.5.92–3) are cut as are concepts such as 'damnation' (4.5.132) and 'grace and mercy' (1.5.178). More generally, 'gods' fill in for an absent 'Heaven' (5.2.316). What is stressed as a result is a sense of the cosmos that accords with a Ghanaian schema of a hierarchy of beings, headed by a Supreme God, comprised of various divine powers – ancestors and lesser divinities – possessing different properties.[47] These pre-Christian

Figure 9: Habiba/Ophelia (Mary Yirenkyi), flanked by the Queen/Gertrude
(Frances Sey), descends into madness in the savannah in *Hamile: The Tongo 'Hamlet'*
(dir. Terry Bishop, 1965). Courtesy of the British Film Institute.

dimensions are seen in shifts in emphasis (the King, standing rather than
kneeling, pleads rather than prays) and in interpolated rituals (before his
work, the Gravedigger pours a gourd of pito on the ground in a libation
indicative of his belief in the supernatural). Above all, it is via the Ghost
that the film's subscription to animism is illuminated. Allusions to the
ambiguities of purgatory are removed (1.5.2–4, 11, 13) and instead the
darkness, from which the figure emerges and to which it returns, pre-
dominates. The implication, at least in a Ghanaian context, is that a soul
or *sia* is restless, funeral rites having proved flawed or inadequate.
Glimpsed on the walls, the Ghost is filmed from a low angle and in
long-shot. Its movements are mannered, the overlaid voice studied and
sepulchral; all that is visible is a helmet-style bead mask capped with
buffalo horns. A cotton and raffia mane obscures the spectral form.
Masks in African culture serve as a manifestation of the spirit world;
at the same time, they function as conduits through which communication between realms – and the demands of the ancestors for retributive

justice – may be enabled.[48] These meanings are bolstered by the horns signifying anger as well as prowess: the ghost is as martial as it is vengeful, with the mask serving as medium and message.[49] Because of the mask, there is no match between mouth and speech (the face cannot be seen), the effect of which is dissociate voice and image.[50] Hence, a greater stress is placed on reaction shots from Hamile/Hamlet's point of view: his bodily responses, as he looks away, contorts in agony and wrings his hands, inform a viewer's reading (these are the points of reference), while the increasing rhythm of the drums on the score suggest a quickening heartbeat.[51] Atypically, Hamile/Hamlet is here manically animated, forceful actions limning how the present is traumatically interrupted by an ancestral return.

A pre-Christian ethos also underpins Habiba/Ophelia's funeral. The play's squabble over truncated obsequies is removed (5.1.206–231) as is the gravediggers' pseudo-legal discussion of suicide (5.1.4–36). As a result, the funeral is discovered as a fully realized occasion, one in keeping with Esi Sutherland-Addy's description of Ghanaian funerals as 'elaborate commemorative ceremonies . . . Legitimacy, pedigree and even sacredness are conferred by sticking to ancient . . . etiquette, modes of dress and ritual procedure'.[52] In a departure from conventional practice, the funeral is filmed as an extended sequence in the outlying savannah: etiquette is instanced in the clutched heads and crowds of mourners ranked in serried rows, and legitimacy is suggested in the studied movement of the participants around the graveside. Chants from an assembly of wailing onlookers – 'O Habiba!' – and the empathetic participation of the Queen (Frances Sey) and her women demonstrate how procedure is honoured. Meanwhile, subtle costume changes – the women wear head-wraps or *dukus* – point up how modes of dress function as indicators of a communal outpouring of grief. Self-evidently, the funeral is of some magnitude, and one made all the more so by a delay in the scene's dialogue.[53] A communal dimension is certainly intimated in the camera's cross-cutting between the faces of the onlookers, the effect of which is to play down Hamile/Hamlet's role, and in the foregrounding of the court musicians, who come to embody a group response. As Habiba/Ophelia is carried towards her grave on a bier, the crowd parting like a guard of honour to assist in the journey to the land of the dead, the *kologo*-playing musician plucks at his instrument and looks on at the departing entourage, his single throbbing notes crystallizing the darkening mood.

The place of ritual is given a more particularized treatment in the representation of Hamile/Hamlet's demise, not least via Karim/Horatio's plea, 'Good night, sweet prince, thy ancestors regard thee well'. Writing on elders in Africa, Igor Kopytoff notes that 'The relation of . . . ancestors to . . . living kinsmen [is] . . . both punitive and benevolent . . . even . . . capricious . . . ancestral benevolence is assured through propitiation and sacrifice; neglect is believed to bring about punishment'.[54] In this connection, Horatio/Karim's words appear not so much injunction as propitiation; he speaks to affirm the crucial interplay between mortal and immortal worlds and to acknowledge the importance of ancestral powers. His proper heeding of the order of things will facilitate the recognition that, to adopt Steven J. Salm and Toyin Falola, Hamile/Hamlet has died 'honourably' and can therefore take his place with his forefathers.[55] Writ large in the request is the idea that the spirit of the father will return to ensure the son's safe passage from one world to the next, and the Ghost's assistance in this respect is felicitously intimated. In the wake of Hamile/Hamlet's death, a voiceover sounds, an amalgam of Fortinbras' reflections on death (5.2.348–51), the order for the body of the protagonist to be accorded military honours (5.2.379–86) and Horatio's promise to rehearse the action we have witnessed (5.2.363–370). The sepulchral tones of the voiceover confirm it as the Ghost's own voice (as played by Sandy Arkhurst), pointing up how the film is framed by instances of ancestral return. What the Ghost's voice asks for is enacted in accompanying business: here, it is implied; Old Hamile/Hamlet is the ultimate arbiter and authority. Hence, matching the four horsemen of the opening, four soldiers lift Hamile/Hamlet's body aloft in a march that brings to mind Habiba/Ophelia's elaborate funeral and underlines the lack of respect that the King's form is accorded. Sacredness now flows to Hamile/Hamlet and, in the arrangement of the grieving parties (men are followed by women are followed by the court musicians), ritual and due process are again to the fore. The procession leaves through the compound's arched entrance, suggesting a union of sorts with Habiba/Ophelia, who is buried beyond the walls, and a destiny that lies outside of the Tongo royal world.

Such formality throws into relief the lack of propriety – and illegality and indecorousness – evinced in the wrestling match which, taking place on mats laid out on the compound surface, substitutes for the play's duel. Any notion of a fair contest evaporates when Laertu/Laertes (Kofi Yirenkyi) produces a poisoned animal claw (or 'ornament') at the fatal moment. Similarly, while royal power is registered in the wooden stage from which the King and Queen watch the proceedings, this is exposed at the moment where the former falls from his costly cushion onto a pile of leopard skins. Traditionally, Ghanaian chiefs occupied stools which served as symbolic repositories of the ruler's power during life and after death, and what is suggested in *Hamile* is that, in collapsing to the floor, the King is de-stooled, removed from office and desacralized.[56] In the Ghanaian political sphere, a *coup* against a King – an act of de-stooling – had a contextual specificity. Nkrumah, the President, had de-stooled Ghanaian chiefs so as to bolster his own rule and was himself overthrown by the police and military in February, 1966, just five months after *Hamile*'s international premiere.[57] Certainly, the film toys with a sense of authority as transient, both through the figure of the King and in scenes in which power is contested from below. (The rebellion of Laertu/Laertes, for example, is envisaged as a grassroots political movement, villagers emerging from and then disappearing into the trees.) At the time of Nkrumah's overthrow, however, such parallels between film and President do not seem to have suggested themselves. Rather, *Hamile* was, along with other films produced by the Ghana Film Industry Corporation, confiscated as an example of work that 'fed the personality cult of Nkrumah', a ruling that was more destructively applied in the banning and burning of his books.[58] The brief heyday of film in Ghana was now over: *Hamile* disappeared from view after its single festival showing and an isolated subsequent public broadcast, and the industry withered, with no further films of substance being made.[59]

Republic of Congo: 2007

The Boyokani *Hamlet* is characterized by a move to integrate African writers within the space of the Shakespearean text. In addition to its speeches being redistributed, the Ghost is given lines from the poem, 'Les Souffles', which are repeated at each of its appearances. 'Listen to things / More often than to people / The voice of the fire is heard / Hear the voice of the water … This is the ancestor breathing', it intones.[60] In the soundscape of the film, these lines function as a private language between Hamlet and the Ghost, the protagonist recapitulating the key phrase – 'The dead are not dead' – to signify, via mantra-like reiteration, filial-spiritual kinship. Revealingly, the phrase that reverberates most in the Boyokani *Hamlet* is not Shakespeare's own. 'Les Souffles' is famous as a key text in the development of the *négritude* movement: the work of the Senegalese poet, Birago Diop, it celebrates African folklore and animism, its very title ('Les Souffles') suggesting, at one and the same time, ancestors, spirits and breath, a principle of unity underlying all things.[61] There are, then, multiple meanings at work here: Shakespeare is not 'dead' to reinvention, and can be brought back and made to work in combinatory capacities that testify to the importance of a specifically Francophone-African means of declaring a shared racial identity.

If the dialogue of the Boyokani *Hamlet* makes space for African poetic voices, it is fitting that it simultaneously foregrounds the role of the African *griot* or storyteller. Historically a feature of African royal courts, the *griot* was a type of bard, acting, in cultural anthropologist Josef Gugler's words, as 'historian, advisor, the voice of the high and mighty, master of ceremonies and praise-singer'.[62] In some ways, the role is encapsulated here by Polonius (Momo Ekissi). Costumed in brilliant orange robes and announcing himself with a harmonica melody, Polonius is more player than politician: he revels in recounting the story of Hamlet's love for Ophélie (Marina Ahoui), dancing and having to be brought to order, and prefaces his discovery with a song that forces Claudius (Abdou El Aziz Gueye) and Gertrude (Maïmouna Doumbia) into the position of reluctant spectators. Similarly, when bringing news of the players, he acts akin to a prologue, mounting the stairs and waving his arms to emphasize his generic points as if he himself were a member of the travelling company. Internal storytelling high points have external equivalents. For David Murphy and Patrick Williams, the alignment of the 'traditional *griot* and the cinematic *auteur* produces a kind of hybrid *griauteur* ... an appropriate figure for contemporary African filmic practice'.[63] And it is just such a role that director and originator of the Boyokani *Hamlet*, Hugues Serge Limbvani, embraces – his opening sequence explanation that *Hamlet* 'offers many possibilities which can be adapted to African culture' is delivered to camera in an auditorium, the effect of which is immediately to establish his interpretive credentials. True to *griauteur* requirements, Limbvani enters once more in the film to offer his story of *Hamlet* and situate his work as filmmaker, although his presence is shadowed in the intertitles – such as 'Several months later, the old King has been assassinated' and 'A Room in the Palace' – that hint at an overseeing organizational personality. Most obviously in the opening sequence, Limbvani focuses on the attractions of *Hamlet*: 'What appealed to me first was the ghost ... the dead man who comes to speak to the living ... that forms part of African culture', he states, before adding, 'I was also interested in the situation of Gertrude, the woman ... she participates ... decides ... because she wants to recover happiness'. Identifying his *Hamlet*'s interpretive motors, Limbvani singles out what he deems important, and what is amenable to adaptation, concentrating on two interlinked figures which he subjects to a distinctive interpretive twist.

Initially, Limbvani's signalling of the importance of the Ghost is reflected in the prominence it is accorded and the rearrangement of the scenes in which it appears. In an embellishment to the play, the Ghost is visible or sensed five times in the film (it is threaded through the action, becoming, in the sense of Diop's 'Les Souffles', an omnipresent force); additionally, its speeches are divided up into smaller units and delivered with more forceful effects (at 3.3, as the King attempts to pray, even an interpolated moan from the Ghost causes him to scream and fall to his knees). Characteristic is how, hard upon the arrival of the players, the Ghost visits a prevaricating Hamlet to suggest the play-within-the-play ('there is your story'), showing how the Ghost's increased involvement is supported by creative revisions to representational traditions. Because of the bandages around its forehead and the warning bell which it holds aloft, the Ghost is imagined as leprous, an identification more self-evident in Jean-Michel Déprats' French language translation, '*Comme une lèpre*' (p. 97), which the film follows, of the 'original' *Hamlet*'s expression, 'Most lazar-like' (1.5.72). Making this identification material, the Ghost's bloody red ear, which it clutches, appears both as the physical sign of the crime and as an index of a diseased – leprous – body. Rod Edmond writes that 'revulsion and fear have been the most common responses' to leprosy, which, judged a 'contagion', is perceived as 'infective, deforming and horrifying'.[64] The same reaction ignites the Boyakani *Hamlet* when terrified characters either seek to flee from the Ghost or are frozen and suspended in movement: it is as if they have been physically incapacitated by its presence.[65]

The Ghost is played by Kaf Malère, the only pale-skinned (French) actor in an all-black cast; complementing this, his skin is artificially whitened. Intertextually, Malère invokes histories of white colonialism and the absent ghost of a white oppressor. 'Colour-blind' casting, then, does not so much neutralize the past here as draw attention to its continuing legacies. Furthermore, as confirmed by the flute and drum score, the white silk *kimono* worn by the Ghost and the chant that announces each of its arrivals, the style of performance is taken from the Japanese *Noh* theatre tradition, and in such a way as to heighten the Boyokani Company's 'union' or 'accord' both between African cultures and theatrical genres in other parts of the world.[66] For Limbvani, Noh, as 'an extreme form of theatre', reverberates with 'mystical aspects of the African past' and offers a way of expressing his sense that 'the dead are not dead, they form part of life, they are with us'.[67] So it is that the Ghost is represented gliding through the colonnades in a stylized walk (*hakobi*), using this section of the palace as a bridgeway (*hashigakari*), the white bandage also functioning as a traditional *Noh* headband (*hachimaki*) that proclaims the spirit a suffering *samurai* warrior.[68] At least in these parts of the film, the action almost takes on the properties of a Japanese *mugen* or supernatural drama, a form indebted to the war epic, the tales of the Heike.[69] Japanese theatrical registers are at work in other parts of the film, too, suggesting the mutually reinforcing contribution of local and global imaginaries and the ways in which the Ghost is made additionally 'present' via imagery and objects.[70]

Traversing the colonnades is of a piece with a creative use of the entirety of the Musée Honmé space. Raised steps, an open yard and adjoining walled gardens play host to, variously, the reception (2.2) of a fawning Rosencrantz (Seidy Abdooulaye) and Guildenstern (Kaf Malère), Hamlet's encounter with Polonius (2.2) and the duel/wrestling match (5.2); in each episode, particular areas suggest sites of influence, as when, for example, Hamlet hides behinds sepia-coloured peeling pillars on the upper steps, finding their physical bulk affords him a refuge from an adversarial court. Intertitles mark act and scene divisions but also fill spaces on screen, encouraging an audience to read the places of action with imaginative latitude. In fact, the Boyokani *Hamlet* makes a virtue of contingency, not least via a soundtrack which showcases the materialities of locale (birdsong and calls to prayer from the neighbouring mosque) even as it overlays background noise with American jazz and African choric chants. We are invited to recognize the realities of filming as constitutive parts of the viewing experience and to appreciate the immediacy of a drama unfolding in the here-and-now.

Historically, the Musée Honmé occupies the site of what was the palace of King Toffa (*c.* 1850–1908), ruler of Hogbonu, now Porto-Novo. During the period of Toffa's rule, closer links were made with local administrators in what was then the French controlled kingdom of Dahomey in the form of educational programmes and initiatives promoting the co-existence of religions. These are among the contexts that shape the Boyokani *Hamlet* – in particular, its choice of a French translation as text and its unifying manifesto. How *Hamlet* came to be at this location, then, a former palace which is now a UNESCO heritage site, is part of an interlinked lineage, and it is one to which the film bears witness.[71] Expressions of 'Africanity', as utilized in the film, are a case in point. In the final scene, for instance, several localizing elements are highlighted – poisoned palm wine is offered, bladed gloves laced with mandragora (interestingly, Gertrude's poison of choice) prove a fatal weapon and, crucially, fencing cedes place to *pongo*, a form of wrestling particular to both the Republic of Congo and the

Democratic Republic of Congo. In the film, *Les Lutteurs/The Wrestlers* (dir. Jean-Michel Tchissoukou, 1982), made in French and *Lingala* in the Republic of Congo, *pongo* features as an index of conflict in the region. By contrast, and honouring its orientation, the Boyakani *Hamlet* extends its allusive remit, *pongo* figuring in concert with signifiers of Japanese theatrical culture (a fan), North African instrumentation and a Mozartian prelude, reinforcing how, through sound and image, the film incorporates European elements, and a *mélange* of histories, in recognition of the complexities of African contemporaneity.

Such localization finds a particularly eloquent articulation in music and dance. Hence, Hamlet purposefully eschews joining in the celebratory song, in the language of the Ivory Coast *Baoulé* peoples, 'Jam-ba-yulé', which accompanies 1.2, the first public appearance of Claudius and Gertrude, since this would be to give assent to the new regime. Instead, the protagonist uses music to affirm alliances between friends, such as Horatio (Macodou Mbengue), the scene in which they meet being characterized by singing in *Dyula* and *Wolof* languages that points up kinship across borders. Similarly, when Laerte (Seidy Abdooulaye) encounters his distracted sister, they sing together: their harmonizing constitutes the only means of communication in Ophélie's afflicted condition. Ceremonial is also revealing, with a switch in the Déprats translation – the expression '*ni ceremonie solennelle*' (p. 273) is altered to 'traditional dance' – emphasizing how the dance forms of Western Africa are imagined as serving vital social and cultural functions. For Hamlet, dance – and song – support communities and networks, as when he greets the players, joining with them in a melody that suggests shared experiences and continuing connections.

Emerging from felicitous localizations is a concomitantly imaginative envisioning of Hamlet (Mamadou Bomou) himself. Wearing varieties of black and purple, he is individualized in the darker tones of his dress and set off from the bright colours (yellow and red) worn by the court. No less distinctive is the clarity of the performance. We are privy to the pretence of his madness, as when he places a sandal on his head with a self-conscious gesture, and to his knowledge, as in the admission, 'a trap is laid for me' (which gains in impact because addressed to camera). At the same time, a strategic use of props – Hamlet wields as weapon an edition of *Dictionnaire des Citations de Langue Française* – foregrounds issues of postcolonial inheritance and linguistic translation. Costume is similarly indicative. For example, Hamlet's distinctive costume, a black robe decorated with cubist shapes, establishes him as a walking work of art, not least when, delivering the 'What a piece of work is a man' (2.2.269) speech, he enacts the idea of a wonderfully imagined creation through his own appearance. His costume also brings to mind a tangled colonial-cultural history. According to Stefan Eisenhofer, commenting on the ways in which artists in the twentieth century experimenting with abstraction and aesthetics responded to African representational practices, the 'pioneers of modernism' drew upon so-called '*art nègre*' as a 'source of inspiration . . . both formal and conceptual'.[72] Around his neck, Hamlet wears a medallion. This, according to a cast member, is an honour bestowed by the President of the Ivory Coast on Bomou, the actor, for his theatrical work and hence is a marker of his investment in, and loyalty to, African performance traditions.[73] The Boyokani *Hamlet* explores through dress and look how notions of 'Africanity' circulate, making visible a cultural journey that leads from Africa to Europe and back again, an itinerary not unlike that of the protagonist himself.

Such individuating features are in sharp contrast to a court elaborated in terms of a common identity. Hence, Polonius bears a cowrie shell on his forehead, Ophélie has a cowrie necklace and earrings, and Claudius and Gertrude wear crowns decorated with cowries in ringed patterns. Historically, cowrie shells functioned in Africa as markers of royalty.[74] In some parts of the Democratic Republic of the Congo, for example, as Anne Van Cutsen and Mauro Magliani write, *kupash* or *mpanu* head-dresses, as sported by members of the 'royal family', were 'covered with cowries and tiny glass beads . . . underlining their wealth in the process'.[75] More generally, indicating affiliations, complicities, hierarchies and dynasties across Africa, the cowrie shell operated as *nzimbu* or currency: bags of cowrie shells served as dowries and for ceremonial and religious payments.[76] In the same way that 'suits of solemn black' (1.2.78) declare Hamlet different, so, in the Boyokani *Hamlet*, does the protagonist's lack of cowrie shells indicate his distance from the structures of the court, with his self-decoration suggesting both resistance and an anti-materialist stance.

Differentiation allows for empathic engagement, not least because Hamlet answers to convention and is discovered in large part as a figure of melancholy. When, for example, in the delivery of the 'To be, or not to be' soliloquy, he combines verse speaking with song (in the *Dyula* language of the Ivory Coast), wailing sustained notes in a minor key, he brings to mind a grief singer setting the mood for a ceremonial occasion. But Hamlet is not the sole point of identification. Recalling Limbvani's *griauteur* role, cast members, in an inset that precedes the film's second half, contemplate their personal connection with the women characters. For Maïmouna

Doumbia (Gertrude), 'the Queen represents all those women ... who have submitted to traditional laws', while Marina Ahoui identifies in her playing of Ophélie 'the weight of obedience ... many things which I often encounter in my culture'. In these twinned reflections, Shakespearean roles are made to speak to women and to resonate in an African *milieu*, and *Hamlet* appears as a resource that touches not only on individual experiences but on gendered norms of a specifically African kind. The Queen is first glimpsed embracing Claudius, the idea being that, rather than the will to political ascendancy, erotic desire propels the action. Above all, she is represented as complicit if not pro-active. As she states on the palace steps (her white robes betokening purity are at odds with her infidelity), 'I can't stand my husband ... He is no longer able to satisfy me. Again, my love ... He must be killed ... Only mandragora ... that mixture of goat's entrails, serpent's venom and frog's blood poured into his left ear will bring death to him'. Indexing *Macbeth*, the interpolated speech discovers Gertrude as instigator and as a witch-like figure of excess. And, if desire is the primary motor in the sequence, this is at one with an emphasis on women's sexuality in the Boyokani *Hamlet* as a whole.

Sexuality is registered in structural parallels. At the start, the guards, Francesca (a gendered switch from Francisco) and Marcellus lustfully embrace: they, too, privilege desire over duty. But, as additional interpolations indicate, this adaptation is as preoccupied with the condition of women in general. Unlike *Hamile*, in which the Queen and Habiba/Ophelia are trimmed to a minimum, the Boyokani *Hamlet* enlists women in interrogations of social and cultural institutions; Gertrude, for example, struggles to rid herself of a husband visited upon her by the traditions of enforced marriage to the extent that it is her guilt, rather than Hamlet's angst, that makes for the dominant impression. During the closet scene (3.4), Gertrude offers a rationale for her extreme measures, extra lines on this occasion establishing her as racked by the pains of physical incompatibility. Elaborating her opening disclosures, she speaks specifically, instancing how acts of rape are legitimated within the arranged marriage structure: 'you cannot understand ... my suffering ... sharing the same bed for many years with a man you don't love', she exclaims. Gertrude's soliloquy, specially composed by Limbvani and addressed to camera, carries an emotive charge. Her self-justifying reflections – 'I had to act ... confronting tradition was the right thing for me to do' – take the form of a confession which displaces Claudius from the spotlight and humanizes her discursive centrality. Moreover, her final interpolation

('I killed to live again'), in its antithetical arrangement, encapsulates the conflicts and contrarieties that impel the fatal decision. In interview, Limbvani maintains that the inspiration for using *Hamlet* to intervene in the practice of enforced marriage came from his personal experience of the dilemma facing a young Senegalese medical student.[77] The prompt to rethink the play also has a legislative context in the 2005 ruling by the African Women's Protocol which outlaws practices that endanger the physical and psychological development of women and specifies that no 'marriage' should take place 'without the free and full consent of both parties'.[78] Inaugurated one year before the ruling came into being, the Boyokani *Hamlet*, at least in its theatrical manifestation, acts to underwrite legal developments in an imaginative form. West African film has frequently highlighted the issue of enforced marriage, as reflected in such women-helmed works as *Femmes Aux Yeux Ouverts* (dir. Anne Laure Folly, 1993), from Togo, and *Mossane* (dir. Safi Faye, 1996), from Senegal, in which women are represented agitating for choice and rights.[79] At least intertextually, the Boyokani *Hamlet* is responsive to these cinematic initiatives, too, meshing African content with Shakespearean narrative to activate its engagements. And, as cast here, Gertrude stands as a representative figure who, through rewriting, takes forward the film's critical project.

The preoccupations of the Boyokani *Hamlet* are amplified in the ways in which Ophélie is figured. Inflected in the light of the film's concepts, Ophélie is realized as initially independent, reading Hamlet's letters in a private space of the palace yard and rolling her eyes at her father's warnings. The relationship, it is suggested, is conflictual (echoing, perhaps, the Gertrude/Old Hamlet marriage), with Ophélie being generally subordinated and debarred from unrestricted expressions of self. Here, Polonius' passive-aggressive harmonica playing is as much a device to still her speech as it is an excuse to indulge in a virtuoso performance. In a film adaptation in which costume is always vital, Ophélie appears in her second mad scene (4.5) dressed in a man's western white shirt and modern ripped jeans, a far cry from the clothes in which she first appears, a lightly decorated African smock in modest pinks and blues. The implication, through costume, is that Ophélie has fallen and lost her virginal status, this being reinforced in her bottom-exposing gesture. (By contrast, Gertrude's embrace of her sexual self is signalled in costumes that are ever more colourful and elaborate.) Crucially, Ophélie appears at this point without her customary cowrie shell necklace and earrings, suggesting adulterating sexual exchange and the loss of her honorary membership of the royal family: no longer valuable, she is robbed of her commodity status and usefulness. The idea is nuanced in the gravediggers' traditional counting song, 'One ham from Bayonne!', which, registering a number at each smack of the spade ('one … two … three … four'), replaces the Shakespearean song of careless youth. 'Bayonne ham', a product of the *pie noir* ('black food') Basque pig, brings to mind a series of animal and racial signifiers. Thus, references to this speciality-cured meat from the south-west of France resonate grimly, not least because the skull of a 'woman … beautiful … adored' is uncovered during the digging process; Ophélie, too, it is suggested, is now treated as foodstuff. In this slippage of identifiers, as woman, pig and human- and non-human categories are muddled, Ophélie's body is both reified and demeaned in value because of its association with meat and carnality.

The fate of woman after death is further thematized during the closing credits. As the action concludes, combined flute, strings and a solitary and melancholy female voice recall the film's woman-centred interests. Introducing the language of *Kikongo*, the song, according to Limbvani, is a popular choice for funerals in the Democratic Republic of Congo; here, it provides a musical correlative for Gertrude's laments. Her posthumous perspective is privileged and her testimony lives on (in the absence of Horatio's final words, music serves as summary) in that it is the Queen's voice that the film has consistently brought out. Or, to adapt the call of the poem, 'Les Souffles', which the film deploys throughout, we are invited to listen, to heed African women trapped in enforced marriages and conditions of adversity. Implied is a force that recapitulates, asks for attention and speaks from beyond, and, in this regard, the film's site of production is additionally suggestive. The Musée Honmé is known for housing the *alounloun*, a stringed musical instrument that, played only by women, is traditionally used to celebrate Porto-Novian royalty, and in the soundtrack to the Boyokani *Hamlet* there is also signalled the idea of a woman who makes music and who exercises a unique responsibility.[80] Writing broadly about Shakespeare's tragedies in Africa, Benaouda Lebdai writes that 'African culture and … languages' are preserved 'through Shakespeare's tragedies', a key part of the process being the contributions of 'storytellers … the keepers of history and legends'.[81] If Limbvani begins in the role of *griauteur*, it is the film's disembodied female voice that has the final word, displacing earlier tellers of the tale and absorbing into itself the task of narrating the continuing drama of Africa's Shakespearean adaptations.

Conclusions

Hamile and the Boyokani *Hamlet* reflect on the mixed complexions of their respective postcolonial inheritances. The films utilize a range of methods for recasting the Shakespearean story, demonstrating, as they do so, the invitation the play extends to reinvention. From Shakespeare's play they extract lessons of value to the struggles and challenges, the ambitions and designs, of African countries emerging from the throes of colonial rule and embracing independence. Both films articulate Hamlet as African, although this is understood in interlocking national and pan-national ways. As *Hamile* suggests, for example, mystical elements work to affirm a national consciousness (Jean Allman and John Parker point out that the deity, Tongnaab, was 'implicated in some of the earliest articulations of Ghana-as-nation'), while such features as clothing and music are indispensable to the upbeat emphasis of the film's newly independent moment.[82] For its part, the Boyokani *Hamlet* is characterized by a combinatory approach that, even as it privileges supernatural belief, gendered narratives and 'Africanity', points up the ways in which Africa is intersected by other forces and imaginaries. Yet *Hamile* and the Boyokani *Hamlet* are also oddities in the history of Shakespeare and world cinema – isolated instances of interpretive responsiveness that reveal the occasional eruption of Shakespeare in African cinematic contexts. These are works that stand as symptoms of their legacies and that, together, point up the vacillating fortunes of Shakespeare in a complex terrain. Unique exemplars, the films do not easily admit an established teleology, more often demonstrating the ways in which *Hamlet* is engaged with for specific purposes in an irregular adaptive process.

Casting his mind back to the achievement of *Hamile* in the context of the withdrawal of the British Council from educational programmes in Ghana after independence, Ernest Abbequaye notes: 'It saddens me when I think back to how much experimentation with Shakespeare we could have done . . . so as to use language as a tool for creativity . . . thinking . . . [and] communication'. Citing, in particular, a never realized film adaptation of *Macbeth* set among the 'African chieftaincy system', he laments the infrastructural realities conspiring against a richer and more sustained embrace of Shakespeare on celluloid. Nevertheless, *Hamile* and the Boyokani *Hamlet* in some regards establish templates for interpretation and creative thinking. Even as they espouse 'Africanity', the films look outside of themselves, ultimately beyond Tongo in the case of *Hamile* and, via traversing nations and cultures, beyond Africa in the case of the

Boyokani *Hamlet* (itself a 'travelling' artefact). The effect is undoubtedly generative. Hence, once he had left Ghana for Kenya, Joe de Graft, the originator of *Hamile*, adapted *Macbeth* as *Mambo*, a theatre work that centred on an entrepreneur competing for the 'crown' of a business empire, that premiered at the West Berlin Academy of Arts in 1979, and that showcased according to James Gibbs and Christine Matzke how some African artistic practices had become 'self-assertive, capable of manipulating' older colonial attachments.[83] Other lines of connection may be more diffuse. The Boyokani *Hamlet*, in the ways in which it mixes and meshes African and world cultures, acts as an unacknowledged precursor to some of the similarly oriented, if ambivalently received, 'African' productions animating the 2012 Cultural Olympiad. Certainly, the notion that *Hamlet* can be accommodated within African frames of reference has a firmly entrenched contemporaneousness. Most distinctive in the 2016 Royal Shakespeare Company Africa-inspired production of *Hamlet*, for example, were motifs of diaspora and loss; in the words of the programme, the play invites comparison with the lot of some African leaders robbed of 'home, family, heritage and a sense of dynastic destiny'.[84] In the kinds of commerce and interaction that these admittedly theatrical productions make visible, a further interpretive turn may be at work. Crucially, most Shakespeare films in Africa are of recent vintage, perhaps part of an additional shift in sensibility, and mark a move away from English and French to a greater if not exclusive use of indigenous African languages, such as Ibo, isiZulu, isiXhosa and Yoruba. *Hamlet* may yet become a part of this trajectory and serve as a platform for further thematic explorations of place and a still evolving story of Shakespearean 'Africanity'.

Notes

1. Jane Plastow, 'Introduction', in Jane Plastow, ed., *Shakespeare In and Out of Africa* (London: James Currey, 2013), p. xi.
2. Kofi Ermeleh Agovi, 'The Origin of Literary Theatre in Colonial Ghana, 1920–1957', *Research Review (Lagon)*, 6.1 (1990), pp. 330–42.
3. See Faisal Fatehali Devji, 'Subject to Translation: Shakespeare, Swahili, Socialism', *Postcolonial Studies*, 3.2 (2000), pp. 181–89; Martin Banham and Eldred Durosimi Jones, '". . . tinap aber we leck giant": African Celebrations of Shakespeare', in Shirley Chew and Alistair Stead, eds, *Translating Life: Studies in Transpositional Aesthetics* (Liverpool: Liverpool University Press, 1999), p. 122; Deborah Seddon, 'The Colonial Encounter and *The Comedy of Errors*: Solomon Plaatje's *Diphosho-phosho*', *The Shakespeare International Yearbook*, 9 (2009), pp. 66–86.

4. Martin Banham, Roshni Mooneram and Jane Plastow, 'Shakespeare and Africa', in Stanley Wells and Sarah Stanton, eds, *The Cambridge Companion to Shakespeare on Stage* (Cambridge: Cambridge University Press, 2002), p. 292; Benaouda Lebdai, 'Traces of Shakespeare's Tragedies in Africa', in Eric C. Brown and Estelle Rivier, eds, *Shakespeare in Performance* (Newcastle-upon-Tyne: Cambridge Scholars, 2013), p. 186.

5. See Colette Gordon, '"Mind the Gap": Globalism, Postcolonialism and Making Up Africa in the Cultural Olympiad', in Paul Prescott and Erin Sullivan, eds, *Shakespeare on the Global Stage: Performance and Festivity in the Olympic Year* (London and New York: Bloomsbury, 2015), pp. 191–225; Kate McLuskie, '*Macbeth/uMabatha*: Global Shakespeare in a Post-Colonial Market', *Shakespeare Survey*, 52 (1999), pp. 154–65.

6. John Akomfrah, 'On the National in African Cinema/s: A Conversation', in Valentina Vitali and Paul Willemen, eds, *Theorising National Cinema* (London: BFI, 2006), p. 274.

7. In Ghana, English is the official – common – language, closely followed by *Twi* (Steven J. Salm and Toyin Falola, *Culture and Customs of Ghana* [Westport and London: Greenwood Press, 2002], pp. 8–9).

8. Interview between Mark Thornton Burnett and Martin Owusu (25 July 2011).

9. For a brief account of the film, see Christine Matzke, 'Afrika', in Peter W. Marx, ed., *Hamlet-Handbuch: Stoffe, Aneiguungen, Deutungen* (Stuttgart and Weimar: Verlag J. B. Meltzler, 2014), p. 337.

10. Anna Cetera, 'Translating Shakespeare for Performance', in Bruce R. Smith, ed., *The Cambridge Guide to the Worlds of Shakespeare*, 2 vols (Cambridge: Cambridge University Press, 2016), II, p. 1378.

11. See William Shakespeare, *Hamlet*, tr. Jean-Michel Déprats (Paris: Éditions Gallimard, 2002), p. 73. All further references to the French language translation appear in the text.

12. Most accounts give the stage production and the film the same date, 1965 (see Kofi Ermeleh Agovi, 'Joe de Graft', in Bernth Lindfors and Reinhard Sander, eds, *Twentieth-Century Caribbean and Black African Writers* [Detroit and London: Gale Research, 1992], p. 138). However, in interview, Kofi Middleton-Mends (who played Hamile in stage production and film alike) observes that the stage production took place 'in 1964 . . . [it] lasted for some weeks' (interview with Mark Thornton Burnett [9 June 2011]). Ernest Abbequaye, who played Ibrahim/Polonius, agrees: 'the stage production was in 1964 and the film the year after' (interview with Mark Thornton Burnett [15 March 2017]). The earlier date of 1964 would match the worldwide celebrations accompanying the 400th anniversary of Shakespeare's birth: the stage production was perhaps envisaged as Ghana's contribution to this international initiative. Unless otherwise stated, all Middleton-Mends and Abbequaye quotations are taken from these interviews and appear in the text or notes.

13. A revival of the stage production at the University of Ghana in 1997 as part of the Golden Jubilee had to be rewritten from scratch, no copy of script or film having survived.

14. Africanus Aveh, 'The Rise of the Video Film Industry & Its Projected Social Impact on Ghanaians', *African Literature Today*, 28 (2010), p. 122; Manthia Diawara, *African Cinema: Politics and Culture* (Bloomington and Indianapolis: Indiana University Press, 1992), p. 5; Tom Rice, 'Gold Coast Film Unit', www.colonialfilm.org.uk (accessed 15 January 2017).

15. Under Nkrumah's aegis, the Ghana Dance Ensemble, the Ghana Drama Studio and the Institute for African Studies were launched and supported, all in the interests of nation-building initiatives. See Paul Schauert, *Staging Ghana: Artistry and Nationalism in State Dance Ensembles* (Bloomington and Indianapolis: Indiana University Press, 2015), pp. 15, 47, 162.

16. Kwame Nkrumah, *I Speak of Freedom* (London: Heinemann, 1961), p. 107.

17. Diawara, *African Cinema*, p. 6; Carmela Garritano, *African Video Movies and Global Desires: A Ghanaian History* (Athens: Ohio University Press, 2013), p. 47.

18. Graham had left Ghana at independence, and the Ghana Film Industry Corporation was managed by the novelist, Kofi Awoonor, but the former's influence remained. (See Obi Maduakor, 'Joe de Graft & the Ghana Cultural Revival', in Martin Banham, James Gibbs and Femi Osofian, eds, *Playwrights and Politics* [Oxford: James Currey, 2001], p. 65; Garritano, *African*, pp. 33, 48, 51; Emma Sandon, Tom Rice and Peter Bloom, 'Changing the World: Sean Graham', *Journal of British Cinema and Television*, 10.3 [2013], pp. 524–36). On Bishop, see Steve Chibnall and Brian Macfarlane, *The British 'B' Film* (Basingstoke: Palgrave, 2009), p. 156.

19. See Rosaleen Smyth, 'Images of Empire on Shifting Sands: The Colonial Film Unit in West Africa in the Post-War Period', in Lee Grieveson and Colin MacCabe, eds, *Film and the End of Empire* (London: BFI, 2011), p. 161. According to Ben Page, citing the director's marginalia on a draft screen-play of *Daybreak in Udi*, Bishop was 'clearly impressed by the visual impact of Igbo culture, particularly in relation to dance: "It is impossible to describe the impression of latent, hardly tapped power which these demonstrations give . . . the whole spirit of the village seems to find expression in an elevated display of strength and *élan*: to be seen and heard to be believed"' ('"And the Oscar Goes to . . . *Daybreak in Udi*": Understanding Late Colonial Community Development and Its Legacy Through Film', *Development and Change*, 45.5 [2014], p. 857).

20. 'Joe de Graft had influence . . . he came on set . . . [and] found time to talk about . . . what it means to be shooting a film as against acting on stage' (interview between Mark Thornton Burnett and Ernest Abbequaye [15 March 2017]).

21. Magali Compan, 'Island Geography as Creole Biography: Shenaz Patel's Mauritian Literary Production', in Freida Ekoto and Kenneth Harrow, eds, *Rethinking African Cultural Production* (Bloomington and Indianapolis: Indiana University Press, 2015), p. 177.

22. Imruh Bakari, 'Introduction: African Cinema and the Emergent Africa', in June Givanni, ed., *Symbolic Narratives/African Cinema: Audiences, Theory,*

and the Moving Image (London: BFI, 2000), p. 5; Briggite Rollet, 'French Funding and Francophone Cinema', in Blandine Stefanson and Sheila Petty, eds, *Directory of World Cinema: Africa* (Bristol and Chicago: Intellect, 2014), p. 37.

23. Nwachukwu Frank Ukadike, *Black African Cinema* (Berkeley, Los Angeles and London: University of California Press, 1994), p. 70.

24. Roy Armes, *African Filmmaking North and South of the Sahara* (Edinburgh: Edinburgh University Press, 2006), p. 55.

25. Leanore Lieblein, 'Nuancing Diversity: The Boyokani Company *Hamlet*', *alt. theatre*, 4.2–3 (2006), p. 24; Kaf Malère, 'Un *Hamlet* africain', *Horizons Maghrébins: Le Droit à la Mémoire*, 53 (2005), pp. 163–71.

26. The film answers both to Ingo Berensmeyer's argument that Shakespeare's play is defined by its history of 'mobility and portability' and Cristina della Coletta's observation that 'travel' is facilitative; as she notes, 'mutual displacement' and 'sustained estrangement' have a '"generative" power on both aesthetic and hermeneutical grounds'. See Ingo Berensmeyer, 'Cultural Ecology and Chinese *Hamlets*', *New Literary History*, 42.3 (2011), p. 421; Cristina della Coletta, *When Stories Travel: Cross-Cultural Encounters Between Fiction and Film* (Baltimore and London: Johns Hopkins University Press, 2012), p. 21.

27. On 'Africanity', see Akomfrah, 'On the National', p. 274.

28. Garritano, *African*, p. 52; 'British Films: *Hamile/Hamlet* (Ghana)', *Variety: Film Reviews 1907–1980*, 16 vols (New York and London: Garland, 1983), XI, n.p. The review is dated 20 October 1965. As antidote, see the review of the film by Isabel Quigly, 'Drums Over Elsinore', *The Spectator*, 7162, 1 October (1965), pp. 410, 412.

29. Emmanuel Sama, 'African Films Are Foreigners in Their Own Countries', in Imruh Bakari and Mbye B. Cham, eds, *African Experiences of Cinema* (London: BFI, 1996), p. 148.

30. See Carola Lentz, *Ethnicity and the Making of History in Northern Ghana* (Edinburgh: Edinburgh University Press, 2006), pp. 175–98.

31. Jean Allman and John Parker, *Tongnaab: The History of a West African God* (Bloomington: Indiana University Press, 2005), p. 5.

32. Allman and Parker, *Tongnaab*, pp. 7, 14, 39, 62, 222.

33. In the *Sisala* language (from which the name, Hamile, stems), place names can often become personal names and vice versa.

34. See A. J. Naden and R. L. Schaefer, 'The Meaning of "Fra-Fra"', *Institute of African Studies Research Review*, 9.2 (1973), pp. 7–12.

35. The only 'southern' reference – to Lagon/Wittenberg – is clearly an in-house university joke.

36. Nkrumah encapsulated the mood of the moment when, speaking at a flag raising ceremony in 1957, he declared, 'we can prove to the world that when the African is given a chance he can show the world that he is somebody'. See Nkrumah, *Freedom*, p. 106.

37. Joe de Graft, 'Interview', in Bernth Lindfors, ed., *Africa Talks Back: Interviews with Anglophone African Writers* (Trenton and Asmara: Africa World Press, 2002), p. 77.

38. Heike Owusu, *African Symbols* (New York and London: Sterling, 2000), p. 159.

39. Peter Adler and Nicholas Barnard, *African Majesty: The Textile Art of the Ashanti and the Ewe* (London: Thames and Hudson, 1992), pp. 44, 8.

40. Kofi Anyidoho, 'Ghanaian *Kente*: Cloth and Song', in Lynn Gumpert, ed., *The Poetics of Cloth: African Textiles/Recent Art* (New York: Grey Art Gallery, 2008), p. 39.

41. Splendour in *Hamile* is all-male. By contrast, women are represented in less ornate dress: notable is the consistent covering of the left shoulder by an upper garment, an index of modesty.

42. See Atta Annan Mensah, 'The Great Ode of History: Music and Dance in Africa', in Don Rubin, Ousmane Diakhaté and Hansel Ndumbe Eyoh, eds, *The World Encyclopedia of Contemporary Theatre: Africa* (London and New York: Routledge, 1997), p. 32.

43. See Suzanne Preston Blier and James Morris, *Butabu: Adobe Architecture of West Africa* (New York: Princeton Architectural Press, 2004), pp. 118, 121, 190; J. Owusu-Addo, 'Traditional Forms of Architecture in Ghana', *International Social Science Journal*, 30.3 (1978), pp. 449, 450, 452–53, 456.

44. See Alisa LaGamma and Christine Giuntini, *The Essential Art of African Textiles: Design Without End* (New Haven and London: Yale University Press, 2008), p. 48; Owusu, *Symbols*, pp. 205, 207–11, 217.

45. On these instruments, see Salm and Falola, *Ghana*, pp. 168, 173; Paschal Yao Younge, *Music and Dance Traditions of Ghana: History, Performance and Teaching* (Jefferson and London: McFarland, 2011), pp. 20, 101.

46. Schauert, *Ghana*, p. 164. Reflecting on the state opening of parliament in 1960, Nkrumah noted that 'my arrival ... was heralded by the beating of traditional drums' (Nkrumah, *Freedom*, p. 238).

47. See Salm and Falola, *Ghana*, p. 39.

48. See Iris Hahner-Herzog, Maria Kecskési and Lászlo Vagda, *African Masks from the Barbier-Mueller Collection, Geneva* (Munich, London and New York: Prestel, 2004), p. 24; Henryk Jurkowski, 'African Puppets and Masks: Links in a Historical Chain', in Rubin, Diakhaté and Eyoh, eds, *Encyclopedia*, pp. 38–39; Peter Stepan, *Spirits Speak: A Celebration of African Masks* (Munich, London and New York: Prestel, 2005), pp. 19, 23, 30, 31.

49. Owusu, *Symbols*, p. 28; Stepan, *Spirits*, p. 24.

50. 'The ghost was Joe de Graft's idea ... in Africa, ghosts are manifested as smoky, shadowy things ... you do not show or see the face' (interview between Mark Thornton Burnett and Ernest Abbequaye [15 March 2017]).

51. Similarly, in the closet (Queen's apartment) scene, the emphasis is on Hamile/Hamlet's reaction to the Ghost: sexual references, and hence Oedipal sub-texts (3.4.43–85, 138–47, 150–53, 165–68, 170–75, 179–97), are conspicuous by their absence.

52. Esi Sutherland-Addy, 'The Funeral as a Site for Choreographing Modern Identities in Contemporary Ghana', in Kwasi Konadu and Clifford C. Campbell, eds, *The Ghana Reader: History, Culture, Politics* (Durham and London: Duke University Press, 2016), pp. 428, 432.

53. This is in sharp contrast to the fate of Ibrahim/Polonius; indeed, Habiba/Ophelia, struck to the quick by how her father is interred in 'haste and secrecy', is driven mad, it is implied, precisely by ceremonial not having been observed.

54. Igor Kopytoff, 'Ancestors as Elders in Africa', in Roy Richard Grinker and Christopher B. Steiner, eds, *Perspectives on Africa: A Reader in Culture, History, and Representation* (Oxford: Blackwell, 1997), p. 412.

55. Salm and Falola, *Ghana*, p. 42.

56. Stephen J. Mock, *Symbols of Defeat in the Construction of National Identity* (Cambridge: Cambridge University Press, 2002), p. 136; Peter Sarpong, *The Sacred Stools of the Akan* (Accra-Tema: Ghana Publishing Corporation, 1971), pp. 13, 34.

57. According to some accounts, Nkrumah exacerbated discontent via censorship of the press, incarceration of dissidents, lavish spending and reliance on a one-party state; he was perceived as having abnegated procedure in favour of a form of a corrupt politics. See Carol Polsgrove, *Ending British Rule in Africa: Writers in a Common Cause* (Manchester and New York: Manchester University Press, 2009), p. 164; Salm and Falola, *Ghana*, p. xviii; Schauert, *Ghana*, p. 168; Kevin Shillington, *History of Africa*, 3rd ed. (Basingstoke and New York: Palgrave, 2012), p. 442.

58. Diawara, *African Cinema*, p. 6. Nkrumah, who frequently had state ceremonies filmed, was all too aware of the uses of media, including cinema, for ideological purposes. See Anne Mette Jørgensen, 'Sankofa and Modern Authenticity in Ghanaian Film and Television', in Mai Palmberg and Maria Eriksson Baaz, eds, *Same and Other: Negotiating African Identity in Cultural Production* (Stockholm: Nordiska Afrikainstitutet, 2001), p. 122.

59. The film's only public broadcast was in 1970 on National Educational Television in the USA.

60. Birago Diop, *Leurres et lueurs* (Paris: Présence Africaine, 1960), pp. 64–66. The translation is mine.

61. As in *Hamile*, 'ancestors' are additionally instanced in repeated references and substitutions (typically, 'By the ancestors' replaces '*Pour l'amour de Dieu*' [p. 67]).

62. Joseph Gugler, *African Film: Re-Imagining a Continent* (Bloomington and Indianapolis: Indiana University Press, 2003), p. 36.

63. David Murphy and Patrick Williams, *Postcolonial African Cinema: Ten Directors* (Manchester and New York: Manchester University Press, 2007), p. 9.

64. Rod Edmond, *Leprosy and Empire: A Medical and Cultural History* (Cambridge: Cambridge University Press, 2006), pp. 1–2.

65. From 2013 to 2017 in Africa, 30,000 new cases of leprosy were reported each year, 66% of which represented particularly severe forms, with the Democratic Republic of the Congo being at a particularly high risk. See 'Leprosy Elimination: World Health Organization Regional Office for Africa', www.afro.who.int (accessed 4 January 2017).

66. On these features, see Kawatake Shigetoshi, Yoshikawa Yoshio and Takekosi Kazuo, *Theatre in Japan* (Tokyo: Japanese National Commission for UNESCO, 1963), pp. 9, 24.

67. Interview between Hugues Serge Limbvani and Mark Thornton Burnett [27 July 2017]. Unless otherwise stated, all Limbvani quotations are from this interview and appear in the text or notes.

68. In interview, Kaf Malère notes that the Ghost's floating, gliding movement was designed to distinguish it from the other – mortal – characters who, earth-bound, walk on their feet (interview with Mark Thornton Burnett [13 April 2017]).

69. See Monica Bethe, 'Interlude: *Noh* and *Kyogen* Costumes and Masks', in Jonah Salz, ed., *A History of Japanese Theatre* (Cambridge: Cambridge University Press, 2016), pp. 63, 64; Shinko Kagaya and Miura Hiroko, '*Noh* and *Muromachi* Culture', in Salz, ed., *History*, pp. 24, 25, 31, 33.

70. In the wordless play-within-a-play, for example, masks, fans, elaborate wigs, *kimonos* and wails point up indebtedness to Japanese *kabuki* theatre. Matching the transgressive charge of the play-within-the-play is *kabuki*'s historical association with unorthodoxy, irreverence and eroticism (see David G. Goodman, 'Japan', in James R. Brandon, ed., *The Cambridge Guide to Asian Theatre* [Cambridge: Cambridge University Press, 1993], p. 147; Julie A. Iezzi, '*Kabuki*: Superheroes and *Femmes Fatales*', in Salz, ed., *History*, pp. 103, 111, 116). The fan, now associated with duplicity and mortality, reappears in the final duelling/wrestling scene.

71. For a discussion of Porto Novo, see Patrick Manning, *Francophone Sub-Saharan Africa, 1880–1995*, 2nd ed. (Cambridge: Cambridge University Press, 1998), pp. 12, 14, 79.

72. Stefan Eisenhofer, *African Art* (Los Angeles and Köln: Taschen, 2010), p. 6.

73. Interview between Mark Thornton Burnett and Kaf Malère (13 April 2017).

74. See Stepan, *Spirits*, p. 31.

75. Anne Van Cutsen and Mauro Magliani, *Powerful Headdresses: Africa/Asia* (Milan: 5 Continents Editions, 2010), p. 177, plate 66.

76. Alisa LaGamma, *Kongo: Power and Majesty* (New York: Metropolitan Museum of Art, 2015), p. 294; Claudia Zaslavsky, *Africa Counts: Number and Pattern in African Cultures*, 3rd ed. (Chicago: Lawrence Hill Books, 1999), pp. 76, 83, 227, 268.

77. See Lieblin, 'Nuancing', p. 22.

78. See Rebecca Brown and Judy Oder, 'The Protection of Women's Economic, Social and Cultural Rights in Africa', in Danwood Mzikenge Chirwa and Lilian Chenwi, eds, *The Protection of Economic, Social and Cultural Rights in Africa: International, Regional and National Perspectives* (Cambridge:

Cambridge University Press, 2016), pp. 121, 139; Simon Ottenberg, 'Artistic and Sex Roles in a Limba Chiefdom', in Christine Oppong, ed., *Female and Male in West Africa* (London, Boston and Sydney: George Allen and Unwin, 1983), p. 77.

79. Melissa Thackway, *Africa Shoots Back: Alternative Perspectives in Sub-Saharan Francophone African Film* (Bloomington and Indianapolis: Indiana University Press, 2003), pp. 151, 155, 157–58.

80. See Michael Bolin, Erika Kraus and Felicie Read, *Benin*, 2nd ed. (Milton Keynes: Other Places, 2014), p. 129.

81. Lebdai, 'Traces', pp. 182, 183.

82. Allman and Parker, *Tongnaab*, p. 181.

83. James Gibbs, 'Joe de Graft: Theatrical Prophet with Strange Honours', in Banham, Gibbs and Osofisan, eds, *Playwrights*, pp. 80–81; James Gibbs and Christine Matzke, '"accents yet unknown": Examples of Shakespeare from Ghana, Malawi and Eritrea', in Norbert Schaffeld, ed., *Shakespeare's Legacy: The Appropriation of the Plays in Post-Colonial Drama* (Trier: WVT, 2005), p. 16.

84. *Royal Shakespeare Company: William Shakespeare, 'Hamlet', RSC Programme* (Stratford-upon-Avon: RSC, 2016), n.p.

CHAPTER THREE

Hamlet *and the Moment of Brazilian Cinema*

The opening sequence to *O Jogo da Vida e da Morte/A Game of Life and Death* (dir. Mário Kuperman, 1971), a Brazilian film adaptation of *Hamlet*, shows a theatre being closed down. Muted applause dies away as the spotlights are lowered onto an empty stage; an elderly caretaker takes in the billboard – the production is *Hamlet* – and brings down the shutters. The idea, emphasized by *noir*-like camerawork and doleful strings, is that an era has come to a natural end. It is the film to ensue, the sequence suggests, that will fill the void vacated by theatre. And it is in the medium of cinema that the play's dominant themes – identified on the billboard as 'A Corrupção no Reino da Dinamarca' or 'Corruption in the State of Denmark' – will find a ready Brazilian expression. As the 1960s concluded, there was certainly reason to feel optimistic about the ascendancy of the Brazilian film industry. The *Cinema Novo* movement, which aspired to establish a revolutionary national cinema that highlighted colonial injustices and social inequities, had placed Brazilian film on the international map; in addition, the creation of government-funded film agencies, such as Embrafilme, provided support for a number of related Brazil-based film projects.[1] Indeed, as the 1970s commenced, no less than four Shakespeare films appeared in quick succession – *Cabeças Cortadas/Severed Heads* (dir. Glauber Rocha, 1970), an adaptation of *Macbeth, Faustão/Faust* (dir. Eduardo Coutinho, 1971), an adaptation of *Henry IV, A Herança/The Inheritance* (dir. Ozualdo Candeias, 1971), a further adaptation of *Hamlet*, and *O Jogo da Vida e da Morte*. In some respects, this engagement with Shakespeare – as shadowed in the scene of the closing of the theatre – marked the culmination of a rich tradition of Shakespearean performance and translation in Latin America in general and Brazil in particular. As critics such as Alfredo Michel Modenessi, Margarida Gandara Rauen and Aimara da Cunha Resende have demonstrated, Shakespeare made his way into Latin America via nineteenth-century performances based on French adaptations, with the plays themselves being subsequently deployed to air questions about postcolonial identity, authentic national cultures, state-sanctioned art and the reverence (or otherwise) accorded 'high culture'.[2] The films above respond to these traditions of interpretation, reworking Shakespeare to assert images and motifs of 'Brazilianness' that sharply contrast with European concepts and forms. But they may also owe their genesis to a more vexed set of production circumstances. During this period, several leading *Cinema Novo* filmmakers had been forced into exile, alarmed by the increasingly authoritarian tenor of the then military regime, which, while it ostensibly enabled the local film industry, was simultaneously prescriptive and only selectively approving.[3] As Darlene J. Sadlier argues in *Brazil Imagined*, 'Film adaptations, especially adaptations of classics, tended to be ignored by the military regime, which regarded the process as simply the transportation of a literary work onto celluloid'.[4] Mário Kuperman, the director of *O Jogo da Vida e da Morte*, puts the point more bluntly: 'when my film was produced ... there was rigorous censorship ... As I feared having my work banned or mutilated (I had a play cut by the censors), I ended up deciding to film a classic', he states.[5] It is possible to suggest that Shakespeare's plays became relevant to directors in Brazil during the early 1970s because the dramatist offered, at some level, a safe outlet for artistic debate.

This chapter discusses *A Herança* and *O Jogo da Vida e da Morte*, identifying in their interpretations of *Hamlet* complementary visions of Brazil.[6] Ozualdo Candeias, the director of *A Herança*, exemplifies the radical *Cinema Marginal*, or 'Underground Cinema', movement which originated in the *Boca do Lixo* or 'Mouth of Garbage' neighbourhood of São Paulo and which, as Daniel Serravalle de Sá states, substituted 'the social didacticism ... of *Cinema Novo*' for a 'more disillusioned and testimonial form of expression [focusing] ... on the lives of subaltern subjects'.[7] Candeias' controversial film, *A Margem/The Margin* (1967), in which dispossessed types scrape a living on the banks of São Paulo's polluted Tiête river, is typical. While he eventually garnered festival awards for *A Opção/The Option* (1981) and *O Vigilante/The Vigilante* (1992), and is now recognized as a seminal filmmaker, Candeias was frequently prevented from directing by a lack of state support, combining technical work with acting and photography in the intervals between regular employment.[8] Unlike Candeias, Kuperman only produced one film, *O Jogo da Vida e da Morte*, and does not fit easily into a particular cinematic category. 'My film is not linked to any movement', he states in interview, keen to resist comparisons. Trained as a sociologist, Kuperman has worked as a screenwriter, commentator and novelist. The better part of his career has been spent in directing documentaries, on such themes as immigration, the rural economy and logging, his work showcasing, in Julianne Burton's words, a Latin American 'preference for raw realism that replicated the compelling immediacy of certain techniques of reportage'.[9] As this chapter will argue, *O Jogo da Vida e da Morte* derives much of its critical impact from its documentary style and from the social and economic analyses it brings to the work of adaptation.

Advertising itself in the credits as 'Baseado em HAMLET de W. Shakespeare', *O Jogo da Vida e da Morte* uses a colloquial form of Brazilian Portuguese to approximate the Shakespearean word.[10] According to Mário Prata, who worked on the film's dialogue, the text of *Hamlet*, in Spanish and Portuguese translations, was the first port of call; these provided a comprehensive basis and the imaginative spur for the film's distinctive verbal lexicon.[11] Characteristic of the method is the rendition of the 'To be, or not to be' soliloquy. As frustrated *Paulistano* João/Hamlet (Walter Cruz) ascends a hill giving onto a rubbish dump, his white shirt throwing the black mass of the landfill into sharp relief, he finds in the detritus around him an advertisement on which is printed part of the monologue's opening line ('*Ser ou não ser*'). Here, via voiceover, the language of the 'original' is realized in amputated synoptic statements ('We do not take risks or do what needs to be done' replaces five lines of the latter part of the soliloquy). 'Local diction' ('Ah, death! Could it be any worse than this shit life?'), 'consistent with' the film's 'socio-cultural situation', surrogates for the more formally turned observation, 'there's the respect / That makes calamity of so long life' (3.1.67–68).[12] As the setting for the soliloquy indicates, the action of *O Jogo da Vida e da Morte* unfolds in the Brazilian metropolis – specifically, the working-class Jaguaré district to the south of São Paulo. Its 'geography and social conditions', according to Kuperman, the director, were, in the early 1970s, 'entirely characteristic of the areas surrounding large-scale Latin American cities'. Within these environs, *O Jogo da Vida e da Morte*, in the spirit of previous shanty town films and with a nod to a documentary tradition centred on the plight of the Brazilian proletariat, identifies João/Hamlet as an archetypal *favelado*, the camera lingering over his angular frame, wavy dark hair and pale looks.[13] Reduced from a palace to a primitive brick bungalow on a crumbling hillside, Elsinore's stark features are emphasized by *ciné-verité*-style cinematography and the use of deep shadows and high contrasts. Against these distinctive backdrops, this chapter argues, *Hamlet* is made to speak to the needs and expectations of a recognizably Brazilian urban *milieu*.

Contrasting in locale and linguistic decisions, *A Herança*, although it publicizes itself as indebted to the well-known 1955 translation of *Hamlet* by Péricles Eugênio da Silva Ramos, represents the play only as a verbal skeleton.[14] At its release, *A Herança* was accused of showing a lack of regard for the 'original' play, no doubt because the film represents an experiment in Shakespeare without words.[15] Language is largely excluded, and in its place *A Herança* substitutes images, compositions and music: the folk score, as played by the Teorema quartet, and alternating between dirge-like laments and jaunty melodies, is jarring and disharmonious, suggestive of a community's struggles and trials. The soundtrack also features diegetic rural noise, the whole operating in a manner akin to a silent film. Judith Buchanan notes that a silent Shakespearean film typically includes in the inter-titles quotations from the plays, or speech summaries, as a means of asserting 'the production's authentic Shakespeareanness'.[16] A parallel suggests itself with *A Herança* in which periodic inter-titles function both as guides to the action and reminders of Shakespearean dialogue (fragmentary quotations suffice to recall a larger textual whole). Even at those points where dialogue is included, the tendency is to downplay speech as a carrier of meaning; for example, when Omeleto/Hamlet delivers the 'To be, or not to be' soliloquy (in English), the anticipated grandeur of the moment is undercut by acoustic distortion. In fact, in *A Herança*, the greater emphasis is on the evocation of a specific time and place. The action unfolds at the turn of the nineteenth century in a street of distinctive whitewashed houses clustered around a church; Elsinore is conjured in the neighbouring *casa grande* or single-story farmhouse. These are the typical characteristics of towns and villages in the *sertão* or scrublands of the north east (*A Herança*'s 'look' suggests variously the states of Minas Gerais, Piauí and Rio Grande do Norte) and, to be sure, the film emerges from an earlier grouping of cinematic works made in the region concerned with the status of landowners and issues of economic hardship.[17] Generically, *A Herança* might be identified as a Latin American Western, as suggested in allusions to Sergio Leone's 'Euro-westerns', a conceptual focus on the lives of *sertanejos* (cowboys), horse-riding sequences and brawls in the dust. The conjunction of Shakespeare and the Western is not unprecedented on film, but, in *A Herança*, the formula is lent a local treatment that illuminates a region-specific set of social and economic circumstances.[18]

Both *A Herança* and *O Jogo da Vida e da Morte* elaborate Hamlet figures who are ill-at-ease in the worlds they inhabit. The João/Hamlet of

O Jogo da Vida e da Morte, for instance, wears a black check shirt that marks him out as different, while his generally hunched pose suggests disaffection. Frequently seen *sola*, the *favelado* is marked by downcast looks, a weary mien and a tight-lipped delivery. Overall, the concentration on João/Hamlet's point of view, which is captured in distorted camera angles, reinforces an individual perspective that the rest of the film prioritizes. In *A Herança*, a like situation is conveyed in the protagonist's appearance (his long hair and city suit distinguish him from his *sertão* counterparts) and in his connection with the industrial process (he arrives by steam train). Instancing the tropes of the Western, in which a wandering hero returns to town, *A Herança* associates Omeleto/Hamlet (David Cardoso), who has been studying law in São Paulo, with an idea of forward progress but also with uncertainty about how he might re-engage with his place of origin – shots of mothers cradling their children in doorways indicate a way of life that the first-generation professional has long left behind. Hence, Omeleto/Hamlet is seen holding back from his mother's embrace and shaking hands with only some of the farm-workers, with inter-title expressions of thought (such as 'You didn't come for any funeral . . . You all came for my mother's wedding') pointing up the condition of an interiorized, reflective protagonist at odds with a rustic environment. Utilizing the familiar construction of Hamlet as an inward-looking and alienated hero, the films simultaneously point up the ways in which he is a cipher for, and a product of, larger kinds of displacement and upset.

    This discussion of these films takes a three-pronged approach to its material. In the first part of the chapter, I explore the ways in which *O Jogo da Vida e da Morte* and *A Herança* deploy locale – the *favela* and the *sertão*. As Ivana Bentes explains, these two environments are not as dissimilar as they might appear, for, as 'frontier territories and social fractures . . . the *sertão* and the *favelas* . . . have always been the "other side" of the . . . positivist Brazil . . . They are places . . . where tradition and invention are extracted from adversity'.[19] Accordingly, I stress the extent to which the films find comparable metaphorical resonances in their respective habitats, highlighting, in so doing, a series of intricate relationships between land, property and poverty. At a time of military rule, these films make a virtue of focusing on occluded communities via a concentration on particular types of setting characterized by scarcity and lack.[20] I go on to suggest, in the second section of the chapter, that the films' intersecting treatment of the communal, the spiritual and the racial is evidenced in their privileging of rituals and celebrations, such as the Claudius/Gertrude

Figure 10: Omeleto/Hamlet (David Cardoso), newly returned to the *sertão*, in
A Herança/The Inheritance (dir. Ozualdo Candeias, 1971). Courtesy of Acervo Heco
Produções/Acervo Ozualdo Candeias.

wedding or the Old Hamlet/Ophelia funerals. Invariably, these occasions are
discovered as divisive. In particular, the black Ophelia figure in *O Jogo da
Vida e da Morte* and *A Herança* is utilized as a significant vehicle through
which Brazil's troubled racial histories are made visible. *O Jogo da Vida e da
Morte* and *A Herança*, I argue, are preoccupied with communities that fail or
are unable to provide for their own, thereby introducing images of Brazil
that run counter to populist conceptions. Michael Chanan suggests that, in
Latin American cinema, the 'periphery' is always inscribed as 'a site of
counter-narrative'.[21] His reading, as I maintain in the chapter's final section,
accords with the ways in which *A Herança* discovers Omeleto/Hamlet at his
death as distributing the estate to the peasantry, thus marking a radical break
with traditions of land ownership in the north-eastern regions. *O Jogo da
Vida e da Morte*, in contrast, visits little capacity for change on João/Hamlet,
stressing his distinctive powerlessness and inertia. While *A Herança* endorses
the ideal of a socialist utopia, then, *O Jogo da Vida e da Morte* assumes
a more nihilistic attitude. Responsive to the straitened political conditions of
Brazil in the early 1970s, *O Jogo da Vida e da Morte* and *A Herança* reveal the
capacity of *Hamlet* to be pulled in two directions at the same time, occupying recuperative and defeatist positions, to address similar sets of difficulties.

Poverty, Place, Landscape

Margreta de Grazia argues that *Hamlet* is 'framed by territorial conflict'; the 'plot', she writes, is fundamentally 'land-driven'.[22] Just such a preoccupation is found in the cinematography of *O Jogo da Vida e da Morte* and *A Herança*: land is limned as a source of power and as a terrain to be fought over. At a time when the rest of the Brazilian film industry was turning to colour, *O Jogo da Vida e da Morte* and *A Herança* cleave to the symbolic resonances of a monochrome palette – aerial shots of a patchwork of gardens in *O Jogo da Vida e da Morte* and pans over abandoned out-buildings in *A Herança* appear all the more stark for being lensed in black and white. More than simply conjurations of Brazilian topography, the landscape-saturated scenes of the films emphasize straitened conditions and material impoverishment. The plight of the *sertão* inhabitants is discovered in a sequence in which the camera arcs over a procession of peasants traversing a dried-up terrain. Drought, it is implied, has com-pelled the common people to migrate, and imaged in the shot is a sense of the economic pressures that force communities apart. More generally, the peasants of *A Herança* appear dwarfed by the landscape, challenged and belittled by its unmanageable size and scale. Symptomatic is the montage that shows silhouetted mourners labouring across a hillside against a threatening backdrop of denuded trees, a visual echo of *The Seventh Seal* (dir. Ingmar Bergman, 1957) and a reminder of psychic tribulations. A woman in a shawl, a labourer riding a cart and workers weighed down with baskets; such 'hungry people', in the words of one inter-title, are typical of the film's imaginary. Consistent with the film's elaboration of landscape is the way in which, invoking the *sertão*, the camera cuts between shots of sagebrush, dry grass, a shallow lake and a parched river bed, features indicative of natural destitution. Nothing here is cultivated, and all is neglected or overgrown, bringing to mind the 'unweeded garden / That grows to seed' (1.2.135–36) of *Hamlet* or, as the inter-titles of the film have it, the suspicion that 'Something is rotten on this big farm'. This, then, is a world that is exhausted, and that has exhausted its own (it is 'stale, flat and unprofitable' [1.2.133]), as is summarized in a widescreen sweep over the disused quarry where Omeleto/Hamlet and Ofélia/Ophelia (Zuleica Maria) conduct their courtship amidst rocks, cacti and thistles. In *Hamlet*, Claudius gains from the murder of his brother a kingdom of crown lands; by contrast, in *A Herança,* the equivalent empire appears as a dispirited acreage that illuminates the uncompromising character of rural arrangements.

The hardships of the *favela* in *O Jogo da Vida e da Morte* have much in common with this unforgiving transposition. In searing natural light, Cláudio/Claudius (Juca de Oliveira) steps out of his bungalow to survey a kind of 'sterile promontory' (2.2.265), the *mise-en-scène* shifting smoothly between starved-looking palm trees, fragile structures made out of wood and cans, a bare washing-line and expanses of sandy wilderness. Repeatedly, the camera dwells on the *favela* as a place poised mid-way between the burgeoning metropolis and a still untouched countryside, discovering an area over which rival powers – of urban capitalism and more traditional rural ways of life – jostle for autonomy. It is a constantly shifting, and unevenly developed, environment. Jagged wooden fences, tangled telephone wires and open sewers – these are the signifiers of a place that has evolved haphazardly. Leisurely panning shots of a shack being disassembled, or a cement factory shuddering into activity, indicate how the architecture of the shantytown is constantly evolving into newer, and less recognizable, forms. A glimpse of discarded tyres, and the movement into the frame of a horse and cart, imply worlds in transit, but they also underline the end-point of the industrial process, the *favela* functioning as a dumping-ground for an exploitative São Paulo economy. Here, the film extracts symbolic capital from one of its chief locales, the rubbish dump, a physical space with metaphorical resonances. The steaming, smoking mass over which the protagonist wanders conjures a landscape benighted and abused, and João/Hamlet, too, is implicated, the gulls that fly overhead serving to emphasize his current stasis and the fact that, for him, these are incarcerating locations, with no immediately identifiable form of escape.

Attention in both *O Jogo da Vida e da Morte* and *A Herança* to domestic interiors affirms an impression of narrowed, desperate existences. Thus, in *A Herança*, interiors are stripped back and unwelcoming: a wash bowl, a pitcher of water, a chipped chest and a worn table all bespeak the reduced living conditions of the *sertão* world. *O Jogo da Vida e da Morte* paints a comparable picture. A cheap carriage clock adorns Cláudio/Claudius and Gertrudes/Gertrude's dining room, the property betraying an unsuccessful projection of a bourgeois lifestyle, while material reality is indexed in the dangling naked light bulb that harshly illuminates the peeling walls. It is all very different from the television studio that João/Hamlet, taking up Tostão/Guildenstern's invitation to meet a samba group making a programme, visits later in the film. Vivian Schelling writes that, during the early 1970s in Brazil, 'television . . . became' an unprecedented 'developmental project' symbolizing the 'status of Brazil as a modern nation'.[23]

Television as a sign of modernity is registered in shots of the manicured lawn outside the building and a shiny, polished interior, with a sleek, moveable set. The contrast is obvious: where the studio points up a cultural movement forwards, the *favela* evokes a sense of stasis born out of impoverishment. More generally in the films, a focus on interiors illuminates gendered constrictions. Indicating their position in the pecking order, the Gertrude figures dwell in the background, dictated to by hierarchies of custom and place. In *O Jogo da Vida e da Morte*, Gertrudes/Gertrude (Odete Lara), flame-haired and wearing an elaborately patterned dress, only enters the dining room, the place of business, to wait on Cláudio/Claudius' visitors. Meanwhile, in *A Herança*, Gertrudes/Gertrude (Bárbara Fazio), dark locks pulled back and modestly attired in a floral skirt and apron, is invariably glimpsed inside the farmhouse interiors. Blocking arrangements clarify where power resides, the Claudius figure either taking up a standing position outside the *sertão* farmhouse or, in the *favela* bungalow, assuming a seat at the head of the dining-table. Themselves types of landscape, these domestic spaces are richly communicative, spotlighting not only the roles to which women are consigned but also the anti-romantic visions of Brazil to which both films subscribe.

In interview, the director of *O Jogo da Vida e da Morte*, Kuperman, sees as the underlying concept of his work 'the exploitation of the weakest', and this is multiply reflected – in the preying attitude of animals, in the treatment of women (one inset shows us Ofélia/Ophelia being dragged by her father across the dump to talk to João/Hamlet), in the marginalizing operations of the city of São Paulo. Most particularly, the concept is captured in *O Jogo da Vida e da Morte* in the representation of Cláudio/Claudius as a petty drug lord who, through his henchmen, presides over a substance-addicted minor empire. Addressed as 'Senhor Cláudio', this brutish-looking type persuades the 'English', a rival gang, to assassinate João/Hamlet, and, behind the scenes, arranges for Fortinbras, a police chief we never see, to be 'sent to another area', 'given early retirement'. The business of the drug empire is both bound up with corruption and born out of the privations that, in the film's cinematography, are writ large in landscape.

A Herança develops ideas of criminality not around Cláudio/Claudius (Rosalvo Caçador) but Manelão (Nivaldo de Lima), the bandit who takes Omeleto/Hamlet prisoner after accidentally foiling the murder plot. A folkloric version of Shakespeare's pirates, Manelão seeks to dominate wild regions rather than tempestuous seas, the inter-titles clarifying the terms on which his authority depends: the bandit, it is stated, is 'a lawless one . . . well-known and terrifying . . . he has killed more people than there are stars in the sky'. Drawing upon literary and filmic traditions, *A Herança* discovers Manelão as a type of *cangaceiro* or social renegade; he operates, it is suggested, according to his own principles of exploitation, as when, in the rural bordello that is his base, he beats a prostitute who is attracted to his captive.[24] In the place of the heroic revolutionary stereotype, however, *A Herança* demythologizes Manelão via his connection with demeaning crimes; the bandit is compromised when he strips Omeleto/Hamlet of his clothes, returning him, in the words of the play, '*naked*' (4.7.43) to the farm (the suit the protagonist wears is a commodity to be seized upon). In common with the Claudius figure of *O Jogo da Vida e da Morte*, Manelão appears, then, as opportunist whose trade is in easy pickings, but, at the same time, the film is insistent on reminding us of the contexts that determine banditry's possibility and perpetuation. Particularly suggestive is the film's brief citation of a musical version of 'The Death and Life of Severino', a poem by João Cabral de Melo Neto which highlights the plight of a peasant from the north-east who, because of a drought, undertakes an arduous trek to the coast.[25] Central to the poem, which, as John Milton argues, is 'fixed in a well-defined Brazilian cultural situation', are the difficulties faced by the dispossessed poor and the challenge of bringing 'to life a dead and deader land'.[26] Within this afflicted landscape, the banditry of Manelão assumes a ready logic, demonstrating not only the precariousness of everyday life but also the difficulties of survival in the face of natural disasters. Working in similar social registers, *A Herança* and *O Jogo da Vida e da Morte* build upon the creative stimulus of *Hamlet* so as to find in practices of criminality responses to, and allegories of, the instabilities and imbalances that characterize rural and urban peripheries.

Community, Spirituality, Race

At the start of *A Herança*, Old Omeleto/Hamlet's funeral is visualized as a *cortège* – oxen pull the cart on which the coffin is displayed – which winds its dusty way across a pitted landscape. The scene emerges from north-eastern funerary conventions wherein the coffin forms part of a procession, mourners following a public route that leads from the *necrotério* (or mausoleum) to the cemetery. Building upon Claudius' line, 'Though yet of Hamlet our dear brother's death / The memory be green' (1.2.1–2), and anticipating by two decades the interpolated scene in Franco Zeffirelli's *Hamlet* (1990) in which the leading players pay their respects to the king (his body is laid out in a vault), *A Herança* uses hat-doffing labourers to point up the enormity of Old Omeleto/Hamlet's passing for the peasant community. Honouring the widow's traditional responsibility for preparing the deceased, Gertrudes/Gertrude places a cross on the face of the corpse, while Claúdio/Claudius' passing glance suggests desire. A sustained filmic emphasis on the proximity of the funeral and Claúdio/Claudius and Gertrudes/Gertrude's wedding is presumably inspired by Hamlet's throwaway comment about how 'the funeral baked meats / Did coldly furnish forth the marriage tables' (1.2.179–80). So, in *A Herança*, a jump-cut moves us immediately from the open grave to a shot of a smiling *padre* officiating at the wedding. The soundtrack to this sequence shifts from tolling bells to a guitar-plucked version of the wedding march; nuptials and obsequies merge inexorably into one, with the inter-title that represents Omeleto/Hamlet's thoughts – 'Only yesterday they were burying my father's body; today, suddenly, they sleep in the same bed' – conveying his sense that a taboo has been broken. In rural Brazil, marriages between the widow and her deceased husband's brother are traditionally a means of keeping an estate intact, and such a scenario is hinted at in *A Herança* in the inter-title, representing Claúdio/Claudius' question, 'Why didn't you tell him our wedding was a necessity?' Yet Omeleto/Hamlet, divorced from *sertão* culture because of his city experience, is discovered as ignorant of the custom. Interestingly, *O Jogo da Vida e da Morte* also elects to represent the proximity of the funeral and the wedding in visual terms. Towards the start, a *montage* of a dead crow, a bottle and a candle (a placatory offering for an *orixá* or deity in Afro-Brazilian religion) dissolves into a shot of a carcass of a roast chicken on a dining-room table (the wedding feast).[27] Implied in the first composition is a post-funeral gift to a 'perturbed spirit' (1.5.180). Expressed in the second is a sense that the traditional mourning period in Brazil has not been honoured, so quickly does one composition give way to the next. Crucially, what is shared between both shots is the body of a bird; symbolic of the body of Old João/Hamlet, the crow and the chicken suggest a family ingesting or cannibalizing its own. Distinctively, João/Hamlet holds back from eating his meal as if in silent empathy with the father whose memory his mother's 'hasty marriage' (2.2.57) has desecrated.

These related sequences in *A Herança* and *O Jogo da Vida e da Morte* derive their impact from juxtaposition, and similar strategies of alignment are at work in the confession scene. Sprawled on his bed in a drunken stupor (this is a 'King' who 'takes his rouse' [1.4.8]), Claúdio/Claudius in *O Jogo da Vida e da Morte* has little to say; instead, the rhetorical onus of the episode resides with a wandering priest who appears on the street below, his homiletic address ('My dearest brothers, what is the purpose of divine mercy, if not to redeem guilt ... We must recognize our faults and confess') echoed in the drug-dealer's sleep-talk. As the director, Kuperman, explains, 'the wandering priest preaches the ideas in the character's monologue'. *A Herança* also lends the confession scene embellishment. Taking off his hat in a demonstration of humility ('I don't know how to pray' is his inter-title admission), *A Herança*'s Claúdio/Claudius respectively addresses himself to a cross in a square, looks upwards to a smaller cross on a church and enters a separate church, these actions connoting a sustained inability to make a connection with the divine. Faced with multiple manifestations of orthodox Catholicism, Claúdio/Claudius cuts an alienated figure, a failed participant in the religious rituals that underpin *sertão* culture and belief.

More generally, *A Herança* and *O Jogo da Vida e da Morte* represent the established church as existing alongside other spiritual and superstition-based traditions. Exemplary are the directives of *A Herança*'s Ghost (Túlio de Lemos), a moustachioed cowboy in hat and long coat who appears and disappears during the day outside the farmhouse. In the Ghost's revelations, Omeleto/Hamlet is given free rein as to how he should proceed ('the choice is yours'), but is also told, 'Don't do anything against your mother ... Leave it to the skies and the spirits'. Arresting in this inter-title formulation is the idea of a quasi-pagan world made up of several inter-related powers, and this is reinforced when Claúdio/Claudius and Laerte/Laertes (Deoclides Gouveia) consult a 'sorcerer', or 'medicine man', as they prepare for the duel. In Claúdio/Claudius' inter-title justification – 'Usually, I don't believe in sorcerers, but it's better if we get support from everywhere' – evidences a typical co-existence of beliefs and faiths. Such *mestizaje* ('intermingling' or 'blending', as Peter Bakewell terms it) finds its expression in Brazil in the continuing alignment of Catholicism and *candomblé*, an African-Brazilian 'spirit possession' religion in which *orixás* or deities take over the bodies of believers, often during festive occasions.[28] Alexander Leggatt writes that the Ghost in *Hamlet* is characterized by its 'fissured ... dislocated identity' and, in *O Jogo da Vida e da Morte*, the idea is intimated in the *candomblé* ritual through which João/Hamlet communes with his 'father's spirit' (1.5.9).[29] Specifically, João/Hamlet visits the shack of Mãe Chiquinha/Mother Chiquinha, an old woman and local priestess whose body the Ghost has entered; as drums sound on the soundtrack, suggesting an ecstatic experience, the camera's focus falls upon the candles and dolls adorning a primitive shrine. Deeply shadowed close-ups on the priestess' wart-encrusted face, swinging head and grasping arms lend the occasion a nightmarish quality, one which is reinforced by the husky, laboured voice through which the Ghost's pronouncement is delivered: 'It is said a snake killed me; it was poison, João . . . take revenge!'. As in *Tardid/Doubt* (dir. Varuzh Karim-Masihi, 2009), the Iranian adaptation of *Hamlet* discussed elsewhere in this book, the ritualistic manifestation of the Ghost implies an entity divided between a number of forms and is of a piece with *O Jogo da Vida e da Morte*'s consistent interleaving of the communal and the spiritual.

Localizing methods are similarly in evidence in the ways in which both films translate the play-within-the-play musically rather than dialogically. Robert Stam notes that 'Brazilian music . . . a collective form of active creation, linked to polyphony and communitarian dance . . . is the dynamic expression of community'.[30] When, in *A Herança*, Omeleto/ Hamlet hires three *sertaneja* (country) musicians from a circus to sing the story of his father's death and his mother's remarriage, the assembled audience of family, farmworkers and cowboys is treated to refrains that reference familiar regional and spiritual motifs. The musicians' song indexes the land ('Our life on earth is full of greed') and the prospect of retribution ('It is God's wish that revenge takes place'), with the camera's close-ups on the main singer's mouth and lips suggesting that the lyrics are all-important. In the setting of the circus tent, the words emblazoned on the backdrop to the stage – '*Música Arte Luz Allegria*' ('Music Art Light Happiness') – become meaningful, for the truth of the murder is illuminated as the internal drama becomes less of an interlude and more of a climax. 'Give me some light, away' (3.2.261) may be Claudius' enigmatic response to the play-within-the-play in *Hamlet*, but, in *A Herança*, Cláudio/Claudius and Gertrudes/Gertrude exchange a series of reaction shots that definitively confirm their guilty involvement: Brazilian country music is proven to have revelatory effects.

Popular culture is again foregrounded in the equivalent set of scenes in *O Jogo da Vida e da Morte*, not least as this is manifested in the performance of the *samba* group that João/Hamlet enlists to 'Play something like the murder of [his] father' (2.2.530). The protagonist's first encounter with the group is at the television studio where they are to appear in a broadcast, their having positively embraced, it is implied, new media so as to preserve and extend older traditions.[31] It is the traditionalism of *samba* that provides the film with a vital interpretive conceit; as the director, Kuperman, explains, because 'stagings of scenes involving historical characters are frequent in the pageants of the samba schools, the play . . . could be turned into a "musical plot" without losing its authenticity'. Presenting their story

Figure 11: A circus setting for the travelling players in *A Herança/The Inheritance* (dir. Ozualdo Candeias, 1971). Courtesy of Acervo Heco Produções/Acervo Ozualdo Candeias.

in a semi-circular external space, the three *sambistas*, who wear glittering costumes, powdered perruques, crowns and tiaras, slip easily into the Shakespearean roles of King, Queen and lover; they are supported by an outer ring of musicians, the whole suggesting an elaborately theatrical undertaking. Historically, samba is a resistant mode of representation; its 'rhythms', states John Charles Chasteen, are 'transgressive', not least because of an association with slave rebellions, with carnival and with a general collapsing of 'categories, groups' and the 'hierarchical principle'.[32] Sub-textually, then, the *sambistas'* performance possesses a dangerous edge and raw energy; it is at several removes from the 'modesty' (3.2.19) and 'discretion' (3.2.17) as recommended by Hamlet in his reflections on the 'purpose of playing' (3.2.20). Certainly, when the *sambistas* approach the audience, uneasiness is in the air, as suggested in Gertrudes/Gertrude's look of recognition, Polônio/Polonius' innocent whistling and Claúdio/Claudius' frantic drinking. Crucially, the Lucianus figure oversteps the mark that keeps performer and spectator apart, coming close to Claúdio/Claudius to deliver with accusatory import his song's climactic line, 'Venom . . . With poison he had changed fate', at which the latter is violently sick. In the same way that the carnivalesque tendencies of samba iron out social distinctions, so is Cláudio/Claudius' criminality exposed in his own fraught physical responsiveness.

Vivian Schelling sees in samba 'a form of transculturation by Afro-Brazilians of the European culture imposed on them' and, in many respects, both *A Herança* and *O Jogo da Vida e da Morte* thematize the ways in which Brazil's racial histories are played out in action and event.[33] Hierarchies in the films are erected on the basis of property ownership and territorial influence, but these, in turn, are entangled in larger narratives of racial segregation and injustice. In this sense, *A Herança* and *O Jogo da Vida e da Morte* are highly attuned to the role of discourse in 'the subjugation of indigenous and African peoples'.[34] Or, to put the point in another way, as does Robert Stam, the 'paternalistic myth' of Brazil as a 'racial democracy' is a 'self-exculpatory' fiction obscuring 'racial oppression'.[35] *A Herança* responds to the contradiction in images of landless types who are not only downtrodden and weather-beaten but also racially differentiated, comprising black and indigenous groupings. In a film centred upon the uses of the land, and land ownership, such visual details are telling and bring to mind the extent to which, as Xavier Albó notes, Brazilian 'African … populations … do not have their own "territory"' and have historically existed as 'a transplanted people brought to the continent as a subordinated labour force'.[36] A revealing piece of casting is suggested in *O Jogo da Vida e da Morte* in the figure of Horácio/Horatio, the black *favelado* who, as João/Hamlet's friend, is, as the director, Kuperman, states, 'specifically identified with' him. Not yet a teenager, this orphan-like individual is discovered as a mostly silent witness, too young to effect a change in the adult world on which he spectates. The film's final montage, for example, shows him running from right to left across the dump and gesticulating wildly in a vain attempt to scare off the vultures that gather about João/Hamlet's corpse. A survivor, but a vitiated one, Horácio/Horatio is unsuccessful in his efforts to protect the body of his friend from the *favela*'s operations and, in this, he incarnates racial trajectories of disempowerment.

But it is in the films' representation of the Polonius/Laertes/Ophelia families that race is made most obviously visible as a barrier to self-expression and mobility. In the play, Laertes' warning to his sister that Hamlet's position of 'greatness' (1.3.17) militates against Ophelia entering a relationship with him is recast in *A Herança* as '[Omeleto] is the boss' son: people like that cannot like people like us'. Given that Laerte/Laertes is black, as are his father and sister, the statement privileges racial difference as the chief factor to be considered in the ill-fated love affair.

The equivalent set of scenes in *O Jogo da Vida e da Morte* – in which the Polonius/Laertes/Ophelia family is also black – takes further the equation between racial designation and lowly status. When, outside a rudimentary café, Ofélia/Ophelia (Yo Braga) reads aloud to Polônio/Polonius (Chocolate) the letter that Laerte/Laertes (Flávio São Thiago) has sent her, the fact of his illiteracy, and the subaltern educational status he occupies as a racial 'other', are highlighted. Polônio/Polonius struggles to keep up with Ofélia/Ophelia's verbal transcription, demanding clarifications in what is, for his daughter, a brief moment of authority. Generational as well as educational issues are held in play; while the youth of Brazil are embracing new opportunities, it is implied, an older demographic has been left behind. Commenting on the 'fishmonger' scene, P. K. Ayers suggests that 'Hamlet exploits the inherent slipperiness of ... written ... language', but, in the equivalent sequence, set on a dusty dirt track, in *O Jogo da Vida e da Morte*, it is Polônio/Polonius' inability to read that becomes the focus of attention.[37] The question, 'What are you reading?', and the reply, 'Words, words, words, yes, words and more words', expose a divide between Polônio/Polonius and João/Hamlet that, in this film, is premised on a history of inequality.[38]

For both films, narratives around race intersect in the figure of Ophelia. *A Herança*, for example, discovers Ofélia/Ophelia as serving coffee, grinding corn and drawing water from a well; rustic corollaries of her dramatic counterpart's 'sewing' in the 'chamber' (2.1.74), these activities confirm an imposed inferiority, one that evokes Brazil's own histories of slavery.[39] At the same time, they suggest the extent to which the continuation of the ruling order (in this case, farmers and landowners) is premised on the labour of underprivileged groups, particularly women. As if in sympathy with her situation, Omeleto/Hamlet is represented as wearing blackface to woo Ofélia/Ophelia; as they withdraw into the undergrowth, she smiles coyly, amused by the impersonation. The 'simulation of negritude', as Virginia Mason Vaughan points out, constitutes a 'mode of representation' which demonstrates intersections between 'racial discrimination' and perceptions of 'skin pigmentation', but this is not to argue that the politics of blackface are always consistent across region, time and space.[40] In Latin America, for instance, 'blacking up' has historically been associated with touring Portuguese and Spanish entertainments, with local adaptations of minstrel shows, with carnival-linked appropriations by elite white constituencies of African music and dance, and with rivalry between racially defined urban groupings, resulting in impersonations within impersonations: to don blackface was to mobilize a concept of *mestizaje* as an oppositional force.[41] Primarily in *A Herança*, the episode, as reinforced by the camera's intense concentration on lips, mouths, hands and caressing fingers, and by close-cropped images of ecstatic faces, suggests Omeleto/Hamlet and Ofélia/Ophelia's consummation; flickering natural light, and a use of deep shadow, make the bodies appear at one. Linda Williams notes that the practice of blackface conjures an attempt to occupy 'the place of the . . . black Other' and to assume 'the mantle of the Other's suffering', and something approximating to this effect is at work in *A Herança*, the blackface sequence pointing up the extent to which this rewriting of *Hamlet* is determined by, even as it counters, local traditions and values.[42]

If in *A Herança* Omeleto/Hamlet pretends to be black, Ofélia/Ophelia in *O Jogo da Vida e da Morte* impersonates being white. As the film reveals, Ofélia/Ophelia is constructed as styling herself on the white, *gamine* models of the 1960s; she has her straightened black hair in pigtails, wears beads and flat shoes, and dresses in a pale *croché* mini-skirt, a 'Twiggy' of the *favela*. 'The imaginary of whiteness' in Latin America, writes Santiago Castro-Gómez, 'was a sign of social status' and, certainly, in the film, Ofélia/Ophelia's looks suggest an aspirational initiative.[43] During a conversation with Ofélia/Ophelia on the rubbish dump, João/Hamlet pulls at her hair, only to find that it is a wig, a device to hide her own close-cropped ethnic appearance. To adopt an argument by Marvin Carlson, Ofélia/Ophelia has been engaged in the performance of 'an appropriate "front" (setting, costume, gestures, voice)' that, now exposed and unmasked, invalidates her 'social role'.[44] Accordingly, at the samba performance, a smaller and more remote Ofélia/Ophelia sits listlessly by, her simple Bahia headscarf declaring an abandonment of European pretensions. In fact, Ofélia/Ophelia as an emblem of humiliation has been prepared for from an early stage. In the play, Hamlet accosts Ophelia, 'Ungartered and down-gyved to his ankle' (2.1.77), in a scene of traumatic intrusion that, in *O Jogo da Vida e da Morte*, is reworked as a sexual tryst. At night, seizing João/Hamlet by the hand in a patch of weedy waste ground, Ofélia/Ophelia takes the erotic lead, encouraging him to make love to her. João/Hamlet, however, haunted by the image of a snake, breaks out of his troubled reverie to strike Ofélia/Ophelia and end the encounter. Stephanie Dennison observes that the '*mulata*' in Brazilian culture is 'traditionally considered to be the seductress, or sexual initiator, who is promiscuous . . . and enjoys sex', and, in *O Jogo da Vida e da Morte*, Ofélia/Ophelia is cast in a similar mould.[45] At the same time, however, the misogynist treatment meted out to her by João/Hamlet, in a sequence that uncomfortably alternates between aggression and passivity, shows up black women's subordinated condition and continuing expressions of stigmatization.

Inside this construction, Ophelia's madness scenes are accordingly nuanced and inflected. *A Herança* and *O Jogo da Vida e da Morte* envision madness as a concomitant part of the vulnerabilities of a black woman who is disenfranchised. From the start of *O Jogo da Vida e da Morte*, for instance, Ofélia/Ophelia is represented as at the mercy of the drug-dealing Claúdio/Claudius, and her increasing helplessness is highlighted when, after Polônio/Polonius' death, she injects herself with heroin, suggesting desperate efforts to anaesthetize herself from reality. The close-up on the vein of her arm, the sounds of pleasure and, crucially, the use of elongated shadows and *chiaroscuro* point up the extent to which Ofélia/Ophelia features less as a 'document in madness' (4.5.172) as a study in addiction. (Hazy point of view shots indicate an extended trip, while the rainstorm scene in which she plays at catching water in her hands prepares us for her drowning in the guise of self-induced distraction.) By contrast, the madness of Ofélia/Ophelia in *A Herança* manifests itself via a fantasy of delighted motherhood. Linking sexualized and reproductive bodies, the film discovers her proudly displaying a shawl-wrapped bundle: the child's cry that punctuates the soundtrack stresses the primacy of Ofélia/Ophelia's damaged perspective. Subsequent shots, shifting to Claúdio/Claudius and Gertrudes/Gertrude's point of view, reveal the baby to be nothing less than a pile of cacti, phallic-shaped excrescences that mock the earlier scene of consummation; the final moments of Ofélia/Ophelia in *A Herança* are read through the natural features of her unyielding rustic environs.

In *Hamlet*, the priest notes that, because '[Ophelia's] death was doubtful' (5.1.216), 'No more' can 'be done' (5.1.224). David Beauregard argues that the passages demonstrate the play's investment in 'a fully Catholic constellation of concerns about ... maimed funeral rites, deprivation of sacraments, and remembrances of the dead', and it is striking that, compared to theatrical productions that often cut the brief exchange, both *A Herança* and *O Jogo da Vida e da Morte* develop it, arguably because Catholic ritual possesses a particular pertinence in a Brazilian context.[46] Thus, in *A Herança*, Ofélia/Ophelia's body is brought to the graveside on a stretcher rather than in a cart. Set alongside the film's opening, and the procession, this is a mean and shrunken affair. Only a few crosses decorate the windswept hillside, suggesting that, on this improvised site, the ground is unconsecrated. A limited number of mourners are in attendance, and the smiling priest of the start is absent, his failure to attend confirming Ofélia/Ophelia's status as a 'lost soul' or *alma penada*.[47] Very different is the cemetery of *O Jogo da Vida e da Morte*, which boasts elongated statues of the Virgin and stark white graves, but the scene similarly underscores the notion of ecclesiastical disapproval in the physical blocking of the characters. Notably, the priest absolves himself from involvement twice – firstly via a dismissive reference to the grave ('It's over there') and secondly through a refusal to grant the funeral party's request ('I cannot sing any requiem to suicidal souls'). Most revealing, perhaps, is the camera's tracking of his withdrawal to the church; a telling *montage* stresses both the priest's closing of the gate and doors and the corresponding actions of an incensed Laerte/Laertes, who spits at his feet. In the imagery of institutional barriers which shut out the people, we see amplified other kinds of exclusion – of race or of class – that reflect back upon both films' portrayals of divided Brazilian societies.

Hamlet Figures, Figuring Change

United in their sensitivity to a segregated Brazil, *A Herança* and *O Jogo da Vida e da Morte* find in their Hamlet figures contrasting prospects for social change. In *A Herança*, Omeleto/Hamlet, as a student of law, is stamped with the potential for redress and reform; what is distinctive about him comes from his education and experience. At the opposite end of the spectrum is João/Hamlet in *O Jogo da Vida e da Morte*; possessed of the will, but lacking the know-how, he is unable to alter his environment. Nowhere is his incapacity more succinctly illustrated than in the scenes in the television studio; here, the criss-crossed pattern of the set and moveable walls invoke an archetypal prison, while the battery of cameras overhead suggests how far his actions are constricted once he moves beyond the *favela*. Here, the film anticipates Michael Almereyda's *Hamlet* (2000), which is similarly preoccupied with the powers of technology, but, in that film, Hamlet is the master of screen and camera, manipulating both for his own ends. In *O Jogo da Vida e da Morte*, João/Hamlet possesses no such expertise; rather, he is represented as cowed by the machinery in his midst (in comparison with the samba group who have embraced television as the medium in which they will thrive). Following a labyrinthine route through a series of studio corridors, he eventually finds himself at a bank of monitors on which there appears a despairing mother who cries '*Meu filho!*' ('My son!'). Less a ghostly Gertrude than a species of player, this soap opera figure prompts the following lament, 'How is it that an artist can control himself ... crying as if the feelings were real?', a version of the

'O, what a rogue and peasant slave am I' (2.2.485) soliloquy. Crucially, what is stressed is the protagonist's failure to act: 'I can't respond … All I can manage are words', he states. Again bringing Almereyda's film to mind, João/Hamlet sees himself reflected in the studio's glass surfaces, the idea being that this is a protagonist who is separated from himself, a schizoid type that, akin to the postmodern 'body' described by Fredric Jameson, is unable to 'map [a] position in a mappable external world'.[48] Thus, in subsequent shots, and in a departure from the film's realist mode, we see João/Hamlet adrift in a variety of spaces – in a surprised actress' dressing-room, on a rain-soaked street, in a darkened hallway, on a bridge – while the soliloquy runs on in voiceover, suggesting discontinuity, dislocation and paralysis. Significantly, in each of these environments, João/Hamlet is still and unmoving, a tortured soul that has lost its way. Having lost not only the 'name' but also the practice of 'action' (3.1.87), João/Hamlet incarnates a fundamental inability to make an intervention, to bring about a difference in the world.

A screen features again in the sequence in which João/Hamlet, having taken refuge in a cinema, watches news footage of the Vietnam war. In the words of Kuperman, the director, the sequence illustrates the workings of 'human ambition' and 'global aims … of … doubtful validity'. Shadowed in the commentary – 'operations are aimed at securing an area without any strategic or economic interest' – is the Captain's admission in *Hamlet* (Q2) that Fortinbras' forces 'go to gain a little patch of ground / That hath in it no profit but the name' (4.4.17–18). At one level, by showing João/Hamlet as absorbed by the newsreel, this interlude functions to imagine the protagonist as participating in the contemporary spirit of disenchantment through which the war was interpreted. So pacifically conceived, João/Hamlet could be said to express an oblique critique of the then military regime, which, as Francisco Vidal Luna and Herbert S. Klein argue, was sympathetic to US imperialism and a 'staunch … ally'.[49] At another level, the episode, as intimated in images of explosions, bodies and casualties, situates João/Hamlet as no less oppressed and powerless. The emphasis is again on his passivity, and, as the newsreel concludes, he is forcibly removed from the cinema by Rosa/Rosencrantz (Benê Silva) and Tostão/Guildenstern (Flávio Porto). While João/Hamlet here serves, in the director's words, as a point of connection between the 'inner' and the 'outer happenings' of the film's 'universe' (we see what is taking place on a global stage through his eyes), it is also the case that he is more observer than agent – the conflict unfolding elsewhere is echoed in the treatment to which he himself is exposed.

A more dynamically conceived Hamlet is offered in *A Herança* and revealed definitively in the *dénouement*. Cousin to Omeleto/Hamlet, Fortinbras (Agnaldo Rayol) arrives at the farm in the wake of the concluding shoot-out and finds on the body of the dying Omeleto/Hamlet a letter, which reads: 'As . . . my days are short . . . it is my wish that my lands be given to those who work on them, who were born on them . . . as they can profit more from the lands than my relatives'. At this moment, in the words of the director, Candeias, the film's major 'social issue: the land' becomes clearly visible.[50] Simultaneously, the meanings conjured by the film's title – translated into English as *The Inheritance* – become evident. Fortinbras, whose characteristic masculine force is registered in a lion's roar and leather attire, is suitably incandescent at being outmanoeuvred: '*Filho da puta*' ('Son of a bitch'), he mouths. As commentators note, Brazil 'never experienced . . . true agrarian land reform in the twentieth century'.[51] Land concentration was most pronounced in the *sertão* of the north-east where forms of 'Indian slavery' persisted and where large domains were enjoyed by a few *coronéis* or landowners.[52] It was a state of affairs that resulted in the emergence of peasant leagues in the 1960s and, over the course of the 1970s, the Movement of the Landless Workers of Brazil, a grass-roots initiative committed to land reclamation.[53] In *A Herança,* the moment of transfer – of inheritance – insists upon a more socially interventionist role for Shakespeare's play. While preserving the discourse of the inward-looking prince for the greater part of the film, *A Herança* finally discovers an Omeleto/Hamlet who all along has been concerned not so much with the self as what lies beyond.

The inheritance engineered by Omeleto/Hamlet is in contradistinction to the argument of a critic such as Linda Charnes that 'with neither offspring nor political structures to entail, Hamlet faces an erasure of existence in both the literal and symbolic realms'.[54] Instead, the overturning of traditional inheritance patterns grants to the film at least a brief utopian impulse.[55] In the last scene, peasants take the place of oxen and pull the cart bearing Omeleto/Hamlet's body in the opposite direction from the *cortège* of the start. The implication is that the protagonist is taken away from the familial graveyard and towards some communal resting-place. *A Herança* focuses finally on Omeleto/Hamlet's body as a requiem sounds in the background, the choral music suggesting both his symbolic significance as a type of sacrificial figure and the 'flights of angels that sing [him] to [his] rest' (5.2.344). Working in these capacities, the film demonstrates how Omeleto/Hamlet incarnates a socialist parable, for his actions mark an end not just to class privilege, as exemplified in

Fortinbras, but also to the ruling class *per se*. The *latifundium* (or large, privately owned estate) is rendered fundamentally altered by a form of common ownership, and an engaged, rather than alienated, protagonist is illuminated as a result: this is a Hamlet who in touch with the life of the indigene. Affirmative politics are reinforced in the final title-card, which reads: 'There are more things in heaven and earth than in our stupid philosophy'. Prioritizing this quotation (in its folio manifestation) above all others, and transporting it from the play's beginning to the film's end, *A Herança* adds to the inter-title an adjectival qualifier ('stupid') so as to suggest that action and materialism must take precedence over philosophy and speech. The 'our' here implies a common bond, its inclusion suggesting a gesture to the audience as a like-minded interpretive constituency, and thus scope for further applications of the adaptation's implications.

As in *A Herança*, the ending of *O Jogo da Vida e da Morte* also points up, via the Hamlet figure, the meanings embodied in its title. Over the course of the film, reference is made, echoing the title (*A Game of Life and Death* in the English translation), to ludic activity, whether this manifests itself in João/Hamlet's playing with a revolver or in his conducting a game of noughts and crosses on the rubbish dump. Rooted in the play's own imagery (such as 'to play at loggets' [5.1.87]), these episodes discover the protagonist as displaying child-like symptoms characteristic of disengagement. A more unsettling iteration of the conceit is reserved for the duel which, taking place on a patch of waste ground, is described by the double-dealing Cláudio/Claudius as 'a friendly fight, a game'. To the musical accompaniment of a *berimbau*, João/Hamlet and Laerte/Laertes engage in *capoeira* combat, a Brazilian martial art characterized by cartwheels and kicks.[56] As Peter Fryer argues, *capoeira* was deployed by African slaves 'in preparation for insurrection ... against their oppressors'; however, more recently, the sport is practised as a type of 'performance' in which dance is privileged.[57] Yet, once Cláudio/Claudius' accomplice slips a knife to the fighting pair (João/Hamlet picks up the knife intended for Laerte/Laertes; Laerte/Laertes draws his own blade), the game assumes its fatal cast. Michael Neill observes how the 'Prince's body' is 'granted the formal dignity of funeral orations', and congruent with this treatment is Horatio's command that the protagonist's corpse 'High on a stage be placed to the view' (5.2.362).[58] But *O Jogo da Vida e da Morte* ironizes the insistence on elevation voiced in the precursor text by discovering the dying João/Hamlet climbing a mountain of cans on the rubbish dump, only to collapse and tumble down its slope, his demise signalled by the vultures that gather overhead, their screams resembling callous laughter.

The final image dissolves to a widescreen shot of the skyscrapers of downtown São Paulo, implying an equation between the birds of prey and the urban scene: the city is dependent on the *favela*, while the *favela*, in turn, is subjected to the city's pitiless gaze. Bringing to mind an earlier image of a dead cat being eaten by rats, the *mise-en-scène* highlights the body of João/Hamlet as just another item of rubbish, to be cast out once its use is expended. Invoking the play's metaphors of rottenness and dissolution, the film elects for its closing montage to realize its protagonist as at one with his landscape in a manner that is as brutal and exploitative as it is visceral and irredeemable.

Conclusions

These are films that centre upon frontier-like spaces and places, and the people inhabiting them, as a means of confronting the paradoxical nature of Brazil's own self-image. As Michael Hanchard comments, 'society' in Brazil is 'in theory committed to liberal-democratic principles, but in practice still struggles with the legacies of patron-clientelism, racial slavery and oppression'.[59] It is here that the films are particularly absorbing – they reimagine *Hamlet* so as to showcase fissures in Brazilian national identity. Illuminating impoverishment as the common denominator linking regions and periods, *A Herança* and *O Jogo da Vida e da Morte* also question the so-called 'economic miracle', which transformed the fortunes of Brazil in the late 1960s and early 1970s, but only for select and privileged groupings.[60] Discussing the place of, and attitudes towards, Shakespeare in the Latin America of modernity, Alfredo Michel Modenessi notes a 'move away from reverence towards a more interesting form of conversation with . . . "Shakespeare"'.[61] He gestures to the ways in which, as a film such as *O Jogo da Vida e da Morte* visualizes, theatre has gradually ceded place to other forms of media representation, such as cinema, although the end-point of the process probably does not, as Modenessi implies, reside with dialogue alone. As a whole, the films demythologize *Hamlet*, stripping it of its accretions of inaccessibility and removing Shakespeare from his pedestal, either by revisions to language and text or via an understanding that sees the play from 'below', from demotic and/or vernacular perspectives. *A Herança* and *O Jogo da Vida e da Morte* are alive to the possibilities of Shakespeare being made to matter in cinema, but they are equally interested in exploring how cinema might be vitalized and continued though Shakespeare, and they join forces in this way as part of a dissatisfaction with a censorious military government at a pivotal moment in the development of the Brazilian film industry. 'All of the art in which we were involved at the time was designed to comment on the political situation', states Mário Prata, who shares a co-credit for the dialogue of *O Jogo da Vida e da Morte*, 'but', he continues, 'there was so little we could actually do because Brazilian censorship assumed such violent forms'. *A Herança* and *O Jogo da Vida e da Morte* are perhaps at their most revealing in illustrating how far *Hamlet* may be reshaped to facilitate its political intervention in a specific time and place. I have discussed reworked endings, fresh beginnings, interpolated scenes, extensions to existing scenes, newly minted characters, omissions, modifications and excisions: in all of these, we see adumbrated a will to point up the interrogative dimension of *Hamlet*'s Brazilian relevancies.

Engaged in such an initiative, *O Jogo da Vida e da Morte* and *A Herança* are ingeniously creative in translating *Hamlet* into local idioms and conventions. Alternating between 'landscapes' and 'deathscapes', the films illuminate their respective environments variously as places of criminality and self-interest, religion and tradition.[62] Many of these transpositions embed critique; for instance, in highlighting the potent cultural force of Afro-Brazilian religions, both films could be said to be working against the then military regime which attempted to criminalize the so-called 'slave-era cults'.[63] Elsewhere in the films, Shakespearean motifs are interwoven with Brazilian cinematic and literary genres, and concerns about land and location, and reflections on the state of the twentieth-century metropolis, are expressed through the adaptive process. *A Herança* and *O Jogo da Vida e da Morte* are born out of the same sets of circumstances, but diverge from each other in the nature of their responses. If Candeias' marginal cinema anticipates possibilities for kinds of land reform, Kuperman's documentary-style realism only intermittently embraces another dispensation (such as in João/Hamlet's passing association with anti-war protest). *A Herança* is able to contemplate a mode of egalitarianism which reverses the fictive nature of discourses of race; by contrast, when *O Jogo da Vida e da Morte* countenances the prospect of social and cultural change, as this is manifested in the scenes in the television studio, the protagonist is represented as at odds with, if not divorced from, the currents that mark new manifestations of popular consciousness. Thus, while *A Herança* and *O Jogo da Vida e da Morte* constitute Shakespearean adaptations deeply invested in the politics of place, and attend to the implications of communities evolving into fresh forms, they move away from each other in the capacity for conceiving of alternatives. With the *favela* remaining locked within an exploitative dynamic, only the *sertão* is imagined as capable of throwing off the yoke of the past, and such a development, it is suggested, is determined by a fusion of city experience and rural practice. *A Herança* and *O Jogo da Vida e da Morte* offer contrasting analyses of the issues they identify, highlighting in the process the cultural-political praxes of their own conditions of production, even as they also distinguish themselves by using *Hamlet* to gesture to very different – utopian and dystopian – futures.

Notes

1. On *Cinema Novo*, see Michael Chanan, 'Latin American Cinema: From Underdevelopment to Postmodernism', in Stephanie Dennison and Song Hwee Lim, eds, *Remapping World Cinema: Identity, Culture and Politics in Film* (London: Wallflower, 2006), pp. 38–43; Randal Johnson and Robert Stam, eds, *Brazilian Cinema*, 2nd ed. (New York: Columbia University Press, 1995); Ismail Xavier, *Allegories of Underdevelopment: Aesthetics and Politics in Modern Brazilian Cinema* (Minneapolis: University of Minnesota Press, 1997).

2. Alfredo Michel Modenessi, 'Meaning by Shakespeare South of the Border', in Sonia Massai, ed., *World-Wide Shakespeares: Local Appropriations in Film and Performance* (London and New York: Routledge, 2005), pp. 104–11; Alfredo Michel Modenessi and Margarida Gandara Rauen, 'Latin America', in Peter W. Marx, ed., *Hamlet-Handbuch: Stoffe, Aneignungen, Deutungen* (Stuttgart and Weimar: Verlag J. B. Meltzler, 2014), pp. 366–73; Margarida Gandara Rauen, 'Brazil', in Michael Dobson and Stanley Wells, eds, *The Oxford Companion to Shakespeare* (Oxford: Oxford University Press, 2001), p. 54; Aimara da Cunha Resende, 'Introduction: Brazilian Appropriations of Shakespeare', in Aimara da Cunha Resende, ed., *Foreign Accents: Brazilian Readings of Shakespeare* (Newark: University of Delaware Press, 2002), pp. 11–41.

3. See Ray Armes, *Third World Filmmaking and the West* (Berkeley, Los Angeles and London: University of California Press, 1987), p. 177; James Chapman, *Cinemas of the World* (London: Reaktion, 2003), pp. 310–11; Talitha Espiritu, 'Multiculturalism, Dictatorship, and Cinema Vanguards: Philippine and Brazilian Analogies', in Ella Shohat and Robert Stam, eds, *Multiculturalism, Postcoloniality, and Transnational Media* (New Brunswick: Rutgers University Press, 2003), p. 290.

4. Darlene J. Sadlier, *Brazil Imagined: 1500 to the Present* (Austin: University of Texas Press, 2008), p. 247.

5. Interview between Mark Thornton Burnett and Mário Kuperman (20 November 2012). Unless otherwise stated, all Kuperman quotations are from this interview and appear in the text.

6. For discussion of these films in the wider contexts of Brazilian cinema and television, see Aimara da Cunha Resende, 'Shakespeare on the Screen: Brazilian

Cinema and TV', *Actes des Congrès de la Société Française Shakespeare*, 33 (2015), pp. 2–13.

7. Daniel Serravalle de Sá, 'Cinema Marginal', in Nátalia Pinazza and Louis Bayman, eds, *World Film Locations: São Paulo* (Bristol: Intellect, 2013), p. 47.

8. See Inácio Araújo, Gabriel Carneiro, Gabe Klinger, Felipe Furtado, Alfredo Sternheim and Matheus Trunk, 'An Abecedarium of the Boca do Lixo', in Gerwin Tamsma, ed., *The Mouth of Garbage/Boca do Lixo: Subculture and Sex in São Paulo, 1967–1987* (Rotterdam: International Film Festival, 2012), p. 12. The beginnings of a rehabilitation for Candeias outside Latin America are hinted at in Aaron Cutler, 'Marginal Revolutionary', *Sight & Sound*, 24.10, October (2014), pp. 50–51.

9. Julianne Burton, 'Toward a History of Social Documentary in Latin America', in Julianne Burton, ed., *The Social Documentary in Latin America* (Pittsburgh: University of Pittsburgh Press, 1990), p. 6.

10. The film's self-identification as a *Hamlet* adaptation is also attested to in the invitation to the premiere, which namechecks the play in a bracket after the title. See Accesso D996 (Miscellaneous), Cinemateca Brasileira, São Paulo.

11. Interview between Mário Prata and Mark Thornton Burnett (16 June 2014). Unless otherwise stated, all Prata quotations are taken from this interview and appear in the text. An interesting linguistic approach to the film is Marcel Álvaro de Amorim, 'Shakespeare no Subúrbio: Uma Leitura Brasileira de *Hamlet*, por Mário Kuperman', *Scripta Uniandrade*, 14.2 (2016), pp. 86–122.

12. Marcel Vieira Barreto Silva, *Adaptação Intercultural: O Caso de Shakespeare no Cinema Brasileiro* (Salvador: Edufba Compós, 2013), p. 311.

13. Examples include *Rio 40°/Rio, 40 Degrees* (dir. Nelson Pereira dos Santos, 1955), *Orfeu do Carnaval/Black Orpheus* (dir. Marcel Camus, 1959) and *Viramundo* (dir. Geraldo Sarno, 1965).

14. In the absence of language, Marcel Álvaro de Amorim fascinatingly discusses the film in terms of intertextual anthropology. See his 'Shakespeare no Sertão: Uma Leitura Brasileira de *Hamlet*, por Ozualdo Candeias', *Cadernos do IL*, 53, January (2017), pp. 10–29.

15. Vítor Angelo, '*A Herança*', in Eugênio Puppo, ed., *Cinema Marginal Brasileiro e Suas Fronteiras: Filmes Produzidos Nos Anos 60 e 70* (São Paulo: Heco Produções, Ltda., 2004), pp. 88–89; Moura Reis, *Ozualdo Candeias: Pedrase Sonhos no Cineboca* (São Paulo: Coleção Aplauso, 2010), p. 96.

16. Judith Buchanan, *Shakespeare on Silent Film: An Excellent Dumb Discourse* (Cambridge: Cambridge University Press, 2009), p. 199.

17. See, for example, *O Cangaceiro/The Bandit* (dir. Lima Barreto, 1953), *Vidas Secas/Barren Lives* (dir. Nelson Pereira dos Santos, 1963) and *Deus e o Diabo na Terra do Sol/Black God, White Devil* (dir. Glauber Rocha, 1964). *A Herança* was actually made in Itapecerica da Serra, a municipality to the south-west of São Paulo, whose parched conditions substituted effectively for the north-eastern *sertão*.

18. See, for example, the Westerns *Broken Lance* (dir. Edward Dmytryk, 1954), an adaptation of *King Lear, Jubal* (dir. Delmer Daves, 1956), an adaptation of *Othello*, and *Johnny Hamlet* (dir. Enzo G. Castellari, 1968), an adaptation of *Hamlet* discussed in Chapter One of this book.

19. Ivana Bentes, 'The *Sertão* and the *Favela* in Contemporary Brazilian Film', in João Luiz Viera, ed., *Cinema Novo and Beyond* (West Haven, Connecticut: Herlin Press, 1998), p. 113.

20. During General Emílio Garrastazu Médici's Presidency from 1969 to 1974, Congress was closed, human rights were violated and military justice played a repressive role. See Francisco Vidal Luna and Herbert S. Klein, *Brazil Since 1980* (Cambridge: Cambridge University Press, 2006), pp. 17–20, 42; Thomas E. Skidmore, *Brazil: Five Centuries of Change* (New York and Oxford: Oxford University Press, 1999), p. 164.

21. Chanan, 'Latin American Cinema', p. 50.

22. Margreta de Grazia, *'Hamlet' Without Hamlet* (Cambridge: Cambridge University Press, 2007), pp. 2, 4.

23. Vivian Schelling, 'Popular Culture in Latin America', in John King, ed., *The Cambridge Companion to Modern Latin American Culture* (Cambridge: Cambridge University Press, 2004), p. 186.

24. *Cangaço* or social banditry was at its height in the north-eastern regions at the end of the nineteenth and the beginning of the twentieth centuries and was romanticized in the so-called 'northern literature' and a number of films. See Sadlier, *Brazil*, p. 151; Breixo Viejo, 'O Cangaceiro', in Alberto Elena and Marina Díaz López, eds, *The Cinema of Latin America* (London and New York: Wallflower, 2003), p. 64.

25. The soundtrack features an extract from Chico Buarque de Hollanda's musical realization of the poem written for a theatrical production staged by Roberto Freire in 1965.

26. John Milton, 'Severino in English', *Cadernos de Literatura em Tradução*, 2 (1998), p. 107; João Cabral de Melo Neto, *Selected Poetry, 1937–1990*, ed. Djelal Kadir (Hanover and London: Wesleyan University Press, 1994), p. 87.

27. See Larry Rohter, *Brazil on the Rise: The Story of a Country Transformed* (New York: Palgrave Macmillan, 2010), p. 45.

28. Peter Bakewell, *A History of Latin America*, 2nd ed. (Oxford: Blackwell, 2004), p. 548; John Charles Chasteen, *National Rhythms, African Roots: The Deep History of Latin American Popular Dance* (Albuquerque: University of New Mexico Press, 2004), p. 34; Robert Stam, *Tropical Multiculturalism: A Comparative History of Race in Brazilian Cinema and Culture* (Durham and London: Duke University Press, 1997), pp. 209, 211.

29. Alexander Leggatt, *Shakespeare's Tragedies: Violation and Identity* (Cambridge: Cambridge University Press, 2005), pp. 55, 81.

30. Stam, *Tropical*, p. 38.

31. The situation of the players in *Hamlet*, forced to 'travel' (2.2.293) because of the popularity of the city children's companies, is echoed in *O Jogo da Vida e da Morte* in the observation that the samba group 'travel' because 'out of the loop', ousted from their usual performance haunts by rival '*música cabeluda*' organizations.

32. Chasteen, *National Rhythms*, p. 5; Roberto DaMatta, *Carnivals, Rogues, and Heroes: An Interpretation of the Brazilian Dilemma*, tr. John Drury (Notre Dame and London: University of Notre Dame Press, 1991), p. 42.

33. Schelling, 'Popular Culture', p. 193.

34. Paul Allatson, *Key Terms in Latino/a Cultural and Literary Studies* (Oxford: Blackwell, 2007), p. 158.

35. Espiritu, 'Multiculturalism', p. 284; Stam, *Tropical*, p. 32.

36. Xavier Albó, 'Our Identity Starting from Pluralism is the Base', in John Beverley, Michael Aronna and José Oviedo, eds, *The Postmodern Debate in Latin America* (Durham and London: Duke University Press, 1995), p. 26.

37. P. K. Ayers, 'Reading, Writing, and *Hamlet*', *Shakespeare Quarterly*, 44.4 (1993), p. 424.

38. As Francisco Vidal Luna and Herbert S. Klein argue, the conjunction of 'race and illiteracy' in contemporary Brazil in part explains why, 'even as late as 1950', over 'half the population' was unable to read and write (*Brazil*, p. 189).

39. Only in 1888, with the introduction of the so-called 'Golden Law', was the institution abolished. See Thomas E. Skidmore and Peter H. Smith, *Modern Latin America*, 6th ed. (New York and Oxford: Oxford University Press, 2005), p. 146.

40. Virginia Mason Vaughan, *Performing Blackness on English Stages, 1500–1800* (Cambridge: Cambridge University Press, 2005), pp. xi, 10.

41. See John Charles Chasteen, 'Black Kings, Blackface Carnival, and Nineteenth-Century Origins of the Tango', in William H. Beezley and Linda A. Curcio-Nagy, eds, *Latin American Popular Culture: An Introduction* (Lanham: Scholarly Resources, 2004), p. 50; Jill Lane, *Blackface Cuba, 1840–1895* (Philadelphia: University of Pennsylvania Press, 2005), pp. 2, 3.

42. Linda Williams, *Playing the Race Card: Melodramas of Black and White from Uncle Tom to O. J. Simpson* (Princeton and Oxford: Princeton University Press, 2001), p. 154.

43. Santiago Castro-Gómez, '(Post)Coloniality for Dummies: Latin American Perspectives on Modernity, Coloniality, and the Geopolitics of Knowledge', in Mabel Moraña, Enrique Dussel and Carlos A. Jáuregui, eds, *Coloniality at Large: Latin America and the Postcolonial Debate* (Durham and London: Duke University Press, 2008), p. 282.

44. Marvin Carlson, *Performance: A Critical Introduction* (London and New York: Routledge, 1996), p. 41.

45. Stephanie Dennison, 'The New Brazilian Bombshell: Sônia Braga, Race and Cinema in the 1970s', in Dennison and Lim, eds, *Remapping*, p. 139.

46. David Beauregard, '"Great command o'ersways the order": Purgatory, Revenge, and Maimed Rites in *Hamlet*', *Religion and the Arts*, 11 (2007), p. 50.

47. See João José Reis, *Death Is a Festival: Funeral Rites and Rebellion in Nineteenth-Century Brazil*, tr. H. Sabrina Gledhill (Chapel Hill and London: University of North Carolina Press, 2003), p. 122.

48. Fredric Jameson, *Postmodernism, or, The Cultural Logic of Late Capitalism* (London: Verso, 1991), p. 44.

49. Luna and Klein, *Brazil*, p. 17.

50. Reis, *Candeias*, p. 93.

51. Luna and Klein, *Brazil*, pp. 102, 103.

52. Ivana Bentes, '*Deus E O Diablo Na Terra Do Sol/Black God, White Devil*', in Elena and López, eds, *Cinema*, p. 90; Nathan W. Warren, *Racial Revolutions: Antiracism and Indian Resurgence in Brazil* (Durham and London: Duke University Press, 2001), p. 11.

53. John Charles Chasteen, *Born in Blood and Fire: A Concise History of Latin America*, 2nd ed. (New York: W. W. Norton, 2006), p. 285; Luna and Klein, *Brazil*, p. 17; Teresa E. Meade, *A Modern History of Latin America* (Oxford: Blackwell, 2010), p. 318; Alfred P. Montero, *Brazilian Politics: Reframing a Democratic State in a Changing World* (Cambridge: Polity, 2005), p. 102.

54. Linda Charnes, *Hamlet's Heirs: Shakespeare and the Politics of a New Millennium* (New York and London: Routledge, 2006), p. 9.

55. In *Brazil on Screen: Cinema Novo, New Cinema, Utopia* (London and New York: I. B. Taurus, 2007), Lúcia Nagib argues for the importance of Brazilian films that pursue 'the utopian myth's trajectory' (p. 20).

56. A *berimbau* is a single-stringed bow attached to a gourd.

57. Peter Fryer, *Rhythms of Resistance: African Musical Heritage in Brazil* (London: Pluto Press, 2000), p. 27.

58. Michael Neill, *Issues of Death: Mortality and Identity in English Renaissance Tragedy* (Oxford: Clarendon, 1997), p. 303.

59. Michael Hanchard, 'Black Cinderella? Race and the Public Sphere in Brazil', in Michael Hanchard, ed., *Racial Politics in Contemporary Brazil* (Durham and London: Duke University Press, 1999), p. 60.

60. See Luna and Klein, *Brazil*, pp. 42, 46, 210.

61. Alfredo Michel Modenessi, 'Of Shadows and Stones: Revering and Translating "The Word" Shakespeare in Mexico', *Shakespeare Survey*, 54 (2001), p. 160.

62. See the discussion of Sharon Emmerichs, 'Shakespeare and the Landscape of Death: Crossing the Boundaries of Life and the Afterlife', *Shakespeare*, 8.2 (2012), pp. 172–73.

63. Miriam Wells, 'Brazil Persecutes Slave-era Cults', *The Sunday Times*, 7 September (2014), p. 28.

CHAPTER FOUR

Pairing the Cinematic Prince: Hamlet, *China and Japan*

This chapter pairs cinematic adaptations of *Hamlet* released in the same year, self-consciously putting into dialogue films with contrasting creative agendas, levels of investment and circumstances of production. In the first section, it examines two Japanese films, *The Bad Sleep Well* (dir. Akira Kurosawa, 1960) and *Castle of Flames* (dir. Katô Tai, 1960), and, in the second, two Chinese films, *The Banquet* (dir. Xiaogang Feng, 2006) and *Prince of the Himalayas* (dir. Sherwood Hu, 2006). In so doing, the chapter extends work already initiated on *The Bad Sleep Well* and *The Banquet* by investigating the films' application of localized modalities of representation and reworking of the Shakespearean source.

The chapter undertakes this discussion by situating *The Bad Sleep Well* and *The Banquet* in relation to the equally ambitious but lesser-known film adaptations, *Castle of Flames* and *Prince of the Himalayas* respectively. Commercially successful, *The Banquet* enjoyed global release, online distribution and awards, all reflective of the film's 'big-budget' credentials.[1] In contradistinction, originally conceived by US-trained Chinese director and screenwriter, Sherwood Hu, with the collaboration of Tibetan screenwriters Trashidawa and Chenaktshang Dorje Tsering (Jangbu), *Prince of the Himalayas* is crafted as an 'art' or niche product; indeed, the director is at pains in interview to identify *The Banquet* as 'too commercial' and his own film as 'more meaningful'.[2] Along a similar axis, *The Bad Sleep Well* enjoyed an international purchase indicative of the ways in which, by the early 1960s, Kurosawa was a firmly established director and general darling of the western film circuit. *The Bad Sleep Well* was co-produced by Toho Studios and the newly established 'Kurosawa Production Company', a sign of the director's increasing influence and independence, and quickly became a core component of the Kurosawa *oeuvre* through sub-titled distribution in English-speaking territories and elsewhere. *Castle of Flames*, however, was only ever distributed in Japan, a result of which is the less elevated place it shares with *Prince of the Himalayas* in Shakespeare on film studies.[3] By reading each film against its dominant twin, this chapter posits the critical worth of juxtaposing familiar Shakespeare works with their less valued siblings – adaptations of the same text, produced within the same timeframe, but to considerably less acclaim. Provoking a conversation between *The Bad Sleep Well* and *Castle of Flames*, and between *The Banquet* and *Prince of the Himalayas*, this chapter uncovers unexpected points of contact and communion while also revealing the unique ways in which each film adapts Shakespeare from the same geographical and cultural space.

Strikingly, in Japan, both Kurosawa and Tai turn to the genre film as a way of reimagining *Hamlet*. *Castle of Flames* (*Hono no Shiro*) is a *jidai-geki* (period genre) adaptation whose title exploits the ambiguities inherent in the Japanese term, *hono*, signifying fire, a destructive element, *and* flame, connoting passion and energy. Both spheres of meaning are at work in the representation of the Hamlet character, Masato, a youthful samurai who joins with the peasantry on an assault on the Omi castle stronghold. Boasting a screenplay by established screenwriter, Toshio Yasumi, *Castle of Flames* has arguably been overlooked because of the occluded status of the director, Katô Tai, briefly an assistant director at Toho and Daiei, but, for the greater part of his career, a director for Toei Studios, working to tight schedules and budgetary constraints.[4] Despite a 1998 retrospective, his work remains under-appreciated in the west, although recent discussion suggests a re-appraisal in the offing (film critic Patrick Galloway describes Tai as a 'bona fide auteur with a vigorous, visceral style all his own').[5] It is possible to see Tai's stylistic uniqueness as part of his rivalry with Akira Kurosawa, and, when he worked as an assistant director on Kurosawa's *Rashomon* (1950), there were frequent clashes.[6] Yet rivalry is more likely embedded in a history of studio competition: Toei Studios, who employed Tai, were the commercially oriented but less successful counterpart to Toho Studios, who employed Kurosawa and were linked to 'prestige' and 'art' filmic products.[7] As a *Hamlet* adaptation, *Castle of Flames*, this chapter argues, is the Toei Studios reply to *Throne of Blood* (dir. Akira Kurosawa, 1957), the *Macbeth* adaptation produced by Toho Studios; even in its title, the former references the latter. In generic contrast, *The Bad Sleep Well* is a *gendai-mono* (or 'present-day') genre film in which contemporaneous references are underpinned by borrowings from *film noir*, the result being an experimental work that references American 'hard-boiled' thriller forms. The action centres on the attempts of Nishi/Hamlet, a company executive, to expose corporate corruption, and the film's Japanese title – *Warui Yatsu Hodo Yoku Nemuru* – plays with the aphorism that it is the just, rather than the unjust, who sleep best. As this chapter argues, Tai responds to *Hamlet* more reverently than does Kurosawa, working closely with the play's form and language. While *The Bad Sleep Well* significantly incorporates *Hamlet*, it does so with greater licence, mobilizing the play in fragments, echoes, reversals and allusions. Both films align themselves with anti-governmental agitations of the late 1950s and the early 1960s and thereby look forward to a wave of Japanese films marked by a politically rebarbative stance. In this endeavour, they are facilitated by, in Tai's case, a relaxation in legislation designed to suppress the *jidai-geki* samurai film (the genre was outlawed during the Occupation as promoting feudal values) and, in Kurosawa's, the opportunities available to a director beginning to operate outside the conventional studio system. Working inside the framework of *Hamlet*, each film differentiates itself, one showing ameliorative impulses and the other highlighting a despairing construction of a repressive and unchanging order.

Situating itself during the bloody period of the 'Five Dynasties and Ten Kingdoms', *The Banquet* deploys extravagant cinematography and epic aesthetics, thereby associating itself with the latest blockbuster *wuxia* (swordplay) and *kung fu* (fist-fighting) movies.[8] Like *The Banquet, Prince of the Himalayas* is set during an ancient time period (the Tang Dynasty); however, it finds its aesthetic impact, and correlatives for Shakespeare's text, in stirring realizations of a snowy and mountainous Tibetan environment. With a closer attention to original dialogue, *Prince of the Himalayas* approximates in Tibetan language many of the familiar soliloquies, exchanges and jokes, overlaying these with references to 'traditional' Tibetan culture.[9] *The Banquet* expresses its Shakespearean indebtedness in parallels, revisions to character types and extensions to key episodes. But both films look to the dysfunctional family as an underlying premise. In *The Banquet*, in spite of her power-affirming marriage to Emperor Li/ Claudius (Ge You), Empress Wan/Gertrude (Zhang Ziyi) pines for the past love affair with her stepson, Wu Luan/Hamlet (Daniel Wu), and gains authority from acting as ruler and stepmother simultaneously. Here, the film inverts and develops Shakespeare's Gertrude (Empress Wan was formerly married to the Old Emperor/Ghost) even as it draws upon various histories of Empress Wu Zetian, the first female Chinese sovereign. A bridge to *Prince of the Himalayas* is afforded in the similarly imagined Queen Nanm/Gertrude (Zomskyid): trapped in a loveless union with the despotic Old King Tsanpo/the Ghost (Lobzangchopel), she pursues an extra-marital relationship with her brother-in-law, King Kulo-ngam/ Claudius (Dobrgyal), marrying him after her first husband's death.

Understanding complex family dynamics as a unifying thematic, *The Banquet* and *Prince of the Himalayas* reify women's roles via a narrative emphasis on female agency, sexuality and space. In this way, they demonstrate how the profiling of China's global visibility and the recasting of *Hamlet* are inter-related – a changing nation-state is shadowed in a new-found confidence in the adaptive process. Across both sets of paired films, different practitioners are inspired to Shakespearean adaptation in context-specific ways. In the case of *Castle of Flames* and *The Bad Sleep Well*, Japan reflects on the implications of its recovery; in the case of *The Banquet* and *Prince of the Himalayas*, China reflects on its global rise, on, to adopt the phrase of Frank N. Pieke, the 'nation' as 'work in progress'.[10] China comes into its own through *The Banquet* and *Prince of the Himalayas*; Japan contemplates what it has become in *Castle of Flames* and *The Bad Sleep Well*. All four films make visible the sometimes continuous, sometimes contradictory, means whereby Shakespeare's franchise assists in the confrontation with emerging Japanese and Chinese realities.

Protesting Japan

Adaptations (translations and performances) of Shakespeare have been a vital part of Japanese culture since the middle of the nineteenth century onwards.[11] At least until the first decade of the twentieth century, Shakespeare was domesticated to suit the *mores* and motifs of the Meiji period, as suggested in a *Hamlet* adaptation of 1886 performed according to the codes of the samurai.[12] Subsequently, in what has been identified as the next phase of Japanese Shakespeare, which lasted from the second decade of the twentieth century to the 1950s, the dramatist 'became the object of academic reading and scholarly translation and annotations'.[13] Inside this *shingeki* or 'new drama' period, 'modern European realism' was 'transplanted to Japan', a process that necessitated theatrical approximations of supposed Renaissance authenticity – the use of padded costumes, props, extravagant sets and orotund delivery.[14] Tai and Kurosawa respond to these traditions but in complementary ways, the former taking his cue from earlier performance conventions and the latter breaking with the imitative trend in contemporary Japanese theatre. For both, a priority was to present Shakespeare *à la Japonaise*, either through vernacularization/modernization or through recognizable constructions of medievalism.

The Bad Sleep Well and *Castle of Flames* both mediate the widespread discontent of the early 1960s in specific generic choices. In *Castle of Flames*, an on-screen announcement states that action unfolds 'some four hundred years ago, on the coast of the inland sea', roughly capturing the period of Shakespeare's drama and establishing the film as belonging to the popular *jidai-geki* genre (characterized by period costuming, 'look' and dialogue).[15] Typically, the *sengoku-jidai* or 'warring states' period (1467–1603) is conjured in the narrative of samurai armies fighting civil wars and *daimyos* or warlords competing for power. More specifically, the film brings home a genre familiar to Japanese audiences in choreographed shots of massing retainers, bearing the *mon* or crest of their clan, and in busy scenes of martial preparations (these also evoking the 'daily cost of brazen cannon / And . . . implements of war' [1.1.72–3]). According to convention, the *jidai-geki* film pivots on a desire to avenge a familial loss. Hence, in terms of motive, Masato/Hamlet is conventionally bent upon exposing the suspected villainy of his uncle, Morokage/Claudius ('Get to the truth, prove that my father died not of illness but by another cause'), played by Denjirô Ôkôchi, despite a brief interlude when he worries that Tokiko/Gertrude (Mieko Takamine) may also be implicated. Similarly, *The Bad Sleep Well* makes its generic debts clear in relying on such *film noir* markers as the doomed love affair, the storage box with unexpected contents and 'the promise of money easily and ill-gotten'.[16] The representational procedure is generically conformist: point-of-view is purposefully muddied, suspense is kept to the forefront, and a slow-drip method of discovery keeps an audience in a state of heightened anticipation. Suiting *noir, The Bad Sleep Well* also prioritizes the revenge motif – Nishi/Hamlet, a solitary vigilante figure cast in the mould of his Shakespearean forbear, is determined to 'get revenge for my father'. Central to his situation are the circumstances surrounding his loss – Furuya/Old Hamlet, an official at the Public Corporation for Land Development, allegedly takes his own life by jumping to his death from a seventh-floor window. Subsequently, Nishi/Hamlet becomes a secretary in the Public Corporation and marries Yoshiko/Ophelia (Kyôko Kagawa), daughter to the company's boss, Iwabuchi/Claudius (Masayuki Mori), as part of a plan to expose the latter's involvement in his father's demise. Linda Charnes writes that the 'detective' figure is always already inscribed as a type of 'revenger'.[17] The identification is underlined in *The Bad Sleep Well* in which Nishi/Hamlet gradually swaps his 'inky . . . suits' (1.2.77–8) for the accoutrements of the fully fledged *noir* detective or investigator (the trench coat and cigarette), emerging from the shadows of his cinematographic representation and suggesting that this is the role to which the tragic protagonist must inevitably gravitate.

Film noir is essentially an urban genre: corruption and the city are seen as synonymous. Appropriately, then, *The Bad Sleep Well* situates its brand of criminality in Tokyo, as instanced in the listing of wards and districts (*Kamimachi, Nishiogikubo, Shibuya* and *Zoshigaya*) and in a resonant establishing shot of the Tokyo Detention Centre. As nocturnal camera sweeps over ill-lit neighbourhoods and fenced-in alleyways indicate, this is, to cite Foster Hirsch, a *noir* city realized in a 'subtly stylized way'; it is a 'symbolic terrain', with no 'sense of a world going on outside the frame'.[18] At an aesthetic level, too, *film noir* elements show themselves in the *chiaroscuro* methods used to represent smoky rooms, tenebrous offices and gloomy bank-vaults, with Kurosawa's compositions typifying a *mise-en-scène* made up of 'encroaching darkness and visual distortions'.[19] By contrast, but equally generically indebted, locations in *Castle of Flames* evoke the opening reference to the Seto Sea – in Donald Richie's words, 'a landlocked, lake-like body of water . . .. entered through four narrow straits'.[20] Exterior work for the film took place in and around the coasts near Kyoto, and glimpses of craggy promontories, a horizon of cobalt blue, horsemen galloping across a swathe of beach, a junk bobbing in the shimmering calm of a harbour and low-lying islands sprouting a profusion of greenery, all caught in blistering light, convey a maritime flavour while privileging natural, non-urban settings in keeping with a historical genre. Such settings make sense of the film's amplification of the role of the pirates (fleshing out the report of the play, *Castle of Flames* installs them as active players), its representation of typhoons that drive Masato/Hamlet away from and back to Omi and the idea of a 'sea-gown scarfed' (5.2.13) protagonist. Imbricating a sense of location still further, and summoning the film's title, the *mise-en-scène* foregrounds images of the seemingly impregnable castle stronghold (Elsinore is succinctly suggested), a gargantuan mass of weighty masonry spiralling upwards to unseen heights. Its presence, as well as reinforcing a period ethos, dwarfs its human actors – even the black-and-white pagodas of the village and interiors with sliding screens looking onto gardens of contemplation appear overshadowed by its bulk.

As *The Bad Sleep Well* and *Castle of Flames* demonstrate, the Hamlet character's relation to location operates as an index of his condition. In *Castle of Flames*, Masato/Hamlet's samurai status is immediately reflected in his formal red (offset by white and gold) *hitatare* costuming: luxuriantly accoutred, the distinctively top-knotted protagonist additionally sports two formidable swords. A samurai designation is just as firmly established in accompanying publicity (the poster for *Castle of Flames* extols in one of two taglines the virtues of the 'beautiful swordsman, Hashizo, who demonstrates the fascination of sorrow and sadness').

Figure 12: Poster for *Castle of Flames* (dir. Katô Tai, 1960).
Courtesy of Toei Company Ltd.

Played by Hashizo Okawa, a *kabuki*-trained performer and former *onna-gata*, Masato/Hamlet appears almost throughout (the film's version of 4.6 and 4.7, when Hamlet has left the stage, places Masato at the centre of the action), thereby affording ample opportunity for expressions of unease.[21]

Illustrative is the scene in which Masato/Hamlet blunders into the castle's formal meeting area to attend the play-within-the-play: his *hatarare* gapes indecently, and he is filmed elongated on the floor, a picture of distraction. Such moments require as accompaniments interpolations ('Forgive me!', Masato/Hamlet whispers to himself, after haranguing Yukino/Ophelia [Keiko Mita]) that explain his madness as pretence. More generally, Masato/Hamlet's regret at his treatment of Yukino/Ophelia frequently combines with his anguish as a bereaved son to construct him as an acutely suffering warrior lord, a type dictated to, and colliding with, his castle environs. In a departure from his previous roles, Toshirô Mifune as Nishi/Hamlet communicates a comparable sense of suffering thanks to a studied performance that stresses psychic repression: contorted lips and strained features bespeak the tension of pent-up emotions, confirming the seemingly imperturbable exterior as a sham. Positioned either against the harsh horizontals of window blinds or the heavy wooden doors of the Public Corporation offices, Nishi/Hamlet only occasionally ruptures the façade of conformity, as when a trembling body and embittered scowl signal an eruption of angry frustration. In fact, the archetypal 'madness' of the play is most often shifted elsewhere – in Yoshiko/Ophelia, psychologically incapacitated once the villainy of her father is revealed, in the 'nervous breakdown' of Shirai (Kô Nishimura), a senior company executive, and in the sweaty anxiety of any number of other officials, suggesting a refracting of central *Hamlet* preoccupations.

A demoralized samurai returning to a world changed beyond recognition in his absence, or a secretary in a corporate machine thwarted in his attempts to articulate his loss, Masato/Hamlet and Nishi/Hamlet would, as the 1960s commenced, have registered as all too familiar personalities. In the wake of World War II, Japan was overtaken by a widespread disillusionment: nationalism had been problematized as ideology, and cities were swamped by troubled soldiers coming back to initially bleak employment prospects. But because figured as at variance with different locales, Nishi/Hamlet and Masato/Hamlet incarnate deeper seams of discontent. A top-down programme of industrial recovery was one cause of dissatisfaction, and the cronyism of corporate organizations another, but the most strident criticisms were reserved for the alliance shared between US and Japanese governments. In the late 1950s and early 1960s, protests opposing the ratification of the US-Japan Security Treaty shook the country. Popular opinion supported Japanese neutrality, the fear being that the Treaty, if renewed, would oblige Japan to support the USA in the event of war. Following a series of general strikes, protesters (students, intellectuals, civil servants and members of labour unions) attacked the Diet on 15 June 1960, breaking through the gates, although on 18 June the Treaty was forced through, still with rioting unfolding in and around government buildings. As an effect of these protests, on 23 June, the Prime Minister, Nobusuke Kishi, popularly seen as the practitioner of grotesquely 'autocratic methods', resigned, leading one historian to dub the unrest 'a turning-point in Japan's post-war political history'.[22] Released on 19 September and 30 October 1960 respectively, *The Bad Sleep Well* and *Castle of Flames* look to the riots for their dissident spirit. In this sense, they form part of a larger critically cinematic whole. Certainly, the impact of the protests was not lost on popular culture representation. In terms of the *jidai-geki* genre, films such as Katô Tai's own *Brave Records of the Sanada Clan* (1963), based on the seventeenth-century siege of Osaka Castle, referenced the disturbances indirectly, while, more openly, Eiichi Kudo's *The Great Mêlée* (1964), set in the *Edo* period (1603–1868), featured recordings of the upheaval on the soundtrack as part of an allegory about the workings of tyranny.[23]

The Bad Sleep Well and *Castle of Flames* anticipate these films in their interrogative energy, but what sharpens their edge is the way in which the death of the father/Old Hamlet is seen to symbolize the operations of corporate interests and militarism. Throughout *The Bad Sleep Well*, we are confronted with the seamy, underlying realities of mutually profitable alliances between business and government: 'Something' is indeed 'rotten' in the 'state' (1.4.90) of modern Japan. In view of the fact that the Public Corporation is a government department, Kurosawa's critique of insider-dealing assumes the illicit diversion of tax-payers' money. The film offers a graphic instance of the culture of what it terms 'bribes', 'graft' and 'kick-backs', not least in the sequence in which Nishi/Hamlet, having raided the company deposit box, plants money on Shirai, lodging it in the latter's briefcase. As with Hamlet's use of the play-within-the-play, Nishi acts here behind the scenes to dupe the unwitting executive into a confession of guilt (itself a Shakespearean plotline). Elsewhere, full-screen montages of news-paper headlines such as 'Building Costs Under Fire' and 'Evidence of "Hospitality"' point up more deeply rooted forms of corruption that Nishi/Hamlet hopes to 'set' to 'right' (1.5.187). In *Castle of Flames*, what is 'rotten' assumes violent appearances. Typical is the way in which Morokage/Claudius is cast in military mould. Rotund, shaven headed and generously bearded, he pursues a policy of aggressive expansionism ('My ambition is to take this castle, then another, then another') which is replicated at a gendered level in his (reported) rape of Tokiko/Gertrude. Expanding upon the sub-texts of *Hamlet,* and elaborating Morokage/Claudius in terms of the 'emulate pride' (1.1.82) of Old Fortinbras and the 'hot ... mettle' (1.1.95) of Young Fortinbras, *Castle of Flames* consistently underscores militarism as motif. Hence, the simmering Norway-Denmark conflict of *Hamlet* is pushed to the fore in the wars waged between Morokage/Claudius (Omi Castle) and Masakiyo/Old Fortinbras (Komano Castle), 'rivals for this domain'. Wars in *Castle of Flames* generate human casualties, and the film equally invests in dramatizing the plight of the oppressed citizenry who, fleeing from Komano, find themselves in Omi tortured as supposed spies. In this way, Masato/Hamlet's suffering is viewed in a wider context, his condition being paralleled in scenes of public humiliation and the persecution of minorities, signs of a feudal society grotesquely overreaching itself.

The Bad Sleep Well and *Castle of Flames* invite particular comparison in the extent to which the Hamletian protagonist embodies a larger representative power. He is discovered as attempting to combat not simply the individual but the order that afflicts a country in crisis. Perhaps echoing Ophelia's idealized realization of Hamlet as 'Th'expectation and rose of the fair state' (3.1.151), the 'Young Lord Masato', returned from China with a wealth of new experiences, is regarded as bringing a 'ray of light' to Omi, over which a 'dark cloud' has been lowering; the implication is that he is a force of revelation and enlightenment. With a name that connotes unimpeachability, Masato/Hamlet is envisaged as capable of remedying the historical isolationism of Omi and progressing his feudal universe into the present. As he states, 'I went in search of knowledge that could help make this a land of peace for all people', a formulation that both conjures his importance as an agent of change and resonates with a move in contemporary Japanese politics towards new democratic processes. Paradoxically, it is to bring about a different dispensation that Masato/Hamlet pledges allegiance to the Omi peasantry rebelling against the taxation laws brought in by Morokage/Claudius to fund his war plans. To Tokei (Bando Kichiya), a rebel peasant leader (the film personalizes a grouping that in the play is largely invisible), he promises to 'do what [he] can' to aid the cause, and, in this, *Castle of Flames* makes central the representation of a Hamlet 'loved of the distracted multitude' (4.3.4), the recipient of 'great love' from 'the general gender' (4.7.19). To adopt Michael Douglas' discussion of the *jidai-geki* genre, Masato/Hamlet acknowledges how he is 'bound to ... the requirement to serve the community'.[24] For example, at the point where the peasants, on a precipitous outcrop jutting into the ocean, are about to be shot for insurrection, Masato/Hamlet rides into the fray on a rescue mission, pointing up how the film conceives of him as 'a reformer prince who saves the people'.[25] Similarly, reflecting in his cell on the pirates' island hideout, Masato/Hamlet berates himself, saying, 'The people are all looking for relief, I can't just sit here'; as Douglas M. Lanier notes, he here recognizes that 'His revenge plot can also serve their revenge'.[26] As elsewhere, the inspiration is Shakespearean, the 'How all occasions do inform against me' (4.4.31) soliloquy being reworked to bring two plotlines into alignment. And, at those points where the film mediates several Shakespearean moments (Masato/Hamlet's 'Something is wrong' aside melds 'I doubt some foul play' [1.2.254] and 'The time is out of joint' [1.5.186]), the samurai lord is filmed from a low angle as if arriving at an awareness of where his social mission resides. His personal tragedy, Masato/Hamlet comes to recognize, is inseparable from a larger cause.

A series of *gendai-mono* ('modern-day') genre films took up the theme of the righter of wrongs who finds his or her personal predicament mirrored in a wider movement. Thus, in *Youth in Fury* (dir. Shinoda Masahiro, 1960), a young woman joins the student insurgency to make reparations for her father's death, while, in *A Full Life* (dir. Hani Susumu, 1962), a dissatisfied actress in a radical theatre group finds that the protests transform her life for the better.[27] Both films, in their agitation for meaningful change, would have struck a chord with Tai, a director active in film unions, frequently at odds with studio bosses and, in his own words, a 'rebel against ... conformity'.[28] They also serve to situate *Castle of Flames* in which the peasants are discovered as a powerful constituency impelled to direct their energies against an autocratic government (the film's climax, when the castle is set alight, would surely have recalled fears, just months previously, that the Diet would suffer a similar fate). In addition, *Castle of Flames* is distinctive, perhaps recalling the mixed composition of contemporary protesters, for highlighting a range of forces affected by, and opposed to, Morokage/Claudius – peasantry, pirates, the Komano citizenry and Masato/Hamlet himself. *The Bad Sleep Well* similarly imagines Nishi/Hamlet in relation to the bigger picture, but within a broader historical timeframe. At once, Nishi/Hamlet finds himself compelled, like Masato/Hamlet, to defend others' interests; as he states, the close-up on his grimace refracting his angst, 'I want those villains brought to justice for the sake of all the helpless people who don't even know they've been had'. His status in this capacity is lent a filmic backstory. At the bombed-out munitions factory that is their hideout, Nishi/Hamlet

Figure 13: Nishi/Hamlet (Toshirô Mifune) negotiates a war-ravaged Tokyo in
The Bad Sleep Well (dir. Akira Kurosawa, 1960). Courtesy of Photofest.

and Itakura/Horatio (Takeshi Katô), his friend, reflect on what their lives
were like in the war's immediate aftermath. Widescreen shots of twisted
metal, amputated structures and piles of debris, about which swirl wind
and dust, recall the firestorms of 1944 and 1945 that laid waste to Tokyo,
leaving 75,000 to 200,000 dead and destroying up to 50 per cent of the
metropolis.[29] More generally, the empty spaces and horizon without end
iterate a lack of reconstruction policy: this is the price the citizenry pays, it
is implied, for the country not being able properly to recover itself. Here,
then, in these *yake-nohara* or 'scorched fields' – a version of the graveyard
from *Hamlet* – is the obverse of the smart-suited, business world Nishi/
Hamlet customarily inhabits. Recalling that they, too, were involved in
racketeering, Nishi/Hamlet and Itakura/Horatio are discovered as the
damaged survivors of an earlier era. Their contest with institutionalism is
in part born out of deprivation and defeat; Japan's contemporary instabil-
ity, it is suggested, finds an echo in the blight of Tokyo's urban scene.

  In the light of the disturbances it refracts, the climax of *Castle of Flames*
carries a powerful charge. The rebellious peasants separate into two pha-
lanxes to set the castle alight, their primitive torches proving more effective

than the *arquebus* weaponry of the samurai. Cross-cut with the general confusion is the duel which, playing up the dexterous swordsmanship of Masato/Hamlet and denying Yugo/Laertes (Izawa Ichiro) even a whiff of repentance, is quickly overtaken by events. At the point where the wounded Masato/Hamlet dispatches Morokage/Claudius in the watchtower, severing his forehead with a fatal blow, the castle's gates are forced apart by the peasants: in these mirrored acts of opening, therefore, the protagonist lives up to the earlier aspiration that he will effect a change in the dominant order.[30] By the same token, bringing very different opening and concluding images into proximity, the film's ending shows the blackened ruin of the castle stronghold.[31] Shot again from below, Masato/Hamlet is now firmly ensconced within the perspective of the victorious populace, while the widescreen format suggests that the screen space around the protagonist is as important as the protagonist himself. Via the alliance with the people, it is implied, the country, phoenix-like, may be reborn from the ashes. Yet any sense of triumph is undercut by the procession of village women bearing the body of Yukino/Ophelia on a bier: peasants kneel and swords are sheathed in a shared response to her death. Displacing Ophelia's funeral (5.1) onto the film's final composition allows for Masato/Hamlet to take centre stage not as swordsman but mourner. As he states, cradling Yukino/Ophelia, 'I wanted to spare you all this . . . I had no other recourse. Cherishing your pure and innocent love, I dedicated my life to the good of the people'. To cite the second tagline of the film's poster, 'Cutting off the evil fire, a pathetic love disappears!', the emphasis is on the costs to the individual of the pursuit of justice. Masato/Hamlet's reflections, in fact, perfectly encapsulate *mono no aware*, the Japanese philosophy which, recognizing love, sadness and loss, simultaneously appreciates the beauty and impermanence of all things.

If *Castle of Flames* brings the Ophelia figure into the final frame, *The Bad Sleep Well* plays in its ending with varieties of ghost. Kurosawa's corporate nightmare is populated not by one ghost but several. One of Nishi/Hamlet's most effective actions against the Public Corporation, for instance, involves his incarceration of Wada (Kamatari Fujiwara), an accountant, and use of him as a ghost to shock other company members into confessing their offences. Pertinent are the two scenes in which Shirai is tricked into thinking that he sees Wada as a ghost, but there are also ghost-like existences, as when the desperately impassioned Wada states, 'Sometimes I don't know who I am, whether I'm alive or dead'. A typical official, Wada emblematizes and incarnates the limbo-like condition generated from the asymmetries of his environment. Something similar might be said of Nishi/Hamlet; as the film reveals in its latter stages, he has, in fact, exchanged identities with Itakura/Horatio so as the more efficiently to execute revenge. (In contradistinction, the Ghost [Akashi Ushio] in *Castle of Flames*, only ever seen by Masato/Hamlet, dressed in white and with a sword protruding from a wound in the side, is an understated and briefly apprehended supernatural presence moving in and out of the shadows).

The insecure foundations of Nishi/Hamlet's identity are spotlighted in the moment of his death. Departing from *Hamlet*, Nishi/Hamlet's actual death occurs off-stage: we are told he was injected with alcohol (the reference is to the poison plot of the duel scene), made unconscious and placed in a car with which a train collided. Unlike *Castle of Flames*, which guardedly looks to a better future, *The Bad Sleep Well* stages a sombre *dénouement* to an even more sombre parable: as Stephen Prince states, 'The intensity of Nishi's protest has not even bruised the institutions of power'.[32] The point is also made aurally in a score in which Nishi/Hamlet's distinctive whistle is drowned out by a cacophonous jazz refrain. The general hopelessness is summed up by Itakura/Horatio when he notes, picking up an earlier sentiment uttered by Tatsuo/Laertes (Tatsuya Mihashi), that Nishi/Hamlet's 'sense of justice' has come to naught.

Part of the final effect of *Castle of Flames* inheres in the fact that Masato/Hamlet lives on to begin the reparative process of making sense of his experience. Occupying a very different interpretive space is *The Bad Sleep Well* in which every teller of the tale is compromised. Attempting, like Horatio, to report his friend's 'cause aright' (5.2.323), Itakura/Horatio aspires to a truthful relation of 'carnal, bloody and unnatural acts, / Of accidental judgements, casual slaughters, / Of deaths put on by cunning, and for no cause' (5.2.365–67). However, he swiftly realizes that this is a resistant narrative. 'I'm Itakura . . . no . . . Nishi . . . now I can never become Nishi again . . . I . . . can say nothing', he states. His accompanying prediction that 'Now all of Japan can be tricked the same way' prepares the way for the subsequent scene in which the previously cynical reporters are represented as accepting at face value Iwabuchi/Claudius' seeming grief. The 'system', it seems, resists attempts from within or without to bring about its reformation while retaining the capacity to shape public opinion. Crucially, as Mitsuhiro Yoshimoto notes, Itakura/Horatio's prediction (current English subtitles do the film a disservice) should more accurately translate as 'All Japan will be fooled again', the detail of 'again' recalling broader national contexts and the 'deception' involved in the 'joint effort by the American and Japanese governments to renew the mutual security treaty in spite of a massive protest'.[33] Nishi/Hamlet's death, in fact, points up the invulnerability of the corporate sphere, reinforcing an ultimately dystopian vision: 'badness', to cite the film's title, is inevitable. In keeping with a *film noir* aesthetic, Nishi/Hamlet fails in his mission; his is imagined as a courageous but ultimately doomed endeavour that illuminates the tensions and the challenges, the ambitions and the contradictions, of Japan's relation to modernity. The film's ending, in fact, appears more despairing in the light of the muted expectancy characterizing the closing stages of *Castle of Flames*, pointing up the mutually illuminating ways in which these two films interact and cross-converse.

China Rising

Variously invoked to 'support or suppress . . . modernity and cultural renewal', Shakespeare's texts were first introduced to China in 1856 via the Lambs' *Tales*, although the first translation of a Shakespeare play did not appear until 1922; thereafter, during the 1930s and 1940s, translations appeared apace.[34] Under communism, Shakespeare's plays were interpreted according to Marxist perspectives to 'stir patriotic spirit in Confucian, moral terms' (and, in the case of *Hamlet*, to draw attention to the ideological unacceptability of a procrastinating type), but, during the Cultural Revolution (1966–76), the works, judged toxic, were banned, meaning that, according to Ruru Li, 'ninety per cent of Chinese Shakespeare productions have appeared since' the Revolution's end.[35] Post-Revolution, China has witnessed an explosion of productions, many centred on notions of 'fidelity' and a recreation of 'authentic' Shakespearean playing styles. Indicating Shakespeare's now mainstream position, a recent counter-movement, which often takes the form of festivals and operatic adaptations, plays up, according to Lingui Yang, Shakespeare's easy recognizability and association with 'cool culture', part of an embrace of 'postmodern sentiment'.[36]

The embrace of Shakespeare, of course, has gone hand-in-hand with the rise of China as a global economic actor, as reflected in its joining the World Trade Organization in 2001, the Beijing Olympics of 2008 and the Shanghai World Expo of 2010. These developments, in turn, are part and parcel of increasing investment in the private sector, the encouragement of the state sector and the production of goods for the world market, all of which have resulted in accelerated economic growth under the banner of socialist governance.[37] Cinema brings these transformations into focus. As Michael Berry notes, 'The rise and ongoing evolution of the Chinese blockbuster runs parallel with and is intricately connected to China's own emergence as an economic superpower', adding, 'cinema [is] an increasingly important component of Chinese "soft" power'.[38] In short, the new Chinese economy has been the precondition for a revitalized film industry, with a combination of domestic consumption and foreign distribution leading to augmented commercial gains and the exploitation of diasporic audiences.[39] And cinema has proved particularly enabling to the business of Shakespearean adaptation. By 2006, when *The Banquet* and *Prince of the Himalayas* were released, it was abundantly evident that Chinese cinemas were able take on Shakespeare with impunity.

Enabled by China's economic rise, and implicitly reflecting on that phenomenon, *The Banquet* and *Prince of the Himalayas* demonstrate complementary strategies of adaptation by choosing, like the *Hamlet* films of Laurence Olivier and Franco Zeffirelli before them, to focus on familial-domestic relations, affect and emotionally laden environs. Both films break with interpretive tradition in furnishing interpolated pre-stories, domestic twists which shift each *Hamlet* adaptation into a fresh interpretive context. Lending unprecedented weight to the ways in which these pre-stories rupture into the present, *The Banquet* and *Prince of the Himalayas* find in volatile familial arrangements an index of a changing China, and nowhere is this more obvious than in the Oedipally fraught relations that obtain between *The Banquet*'s central players – Wu Luan/Hamlet, the Old Emperor/the Ghost, Empress Wan/Gertrude and Emperor Li/Claudius. Where the *Hamlet* adaptations of Olivier and Zeffirelli express a classic Oedipal narrative based on triangulated desire, *The Banquet* pushes at the dynamic, extending the Freudian familial matrix. Wu Luan/Hamlet has lost both his father (he is initially dressed in white to signify mourning) and his former lover (Empress Wan/Gertrude abandons Wu Luan/Hamlet to marry firstly his father, the Old Emperor/the Ghost, and subsequently his uncle, Emperor Li/Claudius). As such, he is figured as afflicted on multiple fronts – torn between a stepmother, a step-father, the spirit of his biological father and the pull of an old love affair. Unsurprisingly, then, Wu Luan/Hamlet appears less as a philosophical prince than an abandoned romantic hero, at one and the same time aesthetically appealing and grieving. As Anne Ciecko notes in a discussion of Daniel Wu (Wu Luan/Hamlet), the 'globalized', 'westernized', 'cosmopolitanized' and 'metrosexual pin-up' image of this American-born Hong Kong star has been traded upon in 'numerous advertising campaigns, fashion spreads and … a fashion design collection'.[40] The notion of a Hamlet to be looked at extends to the film's construction of Wu Luan's skills in calligraphy and martial arts. Critic Sheng-Mei Ma states that 'the calligraphic brush and the sword have long defined masculine strength in Asian culture … and films', and, certainly, in *The Banquet*'s making visible of Ophelia's eulogy to Hamlet as 'soldier' and 'scholar' (3.1.150), Wu Luan is briefly privileged in an action-heavy *mise-en-scène*.[41] With acrobatic aplomb, he outwits armoured opponents, and, in scenes with Empress Wan/Gertrude, shows off his artistic accomplishments in the form of exquisitely cut paperwork. Yet suggestions of Wu Luan/Hamlet's empowerment are quickly dispelled by scenes in which he is represented as sublimating a compromised masculinity in coded behaviours. At the start, for example, having sought sanctuary in an outdoor theatre in the 'southern heartlands', a masked Wu Luan/Hamlet mimes impressions of sufferings and disappointments, suggesting acting as potentially recuperative and physicality as a way of coming to terms with rejection. His love of theatre (the film features not one but three versions of the play-within-the-play) effectively robs Wu Luan of speech, his understated verbal role being mirrored in the dun greys of his costuming. At the film's release, many audiences found Wu Luan/Hamlet too 'passive' and 'lacklustre' convincingly to play a Shakespearean role.[42] However, this is to miss the point that *The Banquet* adapts Wu Luan/Hamlet as a sometime lover, and his more powerful stepmother is the figure that the film consistently prioritizes.

At once, Wu Luan/Hamlet and Empress Wan/Gertrude are closely tied. For example, Empress Wan/Gertrude's reflections on her training with the 'sword of the Yüe maiden' connect her to Wu Luan/Hamlet and his educational absorption in traditional Chinese arts. Casting assists the alliance. Both Daniel Wu (Wu Luan) and Zhang Ziyi (Empress Wan/Gertrude) are close in age, the latter also having established herself as an international Chinese export in big-budget *wuxia* films. But, consistently elevated via blocking, Empress Wan/Gertrude is to Wu Luan/Hamlet an infinitely superior adversary, outmanoeuvring him in swordplay and dominating the frame. Early on, we see her ascending a dais to view her late husband's armour (she acts to claim a stage as her own) and taking a bath in a circular enclosure (its Globe-like associations are intimated in surrounding curtains and arches). At these moments, as elsewhere, Empress Wan/Gertrude is put on display, and, whether it is acts of disrobing or dressing up in finery, an equivalent emphasis on her body is made manifest. Given the four-way relation between the film's characters, *The Banquet* is obliged to double the play's 'closet' scene so as to give optimum opportunity for expressions of Oedipal attraction. In each, the camera focuses on heightened detailing, not least because Empress Wan/Gertrude's 'closet' appears as a large-scale, candelabra-lit and lavishly appointed interior. With the generously sized bed at the centre, surrounded by criss-crossed red voiles and equally elaborate filigree, this female-stamped space is imagined as a court in miniature.

Consistently returned to, the domestic *boudoir* serves to establish both the extent to which the action pivots around Empress Wan/Gertrude and a tangled web of need, will and desire. Again departing from *Hamlet*, Empress Wan/Gertrude is discovered as a proactive and scheming aspirant in an adaptation that places her, and not her male counterparts, in *medias res*. The recalibration of the character is suggested not only in movement (Empress Wan/Gertrude's key position is implied in the scene in which she traverses the full length of the state hall, guards parting before her and the train of her pale yellow dress trailing sinuously and magnificently behind) but also in allusion. To a large extent, Empress Wan/Gertrude is envisioned as Empress Wu Zetian, the seventh-century Tang Dynasty concubine to both Li Shimin (Emperor Taizong) and his son, Li Zhi (Emperor Gaozong), who rose, not without controversy, to become China's first female ruler. The quasi-incestuous parallel with Empress Wan/Gertrude, divided between past and present lovers, finds an echo in *The Banquet*'s absorption in the machinations of women pursuing power.[43] Clarifying the link is the term, *mei*, meaning beautiful. Empress Wu Zetian was termed *mei niang* in recognition of her entrancing eyebrows, while Empress Wan/ Gertrude is described as possessing *wu mei* or soft, charming and attractive eyes, and in both instances an equation is implied between a woman's appearance and political intrigue.[44] As these and linked parallels mount, Wu Lan/Gertrude takes on the characteristics of her royal predecessor even as the film legitimates its period setting via a self-conscious invocation of a turbulent history. Shakespeare, it is implied, is compatible with the struggles and triumphs of China's imperial past.

How women are identified accrues in importance as *The Banquet* develops. Struggles for privilege are at work in the scene where Empress Wan/ Gertrude and Emperor Li/Claudius play, half-threateningly, half-erotically, with nomenclature, while the mutual insistence on the 'correct' forms of 'address' being employed suggests a jockeying for advantage. Gesturing to *Hamlet* and the moment when Gertrude playfully banters with Rosencrantz and Guildenstern (2.2.34), Empress Wan is represented as trafficking in titles to secure political ends. 'Will brother-in-law let the prince go free?', she asks, her question highlighting not only Wu Luan/ Hamlet's imprisonment but also her own. Whether as sexual object or

Figure 14: Empress Wan/Gertrude (Zhang Ziyi) plots her rise to power in
The Banquet (dir. Xiaogang Feng, 2006). Courtesy of Photofest.

sexual agent, Empress Wan/Gertrude is erotically freighted, reflecting the
ways in which, as Mayfair Mei-hui Yang writes, 'the figure of the sexualized
woman has returned in mass-media representation' as a signifier of China's
'current economic reforms and market economy'.[45] In keeping with this
emphasis, and referencing the eventual divide between Claudius and
Gertrude in *Hamlet, The Banquet* envisions Empress Wan in terms of singleness and privileges her decision to be lover-free. Empress Wu Zetian reputedly
entitled herself, *Zhen*, or 'I, the one Man'; with a similar logic, Empress Wan
identifies herself as the Chinese phoenix or *fenghuang*, a mythical creature
embodying an empress' powers and abilities.[46] 'I shall rise', exclaims Empress
Wan/Gertrude in a promise that is as arresting for its glorification of the
individual subject as it is for its exclusion of the male Chinese dragon with
which the female phoenix was conventionally allied. On a later occasion,
Empress Wan/Gertrude reflects on the attainment of power and her titular
trajectory: 'Little Wan ... Empress ... Her Majesty, the Emperor', she
murmurs, rehearsing a biographical journey from child to adult, from dependent to independent, from female to male. Strikingly, this is the one occasion
in the film where a character speaks without others present, the itinerary of
Empress Wan/Gertrude's triumphs here functioning as a filmic soliloquy.[47]

Such a radical modification to Gertrude has a corollary in the ways in
which the father-son dynamic (often a cornerstone of interpretation) is

downplayed. Unlike *Prince of the Himalayas*, the Old Emperor/the Ghost in *The Banquet* is glimpsed only once, its single appearance highlighting its imbrication in the familial-sexual contests at the film's heart. Specifically, the Old Emperor/the Ghost is represented as an emotionally occupied chain-mailed carapace, and, in the scene where Wu Luan/Hamlet explores his father's armour, a POV shot from inside the casing's eyeholes betokens a responsive presence. An accompanying glimpse of blood trickling from the sockets suggests harm or injury, forming a filial bridge between the Old Emperor/Ghost and Wu Luan/Hamlet (whose eyes are seen in close-up behind his mask). Instead of a sustained connection between father and son, however, *The Banquet* points up Wu Luan/Hamlet's ambiguous relation to the Old Emperor/the Ghost who has taken the protagonist's lover for himself. Offering one context for Wu Luan/Hamlet's delay, and to some extent sanitizing the Oedipal dynamic, the film removes the familiar filmic narrative of the son lusting after the mother, replacing it with a stepson and the drama of a Gertrude who moves between three lovers/husbands; Wu Luan/Hamlet gains in innocence, and Empress Wan/Gertrude is marked with opportunism, as a result. Writing on *The Banquet*, Alexa Alice Joubin notes that Qing Nü/Ophelia (Zhou Xun), a figure of 'naïveté and purity', functions as an 'ideal contrast to China's postsocialist society . . . that turns everything, including romance and love, into a commodity'.[48] Crucially, in a film that foregrounds the relationship between Wu Luan/Hamlet and Empress Wan/Gertrude, Qing Nü/Ophelia's guileless protestations of love go unreciprocated. After Wu Luan/Hamlet has assaulted her, Qing Nü/Ophelia cradles him in her arms in a platonic gesture that betokens her chastity. In fact, in that she explains to Wu Luan/Hamlet the circumstances behind his father's death, Qing Nü/Ophelia also operates as a type of Horatio, and here the film recasts the boat girl song associated with her, the sixth-century 'Song from Yüe', which centres on a boatman's longing for his male royal occupant, the ruler of Ngo (the switch in gender is purposeful).[49] Hence, although traces of Ophelia persist in the signature diegetic sound of water heard in the background of her appearances, Qing Nü works as a counterweight to *The Banquet*'s emotional core, a reminder of an alternative scenario which is never realized. The possibilities held in play via Qing Nü/Ophelia are dashed by the stepmother/son bond: it is the pre-story of a thwarted romance that gives the film its energy and impetus.

Romances prevented or unconsummated have become a staple of Asian Shakespearean cinemas. As *The Phantom Lover* (dir. Ronnie Yu, 1995) from Hong Kong, and *Chicken Rice War* (dir. Chee King Cheah, 2000) from

Singapore, attest, *Romeo and Juliet* is popularly reworked, while a nostalgic Chinese film such as *A Time to Love* (dir. Jianqi Huo, 2005) shows how two lovers experience the play mirroring their own lives, caught, as they are, between the end of the Cultural Revolution and a consumerist present. *Prince of the Himalayas* recalls the blueprint of these adaptations when Lhamoklodan/Hamlet (Purba Rgyal), prince of Jiabo, announces early on to Odsaluyang/Ophelia (Sonamdolgar), 'From this day, you shall be my only beloved': the sequence not only streamlines the play's amatory intricacies but also puts romance at the forefront. (The film differentiates itself from *The Banquet* in taking the Hamlet/Ophelia relationship as its point of departure.) Like *The Banquet, Prince of the Himalayas* concentrates on the predicament of a dysfunctional family, only here the drama springs from the revelation that Lhamoklodan/Hamlet is the product of the relationship between Kulo-ngam/Claudius and Queen Nanm/Gertrude (Old King Tsanpo/the Ghost is not his biological father), with the action moving towards the issue of the protagonist's paternity. Taking on board the success of US-financed Tibet-styled films such as *Seven Years in Tibet* (dir. Jean-Jacques Annaud, 1997) and *Kundun* (dir. Martin Scorsese, 1997), and possibly responsive to a less marked move on the part of some Chinese filmmakers to bring Tibet into the cinematic purview, Sherwood Hu in *Prince of the Himalayas* finds the Tibetan *milieu* helps broach perennial Shakespearean questions. An earlier Tibet-set film, *The Horse Thief* (dir. Tian Zhuangzhuang, 1986), is resonant here, combining, as it does, themes of ambition, guilt, betrayal and ostracization with a raw lyricism and hypnotic religious intensity. Within a similar setting, *Hamlet*, according to Hu, 'speaks the same language', so much so that the director's overriding aim was to 'place the protagonist on top of the Himalayas … confronting his destiny'. Interestingly, Lhamoklodan/ Hamlet learns of his paternity only gradually; in between, alternating shots of stupa mounds, still pools, forested mountains and grassy plains work to suggest how the Tibetan landscape is a constituent part of the protagonist's growing realization of himself.

Accordingly, the film's version of the 'To be, or not to be' soliloquy is pushed forward until just before the duel and positioned as a climax. 'Who am I? Where do I come from? Where am I going?', Lhamoklodan/Hamlet asks, having finally learned of parentage. Amidst scudding skies and twi-light prayers, these questions unfold, with the soliloquy delivered as a voiceover split between three locales – a snowy waste ('There is a sea of troubles'), a fire-lit bedroom ('To die, to sleep') and a frozen headland beside a serpentine river ('Who would choose a weary life and perish in the

Figure 15: Queen Nanm/Gertrude (Zomskyid) and King Kulo-ngam/Claudius (Dobrgyal) share an intimate moment in *Prince of the Himalayas* (dir. Sherwood Hu, 2006). Courtesy of Hus Entertainment.

struggle?'). This inside-outside dynamic, coupled with elemental contrasts between fire and ice, mime the psychic situation of Lhamoklodan/Hamlet, split, as he is, between fathers and between claims on his filial loyalty. At several points, too, the sequence hints at a thaw in relations: the ice that encrusts Lhamoklodan/Hamlet begins to melt as a prelude to the bedroom segment in which, flanked by his parents, he is warmed and brought back to consciousness. The accompanying song, 'Celestial Incense', which combines male and female voices and a Buddhist *mantra* in a lyric story of lovers reconciled, further adumbrates possibilities of *rapprochement*.[50] As the soliloquy/voiceover comes to an end, Lhamoklodan/Hamlet looks twice to camera as if seeking approval for having committed himself to the troubled world of his own interiority.

The tensions animating the film's realization of 'To be, or not to be' are expressed more forcefully in the ways in which *Prince of the Himalayas* separates the two fathers into opposing types. For example, the pigtailed and helmeted Kulo-ngam/Claudius is protective towards Lhamoklodan/Hamlet, sending him into exile not to be rid of a troublesome subject, 'full of threats to all' (4.1.14), but to keep him apart from potential enemies. Here, as elsewhere, the biological bond is the source of a pragmatic solicitude. By contrast, Old King Tsanpo/the Ghost, swathed in feathery pale robes, treats his 'son' angrily, rasping out the revelation – 'do not let me die wizened of a broken heart! . . . I was poisoned . . . Take revenge' – in piecemeal fashion. (Old King Tsanpo/the Ghost's speeches are distributed evenly over the course of the film, the effect of which is to keep the pressures of the past continually in play.) In the same way that *Prince of the Himalayas* holds back the facts of Lhamoklodan/Hamlet's paternity, so does it delay clarification of the precise circumstances surrounding the death of Old King Tsanpo/the Ghost (the benevolent 'Spirit of Heaven' provides a poisonous lapdog to be used against the enraged husband when he launches a murderous campaign against the lovers), which reorients moral polarities and disabuses audiences of the expectation that the adaptation cleaves to a familiar narrative course.[51] More significantly, because it reimagines the play's familial nexus, *Prince of the Himalayas* is able to intimate that Lhamoklodan/Hamlet's vengeful mission is misplaced. Congruent with costuming, the vultures that announce the frequent arrivals and departures of Old King Tsanpo suggest the Ghost's preying attitude – a stalking of the living – and deaths in the offing. At each manifestation of the ghostly parent, it is implied, the protagonist's own death is imminent. If *Prince of the Himalayas* uses natural/supernatural rhythms to hint at Lhamoklodan/Hamlet's precariousness, *The Banquet* deploys titular suggestiveness. *Ye Yan*, the Mandarin Chinese title for the film, translates as 'The Night Banquet', which connotes both a political trap and legends about banquets at which rivals were poisoned or military generals plotted to dispatch each other.[52] In both adaptations, the dangers that encircle the protagonists highlight their underlying vulnerabilities.

Given Lhamoklodan/Hamlet's divided condition, questions of responsibility become all important. Resisting classic conventions, *Prince of the Himalayas* steers characters Shakespeare's Hamlet never meets into prominence. *En route* into exile, Lhamoklodan/Hamlet crosses paths with the Subi nation warrior woman, Ajisuji/Fortinbras, played by Luo Sang De Ji (the peacock feathers that decorate her armour indicate an appropriation of male insignia), who is bound for Persia: 'Thousands of us will perish . . . To penetrate the snow-covered mountains and reach the trade routes . . . is worth the sacrifice', she confides. As in the play, the courageous enterprise stimulates Lhamoklodan/Hamlet to reconsider his priorities. Vital here are the ways in which a woman's agency – and honesty – are generative. This accords with a more general emphasis in the film on women as motors of the narrative. For instance, when the Wolf-Woman (Dechendolma), a white-haired and venerable figure accompanied by wolves, appears, she offers a pronouncement that serves to warn Lhamoklodan/Hamlet of the dreadful consequences of honouring Old King Tsanpo/the Ghost's retributive demands. With the 'Wolf-Woman', Hu remarks, 'I wanted to create another unknown universe, to add layers'. Juxtaposed through blocking, Old King Tsanpo/the Ghost and the Wolf-Woman are supernatural 'figures' that, in the words of one of the screenwriters, Jangbu, are part of a 'two-sided aesthetic' exhibiting 'values and tendencies of love and hate, purity and impurity, beauty and ugliness'. Distinctively stepping forward, as Samuel Crowl states, 'like a deity out of Greek tragedy', the Wolf-Woman provides Lhamoklodan/Hamlet with an alternative to retribution – 'I shall break the silence and tell . . . of what happened between two brothers of royal blood . . . the sins of past generations will not cause you to seek revenge in the present' – that exposes male-defined dissimulation, installs female-determined clarity and allows for issues of identity and accountability to be confronted.[53] In this regard, the Wolf-Woman tells the story that Queen Nanm/Gertrude is mostly prevented from disclosing and, in so doing, points up a contrasting model of speaking female action. For, having chosen to be unfaithful and to keep a secret, Queen Nanm/Gertrude is, for much of the film, constricted. Only in the concluding sequences where she joins forces with the Wolf-Woman to tell Lhamoklodan/Hamlet of his origins is she given a more energetic role. At its close, therefore, *Prince of the Himalayas* affirms gendered continuity and confirms women as the narrative's guardians and interpreters.

Women are similarly privileged at the end of *The Banquet* – although far less affirmatively. Stabbed by an anonymous assassin as snow falls, Empress Wan/Gertrude fails in her political endeavour, the cold of the snow symbolically blanketing and changing the heated temperature of her 'desire'. White covers red (the mourning mood associated with Wu Luan/Hamlet returns), effacing her 'flame' of aspiration. What is stressed is the idea that the Empress is 'punished for overreaching', and, in the words of Camilla Chun-Pai Hsieh, there would seem to be offered 'little solace through mutuality in love, friendship or other human bonds'.[54] 'The shimmer of a single dream, and my world is undone', the refrain to the song that sounds over the closing credits, hints at a regretful acknowledgement of the consequences of pursuing ambitions centred on the self and reminds us of how often *The Banquet* has used the lyric form to reorient Shakespeare. On several occasions in the film, Emperor Li/Claudius quotes from the Han dynasty *ko-shih* (song genre) poem about a 'woman from the north' so beautiful that she causes cities and empires to fall. One line is particularly highlighted ('Who cares about losing a kingdom when in the presence of such rare beauty?'), and in such a way as to look forward to the chaos and mayhem that colour the film's final scenes.[55] Wu Luan/Hamlet dies from a poisoned blade after the final performance; Qing Nü/Ophelia collapses, having swallowed the poisoned wine; Emperor Li/Claudius takes his own life; Yin Sun/Laertes (Huang Xiaoming) dies at the hands of Empress Wan/Gertrude; Minister Yin/Polonius (Ma Jingwu) is exiled; and there is no hint of a new dynastic line assuming power. Perhaps referencing the familial annihilations and loss of territories attendant on Empress Wu Zetian's death, *The Banquet* closes with the sense of a world having come to an end.[56] In this sweeping dramatization of the last days of the Tang Dynasty, which has a charged place in contemporary China in the context of anxieties about 'society, economy and . . . politics' brought on by unprecedented 'demographic . . . distortions', the overriding impression is of empires and eras eclipsed.[57]

At the opposite extreme is *Prince of the Himalayas* in which a new family emerges. The idea is found in the prospect of reincarnation that underlies the scene of Odsaluyang/Ophelia's demise. Although taking place in water, this core episode from Shakespeare's play is accompanied in the film by the delivery of Lhamoklodan/Hamlet and Odsaluyang/Ophelia's son, which implies not so much suicide as death in childbirth. The fact that an additional life comes into being at the precise moment when another existence is extinguished is graphically underscored by a *mise-en-scène* that places mother and infant side-by-side in the river (with a subsequent tracking shot tracing the journey of the child downstream). In contradistinction to *Hamlet* in which, as Linda Charnes states, the 'individual bloodline' is erased, *Prince of the Himalayas* stresses renewal.[58] Hu makes the point with a particular poetic flourish when he states that 'tragedy, which enables catharsis and cleansing, helps to reach beyond the darkness to a different horizon, a hope for tomorrow': Hamlet, or a version of him, lives on. As the dying Lhamoklodan/Hamlet is introduced to his son, the precious child is cradled by the Wolf-Woman and Ajisuji/Fortinbras and hailed as the 'King of Jiabo'. The coming together of metaphorical mothers – of the Jiabo and Subi nations – approves a philosophy of harmonious co-existence. Significantly, this culminating moment celebrates the birth of a new dynastic partnership and of a child who will rule in minority: Lhamoklodan/Hamlet's question, 'Who am I?', is finally answered in his offspring's future development. Like his lama forbears, the 'King of Jiabo' will be protected until he reaches maturity, an arrangement to which the closing chants of monks reciting scriptures lend approval. Because assured of what lies beyond, Lhamoklodan/Hamlet is realized as ready to embrace his own destiny, and confidence in succession means that he can finally defeat Old King Tsanpo/the Ghost. Rejecting the Ghost's injunctions, and breaking out of inwardness, Lhamoklodan/Hamlet refuses to 'raise his sword' against his biological father, King Kulo-ngam/Claudius, and, hence, privileges the blood ties of family over and above a false paternal-filial relation expressed as an unthinking reification of authority. Marshalling the energies that have enabled and sustained it, *Prince of the Himalayas* here gestures to the blessings of female Buddha figures of compassion in its realization of a protagonist for whom the 'readiness' is indeed 'all' (5.2.200).[59] The spiritual emphasis is extended in the ways in which the soundtrack references Lhamoklodan/Hamlet's name in such a way as to bring to mind the female Buddhist deity, Palden Lhamo, a protectress of the Dalai Lamas and Tibet and a force archetypally associated with creative power and the ability to overcome destructive emotions.[60] Where *The Banquet* evinces a world spiralling inexorably towards its own demise, *Prince of the Himalayas* gives us a resurrected order and an investment in affirmative future projections.

Conclusions

Placed together, these films demonstrate the multiple ways in which a Shakespeare-inspired cinema responds to, and attempts to understand, the challenges of particular historical moments, with *Castle of Flames, The Bad Sleep Well, The Banquet* and *Prince of the Himalayas* registering solutions and resolutions that vary in scope, depth, nature and style. Two of the films (*Castle of Flames* and *Prince of the Himalayas*) espouse notions of collectivity and human alliance. By contrast, the other two films (*The Bad Sleep Well* and *The Banquet*) contemplate ideas of singleness and individual will, debating the degree of power to which the solitary avenger or aspirant has access. Often, these revisions to Shakespeare's play show themselves in how the Hamlet character is rethought; contrasting conceptual categories (protest and family), too, testify to a range of interpretive requirements. Differences are particularly in evidence in the films' endings. Two films (*Castle of Flames* and *Prince of the Himalayas*) favour ameliorative philosophies; the other two (*The Bad Sleep Well* and *The Banquet*) offer little that is constructive. *The Banquet* and *The Bad Sleep Well* remain rooted in a flawed and broken present; in contradistinction, *Castle of Flames* and *Prince of the Himalayas* project their action forwards into scenarios as yet not realized.

A common denominator is that these pairings of films give voice to anxieties about their respective legacies and are acutely sensitive to the changing faces of China and Japan in the twentieth and twenty-first centuries. *Castle of Flames, The Bad Sleep Well, The Banquet* and *Prince of the Himalayas* are stimulated by their moments of production into creative engagements with *Hamlet*, and, whether through allusion, mediation or trope, allegorize the tensions and the energies, the initiatives and the instabilities, that constitute their own possibility. That said, the precise complexion of each film's engagement with its contexts differs according to praxes of production and distribution – and matters of generic affiliation. Even so, placing them together helps to reveal how, within the same moment of Shakespearean adaptation, there is both homogeneity and asymmetry, how seemingly cognate discourses and metaphors can work in opposite directions, how contemporary questions of belonging and action are taken on board with varying levels of engagement. Above all, the pairing methodology insists upon the critical need to think not so much in terms of the individual output but always in terms of a holistic sense of the depth and diversity of an assembly of Shakespearean responses.

Individually, of course, each of the directors examined in this chapter is stamped as auteur. *Prince of the Himalayas*, for example, was precipitated by director Sherwood Hu's guilt over his inability to attend his father's funeral, and, arguably, the film goes on to exorcise a guilty conscience by cinematically instating what have through recent history been occluded perspectives.[61] In this instance, Shakespearean filmmaking is expiatory. For Feng, director of *The Banquet*, the impetus was imaginative. Shown an early script of a Chinese film adaptation of *Hamlet*, he went back to the play, only to realize, in his words, 'I wasn't interested in directing a pure translation, I wanted there to be creativity': here, *The Banquet* is singled out for its distance from the precursor text, for its capacity to facilitate transformation, for its power as a collocation of parts rather than a whole.[62] Where Kurosawa and Tai are concerned, the different levels of creativity allowed them by their working conditions were both enabling and disabling. Paradoxically, although seemingly enjoying the greater independence, Kurosawa references the Japanese protests only indirectly; by contrast, even though tied to a studio, Tai offers a more searching critique of contemporary unrest, hewing closely to *Hamlet* and providing a particularly acerbic commentary. Dissatisfied with the ending of *Castle of Flames*, and adamant that Masato/Hamlet should perish in the blaze, Tai clashed with studio bosses (who wanted to keep the star alive) to craft a work with a barbed applicability; Kurosawa, with self-insight, regretted after he had completed *The Bad Sleep Well* not 'showing enough'.[63] Discrete visions of *Hamlet* emanate from different systems of production, but also from arguments, serendipity and individual experiential trajectories. *Castle of Flames*, *The Bad Sleep Well*, *The Banquet* and *Prince of the Himalayas* show how Shakespeare is a medium or conduit through which the political crises and economic successes of twentieth- and twenty-first-century Japan and China can be conveyed and communicated. And, if the films highlight the infinitely gradated ways in which *Hamlet* has been relayed and transposed, either through modern media or through redaction, allusion and language, then this is because Shakespeare, whether as long-established tradition or liberated resource, is an integral part of the constitution of modernity. The power of *Hamlet* as idiom and instrument is a shared point of reference, and, as the films conceive of it, the play serves to assist in exploration and self-revelation, functioning as a repository of meaning that facilitates the processes through which Japan and China assess themselves.

Notes

1. Hui Wu records a production investment figure of $20 million for *The Banquet* ('Three Hamlets, Two Gentlemen and One Time to Love: Shakespeare on the Chinese Screen', in Lawrence Raw, ed., *The Silk Road of Adaptation: Transformations from Across Disciplines and Cultures* [Newcastle-upon-Tyne: Cambridge Scholars, 2013], p. 119).

2. Interviews between Sherwood Hu and Mark Thornton Burnett (17–18 November 2014). Unless otherwise stated, all Hu quotations are taken from these interviews and appear in the text or notes.

3. Until recently, *Castle of Flames* was unavailable in subtitled DVD format. Although *Prince of the Himalayas* sold out in Lhasa, Tibet, and premiered at international film festivals (the Adelaide Film Festival, the AFI Los Angeles Film Festival and the Hawaii International Film Festival), it has had a chequered distribution history. However, there was a successful theatrical run in 2011–12 at the Rubin Museum of Art, New York, and a screening at Queen's University Belfast (2014) as part of the national initiative, 'Being Human', a festival of the humanities.

4. The definitive guide (in Japanese) is Katô Tai, Sadao Yamane and Yoshio Yasui, *Katô Tai, eiga o kataru* (Tokyo: Chikuma Shobo, 1994).

5. Chris Desjardins, *Outlaw Masters of Japanese Film* (London and New York: I. B. Taurus, 2005), p. 1; Patrick Galloway, *Warring Clans, Fighting Blades: A Samurai Film Companion* (Berkeley: Stone Bridge, 2009), p. 108.

6. Galloway, *Warring*, p. 109; Mitsuhiro Yoshimoto, *Kurosawa: Film Studies and Japanese Cinema* (Durham: Duke University Press, 2000), p. 188.

7. Desjardins, *Outlaw*, p. 227; Alexander Jacoby, *A Critical Handbook of Japanese Film Directors: From the Silent Era to the Present Day* (Berkeley: Stone Bridge, 2008), pp. 381, 382.

8. These include *Crouching Tiger, Hidden Dragon* (dir. Ang Lee, 2000), *Hero* (dir. Yimou Zhang, 2002) and *House of Flying Daggers* (dir. Yimou Zhang, 2004).

9. For scriptwriting purposes, according to Hu, the play was translated from English into Mandarin and subsequently into Tibetan: 'We didn't work in English, but we had an English text to look at', he states (interviews between Sherwood Hu and Mark Thornton Burnett [17–18 November 2014]). In interview, Chenaktshang Dorje Tsering (Jangbu), one of the Tibetan screenwriters, notes that he 'poured the original idea into Tibetan culture, revised it, pruned its branches and added seasoning' (interview between Jangbu and Mark Thornton Burnett [23 October 2009]). Unless otherwise stated, all Jangbu quotations are taken from this interview and appear in the text or notes.

10. Frank N. Pieke, *Knowing China: A Twenty-First Century Guide* (Cambridge: Cambridge University Press, 2016), p. 141.

11. Translations of Shakespeare (*Julius Caesar*) first appeared in 1884, while the first stage production took place in 1885, *The Merchant of Venice* being presented as a Kabuki-style drama. See Tetsuo Anzai, 'A Century of Shakespeare in Japan: A Brief Historical Survey', *Shakespeare Yearbook*, 9 (1999), p. 3.

12. Izumi Kadono, 'The Kabuki Version of *Hamlet: Hamlet Yamato No Nishikie*', *Shakespeare Yearbook*, 9 (1999), pp. 106–7.

13. Graham Bradshaw and Kaori Ashizu, 'Reading *Hamlet* in Japan', in Jonathan Bate, Jill L. Levenson and Dieter Mehl, eds, *Shakespeare and the Twentieth Century* (Newark: University of Delaware Press, 1998), p. 356.

14. John Gillies, Minami Ryuta, Ruru Li and Poonam Trivedi, 'Shakespeare on the Stages of Asia', in Stanley Wells and Sarah Stanton, eds, *The Cambridge Companion to Shakespeare on Stage* (Cambridge: Cambridge University Press, 2002), p. 261.

15. During the late 1950 early 1960s, over forty new titles belonging to the genre were appearing each year. See David Desser, 'Toward a Structural Analysis of the Postwar Samurai Film', in Arthur Nolletti and David Desser, eds, *Reframing Japanese Cinema: Authorship, Genre, History* (Bloomington and Indianapolis: Indiana University Press, 1992), p. 145.

16. Foster Hirsch, *Film Noir: The Dark Side of the Screen* (New York: Da Capo, 1981), p. 13.

17. Linda Charnes, *Hamlet's Heirs: Shakespeare and the Politics of a New Millennium* (New York and London: Routledge, 2006), p. 29.

18. Hirsch, *Noir*, p. 4.

19. Mark Bould, *Film Noir: From Berlin to Sin City* (London and New York: Wallflower, 2005), p. 60.
20. See Donald Richie, *The Inland Sea* (Berkeley: Stone Bridge, 2002), p. 11.
21. See Galloway, *Warring*, p. 28.
22. Gary D. Allinson, *Japan's Postwar History*, 2nd ed. (Ithaca and New York: Cornell University Press, 2004), p. 97; Elise K. Tipton, *Modern Japan: A Social and Political History*, 2nd ed. (London and New York: Routledge, 2008), pp. 173, 175.
23. See Desjardins, *Outlaw*, p. 33; Jacoby, *Critical*, p. 126.
24. Michael Douglas, '*Jidai-geki*/Period Drama', in John Berra, ed., *Directory of World Cinema: Japan 2* (Bristol and Chicago: Intellect, 2012), p. 226.
25. Douglas M. Lanier, 'Film Spin-Offs and Citations', in Richard Burt, ed., *Shakespeares After Shakespeare: An Encyclopedia of the Bard in Mass Media and Popular Culture*, 2 vols (Westport and London: Greenwood, 2007), I, p. 155.
26. Lanier, 'Film Spin-Offs', I, p. 155.
27. David Desser, *Eros Plus Massacre: An Introduction to the Japanese New Wave Cinema* (Bloomington and Indianapolis: Indiana University Press, 1988), pp. 36–38.
28. Galloway, *Warring*, p. 108; Katô Tai, 'The Fundamentals of My Filmmaking', in Sadao Yamane and Hasumi Shingehiko, eds, *Midnight Surprise: Katô Tai* (Tokyo: The Japan Foundation, *c.* 1997), pp. 10, 15; Hasumi Shingehiko, 'Samurai Loyalty: A Film Geneaology of Katô Tai', in Yamane and Shingehiko, eds, *Midnight*, p. 21; Sadao Yamane, 'A Profile of Katô Tai', in Yamane and Shingehiko, eds, *Midnight*, p. 2.
29. James L. McClean, *Japan: A Modern History* (New York and London; Norton, 2002), p. 505; Tipton, *Japan*, p. 149.
30. In its concluding stages, *Castle of Flames* draws on *Throne of Blood*, not least in the scenes in which Masato/Hamlet, like Washizu/Macbeth (Toshirô Mifune), is pierced with arrows, in which he ascends to the watchtower and in which the castle stronghold is besieged.
31. The ending is alluded to in the film's play-within-the-play, a version of an episode from *The Kojiki*, the eighth-century Japanese chronicle, in which Empress Sahohime, having betrayed her husband, Emperor Suinin, flees with her lover, Lord Sahohiko, to a castle which is then destroyed by fire. See Gustav Heldt, ed., *The Kojiki: An Account of Ancient Matters* (New York: Columbia University Press, 2014), pp. 89–92.
32. Stephen Prince, *The Warrior's Camera: The Cinema of Akira Kurosawa* (Princeton: Princeton University Press, 1999), p. 184.
33. Yoshimoto, *Kurosawa*, pp. 286–87.
34. Alexa Alice Joubin, *Chinese Shakespeares: Two Centuries of Cultural Exchange* (New York: Columbia University Press, 2009), p. 7; Ruru Li, *Shashibiya: Staging Shakespeare in China* (Hong Kong: Hong Kong University Press, 2003), p. 12; Wang Xiangua, 'Shakespeare in China', in Jacob Sutton, ed., *Shakespeare and Friends* (London: Claude & Co., 2012), pp. 80–81.

35. Joubin, *Chinese*, p. 3, Ruru Li, 'Millennium Shashibiya: Shakespeare in the Chinese-Speaking World', in Dennis Kennedy and Yong Li Lan, eds, *Shakespeare in Asia: Contemporary Performance* (Cambridge: Cambridge University Press, 2010), p. 172; Li, *Shashibiya*, p. 51.

36. Li, *Shashibiya*, p. 7; Lingui Yang, 'Shakespeare's Cultural Capital Made in China: From Pre-modern to Post-modern', *Shakespeare Yearbook*, 17 (2010), p. 96.

37. See Pieke, *Knowing*, pp. 50, 51, 53, 55, 59, 164.

38. Michael Berry, 'Chinese Cinema with Hollywood Characteristics, or How *The Karate Kid* became a Chinese Film', in Carlos Rojas and Eileen Cheng-Yin Chow, eds, *The Oxford Handbook of Chinese Cinemas* (Oxford: Oxford University Press, 2013), p. 176.

39. See Michael Curtin, *Playing to the World's Biggest Audience: The Globalization of Chinese Film and TV* (Berkeley, Los Angeles and London: University of California Press, 2007), p. 3.

40. Anne Ciecko, 'Contemporary Meta-Chinese Film Stardom and Transnational Transmedia Celebrity', in Song Hwee Lim and Julian Ward, eds, *The Chinese Cinema Book* (London: BFI, 2011), pp. 186, 187, 190.

41. Sheng-Mei Ma, *East-West Montage: Reflections on Asian Bodies in Diaspora* (Honolulu: University of Hawai'i Press, 2007), p. 42.

42. Camilla Chun-Pai Hsieh, 'Using Sinicised Adaptations for Pedagogy in Taiwan: *The Banquet* and *Bond*', in Kate Flaherty, Penny Gay and L. E. Semler, eds, *Teaching Shakespeare Beyond the Centre: Australasian Perspectives* (Basingstoke: Palgrave, 2013), pp. 194, 197.

43. Ya-Chen Chen, *Women in Chinese Martial Arts Films of the New Millennium: Narrative Analyses and Gender Politics* (Lanham and Boulder: Lexington Books, 2012), p. 117; Jonathan Clements, *Wu: The Chinese Empress who Schemed, Seduced, and Murdered her Way to Become a Living God* (Thrupp: Sutton Publishing, 2007), pp. 36, 112.

44. Chen, *Women*, p. 119; Clements, *Wu*, p. 197.

45. Mayfair Mei-hui Yang, 'From Gender Erasure to Gender Difference: State Feminism, Consumer Society, and Women's Public Sphere in China', in Mayfair Mei-hui Yang, ed., *Spaces of Their Own: Women's Public Sphere in Transnational China* (Minneapolis and London: University of Minnesota Press, 1999), p. 47.

46. N. Harry Rothschild, *Wu Zhao: China's Only Woman Emperor* (New York and London: Pearson/Longman, 2008), p. 3.

47. See Niamh J. O'Leary, 'Ambition and Desire: Gertrude as Tragic Hero in Feng Xiaogang's *The Banquet*', *The Upstart Crow*, 31 (2012), p. 77.

48. Alexa Alice Joubin, 'The Paradox of Female Agency: Ophelia and East Asian Sensibilities', in Kaara L. Peterson and Deanne Williams, eds, *The Afterlife of Ophelia* (New York: Palgrave, 2012), p. 89.

49. See Anne Birrell, ed., *New Songs from a Jade Terrace: An Anthology of Early Chinese Love Poetry* (London, Boston and Sydney: George Allen and Unwin, 1982), p. 231.

50. See *'Prince of the Himalayas': A Sherwood Hu Film*, publicity book (Los Angeles and Shanghai: Hus Entertainment/CineHyte Films, 2006), p. 61. Looking forward to the film's ending, the song features the *mantra*, 'Om Mani Padme Hum' (see Lorne Ladner, 'Practice: Seeing with Eyes of Compassion', in Lorne Ladner, ed., *The Wheel of Great Compassion: The Practice of the Prayer Wheel in Tibetan Buddhism* [Boston: Wisdom Publications, 2000], pp. 8–14).

51. In interview, Jangbu notes that the Tibetan words for '"Spirit of Heaven", *Gnam rgan ma* or *Gnam sngon po*', signify 'a mysterious force that dominates the universe or fate/destiny' (interview between Jangbu and Mark Thornton Burnett [23 October 2009]).

52. Chen, *Women*, p. 122; Clements, *Wu*, p. 88.

53. Samuel Crowl, *Screen Adaptations: Shakespeare's 'Hamlet'* (London and New York: Bloomsbury, 2014), p. 135.

54. O'Leary, 'Ambition', 65; Hsieh, 'Using Sinicised Adaptations', p. 198.

55. The poem is reprinted in Birrell, ed., *New*, p. 41. For provenance, see Luo Yunhun, 'Queen Xiaowu', in Barbara Bennett Peterson, ed., *Notable Women of China: Shang Dynasty to the Early Twentieth Century* (London and New York: Routledge, 2000), pp. 63–64.

56. Chen, *Women*, p. 119; Clements, *Wu*, p. 185.

57. Pieke, *Knowing*, p. 70.

58. Charnes, *Hamlet's Heirs*, p. 9.

59. See Sogyal Rinpoche, *The Tibetan Book of Living and Dying*, ed. Patrick Gaffney and Andrew Harvey (London and Sydney: Rider, 2008), pp. 67, 191; Sangharakshita, *Tibetan Buddhism: An Introduction* (Birmingham: Windhorse, 1999), pp. 91, 109.

60. See Ladrang Kalsang, *The Guardian Deities of Tibet*, tr. Pema Thinley (Laxmi Nagar: Winsome Books, 1996), pp. 25–31.

61. In interview, Hu states: 'I couldn't go back [from the US to China] to attend my father's funeral because of the Tiananmen Square Massacre . . . that hit me hard . . . when I [did manage to go] back, I met one of my father's favourite Shakespeare actors who told me my father wanted to do *Hamlet* as his last play . . . that became my obligation' (interviews between Sherwood Hu and Mark Thornton Burnett [17–18 November 2014]).

62. See *'The Banquet*: About the Production', www.metrodomereleasing.com/films/banquet (accessed 12 May 2009).

63. See Sadao Yamane, 'Filmography of Katô Tai', in Yamane and Shingehiko, eds, *Midnight*, p. 76; Bert Cardullo, ed., *Akira Kurosawa: Interviews* (Jackson: University Press of Mississippi, 2008), p. 18.

CHAPTER FIVE

Hamlet *and Indian Cinemas: Regional Paradigms*

In India, and possibly to a greater extent than in any other part of the world, Shakespeare and colonialism are intricately inter-related. A growing body of scholarship on the late eighteenth-century English language repertories of theatres in Calcutta and Bombay has revealed how pervasively 'Shakespeare's plays' were 'embroiled in the spice and textile trade', with specific productions being targeted at expatriate British commercial communities.[1] From the first, *Hamlet* occupied a special place, looming large in the repertories of the 'Calcutta Theatre' (or 'New Playhouse'): a 1775 production confirms that the play operated as an early reference point.[2] The popularization of Shakespeare went hand-in-hand with educational initiatives as in the curriculum of the Hindu College, Calcutta, where Shakespeare, from 1817 onwards, was integral to the literary studies programme.[3] Shakespeare underwrote the examination process for entry into the Indian civil service, a crucial element of the drive to establish English as the language of colonial administration and to create a citizen, as the 1835 Education Act memorably has it, 'Indian in blood and colour, but English in taste, in opinions, in morals, and in intellect'.[4] As Jyotsna G. Singh has established, English, because vital to the promotion of 'English liberalism' and the principles of empire, was strategically privileged.[5] And, as Shakespeare's plays made a mark on European and Indian mindsets, his cultural uses and significances were granted institutional approval and purchase.

An indication of a growing familiarity with Shakespeare was the increasing number of translations and indigenous productions. Hence, in the nineteenth-century Parsi theatre (which unfolded in several languages, Hindi, Urdu and Gujarati included), Shakespeare appeared in new linguistic and cultural guises, with productions demonstrating spectacular effects, sophisticated technology, flamboyant costumes and an extravagant acting style.[6] A typical Parsi production combined parts of the Shakespearean text with farces, musical interludes, dance and other styles of entertainment.[7] Interestingly, adaptations of *Hamlet* proved popular in this distinctively Indian form, paving the way for the Bengali-language *Hariraja* (1897) and the Urdu-language *Khun-e-Nahaq* (1898).[8] Extended theatrical runs, elaborately presented musical interludes, dance sequences marking ceremonial moments and the removal or addition of characters – these were the watchwords of the Parsi *Hamlet* on stage. In the 1898 production, in particular, ornate prose and *ghazals* (love poems about separation and loss) functioned to approximate Shakespearean language. It is perhaps not surprising that, as the fledging Indian film industries got under way, Parsi theatre productions were to prove formative, both inflecting the first films and exercising a long-term influence at the level of the song-and-dance numbers for which 'Bollywood' became known.

Although it is now lost, extant materials illustrate the extent to which the first sound film adaptation of *Hamlet, Khoon-ka-Khoon* (dir. Sohrab Modi, 1935), is indebted to these earlier stage manifestations. Publicity stills at the National Film Archive of India, Pune, offer a rare glimpse into staging praxes, blocking, costuming and representational decisions. Interestingly, the film is animated by regional detailing. Architectural Islamic motifs on backcloths and the prioritization on posters of the 'Urdu' translation make clear how *Khoon-ka-Khoon* reads the play according to a local vernacular.[9] Images show Hamlet (Sohrab Modi) bowing before Gertrude (Shamshadbai) in the closet scene, indicative of the theatre production's emphasis on the loyalty a son owes to his mother, while a further still captures a pigtailed Ophelia (Naseem Banu) on a bridge about to throw herself to her death (replacing the reports of the play with a sense of the character's agency). The seventeen songs that interspersed the dialogue suggest an intimate relation to Parsi theatre practice; too, the still of a twelve-strong ensemble of children participating in a musical number confirms how, as in original productions, *Khoon-ka-Khoon* was conceived of as a highly choreographed spectacle.

Khoon-ka-Khoon also bears the traces of its European antecedents. The two-level stage, proscenium arch and representation of a black-suited Hamlet leaning disconsolately on a tree reference British theatrical conventions. In a similar way, the Hindi- and Urdu-language film, *Hamlet* (dir. Kishore Sahu, 1954), gestures to Laurence Olivier's adaptation. Olivier's model is primarily intimated in design decisions, particularly the Gothic set and Elizabethan-style dress, although *Khoon-ka-Khoon* is also shadowed in the film's 'look' and structure.[10] In fact, Sahu's *Hamlet* is notable for synthesizing several local and international interpretive trajectories simultaneously. It replaces 'God' with 'Allah' but retains the symbol of the Christian cross; it keeps Denmark as the place of action but introduces context-keyed reflections on affronts to family, honour and parental dignity. Director and star Sahu bills his *Hamlet* in the opening credits as a 'free adaptation', an identification which accords with the ways in which the dialogue is grounded in aphoristic approximations. 'I do not set my life at a pin's fee' (1.4.65), for example, is turned to 'I do not care for hail or fire!' Critic Esha Niyogi De views the film as a '"patchwork" of . . . concepts, ideologies and . . . attractions . . . [a] reflexive hybridization'.[11] But Sahu's *Hamlet* is more purposeful than this. In several scenes (1.3 and 3.1), appropriately gloomy lines from the *ghazals* of nineteenth-century Urdu poet, Ghālib, are cited, the effect of which is to play up Hamlet's dejection and Ophelia's (Mala Sinha) sense of abandonment.[12] These types of citation create a bridge between Indian classical traditions and Shakespeare, making the latter legible via familiar poetic sentiments and tropes. Further connectivity inheres in the mobilization of romantic and philosophical associations. In versions of 4.5 and 5.2, for example, Ophelia and Hamlet quote from the Urdu poetry of Bahadur Shah 'Zafar' and Mohammed Ibrahim Zauq respectively, seeing themselves by implication as tortured souls and fatalistic thinkers.[13] Both characters are thereby cast in a tragic light and discovered in terms of a mutually enriching interplay between literary cultures. Bringing to mind Parsi theatre's heterogeneity, Sahu's film inserts a retrospective romantic scene, derived from the story of Sakuntala, the love-lorn heroine in the *Mahābhārata*, in which Hamlet, hiding in the bushes, watches Ophelia singing with her companions by a lake.[14] Musical interludes and structural rearrangement mean that Ophelia's three songs grant her a greater autonomy than in the playtext, with the director interpolating extended dialogues between her and Hamlet. The relocation of the play-within-the-play to just before the climactic duel also means that the epic battle between Hamlet and Laertes (Kamaljeet) functions as a type of epilogue to the performance, the film underscoring a moment of meta-theatre as its thematic destination point.

In these two *Hamlet* adaptations can be pinpointed both emergent Bollywood tropes (dance, music, song, dialogic experimentation) and marked regional perspectives (a use of classical poetry, set design, linguistic play and epic allusion). Since 1955, when Sahu's film premiered in what was then Bombay, the regional agenda has become increasingly important in how India understands itself. The renewed place of the regional is arguably a response to the growing dominance of conservative caste and social initiatives which, in turn, take their cue from more assertive forms of

Figure 16: Kishore Sahu as the melancholy prince in *Hamlet* (dir. Kishore Sahu, 1954). Courtesy of the British Film Institute.

religious fundamentalism.[15] With Indian political sectors espousing varieties of regionalism as an alternative to a centralized institutionalized system, fresh spaces have increasingly been created for 'popular participation in local government assemblies . . . as well as . . . mechanisms through which citizens can . . . track how government funds are being spent in their . . . districts'.[16] A parallel development involves the growing influence of caste politics, with politicians belonging to the Indian National Congress now more likely to possess a 'distinct regional perspective'.[17]

Sunil Khilnani, his thesis supported through a persuasive range of examples, argues that 'potentially the most far-reaching consequences of this new regionalism lie squarely in the cultural realm'.[18] Yet, in the recent critical focus on Shakespeare and Indian cinemas, the general tendency is for the 'Bollywood' label to serve as a catch-all term, subsuming to itself the depth, range and variety of all Indian cinematic engagements with Shakespeare, and, along the way, obscuring a rich array of film adaptations. In the classic study of 'Bollywood', for example, 'Anglo-Indian, Hindi and diasporic cinema' are unhelpfully lumped together in such a way as to frustrate an engagement with plurality.[19] Following the lead of Poonam Trivedi and Paromita Chakravarti, who argue for the urgency of addressing a broad range of Indian 'cinemas' so as 'to bring their particular histories of literary and theatrical engagement with Shakespeare into the larger and a more interactive picture', this chapter contends that fully capturing the diversity of *Hamlet* adaptations in India involves taking much more account of regional distinctiveness.[20] Between the earliest of the *Hamlet* films and the three adaptations of the play discussed in this chapter – *Karmayogi* (dir. V. K. Prakash, 2012), *Haider* (dir. Vishal Bhardwaj, 2014) and *Hemanta* (dir. Anjan Dutt, 2016) – there are shared approaches which stand as testimony to a revitalized interest in the multiple ways in which *Hamlet* is mobilized. *Karmayogi, Haider* and *Hemanta* contest the usefulness of the 'Bollywood' identifier and go beyond current applications of the label in theme and content, opening fresh ways of accessing Shakespeare inside Indian *milieux*. Each film renders explicit what is involved in the work of adaptation, acknowledging the play as a reflexive prompt for dialogue, iconography and on-screen text.

Karmayogi, a *Hamlet* adaptation set in a pre-colonial period in the northern border parts of Kerala, first declares its difference from 'Bollywood' in the Malayalam-language voiceover that boldly asserts: '*Hamlet* becomes a movie in our language … Shakespeare is immortal … his drama, named *Hamlet*, lives among us'. Clearly, there is, in the declarative power of 'our' and 'us', a keen sense of belonging to a Malayali constituency. A construction of Shakespeare 'for all time' is melded with the suggestion that he can be reincarnated; the idea pushed in the use of the Sanskrit term, '*chiranjivi*', equates a Hindu concept of immortality with Kerala's cultural particularities. Centring on a *kalarippayattu* (martial arts) community, *Karmayogi* demonstrates the extent to which Shakespearean tropes and motifs are mediated through Keralan folkways, and these extend to the film's incorporation of *kelipathram* (imitating Shiva's penance for having beheaded Brahma) and *poorakkali* (a dance ritual). As director V. K. Prakash states, adapting *Hamlet* appealed because of the opportunity to 'layer a connection between the

Shakespearean text and the myths of Kerala' while honouring the 'original's intensity'.[21]

Haider is set in Kashmir in 1995 and situates itself within a contested regional political space characterized by an ongoing history of insurgency. In the wake of independence, Jammu and Kashmir came under the control of India and Pakistan respectively, with both, as Navnita Chadha Behera writes, 'claiming jurisdiction over the whole'.[22] A 'Bollywood' product in the sense that it is the work of an established Mumbai-based director, *Haider* insists at the same time on its distance from 'Bollywood' schema. As part of its representational apparatus, the film takes pre-existing 'Bollywood' constructions (notably, the association of Kashmir with 'love' and a 'traditional' literary 'paradise') only to upturn them.[23] It unsettles a reliance on Hindi as a marker of nationhood in its incorporation of Kashmiri-accented Hindi, Kashmiri terms and an Urdu-language score. And it articulates a departure from expected identifying features in the ways in which it intertextually interrogates 'Bollywood' via insets and poetic quotation. Part of this is reflected in the film's close rendering of (alongside *Hamlet*) one of its sources, *Curfewed Night* (2011) by Kashmiri journalist, Basharat Peer. At several points, *Haider* explicitly aligns itself with the memoir's anti-India politics: the effect is to mark *Haider* out as traversed by resistant ideologies and to complicate any easy reading of its nationalist sympathies.[24]

The most recent example, *Hemanta*, is a Bengali-language film that consistently prioritizes Kolkata, evoking, through its field of reference and specification of locale, the fortunes of a city that, post-1947, suffered years of decline. Known both as the 'dying city' and the 'city of culture', Kolkata, as *Hemanta* imagines it, is a site on which the forces of economic neo-liberalism collide with nostalgia for a lost world. *Hemanta* takes as part of its meta-cinematic setting the contemporary Bengali film industry, utilizing a dialogue chock-a-block with 'Tolly' gossip, cameos and informing detail. The grim joke behind 'Agradoot', the art-house film company founded by Hemanta/Hamlet's father and subsumed by the marketplace, is that it is entirely *unlike* its 'real-life' Bengali equivalent (a co-operative initiative that, from the 1940s to the 1980s, involved film practitioners collectively signing as director).[25] By the same token, the film privileges notions of 'Bengaliness' through hints of West Bengal's communist past, echoes of the 'Bengal Renaissance', the well-known nineteenth- and twentieth-century intellectual movement, and jokes that evoke the city's connections with Shakespearean translation and performance.[26] Consequently, *Hemanta* demonstrates how Bengali cinema, in Sharmistha Gooptu's words, has always existed as a 'domain for the show of regional dynamism . . . a key signifier of "Bengali culture"'.[27] As if to highlight what can be achieved within the thematics of a regional adaptation, *Hemanta* makes a point of furnishing equivalents for the entire *dramatis personae* of *Hamlet*, as is suggested in brief appearances by the announcer/Voltemand, Mrinmoy/Marcellus (Dilip Samajpati), Bobby/Barnardo (Ranjan Roy Chowdhury) and the Lawyer/Norwegian Captain (Souvik Das). The film is one of the very few world cinema adaptations that endeavours to match the roll-call of the play's cast.

This chapter argues forcefully for the point and the pleasures of placing *Karmayogi, Haider* and *Hemanta* – films produced in three different regions – in intimate dialogue. As is argued in the first section of this chapter, deploying regional paradigms as methodology allows for a particularized appreciation of how, in each film, setting and localization are vital components of a subscription to varieties of regional belief-systems. Acts of adaptation, for the individual directors, are, it is suggested, closely allied with the articulation of a regional politics and pride. Out of these alternating regional matrices come three contrasting Hamlet figures, as sections two and three maintain; each protagonist is differently enmeshed in the specifics of the play-text and realized in terms of relations with, variously, friends, lovers and mothers. 'To be, or not to be' functions as a mechanism with which to measure these different Hamlets at the level of their regional attachments and requirements. Section four argues for the importance of the films' poetic registers, which extend to their marshalling of music and dance. If, at times, such features appear archetypal expressions of 'Bollywood', they impress in *Karmayogi, Haider* and *Hemanta* as part of a network of poetry, literature and citation that hinges on precise local and regional signifiers. All three films inaugurate a dialogue with poets and artists originating in their specific places of making to debate past, present and future political formations. In their regional enterprises, *Karmayogi, Haider* and *Hemanta* offer a new paradigm for accessing Indian cinemas and a more variegated application of Shakespeare's utility. They hark back to the *Hamlet* adaptations of an earlier cinematic moment at the same time as they subscribe to regional demands to shape emergent praxes of understanding, interpretation and audience engagement.

Regional Scenes

Literally 'a yogi dedicated to his karma', *Karmayogi* announces its regional *raison d'être* in recurrent shots of the *kalarippayattu* participants, prioritizing scenes of stripped down fighters, costumed in baggy white shorts and decorative red belts, engaged in ritualistic combat with swords and shields on dusty earthen surfaces.[28] The film, then, seizes upon the duelling idea of 'fell . . . points / Of mighty opposites' (5.2.60–61), lending it a new regional colouring. Insets of the sacred *kalarippayattu* flame being extinguished interlace the adapted narrative, while staged competitions between the houses of Chathoth/Denmark and Chirikandoth/Norway in Ekarajyam/ Elsinore ('one country') reinforce local power dynamics. Because, as Phillip B. Zarrilli notes, *kalarippayattu* embodies 'history, kingship and [a] heroic' ideology even as it also points up 'an idealized image of Malayali manhood . . . central to the formation of the modern Kerala as a political entity', *Karmoyogi*'s centring of martial arts serves a regio-centric purpose.[29] Distinctively, the combatants are decorated with a *bindi* or *tilak* to signify sacred energy, and, throughout, the connections between *kalarippayattu* and the cult of Shiva are affirmed. The myth of Shiva, who was forced to beg and wander the earth in penance for beheading Brahma, is often invoked in the dialogue, while Shiva's presence is conjured in scenes of *teyyam* (in which a temple dancer comes to incarnate 'the spirit of the deity'), in holy sites (where votive candles bathe the action in a shimmering glow), in festive occasions (such as *Shivaratri*) and in the score (the opening hymn, with its Sanskrit references to 'Lord Shiva . . . greatest among gods . . . Om!', establishes a foundational narrative as pretext).[30] In this way, *kalarippayattu*'s involvement in the mythology of Shiva is highlighted, with the concomitant effect that the motifs and styles of South Indian Hinduism take on a symbolic significance inside the filmic aesthetic. The particularization of Shiva as regionally encoded is echoed in the film's warmly lit, liquid landscapes – slow-moving Keralan waterways that surrogate for the corridors of Elsinore and lushly carpeted hillsides and lofty palms that hint at a castle's battlements. Leafy banks running steeply down to overflowing rivers and densely forested glades approximate the idea of an impenetrable, crenelated Gothic edifice. These typical features of the Malabar regions of northern Kerala, where much of *Karmayogi* was filmed, belong with the film's circulation of local place- and group-names (*Kunnathoor Padi* and *Thiyyas*, for example) as iterations of past and present cultures. Both through suggestive location shooting and dialogic reference, *Karmayogi* elaborates an interplay between 'same' and 'other', interior and exterior, south and north, 'here' and elsewhere. The representational strategy is particularly in evidence in the character-ization of the quivering, effete Sathyan/Fortinbras (Manikuttan), of the house of Chirikandoth/Norway, who employs 'Assamese warriors' (their distinctive loose brown tunics mark out their difference) as part of his fighting retinue. Assam, in the north-east of India, could not lie further away from Kerala, in the south, with *Karmayogi* foregrounding in figures of emasculation and alterity threats to Keralan integrity. The film's *mise-en-bande* also contributes. Overlaying the hymn to Shiva is the sound of a conch being blown, the conch being the emblem of Kerala and a potent indicator of the state's values.[31] It is as if the conch is taken up as a rallying call – an aural invitation to recognize what is at stake in transposing *Hamlet* to a South Indian setting and situation.

Because *Haider* situates its action in 1995, the film makes manifest a time when instability in Kashmir was at its height.[32] Pushing at Shakespearean rivalries, the film presents the valley as a divided region which, plagued by factionalized modes of belonging, faces the threat of disintegration. The temporal-specific representation is abetted through an extended montage of surveillance, incarceration and torture, while filming locations – such as the stately ruins of the Martand Sun Temple near Anantnag which provide the backdrop to the 'play-within-the-play' – invest the adaptation with a spectacular visibility. Above all, *Haider*'s interest in graphically illustrating the internecine conflicts of Kashmir shows itself in a *mise-en-scène* comprised of the instruments of a controlling state apparatus. Detention centres, grilles and road blocks are signature images, bringing to mind the archetypal Hamletian metaphor of Denmark as a prison. The apprehensions underlying *Hamlet*'s opening exchange – 'Who's there? ... Stand and unfold yourself' (1.1.1–2) – are, then, in *Haider*, radically amplified. In a more directly politicized way than *Karmayogi*, *Haider* turns to nomenclature to debate the implications of the contested *habitus* to which *Hamlet* is transposed. At the Jawahar Tunnel border post (an icy peak frames a line of cars waiting to be searched and soldiers bristling with firepower) postgraduate student Haider/Hamlet (Shahid Kapoor), newly returned to Kashmir from Aligarh Muslim University, announces that he is from 'Islamabad', his deliberate confusion between Anantnag, a city and district in Jammu/Kashmir also known as 'Islamabad', and 'Islamabad', the capital of Pakistan, heightening his anti-Indian sentiments, the politics of allegiance and the ambiguated status of categorizations, classifications and regions. English, in particular, is equated with repressive Indian military forces. Hence, it is revealing when Haider/Hamlet, responding in English to the lieutenant's question about his research topic, states: 'Revolutionary poets of British India', his provocative reply giving rebellion (art and resistance) a dangerous pre-eminence. Interweaving documentary-style establishing shots and yellow-filtered sequences showing marching boots and backstreets (there is something 'sulphurous' [1.5.3] in this envisioning of Elsinore), *Haider* limns Kashmir as a vast military encampment characterized by an edgy, intimidatory mindset.

As part of its elaboration of setting, *Haider* temporarily mobilizes another Kashmir, one that smacks of the 'Bollywood' cinematic tradition, only to problematize its associations. A rhythmical pause over snow-capped mountains, for instance, is accompanied by a glimpse of severely pollarded trees, standing forlornly like grotesquely amputated bodies; similarly, a later lingering on frozen wastes works as a visual prelude to the bloody, bespattered slaughter by Haider/Hamlet of Salman/Rosencrantz (Sumit Kaul) and Salman/Guildenstern (Rajat Bhagat). More directly, the film's referencing, via extracts from 'Bollywood' movies, of the actor, Salman Khan, is interrogatively acerbic. One of the industry's Muslim stars, Khan, a 'bad-boy' known for his 'masculine bodily ideal', occupies a charged space in *Haider*, not least through a flashback scene in which, in the Faraz Cinema, Indian army officers watch a clip from *Sangdil Sanam* (dir. Shomu Mukherjee, 1994), one of his romantic comedies.[33] The key song-and-dance number, '*Main Hoon Deewana Tere Pyar Ka*' ('Give Me a Kiss'), plays at the point where prisoners (including Hilal/Old Hamlet [Narendra Jha]) are paraded before the screen for inspection, the juxtaposition functioning to correlate the actions in the inset film and the predicament of the cinema's captives. Critically, the Indian army are elided with the inset figure of Kishan/Khan, who, wearing a black singlet with a 'FIST' slogan, accosts a group of women swimming in a river, turning the invitation of the episode into an exercise in harassment.[34] In Kashmir in the 1990s, Khan was a much-imitated popular celebrity figure.[35] Via self-conscious allusion, therefore, *Haider* both gestures to the historical effects of the circulation of the 'Bollywood' product and broadens its representation of intimidation and torture. Implicitly, the Faraz Cinema, a stage for the exercise of power, is another version of the 'MAMA 2' detention centre in which electric shock treatment and solitary confinement reduce inmates to emasculated parodies of their former selves. *Haider*'s signal achievement is to take images and imaginaries so as forcibly to realign their applications.

Karmoyogi's regional dialectic mediates between south and north; by contrast, *Hemanta*'s equivalent engagement with setting shows itself in a global juxtaposition of the east and the west. In the interpolated opening scene – a backstory approximating the Wittenberg experience – the pro-tagonist is seen inhabiting a swanky New York apartment, its walls adorned with homages to Martin Scorsese (posters of *Scarface* and *Taxi Driver*). Hemanta/Hamlet (Parambrata Chattopadhyay), it is suggested, has eschewed the demands of Kolkata and his Kolkata commitments by escaping to New York where he has forged a successful career as a film director (in a Hamletian joke, he is poised to direct a season of the prime-time TV show, *Psychopath*). The incompatibility of his New York-based professional life and his Kolkata-based familial life are made apparent when Ananta Sen/the Ghost (Anjan Dutt) sends an urgent text message ('The artist's job is to play the role, / Thy role is defined by thy goal'), thereby catapulting Hemanta/Hamlet into the demands of family and region.[36] His return is constructed as a professional movement backwards that compromises creative independence. And from this point on, compared with the range of locations summoned in *Karmayogi* and *Haider*, *Hemanta* confines itself to a strictly delimited Kolkata locale, taking its cinematic cue from other recent Kolkata-set (but theatrical) *Hamlet* productions, such as Asit Basu's *Kolkatar Hamlet* (1973), Bratya Basu's *Hemlat* (2006) and Bibhash Chakraborty's *Hamlet* (2011), interpretations which, via Shakespeare, map the city's 'political cartography'.[37] Reifying the Kolkata *habitus*, *Hemanta* expresses the present predicament of a city that, thanks to the extraordinary influence wielded by the East India Company, had been not only the capital of the British Raj but also 'the wealthiest and most industrialized' state 'in India'.[38] The very different Kolkata of today is characterized by Kushanava Choudhury as a 'rust-belt on the Ganga' littered with the 'skeletons of its machine-age past'.[39] Resonant here is the mildewed mansion, once the property of a 'Maharaja' and now in the ownership of Kalyan/Claudius (Saswata Chatterjee), to which – in a version of 2.2 – Hemanta/Hamlet is taken by Gupi/Guildenstern (Vivan) and Raju/Rosencrantz (Sagnik): its cracked marble detailing, rickety staircase, crumbling stucco work and delapidated air instantiate faded glories in the same moment as they hint at neglect. *Hemanta* is set in the Bengali film industry (or 'Tollywood', as it is sometimes known), but, in common with the mansion, this is a world in terminal decline. 'All your screens … are like graveyards', Rakesh/the Player King (Shantilal Mukherjee) opines, his theme being that the art-house production house ('Agradoot') created by Ananta Sen/the Ghost is facing bankruptcy. 'Agradoot', in Ananta Sen/the Ghost's hands, has been forced to compete with 'Bollywood', with both city (Kolkata) and region (West Bengal) being vitiated in the process. Typical is how aspiring Bengali actor Lalit/Laertes (Souptik Chakraborty) has no other option than to transplant himself to Mumbai/Paris, learn Hindi and accept villains' roles: he is obliged to submit to a rival, and his attachment to his cultural and linguistic authenticity is compromised. The trajectory that *Hemanta* eventually traces is how 'Agradoot' is pushed into diversifying in a betrayal of its artistic and aesthetic mission.

Embracing the fabled reputation of Kolkata as, in Krishna Dutta's words, 'a City of Palaces', and mirroring its regional imperatives, *Hemanta* organizes itself around key internal and external urban environs.[40] In the family home, Ananta Sen/the Ghost's library, to which Hemanta/Hamlet withdraws, is filled with the contents of the past. A gramophone, leather-bound tomes, a toy cannon and stuffed animal heads index both nostalgically tinged remnants of an earlier era and the detritus of postcolonialism. The library bespeaks the film's backward-looking stance and, through an hour-glass perched on a bookshelf, alerts us to the fact that, for the revenge-seeking Hemanta/Hamlet, only so much time is left. At odds with old wealth is the *parvenu* wealth on display at the Kalyan/Claudius residence to which Gayatri/Gertrude (Gargee Roy Chowdhury) moves after her husband's death in what is seen as an unseemly abandonment of the widow's mourning duties. Full of brash statuettes, fake Andy Warhols, purple flocked wallpaper, extravagantly-swagged velvet and kitsch figurines from the Buddhist and Hindu pantheon, Kalyan/Claudius' rooms suggest the condition of a CEO newly risen to vulgarized ascendancy. As the film unveils, Kalyan/Claudius is successful not only because he has left traditional Bengali films behind but also because he uses charitable NGOs covertly to support terrorist organizations, his venality being defined through regionally destabilizing religious identifications. Between, and interleaved with, these two spaces, *Hemanta* turns its gaze onto traffic-choked streets and dingy roadside eateries as illustrations of the city's material underside. For example, in a registration of the complexities of Kolkata society, director Anjan Dutt has one scene towards the upper end of the class spectrum (the Hotel Wellesley on Park Street) and another towards the lower end (a nameless roadhouse on Sudder Street), the effect of which is to present the city as a variegated social grid onto which the polarities and tensions of *Hamlet* can be projected. As is symptomatic of the film, many of these sites are historically as well as regionally freighted. The film's transposition of 1.4 takes place on the banks of the River Hooghly at night-time, the majestic waterway's blue hues being offset by pinpoints of light and the setting evoking not only east-west encounters but also the founding of company buildings on the swampy environs of the delta. Here, in a classic car, Hemanta/Hamlet and Hirak/Horatio (Jisshu Sengupta) share a joint in a male bonding moment that takes its imaginative impetus from other kinds of exchange and Kolkata's historical trade in products and substances – calico, indigo, jute. All is of a piece with the film's summoning of the anterior, its subscription to what has been. As Hirak/Horatio notes in conversation with Hemanta/Hamlet, 'if anything survives it will be the books in your dad's library . . . theatre . . . films'. His comment highlights the film's subscription to Bengali art and literature – its rich cultural legacies – as antidote to, and bulwark against, a corrupting modernity.

Hamletian Appearances

Emerging from these contrasting regional realizations are three very different Hamlets. In each film, the Hamlet figure is accented in such a way as to bring to the surface the individual film's localized vision and identity. The recasting shows itself in the repurposing of soliloquies; it is also manifested in appearances and particularly in the ways in which costume changes consistently affirm a regional coming to consciousness. For example, in *Haider*, the green bomber jacket with tartan detailing that Haider/Hamlet initially wears is put aside for a chequered Kashmiri *pheran*. This local clothing item (one loose cloak worn over another) is the garment of choice for Kashmiri separatist leaders and signifies accordingly. Haider/Hamlet's switch proclaims a shift – a radical alteration in how he envisages himself and his *dharma* in relation to his political allegiances – in the wake of his confrontation with the army, the disappearance of his father and the flattening of his family home. A parallel scene is when Haider/Hamlet, immediately after the discovery of his father's grave, appears with his head shaved: the loss of his locks connotes a shedding of a western lifestyle as much as a new vulnerability. The film thus knits together appearances, awakening and politicization, showing how a change of heart – and commitment – have intimately visual correlatives and consequences.

In *Hemanta*, Hemanta/Hamlet's propensity for black (black T-shirts, open-neck black shirts and two-tone tops) initially suggests the 'inky cloak' (1.2.77) of his Shakespearean counterpart as a constant. Smoking and downing whiskey to desensitize himself to revelations that accelerate in their awfulness, Hemanta/Hamlet, ear-ringed and bearded, is invariably ireful, bouts of angry mania testifying to a never-out-of-mourning condition. But two minor costume changes subtly signal his developing moral parameters. After he has stage-managed the deaths of the drunken Raju/Rosencrantz and Gupi/Guildenstern by lacing their drink with rat poison, Hemanta/Hamlet conceals himself in a dark hoodie to leave the derelict palace. Here, in the film's rendition of Hamlet's account of reversing the 'grand commission' (5.2.18) designed to remove him, *Hemanta* presents us not so much with urban 'cool' as an anonymous protagonist defined as an underground artist enveloped in Kolkata criminality. A fight with Lalit/ Laertes results in Hemanta/Hamlet being taken to hospital and a second significant moment in costuming. Coming to on the ward, a bandaged Hemanta/Hamlet finds 'customary suits of solemn black' (1.2.78) replaced by a plastic blue gown, the transformed appearance functioning to stress the beginnings of a sanitizing process. Forthwith, as the film demonstrates, Hemanta/Hamlet takes a proactive role, ridding himself of the taint of the new-look 'Agradoot' by engineering a defining confrontation with Kalyan/ Claudius.

Karmayogi is structured according to five psychic phases, each corresponding to five costuming moments, that mark a journey towards revenge, resolution and yogic harmony. A still and dejected Rudran/ Hamlet (Indrajith) is first seen in funereal black robes, with only his arm bracelets hinting at the muscled *kalarippayattu* combatant he is to become. Secondly, he transforms himself into a mendicant in an expression of *kelipathram*. His cobra head-dress, red sash, necklace of conches, staff with a skull handle and ashen make-up index not only the demands required of a devotee of Shiva but also Hamletian concerns of transience and mortality.[41] At the point where he commits himself to his new role, his cleansing tantric rituals and wordless actions of investiture are mediated through the lyrics of the sitar-stringed score which, associating Rudran/ Hamlet with the son of Shiva, Ganesha, the elephant deity worshipped as the remover of obstacles and the facilitator of new beginnings, traces a movement from objective description ('spring blossoms in the valleys') to subjective appeal ('Please bless me!'). In this way, the song's lyrics function as a musical registration of several soliloquies where the protagonist steels himself to be emotionally centred in pursuit of his cause ('this thing's to do' [4.4.43] and 'heart, lose not thy nature' [3.2.383]). The change in appearance demonstrates how Rudran/Hamlet spectacularizes the bonds with his father, Rudran Valiya Gurukkal/Old Hamlet (Indrajith), also a penitent, while simultaneously endowing the protagonist with sacrality through the ascetism of Indian epic narratives.[42]

Once the lessons of Shiva's penance have been internalized, Rudran/ Hamlet appears in dark ochre *kalarippayattu* attire, the effect of which is to ratify his status as a cipher of Keralan masculinity and to lend him a guru-like gravitas. Interestingly, these developments are again soliloquy-inspired. Accompanying a backlit upper body shot, for example, Rudran/ Hamlet's voice sounds in a vernacular rendering of ''Tis now the very witching time of night' (3.2.378). Becoming a combatant brings with this third phase authority and insight: 'Let my mind grow calm . . . I will fulfil my vow'. Finally, on the eve of the duel, Rudran/Hamlet wears a studded brown outfit that proclaims a surpassing warrior-like confidence ('I have been in continual practice. I shall win' [5.2.188–189]). The donning of duelling garb in this fourth phase not only allows for the affirmation of purpose; it also clarifies the energies associated with Rudran/Hamlet's namesake. Likened to Shiva, Rudran, the deity known as 'the howler', connotes, as Alain Daniélou writes, the 'remover of pain . . . the uplifted thunderbolt . . . the fearful destroyer . . . the god of fire'.[43] As analogue, then, Rudran's name contextualizes *Karmayogi*'s hero as an Indianized revenger, an avatar whose mission is dependent on the successful exercise of a regional fighting form.

In an eloquent discussion, Thea Buckley argues that the film demonstrates how Rudran/Hamlet's 'self-realization through *karmayoga*, or the selfless performance of one's duty', empowers him to achieve 'liberation from the karmic life-cycle'.[44] This is writ large in the penultimate scene which, taking place in the *Rudrabhumi* cemetery (the name combines Shiva and a place of last rites), shows Rudran/Hamlet dispatching Bhairavan/Claudius (Thalaivasal Vijay) with a unique *kalarippayattu* blow. Significantly, the cemetery is adorned with signs of Shiva (the *trishula* or trident) which, in its three-part arrangement, implies a contest between forces – creation, sustenance and destruction, the past, the present and the future. At the point where Rudran/Hamlet throws the trident away (it is swallowed up by a neighbouring lake), it is suggested that he is no longer defined in terms of restless energy and has moved to a higher plane. ('[L]et it be' [5.2.322], Hamlet announces in one of his final reflections.) The closing tableau pushes the idea to its logical extreme. 'When I stand before the other, all my pride vanishes. The "I" in me vanishes', Rudran/Hamlet states, the new-found relation to self being visibly rendered in the protagonist's reappearance in *kelipathram* costuming. Contrary to readings that suggest 'discomfort with the ethical vacuum' created by Shakespeare's tragic conclusion, attention to costume suggests instead that *Karmayogi* works towards a sense of closure.[45] Ready to embrace his destiny, Rudran/Hamlet enters in the fifth phase on a new experience which, given the disappearance of the 'I', entails a corresponding loss of speech: the ending is without dialogue, as his figure gradually moves out of shot, and the 'rest is silence' (5.2.342). The sun sets, and the camera lifts heavenwards, implying that the yogic transformation is complete.

How we read these various representations of Hamlet is determined by, and mediated through, each film's approach to the 'To be, or not to be'

Figure 17: Rudran/Hamlet (Indrajith) strikes a yogic pose in *Karmayogi* (dir. V. K. Prakash, 2012). Courtesy of Trends Ad Films/Creative Land Entertainment.

soliloquy. In the hands of three different directors, the Shakespearean set-piece assumes mythological, political and familial dimensions. 'Our approach ... was to communicate the emotion of "To be, or not to be" through the narrative, through silences and through moments of intensity', states director V. K. Prakash, director of *Karmayogi*, and this is registered in a reluctance to transliterate the soliloquy's specifics. Rather, as Rudran/Hamlet makes his 'vow', the drums rise to a crescendo and the camera fades to black, the two parts of the opening lines appear on screen in opposite corners, the sequence suggesting that, until he acquires a state of yogic oneness, the protagonist, and the polarities of his universe, will remain in a divided state. True to its regional cultivation of divinity, the film returns to the famous crux in the scene where Shankunni/Horatio (Ashokan), recognizing the conflicting demands placed on Rudran/Hamlet, states: 'It is like the plight of Lord Shiva who can neither gulp the poison nor spit it out ... To be or not to be'. The reference is to the myth in which Shiva comes to the rescue of humanity by drinking the poison that a snake has emptied into the sea, and its inclusion in *Karmayogi* operates to push into the cosmic realm the speech's philosophical questions.[46] According to popular lore, Shiva controlled the negative effects of the poison – and exercised his saviour function – by retaining it in his throat (thereby taking on his blue colour); by the same token, it is implied, Rudran/Hamlet through his actions will assist in the preservation of the Keralan *communitas*.[47]

If *Karmayogi* diffuses 'To be, or not to be', *Haider* separates it out further into discrete articulations. 'To be, or not to be' (or versions of it) sound several times over – in protest slogans ('Do we exist or do we not?'), in a harangue to the crowd at the Lal Chowk traffic intersection, Srinagar ('If we [exist], then who are we? If not, then where are we?'), and in legal phrases from the Armed Forces Special Powers Act (a 'commissioned officer . . . in a disturbed area . . . may use force'). Interestingly, Haider/Hamlet's address underlines location as a key to interpretation, his specification of 'where' and 'area' suggesting that 'To be, or not to be' can only ever be read in relation to a particular time and place. Legal signifiers are illuminating, with a term such as 'disturbed' reflecting back on Haider/Hamlet's crazed state of mind. Referencing 'To be, or not to be', Haider/Hamlet's situation implies a precarious hold on life – as his parodic, noose-like use of the rope hanging around his neck makes clear. Because delivered as part of 'a chorus', writes Brian Walsh, the soliloquy in these episodes conjures a public 'experience of oppression', so it is in marked contrast with the 'To be, or not to be' which returns in more conventional guise in an intimate dialogue between Haider/Hamlet and Arshee/Ophelia (Shraddha Kapoor).[48] Haider/Hamlet reflects, 'To believe or not to believe . . . To kill or to die . . . To be or not to be', his statements gaining strength from the fact that they signal here a meeting of minds rather than, in the play, solitary self-analysis. For Bhardwaj, then, the soliloquy is a symptom of a regional condition that cuts across political and personal categories, that entangles inextricably the fortunes of the individual and the state. As he remarks in interview, 'Kashmir itself becomes Hamlet: the whole of Kashmir is about "To be, or not to be"'.[49]

Where *Haider* embeds 'To be, or not to be' in politics, *Hemanta* situates it as a desperate confessional interlude. The Kolkata-set adaptation makes the soliloquy legible by staging it as a three-way conversation between Hemanta/Hamlet, Olipriya/Ophelia (Payel Sarkar) and Hirak/Horatio, the common theme being the loss of fathers. Crucially, the film repurposes 'To be, or not to be' as series of questions ('To care or not to care? To do or not to do? To be or not to be?') that occurs *after* the accidental killing of Pulak/Polonius (Pijush Ganguly), the effect of which is to point up both Hemanta/Hamlet's reflections on his actions and his attempt to take his own life (abundantly adumbrated in a fade to tears, the crashing to the floor of a light and subsequent Stygian darkness). The mirrored dialogue (Olypriya/Ophelia bursts in, having been unable to locate Pulak/Polonius, while Hemanta/Hamlet replies, 'I've also been searching for my dad for a long time') emphasizes a point of connection, with Hirak/Horatio taking the role of a confessor in an epilogue to the encounter. 'I killed someone', cries Hemanta/Hamlet, adding, 'What should I do? Just fall asleep?'. Here, one of key motifs of 'To be, or not to be' is continued, the film filling in for a gap in the text by discovering a Hemanta/Hamlet who is racked by self-destructive guilt. Expressing himself in English and Bengali, Hemanta/Hamlet gives voice to a mixture of identifications. Delivered in the library during a storm, the confession incorporates into itself site-specific freight – Hemanta/Hamlet's fraught relation to Kolkata, his ties to the city's past, and their lingering effects on his unresolved present.

Hamletian Relations

If *Karmayogi, Haider* and *Hemanta* test regional questions via adaptations of 'To be, or not to be', then they also realize the protagonist's immersion in his location in terms of personal relations – with lovers, mothers and friends. Each film prioritizes a different intimate connection, thereby pointing up what becomes regionally significant in heterosexual, homo-erotic and Oedipal scenarios. In *Karmayogi*, Rudran/Hamlet rises above his surroundings in his moral blamelessness, and this extends to his relationship with Moonumani/Ophelia (Nithya Menon) who balks at her lover's change in manner, his penitent course of action appearing to her a kind of 'antic disposition' (1.5.170): 'Why is your appearance like this?', she asks. Her distress is registered multiply (a moment of mourning before broken religious icons, the torching of her living quarters), heightening a deteriorating condition that culminates in an appropriation of the *sati* ritual. The film stresses a tragically loaded connection between Rudran/Hamlet and Moonumani/Ophelia through suggestive costuming decisions. The flaming oranges and reds of worn by Moonumani/Ophelia are predictive; similarly, when she appears later in ill-fitting pale purples and pinks, her weakening psychological grasp is highlighted.[50] Paralleling the appearances of Rudran/Hamlet's yogic oneness, then, is the corresponding visualization of Moonumani/Ophelia's disintegration.

The underpinning logic of the Rudran/Hamlet and Moonumani/Ophelia relationship is a romantically eroticized one, and this is captured in the sequence in which they dance by a waterfall to a background score. Sangita Gopal and Biswarup Sen argue that such 'song-dance' numbers posit 'exterior and interior scenarios of modernity that the narrative is unable to depict', envision 'ways of acting and behaving not coded into the text' and afford 'the possibility of *jouissance* or joyous release that cannot be spoken by any character or voice'.[51] Usually shot against barred windows, Moonumani/Ophelia at this moment is permitted just such 'release'. The song, 'O moon-faced darling, come hither', comprises a male and female voice which sound separately and in unison, but, significantly, it is the female voice that inaugurates and closes the whole. As the lyrics suggest, Moonumani/Ophelia's invitation is accepted and acted upon, allusions to 'desire', the abandonment of the night's 'silk dress' and being 'tired from love-play' reinforcing the notion of a shared *jouissance*. Foregrounding the adaptive approach, the dancing bodies are lensed against the verdant green forests characteristic of northern Kerala, the sequence shifting in the second half to a ruined temple complex. Here, the focus on the Dravidian architecture – soaring *gopurams* (towers), inner shrines, steep steps and sacred motifs – suggests both that the Rudran/Hamlet and Moonumani/Ophelia union is blessed and that their love-making has epic correlatives. Particularly expressive are the ways in which Rudran/Hamlet and Moonumani/Ophelia assume, through doubled blocking and interlocking arm movements, the classic pose of Ardhanarisvara, the hermaphroditic combined form of Shiva and his consort, Parvati, and an emblem of the melding of male and female energies. The effect is to highlight a moment of synergy, which is bounded by physical pleasure, the lovers inhabiting the same sphere. Cross-cutting is thematically resonant, too, with the camera alternating between establishing shots of Rudran/Hamlet and Moonumani/Ophelia and bas-relief carvings of Shiva and Parvati in the rocks and temple walls (these are referenced in the lyrics). In this way, nature and artifice, and overlapping modes of being, are harmonized in the structures and choreographies of a localized experience.

In interview, Vishal Bhardwaj confesses that making *Haider* afforded the opportunity to 'look for [his] roots . . . I feel homeless at times', and, in *Haider*, the emphasis is on homes that are lost. 'What is a home? . . . What is a house?', Ghazala/Gertrude (Tabu) asks her schoolgirls in an opening scene that is echoed in Khurram/Claudius' (Kay Kay Menon) welcoming remarks to Haider/Hamlet: 'You are home'. Suggested here is the notion of 'home' as a protective, nurturing space, but *Haider* mainly shows only ruined remnants of the domestic, gaps and blown apart shells. Consistently, the film's gaze lights upon Hilal/Old Hamlet's wrecked surgery, or the gravediggers' desecrated dwelling in the Islamic graveyard, meaning that it is these ravaged reminders of 'home' that lodge in the imagination. Coding the domestic in terms of a dominant colour-scape belongs with *Haider*'s political orientation. Thus, a prevailing red – iterated in the bloody bowl cradled by Ghazala/Gertrude, the red thread she leaves as an offering at the shrine and the red muffler knitted by Arshee/Ophelia for her father – analogizes the wounded condition of the valley, the suffering of Kashmir. In Shakespeare's play, Hamlet imagines the 'distempered' Claudius as in need of 'purgation' (3.2.294, 299), and the conceit is extrapolated in *Haider* in the figure of Hilal/Old Hamlet, a doctor who, treating all patients with the same degree of care, ministers to the region's afflictions. Bringing sick militants to his 'home' or surgery under cover, Hilal/Old Hamlet is represented as putting politics before family, alienating himself from Ghazala/Gertrude in the process. The lesson that Ghazala/Gertrude learns is that family and politics cannot be so easily separated out, and this is an argument that she has, too, with Haider/Hamlet as he agitates for autonomy.

Playing a Kashmiri variant on an Oedipal tradition of interpretation, the film fills in details of Haider/Hamlet's childhood through inset recollections. These encompass the young Haider/Hamlet (Anshuman Malhotra) polishing his father's shoes (service to the patriarch), anointing his mother with perfume before a mirror (sublimating sexual pleasure by enacting the role of a lover) and crawling into bed with his parents (the three bodies forming an archetypal Oedipal triangle). A key connective is a compulsion to break with the mother's influence. Hence, in a related inset, we see the teenage Haider/Hamlet being slapped by Ghazala/Gertrude who has discovered a pistol in his bedroom. 'Going for arms training in Pakistan?' she demands. At issue here is the narrative of Haider/Hamlet growing up and achieving manhood. Such a trajectory is conveyed not through the journalist, Arshee/Ophelia, who is imagined more as friend than lover. (Her major function is to surrogate for Horatio, the only player in Shakespeare's *dramatis personae* missing from *Haider*'s cast.) Instead, the film takes the measure of Haider/Hamlet by explaining the relationship with his mother more intensely and fully than in other screen *Hamlet* adaptations – whether in a heavily veiled reception room or a *chinar* tree-lined avenue, the closet scene is played several times over, suggesting a dynamic that has to be repeatedly negotiated. Reified as substitute husband, Haider/Hamlet, it is implied, is forced into confrontations with his mother so as to reverse a pattern of arrested development.

Identifying herself as a 'half-widow' (a Kashmiri expression signifying a wife whose husband is missing or who has disappeared), Ghazala/Gertrude emerges as a figure of 'premeditated agency' wielding power 'on her own terms'.[52] For instance, in Hilal/Old Hamlet's absence, her

Figure 18: A tree-lined avenue serves as a closet scene in *Haider* (dir. Vishal Bhardwaj, 2014). Courtesy of Vishal Bhardwaj Pictures/Jaisingh Nageshwaran.

relationship with Khurran/Claudius accelerates, as reflected in increasingly confident blue and purple costuming, cosmetics and a 'hasty marriage' (2.2.57). Once the marriage founders, however, Ghazala/Gertrude joins forces with Roohdaar/the Ghost (Irrfan Khan), the ambiguous, robed figure who, bringing with him the father's demand for 'revenge', announces himself as 'the doctor's soul'.[53] And, arming herself with a body-vest of grenades, Ghazala/Gertrude declares her identification with the rebel contingent she had previously railed against. During her final encounter with Haider/Hamlet, Ghazala/Gertrude repeats to herself a mantra first articulated by his grandfather: 'Revenge begets revenge. Revenge does not set us free. Freedom lies beyond revenge. True freedom', she murmurs. Enacting a form of self-determination directed towards reversing the tide of injustice, Ghazala/Gertrude is represented as finally determined by regional politics, her *modus operandi* recalling 'suicide bombings' in Kashmir directed at military and government installations.[54] In the same moment, her renunciation of revenge brings to mind Gandhi's reflections on the dangers of retaliation, the effect of which, and notwithstanding the carnage of the conclusion, is to imbue the ending with a pacifist aspiration.[55] (This is additionally reflected in the fact that *Haider* was released in India on *Gandhi Jayanti*, a national holiday.) In *Haider*, then, Ghazala/Gertrude uses her body to announce her conversion, going from an espousal of the domestic-political divide to the very opposite belief-system. In so doing, she is figured as accommodating the son she had long resisted and enabling his own journey.

Where Oedipal mother-son relations are prioritized in *Haider*, homo-erotic affiliations take centre stage in *Hemanta*. With Gayatri/Gertrude and Olipriya/Ophelia pushed to the side-lines, the primary relationship is between film director, Hemanta/Hamlet, and journalist Hirak/Horatio, who, in this adaptation, is both friend and half-brother, having been raised by Ananta Sen/the Ghost as ward. In this sense, *Hemanta* makes manifest Hamlet's paean to Horatio, 'I will wear [you] / In my heart's core' (3.2. 68–9). But, while the Hemanta/Hamlet and Hirak/Horatio relationship is platonic, Hirak/Horatio and Yuri/Yorick (Subhra Sourav), a young Bengali Christian, are lovers, meaning that the three are intimately allied, entangled in a nexus of – sometimes sublimated, sometimes open – sexual energies and rivalries. Despite the 'Rainbow Pride Walk' and the 'Dialogues' film festival, established in 1999 and 2006 respectively, there is no real LGBTQ culture in contemporary Kolkata, mirroring, arguably, the Indian Supreme Court's decision of 2013 overruling the decriminaliz-ing of homosexuality.[56] Backlashes and expressions of hostility have driven expressions of male-on-male desire in Kolkata to the edges of the urban scene.[57] Media representations have followed suit, Thomas Waugh writing that, in a 'tightening political atmosphere', Bengali-language cinema demonstrates an 'avoidance pattern with regard to explicit same-sex dis-courses and identities' and camouflages 'homoeroticism in particular'.[58] In this context, *Hemanta* represents a cinematic 'first' in its figuration of Yuri/Yorick, a queer 'computer hacker' who uses his skills (or 'fancy' [5.1.175]) to identify corruption and malpractice. Suiting a drug-raddled covert investigator who delves into dark places to uncover buried evidence, Yuri/Yorick is defined through typologies of counter-cultural energy that refract his stigmatization, including (to judge from the images decorating the green walls of his rooms), the Dalai Lama, Bob Marley, the Velvet Underground's Lou Reed and, as the Joker, Heath Ledger. The picture/poster montage localizes the alienated and alienating situation of Yuri/Yorick's Kolkata *milieu* at the same time as it establishes an affiliation with Hemanta/Hamlet who, through filmmaking, is similarly conjoined with dissident, subversive personalities. After an argument with Hirak/Horatio, Yuri/Yorick overdoses, his body ending up in the hospital in the bed next to Hemanta/Hamlet's, who, following his fight, has lost consciousness. (Here, the 'quick and dead' [5.1.240] are juxtaposed.) Their parallel situa-tion is earlier indicated in narrowly missed meetings (in the street), in the score (sounding over sequences involving both characters, the lyric, 'Everybody knows when you say goodbye', emphasizes a connection) and in the corroborating words of the hospital nurse, Sister Dome/the gravedigger (Sudipa Bose): 'Finally, everyone will be either buried or burnt. We all have to go. Life is very short'. Her philosophy of impermanence, a key feature of Hindu thought, underwrites how Hemanta/Hamlet is imagined according to a grammar of homoerotic relationality.[59] It points up the ways in which the key players inhabit a similar urban space, and it illuminates the local and regional situatedness of the film's imaginative envisioning of Shakespearean sexuality.

Regional Intertextualities

In all three films, the 'play-within-the-play' is mediated through regionally based artistic praxes. Variously, poetry, performance traditions and distinct cinematic cultures are referenced in intertextual treatments of *The Mousetrap* that reverberate with indigenous imperatives, thereby complementing and furthering each film's interpretive particularity. With *Karmayogi*, the 'play-within-the-play' is staged as a *poorakkali*, a men-only festival performance that takes place in temples, includes participants as deities and is directed to Kama, the deity of love. The appropriative strategy works both to prioritize the virtues of Kerala as location (the gods are enjoined 'To see this part of the world') and to mediate Shakespearean thematics of memory. Pertinent here is the fusion in the *poorakkali* between gestures (such as foot-stamping) that echo the martial movements of *kalarippayattu* and dialogic insets that, as in the 'play-within-the-play', hark back to past events. If Hamlet uses theatre to reconstruct 'the image of a murder done' (3.2.232), then, honouring the father's injunction to 'remember', the typical *poorakkali* gives voice to the memories of the inhabitants of a mythological realm. So it is that, in this adaptation, the *poorakkali* alternates between scenes of loin-clothed dancers circling around the sacred *nilavilukku* lamp, flashbacks of Rudran/Hamlet's ghostly encounter with his father (1.5) and the equivalent murder in the orchard scene. In this sense, *Karmayogi* imagines *Hamlet*'s metatheatrical centre-piece as both psychically generative and traumatic, igniting separate and intersecting recollections. As the verbal contest between two *panikkars* (player-masters or scholar-artists) makes clear ('I was murdered . . . Who murdered you?'), the ritual also includes a *maruthukali*, a verbal competition in Sanskrit traditionally centred on the demonstration of scriptural knowledge but here recast as an exercise in the exposure of guilt. Thus, within the context of a departure from localized convention, Bhairavan/ Claudius' objections are revealing: he storms out, branding the performance generically anomalous: 'Stop it! Do you call this *poorakkali*? Get lost!'[60]

Similarly, *Haider*'s realization of the play-within-the-play (the 'Bismil' number) bristles with local detailing. For example, the critical marshalling of place-names in the song lyrics (the Jhelum river and Kashmir itself) chimes with the ways in which, in Kashmiri folk theatre (known as *bhand pather*), 'satire and mimicry' are crucial components.[61] As in *bhand pather*, 'Bismil' exploits the punitive power of 'masks . . . dance, drama, mime, puppetry and music', spinning an interwoven narrative in which a falcon-devil (the two-faced puppet suggests a 'smiling damned villain' [1.5.106]) invades the 'palace' of a 'simple . . . nightingale', consigning the bird to a 'watery grave'.[62] The lyrics play a variation on some of the film's dominant images (the 'nightingale' that lends its name to the Indian army's counter-operations and the river that, once 'saline', is now red with the blood of the 'disappeared'), thereby bringing to a head a series of key political signifiers. 'Bismil' deploys a folktale discourse that recalls moments of the film's soundscape as signature features of its regional landscape.

In *Hemanta*, the 'play-within-the-play' is not a performance as such; rather, Hemanta/Hamlet repeatedly directs portions of a short film (*Protisodh/Revenge*) designed to reveal his uncle's villainy. Tellingly, this film-in-process combines references to 'our Bengal film industry' and Bengali film collectives (such as 'Agragami'). Anchoring things in the particular is the way in which Hemanta/Hamlet crafts a work characterized by symbolic lighting and neo-realist effects in the tradition of Bengali 'parallel cinema'. The imitation is critically purposeful. Crucially, Kalyan/Claudius' predilection for 'copying South Indian films to make money' deepens and reinforces the malaise afflicting 'Agradoot': awash with 'lousy remakes', the studio, it is implied, has lost its sense of proper purpose. Cigar-chewing, linen-shirted and expensively perfumed, Kalyan/Claudius defends his imitative practice, holding up Martin Scorsese as a perfect example of a director who 'cheats', an attitude that is parodied in the slogan emblazoned on Lalit/Laertes' T-shirt, 'Don't copy my attitude: it's my copyright'. *Protisodh/Revenge*, then, shows Hemanta/Hamlet agitating to bring down Kalyan/Claudius by playing his own game. He is represented as taking up the 'remake' so as to react against what it signifies, working in the style of his Bengali cinematic forbears to arraign the industry for its artistic – and moral – derelictions.

Figure 19: Kalyan/Claudius (Saswata Chatterjee) and Gayatri/Gertrude (Gargi Roy Chowdhury) express discomfort in *Hemanta* (dir. Anjan Dutt, 2016). Courtesy of Green Touch Entertainment/Lundia Group.

By contrast, *Haider* and *Karmayogi* depend, for their localized effects, on a variety of poetic – rather than filmic – registers. It is poetry, in the form of extracts from the songs of sixteenth-century female Kashmiri mystic, Habba Khatoon, that underpins the scenes of Arshee/Ophelia's madness in *Haider*, this regional analogue foregrounding the Sufi poetess' fabled experiences of separation, suffering, renunciation and loss.[63] *Hamlet* is enfolded into a construction of Kashmiri history via the connection, with comparable literary figures, and historical junctures, intertextually speaking to each other. *Karmayogi*'s poetic intertexts are also historically suggestive. Overlaying the scene in which Rudran/Hamlet lies supine on the sepulchre is the accompanying Malayalam lullaby, '*Omanathinkal Kidavo*', with its questioning lyrics ('Are you an offspring of the moon? Or a beautiful lotus?'). '*Omanathinkal Kidavo*' was composed in celebration of the birth of Maharajah Swathi Thirunal of Travancore in 1813, a key event in the South Indian region as it enabled the royal house to avoid the British annexation of its powers and territories in the absence of a male heir.[64] Germane here is the comment of an official towards the start that, were it not for the custom of remarriage, the house of Chathoth 'would get ruined'. *Karmayogi* demonstrates its investment in a region-oriented undertaking by repurposing a well-known Malayalam lullaby, suggesting vernacular expressions of a resistance to incorporation and post-colonial assertions of Keralan statehood.

Hemanta does not depend on the poet, but it does subscribe to the significance of the artist-filmmaker, who is reified as embodying values and meanings with regional currency. In the movie memorabilia on display in Olipriya/Ophelia's creamy-yellow rooms, Bengali film director Satyajit Ray, who came to international attention with his Apu trilogy (1950–59), is privileged – his likeness hovers over the proceedings like a benevolent god, and his association with 'social conscience' films marks him out as the embodiment of an empathetic creativity. As Sharmistha Gooptu writes, 'Ray . . . had a singular resonance for the Bengali cinema and its audiences', making available an 'affective domain . . . which . . . effected the Bengali sense of self'.[65] Other practitioners form part of the texture of *Hemanta* as illustrations of how film can be marshalled for critical ends. Typical is a scene in the library in which Hemanta/Hamlet is lensed for several beats against a poster of Ritwik Ghatak, a Bengali director who, according to Manishita Daas, combined 'an eclectic mix of . . . leftist critique . . . creative appropriation of Indian folklore/mythology . . . and avant-garde formalism'.[66] Operating outside of commercial networks, and destroyed by alcohol and illness, Ghatak was a fecund and doomed personality denied international exposure. Cast in this mould, Hemanta/Hamlet faces an insuperable challenge, it is implied, in his attempt to root out the rot at the heart of 'Agradoot'.

The world of cinematic sleaze is ultimately combated via Hemanta/Hamlet's combination of US models and Bengali influences (a suicidal car-crash that precipitates Kalyan/Claudius' death and his own). Typically, the climax is staged as a joke, the protagonist undertaking, as driver, his own remake of *Taxi Driver* and, in so doing, alerting an audience to the fact *Hemanta*, too, is a Shakespearean remake. A Bengali cosmopolitan, Hemanta/Hamlet finally brings together the different realms of his experience. Previously enjoined to 'take this [memory stick] . . . print it all . . . your job is to tell the truth', Hirak/Horatio is the ultimate instrument of exposure, as indicated in a *mise-en-bande* comprised of a radio broadcast spelling out the company's desperate dealings. Hirak/Horatio, departing from his Shakespearean equivalent, has done his investigative job well, allowing Yuri/Yorick's skills to shine, bringing the 'original' into full view and exercising his writerly craft to reveal the underbelly of a Kolkata that has been contaminated. The montage, which shows Hirak/Horatio in the library and in Yuri/Yorick's apartment, strikes a balance between the book and modern media, between old forms of cinema and new modes of representation. Arrestingly, the alternating between two scenarios hinges on the prioritization of male-on-male relations, the focus on Hirak/Horatio pointing up his lament for lost loves. The concluding shot is of a cracked, framed photograph of Hirak/Horatio and Yuri/Yorick together as light, for the first time, pours into the computer hacker's rooms. Previously shuttered and shadowy, like the grave, this Kolkata *habitus* is now open and illuminated.

Hemanta and *Haider* both mobilize filmmakers and poets to support an anti-hegemonic agenda. In *Haider*, the Urdu-language poetry of twentieth-century Pakistani author and poet, Faiz Ahmed Faiz, fills the soundscape; his 'life and work', writes Jyotsna G. Singh, 'reflect the political struggles for social justice following the partition of the subcontinent'.[67] His *ghazal*, 'Let the petals fill with colour ... Awake the garden to life', is first cited in flashback, this spring-themed address to a beloved functioning as a call-and-answer that bonds Haider/Hamlet to his father (the protagonist repeats lines from the poem in an affectionate paternal-filial game).[68] When we next hear the poem (Roohdaar/the Ghost cites the opening in an attempt on Haider/Hamlet's conversion), therefore, the idea is both of a continuing conversation and of a voice that sounds from beyond the grave. Urdu, writes Ananya Jahanara Kabir, is 'the language of North Indian Muslim high culture, revolution, glamour and romance ... subsequently politicized and romanticized through the exposure of Kashmiri Muslim leaders to anti-colonial, Islamist intellectualism'.[69] These associations are traced in *Haider* in a dissolve to a chained Hilal/Old Hamlet singing the *ghazal's* second verse in the detention centre (with its telling reference to 'The prison is a sullen ghost') which works to suggest a shared recital and to transition Faiz's poetry from romantic recollection to prompt to political action: Haider/Hamlet, involved by proxy, it is hinted, will be 'awakened' to his responsibilities.[70] Such a reorientation is affirmed in Hilal/Old Hamlet's simultaneous – mumbled and pained – delivery of the Faiz *nazm*, 'The Face of Thy Lord', which, with its stirring allusions to witnessing the 'promised day ... of the blessed word', introduces the prospect of divinely backed resolution and judgement.[71] If only as part of an as yet unrealized scenario, the lines adumbrate an aspiration for a better order. The affirmative note continues over the closing credits. The Faiz poem, 'Dedication', sounds as a specially composed musical arrangement that, omitting verses about the repressed state of the 'office workers ... railwaymen ... tonga-wallahs ... postmen

[and] . . . call-workers', concentrates instead on the plight of 'sad mothers . . . beauties . . . brides [and] . . . widows'.[72] The change emphasizes the importance of Ghazala/Gertrude who, over the course of the film, fulfils all four roles. The lack of subtitles for the poem in internationally distributed versions of the film demonstrates the significance of the indigenous, unadulterated statement; what Faiz articulates in Urdu, it seems, is for a select grouping of listeners and interpreters.

The fittingness of the *ghazal* belies the fact that director Vishal Bhardwaj struggled with bringing *Haider* to a close. The published screenplay contains two endings, neither adopted in the film proper.[73] And, in interview, Bhardwaj testifies to a racked decision-making process. 'I was so frustrated that I asked my dear friend, Sabrina Dhawan, "What do you want me to do? Shouldn't Haider kill his uncle and walk away?"', he recollects. In the spirit of Faiz's call in 'Dedication' for recognition of the neglected constituencies of a 'homeland', he confronts the issue thanks to a layered sequence that looks backwards and forwards in Kashmiri time. With the refrains of his father ('Avenge me') and mother ('Freedom lies beyond revenge') ringing in his ears, Haider/Hamlet elects not to kill Khurram/Claudius, who has been devastatingly injured in the explosion triggered by Ghazala/Gertrude, instead leaving the blood-bestrewn, snowy cemetery. He moves towards a future that is not directly dependent on parents or the previous generation, and in this suggestion of resolution there is perhaps an echo of the scene of welcome introduced at the close of Basharat Peer's memoir, *Curfewed Night*.[74] Just as it seems that *Haider* is over, however, an on-screen announcement, mirroring the film's opening, appears: 'In the recent devastating floods in Kashmir, the Indian army saved the lives of thousands of civilians. We salute their efforts and their valour'. The statement brings things forward by almost a decade to the present-day, underscoring that the story of India's relationship to Kashmir is not necessarily confined to 1995. Here is a downplaying of familial conflict in favour of political *rapprochement*, with the vulnerability of the valley to ecological disaster taking on a shaping significance. In this context, a fourth ending, never filmed, is pertinent. As Bhardwaj intimates, he had planned for a spring-set epilogue featuring Haider/Hamlet, ten years on, teaching in the rebuilt school where his mother had also taught: 'I liked this option the most', the director notes. In spirit, the epilogue operates to recall Faiz's *ghazal* about awakening the garden (for which we may read 'homeland'). It also alerts audiences to the reverberations of familial continuity; Haider/Hamlet is represented as having finally reconciled with Ghazala/Gertrude and taken up her pedagogical vocation. The specification of spring in the epilogue replaces the wintry condition of the vale with a season that confirms a new life-cycle. In this imagining of *Haider*, we are returned to the sentiments of the garden *ghazal*'s invitation to work and industry in the realization of a protagonist conscious of, and committed to, an ongoing process of education, collaboration and development.

Conclusions

In this unique cluster of three film adaptations, we see the colonial legacy working itself out in diverse ways. Within Indian contexts, Shakespeare is freighted with a gamut of associations – educational and institutional as well as theatrical – meaning that the forms his work inhabit are inevitably wide-ranging, differently inflected and multiple. *Karmayogi, Haider* and *Hemanta* bear witness to the historical pasts that generated their possibility first in the extent to which Shakespeare works as symbolic capital. They demonstrate how far Shakespeare has come since his first Parsi theatre incarnations and showcase, in their variety, a spectrum of audiences and a remit sensitive to the vitality of continuing cultural transfer. *Karmayogi, Haider* and *Hemanta* synthesize trajectories that move between east and west and India and Europe. They demonstrate, too, energies running within and across India itself, *Hamlet* being rewardingly recast through the lens of place-specific creative praxes and shaped to speak from the past to the present.

In the ongoing trade with Shakespeare, regional agendas take pride of place. The three adaptations discussed here continually revert to their sites of making and representation. Their inventive indigeneity is reflected in the use of the epics and in mythological reference. All three adaptations inject into 'To be, or not to be' and *The Mousetrap* vernacular idioms attuned to location yet they do so distinctively. Operating thus, they point up what is to be gained in thinking about Shakespearean adaptation according to regional logics. By assessing *Hamlet* in terms of a rubrics of the region we gain a better appreciation of each film's unique mobilization of sound, sense and image. As earlier parts of this chapter have argued, critically embracing *Karmayogi, Haider* and *Hemanta* necessitates an attuned absorption in music, score, 'look', language, poetry and literary tradition, whether that comprises hymns to Shiva, a repurposing of the classic *ghazal* or a strategic focus on an urban *milieu*: we read simultaneously landscapes and soundscapes. The regional emphasis allows for gendered reflection, and in more than one way these three adaptations make visible how the dynamics of parent-son relations, or same-sex desire, are mediated through conventions and constructions forged in particular circumstances. A film such as *Hemanta*, for example, illuminates how articulating a gay subject position signifies in a Kolkata context. The common denominator shared by *Karmayogi, Haider* and *Hemanta* is a dialectic whereby the region is pitted against, or figured through, an 'other'. This may be Mumbai/Bollywood, as in *Hemanta*; it could be Assam, as *Karmayogi* evidences; it is the Indian army (and Delhi), as *Haider* intimates. The effect is to centre the region within India in terms of a geographical matrix that runs from north to south, and from west to east, with related points on the compass also being applied. Such movement and referencing open a window onto the social, cultural and political determinants animating India as a modern nation-state. This is not to suggest that these films are resistant; rather, they use regionalism to reflect on the place of particular environments within India, and within democratic processes, thereby facilitating discussion about the contributions of the different parts of India to a larger whole. The regional dialectic that underpins and informs these three *Hamlet* adaptations enables us, therefore, to think anew about a state such as Kerala, with its high literacy rates, or to cogitate the situation of Jammu/Kashmir and its current predicament. The timeliness of *Haider*'s holistic vision is all the more urgent given recent unrest in Kashmir and ongoing killings, raids and cross-border attacks.[75] To appreciate *Karmayogi, Haider* and *Hemanta* is to become versed in the subcontinent's continuities and discontinuities, its hopes and regrets, its triumphs and struggles. Pursuing a regional methodology allows us to situate Shakespeare's utility and to contextualize *Hamlet* inside a fresh constellation of Indianized habitations.

Notes

1. Poonam Trivedi, 'Introduction', in Poonam Trivedi and Dennis Bartholomeusz, eds, *India's Shakespeare: Translation, Interpretation, and Performance* (Newark: University of Delaware Press, 2005), pp. 13–14.
2. Bhaben Barua, 'Shakespeare, Indian Renaissance in Bengal, and Assamese Literature', in D. A. Shankar, ed., *Shakespeare in Indian Languages* (Shimla: Institute of Advanced Study, 1999), pp. 89, 90; Jyotsna G. Singh, *Colonial Narratives/Cultural Dialogues: 'Discoveries' of India in the Language of Colonialism* (London and New York: Routledge, 1996), p. 121.
3. Supriya Chaudhuri, 'Remembering Shakespeare in India: Colonial and Postcolonial Memory', in Clara Calvo and Coppélia Kahn, eds, *Celebrating Shakespeare: Commemoration and Cultural Memory* (Cambridge: Cambridge University Press, 2015), p. 102.

4. Thomas Babington Macaulay, 'Minute of 2 February 1835 on Indian Education', in G. M. Young, ed., *Macaulay: Prose and Poetry* (Cambridge, Mass.: Harvard University Press, 1957), p. 729.

5. Singh, *Colonial*, p. 133.

6. Chaudhuri, 'Remembering', p. 114.

7. Somnath Gupt, *The Parsi Theatre: Its Origins and Development*, tr. Kathryn Hansen (Calcutta and New Delhi: Seagull Books, 2005), p. 20; Rosie Thomas, *Bombay Before Bollywood: Film City Fantasies* (New York: SUNY Press, 2013), p. 36.

8. Vikram Singh Thakur, 'Parsi Shakespeare: The Precursor to "Bollywood" Shakespeare', in Craig Dionne and Parmita Kapadia, eds, *Bollywood Shakespeares* (New York and Basingstoke: Palgrave, 2014), pp. 28, 30, 33.

9. See Rajiva Verma, '*Hamlet* on the Hindi Screen', *Hamlet Studies*, 24 (2002), pp. 84–85.

10. Andrew Dickson, *Worlds Elsewhere: Journeys around Shakespeare's Globe* (London: Bodley Head, 2015), p. 228.

11. Esha Niyogi De, 'Modern Shakespeares in Popular Bombay Cinema: Translation, Subjection and Community', *Screen*, 43.1 (2002), pp. 31, 32.

12. The specific *ghazals* are 'No hope ever comes to fruition' and 'What is ailing thee, my simpleton heart?' See Mirza Ghālib, *Love Sonnets of Ghālib*, ed. Sarfaraz K. Niazi (New Delhi: RUPA, 2011), pp. 612, 615.

13. Bahadur Shah 'Zafar', 'I am no eye's light', in Khwaja Tariq Mahmood, ed., *Selected Poems* (New Delhi: Star Publications, 2003), p. 21; Mohammed Ibrahim Zauq, 'Commissioned by Life We Come, Commanded by Death We Go', in K. C. Kanda, ed., *Urdu Ghazals: An Anthology from 16th to 20th Century* (New Delhi: Sterling, 1995), p. 135.

14. A. L. Basham, *The Wonder That Was India*, 3rd ed. (London: Sidgwick and Jackson, 1988), pp. 435–40; *The Mahābhārata*, ed. John D. Smith (London and New York: Penguin, 2009), p. 24.

15. More extreme expressions of some of these developments took the form of territorial violence in Kashmir, Punjab and North-East India during the 1980s, 1990s and beyond, discontent offering a window onto demands for autonomy which were regionally rooted.

16. Stuart Corbridge, John Harris and Craig Jeffrey, *India Today: Economy, Politics and Society* (Cambridge and Malden: Polity, 2013), p. 18.

17. Sunil Khilnani, *The Idea of India* (London and New York: Penguin, 2012), p. 192.

18. Khilnani, *Idea*, p. 193.

19. See Craig Dionne and Parmita Kapadia, 'Shakespeare and Bollywood: The Difference a World Makes', in Dionne and Kapadia, eds, *Bollywood*, p. 7.

20. Poonam Trivedi and Paromita Chakravarti, 'Shakespeare and Indian Cinemas: "Local Habitations"', in Poonam Trivedi and Paromita Chakravarti, eds, *Shakespeare and Indian Cinemas: 'Local Habitations'* (London and New York: Routledge, 2018), p. 4.

21. Interview between V. K. Prakash and Mark Thornton Burnett (16 May 2018). Unless otherwise stated, all Prakash quotations are from this interview and appear in the text or notes.

22. Navnita Chadha Behera, *Demystifying Kashmir* (Washington, D.C.: Brookings Institution Press, 2006), pp. 1, 2.

23. Rachel Dwyer and Divia Patel, *Cinema India: The Visual Culture of Hindi Film* (London: Reaktion, 2002), pp. 60, 61. Several films, such as *Roja* (dir. Mani Ratnam, 1992) and *LOC: Kargil* (dir. J. P. Dutta, 2003), represent Kashmir's political instabilities but generally in terms of a 'distorting emplotment' and 'dominant problematics'. See Patrick Colm Hogan, *Imagining Kashmir: Emplotment and Colonialism* (Lincoln and London: University of Nebraska Press, 2016), pp. 81, 86.

24. Descriptions of 'disappeared persons', ghosts, graveyards, names and protests make their way into the *Haider* narrative. See Basharat Peer, *Curfewed Night: A Memoir of War in Kashmir* (London: HarperCollins, 2011), pp. 16, 30, 48, 63, 121, 128, 145, 149, 211, 200.

25. See Ashish Rajadhyaksha and Paul Willemen, *Encyclopaedia of Indian Cinema*, rev. ed. (New Delhi: Oxford University Press, 1999), p. 40.

26. See Singh, *Colonial*, pp. 141, 142.

27. Sharmistha Gooptu, *Bengali Cinema: 'An Other Nation'* (New York and London: Routledge, 2011), p. 6.

28. Commenting on etymology, Phillip B. Zarrilli notes that '*kalari* means "open space ... battlefield" ... *payattu* ... [means] "fencing, exercise, a trick"' (*When the Body Becomes All Eyes: Paradigms, Discourses and Practices of Power in Kalarippayattu, a South Indian Martial Art* [New Delhi: Oxford University Press, 1998], p. 25).

29. Zarrilli, *When*, pp. 23, 24.

30. See T. V. Chandran, *Ritual as Ideology: Text and Context in Teyyam* (New Delhi: Indira Gandhi National Centre for the Arts, 2006), p. 72.

31. See Theodore Gabriel, *Playing God: Belief and Ritual in the Muttappan Cult of North Malabar* (London and Oakville: Equinox, 2010), p. 5.

32. Rajnarayam Chandavarkar, *History, Culture and the Indian City* (Cambridge: Cambridge University Press, 2009), p. 104.

33. Ann R. David, 'King of Bollywood? The Construction of a Global Image in Shah Rukh Khan's Dance Choreography', in Rajinder Dudrah, Elke Mader and Bernhard Fuchs, eds, *SRK and Global Bollywood* (Oxford and New Delhi: Oxford University Press, 2015), p. 299. Khan is also referenced in a dance sequence from the film, *Maine Pyar Kiya* (dir. Sooraj Barjatya, 1989), which is imitated by the Salman brothers.

34. Women in the episode are reprehensibly treated in an orgy of *machismo* presented as courtship.

35. See Peer, *Curfewed*, p. 210.

36. Ananta Sen/the Ghost as spectral entity is embedded throughout via the semi-verse in which it text-messages (a parody of iambic pentameter), five messages evenly spaced over the course of the film.

37. Paromita Chakravarti, 'Urban Histories and Vernacular Shakespeare in Bengal: *Kolkatar Hamlet, Hemlet* and *Hamlet 2011*', in Shormishtha Panja and Babli Moitra Saraf, eds, *Performing Shakespeare in India: Exploring Indianness, Literatures and Cultures* (London and New Delhi: Sage, 2016), pp. 41–59.

38. Kushanava Choudhury, *The Epic City: The World on the Streets of Calcutta* (London and New York: Bloomsbury, 2017), p. 144.

39. Choudhury, *Epic*, pp. 144, 145.

40. Krishna Dutta, *Calcutta: A Cultural and Literary History* (Oxford: Signal, 2003), p. xv.

41. According to A. L. Basham, Shiva, 'a great ascetic', is often depicted wearing 'a garland of skulls … snakes … encircle his neck and arms … his body is covered with ashes' (*Wonder*, p. 307).

42. In *The Rāmāyana*, Rāma's heroic qualifications are reinforced when he takes 'the vow of the ascetic' and assumes 'matted hair' and 'simple clothes', while, in *The Bhagavad Gita*, the yogic practitioner who makes 'sacrifices', renunciates 'desires and acts free from longing' achieves 'insight', 'purity of spirit' and 'peace'. See Vālmīki, *The Rāmāyana*, ed. Arshia Sattar (New Delhi: Penguin, 1996), pp. 162, 165; *The Bhagavad Gita*, ed. S. Radhakrishnan (London: George Allen and Unwin, 1948), pp. 122, 126, 128, 166.

43. Alain Daniélou, *The Myths and Gods of India: The Classic Work on Hindu Polytheism* (Rochester: Inner Traditions, 1991), pp. 192, 194, 195, 197.

44. Thea Buckley, 'Hero as Avatar: *Karmayogi*, Kerala's Kalarippayattu *Hamlet*', *The Shakespeare Institute Review*, 2, Spring (2013), p. 46.

45. C. S. Venkiteswaran, 'Shakespeare in Malayalam Cinema: Cultural and Mythic Interface, Narrative Negotiations', in Trivedi and Chakravarti, eds, *Shakespeare*, p. 89.

46. Basham, *Wonder*, p. 307.

47. Rachel Storm, *Myths and Legends of India, Egypt, China and Japan* (Wigston: Anness, 2011), pp. 156–57.

48. Brian Walsh, 'Resisting Hamlet: Revenge and Nonviolent Struggle in Vishal Bhardwaj's *Haider*', *Literature/Film Quarterly*, 46.2 (2018), p. 6.

49. Interview between Vishal Bhardwaj and Mark Thornton Burnett (30 April 2016). Unless otherwise stated, all Bhardwaj quotations are from this interview and appear in the text.

50. As director V. K. Prakash observes, the design reflected an aim 'to communicate the thin line between reality and fantasy' (interview between V. K. Prakash and Mark Thornton Burnett [16 May 2018]).

51. Sangita Gopal and Biswarup Sen, 'Inside and Out: Song and Dance in Bollywood Cinema', in Rajinder Dudrah and Jigna Desai, eds, *The Bollywood Reader* (Maidenhead and New York: Open University Press/McGraw-Hill, 2008), p. 147.

52. Paromita Chakravarti, 'Theatre Reviews: *Haider*', *Shakespeare Bulletin*, 34.1 (2016), p. 131.

53. When Roohdaar/the Ghost states, 'I always was … I am … I always will be', the appropriation of Krishna's counsel in *The Bhagavad Gita* ('I know the

beings that are past, that are present ... and that are to come'), sounds a warning note. See *Gita*, p. 224.

54. Suba Chandran, 'The First Suicide Bomb in Kashmir', *IPCS: Institute of Peace and Conflict Studies*, 11 May 2000, www.ipcs.org/focusthemsel (accessed 27 July 2018).

55. Mahatma Gandhi, *The Writings of Gandhi*, ed. Ronald Duncan (London: Fontana/Collins, 1983), p. 54.

56. Homosexuality was only finally decriminalized in India in 2018. See Michael Safi, '"A Great First Step": Elation in India after Gay sex is Legalized', *The Guardian*, 7 September (2018), p. 27.

57. Shaminder Dulai, 'Back in the Shadows: The Perils of Being LGBT in India', *Newsweek*, 29 December 2014, www.newsweek.com/india-gay-lgbt (accessed 20 July 2018).

58. Thomas Waugh, '"I Sleep Behind You": Male Homosociality and Homoeroticism in Indian Parallel Cinema', in Ruth Vanita, ed., *Queering India: Same-Sex Love and Eroticism in Indian Culture and Society* (London and New York: Routledge, 2002), p. 193.

59. See Richard King, *Indian Philosophy: An Introduction to Hindu and Buddhist Thought* (Edinburgh: Edinburgh University Press, 1999), p. 117.

60. There may also be a caste implication. *Karmayogi* establishes Bhairavan/ Claudius as a Brahmin, while, as K. K. N. Kurup writes, *panikkars* tradition- ally belonged to the 'lower castes' (*Poorakkali and Maruthukali: A Performance of Male Dancers in the Bhagavati Temples of Malabar* [New Delhi: National Mission for Manuscripts, 2017], p. 4).

61. See Mohan Lal Aima, 'Kashmiri Drama', in K. L. Kalla, ed., *The Literary Heritage of Kashmir* (Delhi: Mittal Publications, 1985), p. 117.

62. See Sushma Jatoo and Sudhir Lall, 'Introduction', in Sushma Jatoo and Sudhir Lall, eds, *Bhand Pather: The Folk Theatre of Kashmir* (Delhi: B. R. Publishing, 2016), pp. 3, 4.

63. See Vishal Bhardwaj, with Basharat Peer, *'Haider': The Original Screenplay* (New Delhi: HarperCollins, 2014), p. 193; Ananya Jahanara Kabir, *Territory of Desire: Representing the Valley of Kashmir* (Minneapolis and London: University of Minnesota Press, 2009), pp. 51, 190; S. N. Vakhlu, 'The Nightingale of Kashmir (Habba Khatoon: Her Life and Work)', in Kalla, ed., *Kashmir*, pp. 198–208.

64. A. H. Fox Strangways, *The Music of Hindostan* (Oxford: Clarendon, 1914), pp. 62–63.

65. Gooptu, *Bengali*, p. 139.

66. Manishita Daas, 'The Cloud-Capped Star: Ritwik Ghatak on the Horizon of Global Art Cinema', in Rosalind Galt and Karl Schoonover, eds, *Global Art Cinema: New Theories and Histories* (Oxford: Oxford University Press, 2010), p. 240.

67. Jyotsna G. Singh, 'Introduction', in Jyotsna G. Singh and David D. Kim, eds, *The Postcolonial World* (London and New York: Routledge, 2017), p. 25. For a rich discussion of the place of Faiz's poetry in *Haider*, see Jyotsna G. Singh,

Shakespeare and Postcolonial Theory (London and New York: Bloomsbury, 2019), pp. 177–94.

68. See Faiz Ahmed Faiz, *The Rebel's Silhouette: Selected Poems*, tr. Agha Shahid Ali (Amherst: University of Massachusetts Press, 1995), pp. 35–37.

69. Kabir, *Territory*, p. 140.

70. 'Let the petals fill with colour' was written in 1951–55 while Faiz was imprisoned, having been accused of a plotting a coup against the Pakistani government (Ralph Russell, *The Pursuit of Urdu Literature: A Select History* [London and New Jersey: Zed Books, 1992], p. 242).

71. See Ali Madeeh Hashmi, *The Way It Once Was: Faiz Ahmed Faiz – His Life, His Poems* (New Delhi: HarperCollins, 2012), pp. 199–201. The *nazm*, written in 1979, draws on the Qur'an's description of the Day of Reckoning to criticize Muhammad Zia-ul-Haq, President of Pakistan.

72. Ali Madeeh Hashmi, *Love and Revolution: Faiz Ahmed Faiz, the Authorized Biography* (New Delhi: Rupa, 2016), p. 148. 'Dedication' was composed in the 1940s in support of the Lahore postal workers. See Hashmi, *Way*, pp. 101–3.

73. Bhardwaj, with Peer, *'Haider'*, p. 212.

74. 'There were only hands reaching out of the bus windows, waving in the air, as if each wave would erase the lines of control' (Peer, *Curfewed*, p. 221).

75. Agence Presse-France, 'Indian Forces in Kashmir Kill Top Commander of Militant group', *The Guardian*, 27 December (2017), p. 21; Jon Boone and Michael Safi, 'India Strikes Back at Pakistan with Deadly Night Raids as Kashmir Dispute Escalates', *The Guardian*, 30 September (2016), p. 19; 'Kashmir Clashes Kill 7', *The Guardian*, 10 July (2017), p. 32.

CHAPTER SIX

Gendering Borders: Hamlet *and the Cinemas of Turkey and Iran*

In discussing adaptations of *Hamlet* in Middle Eastern cinema, this chapter focuses on *İntikam Meleği/Kadin Hamlet*, or *Angel of Vengeance/Female Hamlet* (dir. Metin Erksan, 1976), from Turkey, and *Tardid/Doubt* (dir. Varuzh Karim-Masihi, 2009), from Iran. Despite the fact that these works are separated by over thirty years, shared preoccupations make it productive to read the films side-by-side. As this chapter maintains, both films draw on well-rooted Shakespearean translation and performance traditions, a process enabled by the fact that Iran and Turkey share one of the oldest borders in the Middle East. Over the course of the twentieth century, a flood of translations and stage adaptations bears witness to the popularity of Shakespeare in Turkey (his name has been linked to a modernizing process that eschews Ottoman influence in favour of a European-looking national sensibility), while, in Iran, familiarity with Shakespeare is attested to in translation, a thriving stage tradition and the everyday use of well-worn Shakespearean phrases.[1] *Hamlet* in Iran has attracted more translations into Farsi than any of Shakespeare's other works, possibly because of the ways in which the play chimes with myths about the overthrow of despotic rulers and narratives of martyrdom.[2] A complementary case is offered in Turkey where, as Savaş Arslan argues, *Hamlet* has formed part of 'a republican discourse which invariably sides with secularism and modernization against religious and conservative movements'.[3] To judge from the literary histories of Turkey and Iran, then, adapting *Hamlet* for the screen was a natural development, one that was healthily established in terms of the play's long-standing cultural position and ready recognizability.

In his absorbing study of women who have played Hamlet on stage and screen, Tony Howard notes of *İntikam Meleği* that 'To European (and many Turkish) eyes it is a bewildering cross of Shakespeare, the avant-garde, and low-budget exploitation cinema'.[4] More critically, according to Monika Seidl, the film fared ill with the 'local audience', with Turkish commentators labelling it 'curious' and 'surreal'.[5] Taking the play-within-the-play and extending it, the film constitutes a series of performance insets enacted by a female Hamlet, played by Turkish actress, Fatma Girik. (Matching the gendered complexions of the central casting, Osman/Ophelia [Ahmet Sezerel] is male.) In this adaptation, Hamlet is envisaged as the devoted daughter of wealthy, landed family; she is a professional woman and 'rich girl', to cite one character's assessment. Her privileged position in the community is attested to by her frequent changes of outfit, making her symbolic of emancipated modernity. Filmed in strident colours, chiefly bright blues and reds, and revelling in vertiginous camera work, *İntikam Meleği* replaces Elsinore with a ranch in the semi-feudal eastern Turkish backlands, with the majority of the scenes occurring externally; the importance accorded the stockade and the watchtower suggest that this is a society under siege or, at least, fearful of the threat posed by its immediate neighbours. The ranch itself is envisioned both as a vast church-like white hall with an arched ceiling and as a forest terrain; the camera's leisurely sweep over green hillsides, or pausing over sunny clearings, thus approximates early modern notions of empire via the spectacle of a rural fiefdom.

By contrast, the world of *Tardid* is a cityscape – modern Tehran – as established in shots of traffic-choked roads, palatial residences, high-walled alleyways and deserted rooftops; also filmed in colour, but with a reliance on muted, sombre shades, the film displays many of the sterling qualities of Iranian cinema, such as sharp dialogue and arresting cinematography. A creamy mansion in a wealthy suburb stands in for Elsinore. In the spirit of *İntikam Meleği*, and possibly with a nod to *Hamlet* (dir. Michael Almereyda, 2000), *Tardid* conceives of the Hamlet figure, Siavash (Bahram Radan), as a type of artist, a photojournalist whose interest in culture and representation reveals itself in the images, puppets and African masks that adorn his apartment's walls.[6] Crucially, although Siavash/Hamlet lives in the family mansion – the focus on a winding staircase and luxuriously appointed interiors is typical of the ways in which Iranian cinema details the lifestyles of elite Tehranis – the suggestion is that he has been schooled elsewhere and has recently returned to the city (suitcases litter his room), making him an outsider in the family drama that ensues. Other sites in the film include a downtown cinema undergoing restoration; the project is overseen over by the Armenian, Garo/Horatio (Hamed Komeyli), whose fearless commitment to the arts makes him and Siavash/Hamlet natural companions. Here, it is interesting that Armenian director Karim-Masihi identifies with the character and his capacity to 'see things differently'.[7] Difference also characterizes other casting choices, including that of Mahtab/Ophelia (Taraneh Alidoosti) and her disabled half-brother, Danial/Laertes (Yahya Tavassoli), a pairing that reverses *Hamlet*'s typical power dynamic. This is, rather in the manner of *İntikam Meleği*, a self-enclosed world that mirrors the claustrophobic conditions of the play, but *Tardid* is distinctive in the way in which it presents Siavash/Hamlet as slowing waking up to the fact that his life, and that of Shakespeare's Hamlet, run along parallel lines. Finding his rationalist beliefs threatened, for Siavash, the only certainty becomes the uncanny spiritual force of *Hamlet* repeating itself.

İntikam Meleği and *Tardid* are perhaps most like each other in their recasting of the play's language. *İntikam Meleği* eschews an original language translation and versification, relying, instead, on a contemporary, vernacular paraphrase. At times, however, it retains shards of the 'original dialogue', as in the play-within-the-play, and it also elects to render a substantial part of 'To be, or not to be', suggesting that, *outré* characteristics notwithstanding, the film aspires to fidelity and authenticity. As much is indicated, indeed, by the on-screen credit, 'William Shakespeare'. Where the language is missing in the film, visual motifs suffice, as in the robe patterned with skulls, referencing Yorick, in which Hamlet presents herself during the play-within-the play. *Tardid* demonstrates a like strategy, offering visual clues that recall the precursor text (Siavash/Hamlet's table is also decorated with that archetypal skull) and elaborating echoes (Horatio's 'Goodnight, sweet prince' [5.2.343] appears in attenuated form in the characterization of the protagonist as a 'lost prince') that invite us to ponder both the presence of the play and the pressures it exerts. A number of speeches – the Ghost's confession to Hamlet, the 'providence in the fall of a sparrow' (5.2.197–98) speech and 'To be, or not to be' – feature intact, illuminating how *Tardid* mediates Hamletian language, like *İntikam Meleği,* through a complex network of reproduction, suggestion and allusion.

Language choices, this chapter argues, are politically inflected. *İntikam Meleği* emerges from, even as it intervenes in, the turbulence of its times. The 1971 military coup in Turkey heralded a period characterized by impositions of martial law, escalating terrorism, collapsed coalitions, a failure to form a government, a war with Cyprus and a rising tide of violence; as this chapter argues, the film is responsive to its conditions of production in the ways in which it deploys types of performance art to pass satirical comment.[8] During a decade that bore witness to what Kevin Robins and Asu Aksoy have described as a 'progressive disordering of the ideal of the ... nation', there were thousands of deaths resulting from conflicts between Islamists and left- and right-wing organizations, to the extent that, when the military staged another coup in 1980, the takeover was greeted with popular relief.[9] Subsequent to the Revolution of 1978, and the assumption of power by the Ayatollah in 1979, Iran has been overtaken by changes no less far-reaching in import: a war with Iraq, tensions with the USA and largely unsuccessful efforts at political reform. As recent history implies, Iran, as a nation-state, is still caught in the process of finding the appropriate social and political balance in the wake of the Revolution's 'populist and anti-imperialist' aspirations.[10] From 2009 to 2010, Iranian cities were shaken by a series of violent protests objecting to irregularities in the presidential elections. Labelled the 'Green Movement', these protests constituted not only a demand for improved citizens' rights but also for women to be treated with greater equity and, as such, represented a 'defiance', in Fatemeh Sadeghi's words, of 'the systematic gender discrimination of the post-revolutionary Islamic apparatus'.[11] Poised on the cusp of the electoral discontent, *Tardid*, this chapter suggests, is distinctive for debating women's roles inside a constraining system, and, in so doing, makes a contribution to larger questions about national self-determination.

'Every [Iranian] art-house film', writes Hamid Naficy, 'is not only about its ostensible topic but also about cinema'.[12] During the Revolution, cinema was perceived as a sign of the decadence of the Shah's regime, with more than 180 cinemas having been destroyed nation-wide by the time the Ayatollah assumed power. Most famously, in August, 1978, the Rex Cinema in Abadan was burned to the ground by radicals, killing over 400 spectators in the process.[13] In the immediate wake of the Revolution, production arrangements were dismantled and scores of filmmakers and actors exiled, resulting in a general dearth of creativity.[14] *Tardid* makes the period an integral part of its subject matter, not least in the ways in which the cinema, which Garo/Horatio restores, is imaged as a wreck: broken chairs litter the foyer, smashed fittings are everywhere apparent, defaced lobby cards adorn the exterior and loose beams endanger the workers. On the one hand, Garo/Horatio and Siavash/Hamlet are represented as conservationists in their will to preserve cinema as an art; on the other, they are conceived of as embodying the energies that have brought about a cinematic revival. Thanks to state investment in local companies, the establishment of co-production partnerships and a relaxation of regulations, Iranian cinema revived from the mid-1980s onwards; as a result, even though there is still a general lack of exhibition spaces, there currently obtains a thriving national film industry that has garnered international recognition and acclaim.[15] As part of its reconfiguration of *Hamlet*, this chapter suggests, *Tardid* reflects upon the changing political landscape within which cinematic representation has been both adversely affected and productively enabled.

When *İntikam Meleği* was made in the mid-1970s, the heyday of Turkish cinema – the so-called 'golden age' of the 1960s and the 1970s – was coming to an end.[16] *Yeşilçam* cinema, named after the district in Istanbul where a number of studios and production facilities were located, defined a prosperous industry which included popular melodramas and 'social realist' filmmaking traditions.[17] *İntikam Meleği* was made on the eve of the decline of *Yeşilçam* and the advent of a new style of cinema devoted to women's issues and the use of women, in Ahmet Gürata's words, to symbolize the 'clash between modern and traditional values'.[18] Turkish cinema is historically positioned in 'a triangular relationship with both the US and Europe' and, as this chapter argues, *İntikam Meleği* elaborates its characterization of a female Hamlet by consistently invoking cultural markers from beyond its own borders.[19] Adapting Shakespeare in such a fashion, *İntikam Meleği* reveals itself as sensitive to, in Dimitris Eleftheriotis' formulation, 'the profoundly ambivalent relationship between Turkish and western identities'.[20] Crafting *İntikam Meleği* from a range of histories, sources, influences and tendencies, director Metin Erksan uses Shakespeare to look back upon a local film industry and its implication in debates around national identity.

Both directors came to their filmic undertakings with differing degrees of experience. Exemplary works by Erksan, 'the first auteur of Turkish cinema', are 'social realist' films such as *Revenge of the Snakes* (1962) and *A Dry Summer* (1963), which centre on a visceral discovery of the harshness of rural peasant life; the latter received the Golden Bear Award at the Berlin International Film Festival.[21] Although there are some overlapping pre-occupations with these earlier productions, *İntikam Meleği* does not readily bear the 'social realist' stamp; rather, emerging from a period in which the director had turned to purely commercial cinema, the film constitutes a unique 'art-house' statement, perhaps a factor in the poor reception it was accorded on release. By contrast, Varuzh Karim-Masihi is known for only one other full-length feature prior to *Tardid, Parde-ye Akhar/The Last Act* (1991), which concerns a frustrated actor's attempts to secure his sister-in-law's inheritance.[22] The film anticipates many of *Tardid*'s comparable characteristics, not least its deployment of a play-within-the-play and metatheatrical motifs. While the film garnered awards for the director in

Iran, it did not herald a period of artistic productivity or commercial success. Karim-Masihi's output, it might be suggested, has been shaped by fluctuating support for the arts in post-revolutionary Iran, and in the interval that separates *Tardid* from *The Last Act* might be glimpsed both a repression of local cinema and the gradual process of its rehabilitation.

This chapter is divided into two interrelated sections. The first section argues that *İntikam Meleği* and *Tardid* are distinguished by elaborating different constructions of the Old Hamlet/Ghost figure, which is foregrounded in such a way as to address ideas about the execution of justice, the mission of the Hamletian protagonist and the status of the image. As discussion suggests, by purposefully reworking key debates sparked by the play, the films show themselves as acutely self-conscious, whether this reveals itself in *Tardid*'s concern with *Hamlet* as a drama from the past whose action recurs in the present or in *İntikam Meleği*'s surrealist recreations of famous Shakespearean moments. Acknowledging the adaptive process entails a corresponding focus on issues of performance. In the second section, I unpick the political valences of both films' immersion in performance idioms, identifying the significations of the play-within-the-play in *İntikam Meleği* and the coded ways in which metaphors of water in *Tardid*, and Siavash/Hamlet's photojournalism, intimate resistant ideologies. Even as *İntikam Meleği* and *Tardid* conjure expectations about the trajectory of the play, I maintain, they also subject them to scrutiny and reversal. This is nowhere more obvious than in both films' privileging, via casting or rewriting, of women's roles: *İntikam Meleği*'s dynamic female Hamlet, for example, is matched by an equivalently pro-active Mahtab/Ophelia in *Tardid*, who is granted an agency beyond the constrictions of her Shakespearean equivalent.[23] And, even as women's roles are being extended or invented, the Hamlet figure at the centre of both films is reconceived, with a particular emphasis falling on split and bifurcated conditions. Purposefully forestalling the deaths of the protagonists, the chapter contends, *İntikam Meleği* and *Tardid* reify their respective Hamlets as wounded icons, continuing the notion of a divided self and voicing mixed hopes for future reconstitution and reform.

Fathers, Traditions, Adaptation

Immediately apparent in *Kadin Hamlet*, the title of *İntikam Meleği* reserved for international distribution, is the idea of a gendered reversal, one that originates in a long-standing tradition of female Hamlets on the twentieth-century Turkish stage.[24] By casting actress Fatma Girik in the central role,

Erksan was also able to draw on a wealth of intertextual resonances. Known as *Erkek Fatma* or the 'Male Fatma' (a term which approximates not so much masculinity as straightforwardness), Girik made her name playing earthy, strong-willed peasant women battling with adversity.[25] Most at home in – and associated with – *Yeşilçam* melodrama and that genre's absorption in familial issues of 'infidelity, revenge and honour', Girik easily donned the mantle of a Shakespearean protagonist realized in comparably bold terms.[26] By the time she came to Hamlet, Girik was at the height of her powers; her co-production credit on the film suggests that, as a woman, she was able to materially invest in the production. That a female Hamlet is the film's conceptual point is made clear in the opening credit sequence, which shows a series of close-up stills of the protagonist playing a variety of parts – conductor of an orchestra, dramaturge and wounded victim – the effect of which is simultaneously to underscore Girik's centrality, an illusion of Shakespearean interiority and the cycle of violence and retribution which determines the action. In interview, Erksan notes that the idea for the film came from his reading of François de Belleforest and, in particular, the tale of a daughter delivered to Gertrude brought up as a son.[27] Certainly, Hamlet appears in *İntikam Meleği* in a transsexual guise; Girik's long dark hair, and strikingly lashed blue eyes, establish her as female, while her attire suggests male. Costume changes and filmic properties underscore the cross-gender motif, as when Hamlet smokes a cigar with phallic insouciance, for all the world like a Turkish roaring girl. Simultaneously in *İntikam Meleği*, costumes sound Shakespearean notes. Hamlet's black suit at the start, for instance, brings the 'nighted colour' (1.2.68) of the Shakespearean protagonist's funereal garments to mind, while, in the scene where she meets the female Rezzan/Rosencrantz and Gul/Guildenstern, she appears dressed as a convict in a material manifestation of the play's prison metaphor. *İntikam Meleği* both references critical readings of a 'feminized . . . man', therefore, and inverts the notion, in James W. Stone's words, that the Shakespearean protagonist's 'tragedy lies in his having to expel the woman in himself in order to take manly action and to re-establish sexual difference'.[28]

Imagined in this way, *İntikam Meleği* establishes itself as a narrative centred on the *gendered* execution of justice; as such, it works largely to bypass the questions that haunt the protagonist in the text. The fact that the action is inaugurated with the murder of Ahmet/Old Hamlet, who is mercilessly gunned down in the forest by his rifle-wielding brother, Kasim/Claudius (Reha Yurdakul), means that there can be no debate about the Ghost's claim that the uncle is culpable. Meanwhile, a shot from Ahmet/

Old Hamlet's posthumous point of view as the coffin is lowered into the ground confirms the vengeful role that, as a daughter impersonating a son, Hamlet has been enjoined to execute. And honouring the 'dear father' (1.5.23) is envisaged as a task that is both heroic and historically resonant. Thus, before his death, Ahmet/Old Hamlet is represented as a frontiersman (complete with cartridge belt and cowboy hat) exploring the wilderness, suggesting the codes of the Western and the myth of an epic journey. In his spectral incarnation, Ahmet/Old Hamlet enters in a black cape to deliver his injunctions in an echoing baritone, all of which stresses his other-worldliness. Throughout, indeed, Ahmet/Old Hamlet seems a construction from another era. A flute refrain (traditional Anatolian *ney* music) is heard during his funeral, while the booming, orchestral accompaniment reserved for the encounter with Hamlet is taken from Dmitri Shostakovich's score for Grigori Kozintsev's 1964 Russian film adaptation of the play, a quintessentially classic soundtrack endowing the Ghost with a suitably august stature. Both the romantic reification of Ahmet/Old Hamlet, and the retrospective mode of his representation, point up the film's nostalgia, in Tony Howard's eloquent phrase, for a 'Herculean Father', namely, 'Mustafa Kemal, who founded the modern Turkish state by military force ... took the name of Atatürk – "Father of Turkey" – [and] was systematically mythicized after his death'.[29] To avenge the father in *İntikam Meleği*, then, is both to rectify a present injustice and, given the associations that gather about Ahmet/Old Hamlet, to hark back to republican ideals. In the place of an ennobled father figure, the film posits the corpulent and bushy-bearded Kasim/Claudius, a landlord whose hypocrisy is discovered not only through camera work (a jump-cut from his grieving countenance to his laughing mouth stresses his dissimulating ways, an interpretive effect emphasized by the use of a distorting fish-eye lens) but also, as with Ahmet/Old Hamlet, via the score. The music to which he is linked is that of European disco, a genre associated with bland and empty contemporaneity.[30] Adumbrated in the vacuity of the music is a betrayal that signals a new era of shallow modernity.

Tardid offers a contrasting perspective on its equivalent father figures and muddies rather than clarifies the issue of Siavash/Hamlet's central mission. 'I'm full of doubt', Siavash/Hamlet states early on, continuing, later, 'I've never been very good at making decisions'. In this sense, he is elaborated as manifesting in his behaviour and thinking the multiple meanings enshrined in the film's title. For *tardid*, the noun, translates as both 'doubt' and 'hesitation', while a cognate term, *taraddod*, signifies 'perplexity' and 'confusion'.[31] Director Karim-Masihi, rationalizing his attraction to the play, admits that he has 'always found Hamlet's indecisiveness – his wavering – fascinating'. And immediate access to this conflicted state of mind is provided via the opening sequence, which, when set alongside İntikam Meleği, appears all the more distinctive for blurring Shakespearean 'delight and dole' (1.2.13). In the play, Hamlet reflects ironically on how 'the funeral baked meats / Did coldly furnish forth the marriage tables' (1.2.179–80), and, in *Tardid*, it is precisely such an unseemly proximity of occasions that strikes the dominant note, as the camera, tracking from left to right across the walls of a village, reveals bearers carrying a coffin, scarlet-draped women holding aloft blank photograph frames, clapping onlookers, swaying participants and, in the middle, Siavash attempting to take photographs. The whole suggests a textually-rooted amalgam of activities (wedding, funeral and exorcism), with the frenzied rhythms of an incantation sung by seated musicians underscoring a sense of disorientation. It is only when, in a rapid cut, Siavash/Hamlet wakes up that we realize that the montage has been a dream, a nightmare induced by the collision of the father's death and Roozbehan/Claudius (Ali Reza Shoja-Nuri) and Mah Tal'at/Gertrude's (Atash Garakani) imminent marriage. Marjorie Garber discusses Shakespearean dreams as 'fundamentally psychological' phenomena that mix 'canons of experience', revealing 'character' and permitting 'speculation, insight, and self-delusion', and her summary aptly captures the complexions both of the film's inauguration and Siavash/Hamlet's troubled imagination.[32]

The dream sequence also launches the film on a supernatural trajectory. From the crowd rises an angry, loose-haired, wild-eyed and bearded figure – Father 'Baba' or a ghostly visitation (Anoshirvan Arjomand) – who points at Siavash/Hamlet with an accusatory finger. The identification of the figure as the play's 'spirit of health or goblin damned' (1.4.40) is made explicit half-way through the action when Siavash/Hamlet, summoned by his friends, Yassin and Calif, versions of Bernardo and Marcellus, to a seedy downtown hotel, is told that their religious ceremonies are 'haunted' by a strange force, a 'genie, a human being or the wind'. What ensues equates with 1.1 and 1.4, as, despite rationalist objections, Siavash/Hamlet reluctantly participates in his friends' ceremonials. His initially sceptical stance is revealed as inadequate when, via a trance, Siavash/Hamlet finds himself returned to the village of his nightmare and confronted by the same musicians and clapping onlookers. Here, he is again faced with the angry, bearded figure of the opening, who this time exclaims, 'I'm your father . . . I didn't commit suicide! I was killed!', the revelation confirming

Figure 20: Father 'Baba' (Anoshirvan Arjomand) exerts his influence in *Tardid/ Doubt* (dir. Varuzh Karim-Masihi, 2009). Courtesy of Varuzh Karim-Masihi.

the Ghost's identity and Siavash/Hamlet's 'prophetic soul' (1.5.40). In keeping with local spiritual conventions, the force speaks not as a spectral entity but through Calif/Marcellus' body, making of the encounter a *zār* or spirit possession ritual.[33] Director Karim-Masihi cites these rituals, 'which are still very much alive in parts of Iran's southern provinces [such as] Baluchestan', as a direct inspiration. Creatively deployed, the *zār* ritual transposes the idea of a 'spirit, / Doomed . . . to walk the night' (1.5. 9–10), interweaving dreams with demonic possession, placing the Ghost in a recognizable community context and underlining doubts about the deceased father's status and intentions.

Where *İntikam Meleği* ennobles the father, *Tardid* subjects him to ambiguation. Various claims about the father's death circulate in the film – that Hemmatollah/Old Hamlet was unfaithful, that he paid to have the jealous husband of his mistress murdered, that he was involved in extortion and the drug trade, and that he committed suicide because his crimes were on the point of being exposed. If *Hamlet* begins the process of interrogating the high regard in which the son holds his father, *Tardid* completes the trajectory, offering a multiply critical elaboration of Hemmatollah/Old Hamlet, which in turn introduces additional questions touching upon guilt, accountability, agency and justice.[34] Deepening its anti-romantic notes still further is that fact that all claims made about the father emanate from untrustworthy sources such as Ansari/Polonius (Mohamad Motie) and Roozbehan/Claudius: double-dealing and venality are common denominators. An audience is denied firm vantage-points from which to adjudicate, with Siavash/Hamlet's own confusion thereby becoming a shared experience. As the film progresses, its slow-drip method of releasing truths means that the questions surrounding Hemmatollah/Old Hamlet's death are only answered at the close, a structural re-ordering of the play that makes a virtue out of delay.

At a number of levels, the image of Siavash/Hamlet's father is discovered as adulterated. Commenting on aniconism in Islamic art – the proscription against the pictorial representation of divinity, the prophets, human and animal forms – Oleg Grabar notes that, traditionally, 'all aesthetic creativity that is tied to the material world' is judged 'a vanity and an evil'.[35] Although these principles vary hugely across the Middle Eastern world, an echo of the underlying belief system sounds in *Tardid* – in the objections of Calif/the Ghost to Siavash/Hamlet's attempt to capture on film ritualistic practices, in the despoiled state of the cinema and in the ways in which images are correspondingly foregrounded as significant sources of meaning and emotional attachment. At the most immediate level, Siavash/Hamlet is represented as using his skills as a photographer in an attempt to penetrate the mysteries at the heart of the family business, as when he creeps behind a pillar to photograph the audience watching the play-within-the-play from the mansion's balcony. Here, the idea is that the image will take precedence as a form of proof over any hoped-for verbal confession or response. But, to his disappointment, Siavash/Hamlet finds that such efforts are constantly thwarted. Crucially, the protagonist is discovered as unable to recollect his father via visual representation; Siavash/Hamlet's framed photograph of his father crashes to the ground, while Mah Tal'at/Gertrude demands that the large portrait of Hemmatollah/Old Hamlet hanging in the mansion's entrance hall be covered and removed. It is in a wry anticipation of this iconic lack that the photograph frames in the nightmare sequence are represented as empty. A more affirmative relation to the image is suggested in Siavash/Hamlet's work assisting Garo/Horatio in the cinema's restoration. At once, of course, the ruined cinema stands as an exemplar of the worst excesses of the impulses to aniconism (revenge meted out by clerical forces against the Pahlavi regime's modernizing derelictions); in the film, however, the project becomes indissoluble from Siavash/Hamlet's commitment to honouring the past. Rhodri Lewis writes that Hamlet controls 'what ... he will and won't remember' via a manipulation of 'the ... metaphors around which ... early mnemonic ... discourse was framed'; playing a variation on the idea, *Tardid* represents Siavash, with Garo/Horatio, rescuing negatives, films and photographs, thereby engaging in a resurrection of history.[36] By recovering the products of what has been, they are imagined both as dedicating themselves to the value of the image and as paying homage to the ghosts of a pre-revolutionary Iranian cultural scene.

Images are also to the fore in sensitizing audiences to internal *Hamlet* correspondences. As the narrative of *Tardid* understands it, the moment at which Siavash/Hamlet recognizes the contiguity between his own situation and that of the melancholic Dane occurs when the archivist hangs on his office wall a framed text in Farsi, the quotation being not a verse from the Qur'an, as might be expected, but the Shakespearean 'To be, or not to be' soliloquy. 'Could it be a case of brothers murdering each other?', Siavash/Hamlet wonders, the dissolve to the cinema and a light being switched on suggesting a transformative moment of illumination. In *İntikam Meleği*, 'To be, or not to be' is anticipated by Hamlet who, sporting a tuxedo and standing on a dais in a field at sunset, conducts an orchestra in a performance of the famous Shostakovich score. In a sense, the conductor role suits Hamlet well, for, throughout, she has orchestrated things according to her own imperatives. Typically, this is a surrealist performance (the musical instruments hang suspended, unplucked and unblown, from music stands), while the music itself, as revealed in a debunking shot of a tape-recorder, is pre-recorded. Even the applause is canned, suggesting both a pre-meditated arrangement on Hamlet's part and the brute realities of her isolation: there is no audience, except for a passing Osman/Ophelia, whose confused expression speaks volumes. The episode functions as a portentous prologue to a realization of 'To be, or not to be', with the bombast and grandiloquence of the Shostakovich score being deployed to pave the way for the famous soliloquy. Appropriately, then, the soliloquy is performed as a set-piece, mid-shots, close-ups and soundtrack privileging flailing arms, furious movements and a wild-eyed, high-decibel delivery. In this sense, 'To be, or not to be', as *İntikam Meleği* imagines it, takes us away from the convention of a quietly philosophizing prince. Although the first four lines remain intact, the section on sleep and dreams is excised. Instead, thanks to a carefully filleted reworking of the two questions that culminate in 'Thus conscience does make cowards of us all' (F, 3.1.83), the soliloquy is accented towards the articulation of an intolerable state of affairs. As Hamlet demands, 'Who would bear the oppressor's wrong, the proud man's contumely ... the insolence of office ... Who could bear it?' For Hamlet, these questions ring out in desperate registration of the present condition: it is not so much the option of 'not being' as the material fact of 'being' that is prioritized.

The use of the Shostakovich score in *İntikam Meleği* showcases a self-consciousness about the appropriative tradition; in featuring music from an earlier *Hamlet* film, Erksan's screen reading of the play admits of the fact that Shakespeare's tragedy is always already mediated. In this regard, *İntikam Meleği* joins with *Tardid*, both privileging a sense of their distinctive con-tributions to a continuum of reinvented Shakespeares and a series of adaptive encounters. These may be pictorial. In *Tardid*, for instance, a horizontal wipe shows Siavash/Hamlet, on the cinema's rooftop, reflecting upon the implications of the famous Sir John Everett Millais portrait of the drowned Ophelia. Or they may be cinematic. On the walls of the cinema foyer is displayed a tattered poster for *West Side Story* (dir. Jerome Robbins and Robert Wise, 1961), the musical adaptation of *Romeo and Juliet*, its presence alerting us to the fact that *Tardid*, in common with its filmic predecessor, participates in a boldly conceived reworking of a classic play. Like *İntikam Meleği* before it, *Tardid* also gravitates to Grigori Kozintsev's classic *Gamlet*. As he expounds his thesis that the events of *Hamlet* are being re-enacted, Siavash reclines on a sofa, a wide-screen shot showing, behind him, a vast poster for the film, an adaptation that, as Margaret Litvin argues, portrays a 'political Hamlet', a 'decisive and heroic figure, a fighter for justice brutally martyred by an oppressive regime'.[37] The juxtaposition of two Hamlets from different nations, cultures and periods makes for an ironic counterpoint, for *Gamlet* is the film that *Tardid* is not. Via citation, *Tardid*'s dissension from previous Shakespearean adaptations is illuminated; the film is neither a musical nor a socialist parable, and its reading of *Hamlet*, it is suggested, is to take another direction.

Performativity, Politics, Play

If *Tardid* is interested in the cultural purchase of cinema, *İntikam Meleği* is absorbed by theatre. The central external spaces in the latter film – the stockade and the watchtower – resemble raised stages and, inside these favourite haunts, Hamlet acts histrionically, suggesting that metatheatri-cality is integral to the film's conception of the character. However, it is important to recall that, when *İntikam Meleği* was released, a repressive censorship apparatus held sway: left-wing organizations were attacked, intellectuals imprisoned (academics and writers) and newspapers shut down.[38] Judged against these contexts, *İntikam Meleği*'s reification of performance appears both culturally recuperative and politically interrogative, forming part of a conceptually specific plea for the importance of the artist-intellectual.

To this end, the film embraces a series of theatrically inspired tableaux that reference the play's motifs and themes. Tony Howard argues that 'Girik's Hamlet uses performance to disconcert', but, in fact, the play-like insets that structure *İntikam Meleği* both surrogate for the protagonist's delay (they stand between the act of murder and the execution of revenge) and thematize delay as a governing principle.[39] Germane are episodes in which the Arcadian idyll of the ranch is fractured by militaristic performances characterized by cross-generic components. The first example finds its inspiration in Ophelia's report of having been surprised in her closet by Hamlet, 'with his doublet all unbraced' (2.1.75); it draws, too, on the misogynist metaphor of the 'lady' who 'paint[s] an inch thick' (5.1.182, 183). For, as Osman/Ophelia paints a picture of the forest, he is confronted by Hamlet, here dressed as a nineteenth-century bugler declaring, it is suggested, a military campaign. Distinctive is the disparity conjured by the studied contrast between Hamlet's call to action and Osman/Ophelia's passivity and stillness. Playing upon the stage uses of trumpets and alarums in early modern dramaturgy, Hamlet's assumption of the bugler role brings to mind the etymological derivation of bugle (from the Latin, *buculus*, or bullock) and, hence, ratifies the gendered switch at the film's conceptual core. The second example takes as its point of departure the Shakespearean notion of art's capacity to 'hold ... [a] mirror up to Nature' (3.2.21–22). Once again dressed as a soldier, but now a Roman centurion with a plumed helmet, Hamlet breaks in on Kasim/Claudius and Gönül/Gertrude (Sevda Ferdag), who are relaxing on hammocks. Making a mockery of the sylvan scene, Hamlet aggressively brandishes the mirror in which she demands her uncle and mother inspect their own reflections. Disturbing is the sense of temporal dislocation; Hamlet's Roman costume takes us back in history, highlighting a non-linear trajectory that indexes both a 'time' that is 'out of joint' (1.5.186) and a 'state' that is 'out of frame' (1.2.20). The taking on of different soldierly identities in these episodes, it might be suggested, brings to mind the military coups that bracketed the 1970s in Turkey. As a result, Hamlet's role-play, as much as it blurs temporal distinctions, smacks of the contemporary, lending her acts and appearance a recognizably political cast.

For *İntikam Meleği*'s Hamlet, theatre is a particularly powerful vehicle, one that can function, in Meredith Anne Skura's words, to bring to light 'a hidden evil, the unflattering truth *beneath* the surface'.[40] Each of Hamlet's performances takes as a premise critical constructions of the play's inner-outer dynamic. Interestingly, her desire to access occluded realities – she smashes the mirror she presents to Kasim/Claudius and Gönül/Gertrude because it shows only 'the exteriors of people', while she defaces Osman/Ophelia's picture in that it is concerned with the 'visible' and does not capture the 'true essence' – has a counterpart in *Ṣūfī* philosophy (an aspect of Islamic mysticism) and the tradition of, in Andrew Rippin's words, 'looking inward' as a 'goal and quest'.[41] Key to the initiate's quest, as David Waines explains, was progressing through a number of 'stations' in order to achieve 'an esoteric or inner dimension . . . the true state of the heart'.[42] Performance insets in *İntikam Meleği* suggest variations on such 'stations' and, as she moves through phases of theatricality, Hamlet's delay in meting out vengeance is accounted for; only when art has fulfilled its purpose can her father's injunctions be executed. In the light of the film's insets, the play-within-the-play becomes more openly accusatory. 'Let the guilty wince', adapted from 3.2.236, is the dominant notion in an overblown Ottoman drama in which the players appear as comic sultans and sultanas. All of *The Mousetrap*'s characters are dressed to resemble their audience equivalents, and this, along with the film's disambiguation of Ahmet/Old Hamlet's and Kasim/Claudius' roles, means that the effect is more con-frontational than investigative, with Hamlet intervening frequently and hammering points home via admonishment. Commentators such as Gülşen Sayin argue that, in the play-within-the-play, Hamlet is akin to the performers of the Turkish *tulûat* (or improvisational) drama; however, it seems more suggestive to see her as assuming the role of *Meddah* or story-teller who, in traditional Turkish theatre, as Metin And notes, 'introduced . . . stories by means of couplets or proverbs, saying that each story had a moral for those who understand'.[43] The aphoristic statements deployed by Hamlet, coupled with her explanatory comments, clarify her appropriation of the *Meddah*'s functions in such a way as to privilege female control over narrative extrapolation.

The scatological anti-masque to *The Mousetrap* – Hamlet struts up and down to Timur Selçuk's popular song, 'Bu Düzen Böyle Mi Gidecek?' or 'Is this System Going to Last for Ever?' – brings us back to a military frame of reference. As Gönül Dönmez-Colin notes, including the song 'was courageous considering the film was made in the precarious period between two military interventions'.[44] Certainly, the lyrics – 'Who do we tell our problems to?' and 'Some don't wear underwear over their arses' – are possessed of a raw, demotic energy (encapsulated by Hamlet herself when she pushes her bottom towards the audience). If elsewhere Hamlet's different military uniforms carry a potentially subversive charge, here it is her appearance in a striped top and bowler that recalls the distinctive get-up of Sally Bowles (Lisa Minnelli) in *Cabaret* (dir. Bob Fosse, 1972), a film that, set in 1930s' Germany, anatomizes the role of the arts under a fascist dictatorship. In this sense, *İntikam Meleği* harks back to the director's own political credentials (Erksan was the founder of trade unions for Turkish cinema workers and directors alike), with the anti-masque music, in particular, articulating auteurial disillusionment.[45] Of course, as Kasim/Claudius' response to Hamlet in the play-within-the-play indicates, he has little grasp of the performance's underlying message: as he admits, 'I don't really get philosophy'. Here, performance indicts, through the figure of Kasim/Claudius, a general current of philistinism and cultural illiteracy.

In part, Hamlet's performances are greeted with incomprehension within the contexts elaborated by the film because of the ways in which she is discovered as an artist who is internationally oriented. Her outward-looking profile is shaped, it is suggested, by her having pursued a US 'theatre education'; modalities of performance appeal to Hamlet in that they provide an opportunity to demonstrate skills honed as a drama student.[46] Similarly, in the scene with the house manager/Polonius (a version of 2.2), although an *alla turca* classic song, 'Makber' or 'The Grave', plays on the gramophone, the underlying idea is of Hamlet's embrace of European models of representation. As she lolls on a bed in a purple *négligé* in a bedroom with a door but no walls in an open field, attention focuses on the ways in which the bizarre design echoes the paintings of artists such as Dalí and Magritte. Pulled inwards and outwards in this manner, Hamlet is established as a conflicted type; hence, it is appropriate that she is the only character who bears a non-'Turkified' name, which implies that she is less a citizen of her own country than a citizen of the world (an inflated toy globe decorates her firing-range). Yet, even here, there are ambivalences; the USA, for instance, is represented contradictorily in the film, as a place of personal liberation and a haven for organized crime, meaning that there is no clear-cut representation of the relationship between cultural values and a particular nation-state. More generally, Turkey itself in *İntikam Meleği* is rendered in terms that place the old and the new in a tenuous proximity. Typically, the two funeral services in the film highlight as a key property a pall embroidered with Arabic script, yet Hamlet is represented as communing with her father by kneeling next his gravestone on which his name and dates appear in Roman letters.[47] Via such slippages among times and forms, the film illuminates, as does *Tardid*, the in-between status of the Hamlet figure at its core. In particular, both Girik's Hamlet and Siavash/Hamlet are conceived of inhabiting conditions that draw attention to questions about where to look, how to act, in what ways to 'be'.

To an even greater extent, *Tardid* discovers Siavash/Hamlet as pincered between different allegiances. Most obviously, he battles to privilege the authenticity of self-belief and his own intellectual instincts in the context of traditional Middle Eastern notions of honour promulgated by those whose opinions he values most. For Mahtab/Ophelia, the 'daydreaming' Siavash/Hamlet is 'irresponsible towards [his] family'; 'It will all end in your disgracing your family!' is Garo/Horatio's equivalent pronouncement. These objections index the ways in which, as Minoo Moallem writes, the 'ideology of the patriarchal family' in Iran is mediated through the 'spaces' of 'home' and 'submission to normative respectability'.[48] In *Tardid*, Siavash/Hamlet, dishevelled, rough-haired and rarely out of a scruffy jacket and shirt, is singularly at odds with the domestic sphere, missing the wedding of Roozbehan/Claudius and Mah Tal'at/Gertrude and absenting himself from the mansion's activities. The air of displacement and distraction that gathers about Siavash/Hamlet, it is suggested, emerges from his difficulty in coming to terms with what he told about his father: seeking further information, he discovers only that Hemmatollah/Old Hamlet appears little different from the rest of his corrupt associates. Whether it is the adulteration of baby food, or payments to criminals, the Iranian business world, Siavash/Hamlet begins to realize, is 'rotten' (1.4.90) to the core, with his own naivety being highlighted as a consequence.

'Denied the possibility of openly criticizing their government', Christopher Gow remarks, 'post-revolutionary Iranian filmmakers have opted instead for a mode of storytelling that is open to multiple levels of interpretation'.[49] Corruption in *Tardid* is a case in point, with metaphors of water and images of ponds serving to express its manifold manifestations. Functioning as an amalgam of the gravedigger and Yorick, the company archivist describes Tehran's business world as a 'stagnant pool' with a 'dirty stink'.[50] 'Money' is the 'slave of ... [the] pool's rules', Siavash/Hamlet is informed, the archivist continuing, 'somebody will eventually stand on your shoulders ... and you will drown'. Emerging from these formulations is a vivid sense of moral besmirching and unnatural pollution that owes its genesis to *Hamlet*'s 'unweeded garden / That grows to seed' (1.2.135–36). Specifically, the archivist's warning brings back into the film's consciousness the river in which we glimpse the corpse of Hemmatollah/

Old Hamlet; choked with detritus and the froth of effluent, this slow-moving waterway is used to suggest something 'rank and gross' (1.2.136) in the 'state' (1.4.90) of modern-day Iran. At other points in *Tardid*, water is associated with entrapment, as when, in a reworking of the 'fishmonger' scene, Siavash/Hamlet, pretending madness by attempting to catch fish in an ornamental pond on the family estate, finds himself reprimanded by the sleek lawyer, Ansari/Polonius, for not using the appropriate 'fishing net'. Identifying corruption is a challenge for the protagonist, not least because his preferred forms of proof (a 'contract . . . a film . . . photos . . . a recorded conversation') are at odds with the types of practice that enable company operations; as the archivist states, in answer to Siavash/Hamlet's enquiry, 'I don't have . . . evidence'. The same lack is highlighted in the meeting with the Police Chief (Farrokh Nemati) who makes it clear that he is unwilling to act on Siavash/Hamlet's unsubstantiated allegations. Before throwing him out of his office, he asks: 'But can you give me some evidence for at least a couple of these accusations?' For Siavash/Hamlet, the chief instrument with which he holds a 'mirror up to Nature' (3.2.22) – so as to access fundamental 'truths' – is the lens of the camera. Yet the fact remains that, even with his expertise, his family's affairs remain as murky as the water in which his father meets his demise. *İntikam Meleği* shows us Girik's Hamlet smashing her mirror as a sign of her frustrations; a complementary moment is *Tardid*'s opening sequence which discovers Siavash/Hamlet standing next to a broken mirror, a cipher for his inadequacy.

Interestingly, within such a situation, it is women (with the exception of Mah Tal'at/Gertrude) who are envisaged as possessing a greater capability, their qualities of self-assurance and conviction throwing characters such as Siavash/Hamlet into sharp relief. Women in Iran have been able steadily to gain in influence in recent years, as testified in an increased demand for greater rights, participation in education and the professions, and the emergence of women as directors and filmmakers.[51] Important extra-textual female characters in *Tardid* include Anna, Garo/Horatio's mother, a theatre director. Her ambition is implied in her scheme to create a cultural centre in Isfahan, and her innovative ideas for staging Shakespeare are bodied forth in her performance of the Ghost in a version of the play-within-the-play: 'I was murdered [in] . . . a disastrous, horrible conspiracy', she announces, breaking with tradition in taking on a role archetypally identified as male. Women with roles that are amplified from the text and switched in terms of gender include the pragmatic Rana/Guildenstern (who converses seductively with Siavash/Hamlet fingering a loose purple headscarf, a code in Iranian cinema for immorality); she, unlike her Shakespearean counterpart, weathers the intrigues and survives the final bloodbath.[52] Encapsulated in both figurations are responses to the gendered potentialities of *Hamlet* and a re-envisioning of the play that accords with an increasing focus on women in Iranian cinematic culture.

Woman as independent agent finds its most complete statement in Mahtab/Ophelia, who is possessed of an immediately identifiable capability and acumen; arguably, in adaptations of *Hamlet*, the female Hamlet of *İntikam Meleği* is her closest relative. Despite the changes that have overtaken women's roles in contemporary Iran, types of 'discrimination and segregation', notes David Waines, continue.[53] The idea is illustrated in *Tardid* in the ways in which, when men and women gather in the mansion, they are grouped in separate areas; Mahtab/Ophelia refuses these distinctions, forging a route through demarcated spaces and traversing forbidden boundaries. Her athleticism (despite the restrictions of the *hijab*), and the busy and lively score that characterizes her, register a capacity for action and sense of purpose. Like Siavash/Hamlet and Garo/Horatio, Mahtab/Ophelia is immersed in the arts; she aids Siavash/Hamlet in his eavesdropping activities and acts as prompter during the play-within-the-play, suggesting not only support for the plan to have Roozbehan/Claudius exposed but also an alliance with women theatrical practitioners. Elsewhere, Mahtab/Ophelia emerges as distinctive in Shakespearean adaptations of *Hamlet* in that she is represented as caring for her stepbrother, Danial/Laertes, who has Down's Syndrome, arranging driving lessons for him and generally ensuring his welfare; here, by foregrounding disability, *Tardid* reverses a film and stage tradition of a brother-sister dynamic based on the former's domination of the latter.

Crucially, once the parallels between the unfolding action and Shakespeare's *Hamlet* are pointed out to her, Mahtab/Ophelia is quick to resist the momentum that threatens to shape events according to a seemingly inexorable Shakespearean dramatic logic. On the starry rooftop of the ruined cinema, strewn with rubbish and bathed in an eerie blue light, she balks at seeing an exhausted Siavash/Hamlet supine on a coffin-like box. Extinguishing the candle, she exclaims, 'I'll prevent this tragedy . . . from happening . . . I'll make your uncle drink that poisoned chalice!', a statement that underscores her defiance of fate and espousal of agency. A similar moment occurs in the same sequence when 'To be, or not to be' is referenced; as Siavash/Hamlet lies down to sleep; Garo/Horatio, whose mind is running on the theme of slumber, intones, 'to die: to sleep' (3.1.59), only to be interrupted by Mahtab/Ophelia, who exclaims, 'Now

Figure 21: Mahtab/Ophelia (Taraneh Alidoosti) refuses to capitulate to gendered expectations in *Tardid/Doubt* (dir. Varuzh Karim-Masihi, 2009). Courtesy of Varuzh Karim-Masihi.

I see why Hamlet gets killed; because he too has a pessimistic friend like you!' Her note of reprimand and bathetic deflation of Garo/Horatio's pseudo-philosophizing, as well as the fact that, contrary to expectation, the famous soliloquy is removed from Siavash/Hamlet's discursive owner-ship, clarify the nature of *Tardid*'s appropriation of the play – in part irreverent, in part deferential, wittily invoking assumptions in order to undermine them, sculpting new traditions out of old.

As befits this kind of representation, *Tardid* unshackles Ophelia from her association with madness, stressing throughout the strength she derives from a rationalist outlook. The same might be said for both of the Hamlet figures under discussion. *İntikam Meleği* has Girik's Hamlet confess at an early stage, 'I want people to think I'm crazy . . . I'm going to make myself look insane', so as to clarify her enlistment of madness as a device, while *Tardid* discovers Siavash/Hamlet as also impersonating an 'antic disposi-tion' (1.5.170), not least in the scene where he provokes Saboori/Rosencrantz, saying, 'Imagine hundreds of horses flying together . . . all neighing', in a ploy to encourage the lawyer to leave him so that he might the better explore his father's office. The strain of rationalism that runs between Mahtab/Ophelia and Siavash/Hamlet binds them, establishing both, as the action approaches its climax, as united in an endeavour to forestall *Hamlet*'s tragic conclusion.

Unmooring Mahtab/Ophelia from the threat of breakdown, *Tardid* locates madness instead in Mah Tal'at/Gertrude, showing itself sensitive to the ways in which Iranian cinema, as Saeed Zeydabadi-Nejad notes, has tended to gravitate to the figure of the 'woman' afflicted with 'madness' as a 'reaction to life conditions in [the] post-revolution' nation-state.[54] To be sure, in *Tardid*, Mah Tal'at/Gertrude is conceptualized in terms of victim-hood – she does not leave the domestic sphere, appears traumatized during the closet scene, plays cards alone and, later, veiled from head to toe in blue, fixedly dusts the mansion's artefacts, reinforcing a sense both of her isolation and an obsession gone crazily awry. The association of Mah Tal'at with cleaning limns her as a casualty of the dirty pool system; at the same time, it introduces a connection with that 'hysterical somnambulist', as Joanna Levin describes Lady Macbeth, pointing up the spectral power of the Scottish tragedy at the edges of the Iranian adaptation.[55] In the final image of Mah Tal'at/Gertrude's body hanging from the mansion's roof is implied the end-point of process of ostracism that culminates in her taking her own life.

İntikam Meleği is conventional in maintaining the knot that ties Ophelia and madness, although, given the fact that the Ophelia figure, Osman, is male, the process of decline is treated differently. At first, Osman/Ophelia, who is associated with feminine pursuits such as painting, appears as a pining lover. His admission to Hamlet, 'I can't exist without your love in my heart', is typically framed in the negative and sounds a note of foreboding that is also picked up in the setting, a ruined jetty next to a lake. Later, after the play-within-the-play, which has driven Osman/Ophelia ever inwards, he can only mutter, disconsolately, 'I am helpless, troubled and useless', a further negative formulation that highlights a crisis of impotence. The match-cut between Hamlet's departure and the spectacle of Osman/Ophelia drowned in the lake confirms the latter's deathly association with water and completes a psychic trajectory that from the start has been marked as inevitable. If, in Shakespeare's *Hamlet*, there are stereotypical womanly tendencies in the protagonist (he states he suffers from a 'kind of gaingiving as would perhaps trouble a woman' [5.2. 193–94]), *İntikam Meleği* locates these in Osman/Ophelia, playing up the text's queer suggestiveness and discovering madness as a consequence of male disempowerment.

Tardid observes the conventions of the Hamlet-Ophelia relation by emphasizing a heterosexual attraction, although this is conducted within prescribed filmic codes. Commenting on the representation of sexuality in Iranian cinema, Hamid Naficy notes the deployment of a unique 'system of looking – veiled, averted, and pornographic' that finds its most eloquent articulation in the ways in which 'women's faces become the stage and their gazes become primary agents of complex communication'.[56] In privileging the erotic charge that brings Siavash/Hamlet and Mahtab/Ophelia together, *Tardid* adapts just such a 'system', and this is particularly in evidence in the scene where they walk slowly down a dingy, high-walled alleyway trading confidences. Interestingly, in the exchange of shy glances, it is Ophelia's face that is privileged; the camera dwells upon her responses and focuses on her pale, delicately framed features as an index of intimacy. As the romantic pair glides away from Garo/Horatio, who hovers anxiously as a chaperone in the background, the blocking of the characters demonstrates how Mahtab/Ophelia rejects the protection assigned to her in favour of her own romantic trajectory. In the process, material properties as well as emotion-laden looks are exchanged. At night, on the cinema's rooftop, Mahtab/Ophelia places her distinctive purple shawl over a freezing Siavash/Hamlet; he, in turn, wraps the same item around his lover's shoulders, only to find that she allows it to fall leisurely to the ground. With this gentle ballet around possession of the shawl, an example of Iranian cinema's '"no touching" rules', Siavash/Hamlet and Mahtab/Ophelia play a flirtatious game, participating in a performance that, while culturally specific, bears witness to their deepening attachment.[57]

The ways in which Mahtab/Ophelia and Siavash/Hamlet grow together (as opposed to apart) is typical of *Tardid*'s simultaneous summoning and dismantling of expectations about *Hamlet*, and nowhere is this more obvious than at the close. Prior to the *dénouement*, the Police Chief, briefly glimpsed earlier responding to enquiries, is seen as having grown into a Fortinbras-like role, and, in this, he brings to mind a 'positive' assessment of Shakespeare's Norwegian prince as an 'activist' distinguished by his 'decisiveness and courage'.[58] Such a reading is implicit in the subsequent conversation between the Police Chief and Siavash/Hamlet; here, he shows himself as invulnerable to bribery and now able clearly to identify the villainy of Roozbehan/Claudius ('He has had a hand in hundreds of criminal cases'), including his role in the murder of Hemmatollah/Old Hamlet. The Police Chief is distinctive for promising a wholesale exposure of the system, for working within the law to bring about an unravelling of what has been hidden and unproven. Richard Tapper notes that there has recently obtained in Iran 'a strong movement . . . to reject the traditional politics of monopolization of power, control, secrecy and violence, in favour of democracy, transparency and political, religious and ethnic pluralism'.[59] *Tardid* derives energy from its political cross-currents, readjusting the play's suggestions of a military takeover and identifying in the representation of properly functioning police mechanisms the hope for parity of justice and a greater equity.

The *dénouement* itself revolves around Roozbehan/Claudius' plot to convince Danial/Laertes, Mahtab/Ophelia's Down's Syndrome sibling, to shoot Siavash/Hamlet at Ansari/Polonius' memorial service. However, Danial/Laertes wounds rather than kills Siavash/Hamlet, gunning down instead Roozbehan/Claudius, one of his aides and a passing guest. On the magnificent staircase of the family mansion, shocked guests swarm in different directions, the stabbing and violin-heavy score registering a sense of traumatic confusion. Profusely bleeding, Siavash/Hamlet is incapable of saving Danial/Laertes, who is spirited away by Roozbehan/Claudius' henchmen, dying in a rigged car crash on the estate's grounds. The film climaxes, then, with 'casual slaughters ... deaths put on by cunning, and for no cause ... purposes mistook' (5.2.366–68), and any revenge achieved is meted out accidentally. In keeping with the Shakespearean idea of tragic contingency, we do not witness Siavash/Hamlet's death within the film proper; fatally injured, he is pictured bleeding on the bench next to the estate's ornamental pool. Having freed himself of the corrupt constrictions of family, and now confirmed in the loyalties between lovers and friends, his doubts, it is suggested, are finally resolved. But the still image on which we come to rest in the concluding montage is Mahtab/Ophelia's; she assumes the film's thematic focus and stands as the action's inheritrix. Her position at the edge of the pool shows her once again resisting both the thrust of *Hamlet* and the film's association of water with corruption. As the camera pans from head to toe, resting finally on Mahtab/Ophelia's upside-down reflection in the pond, the film showcases the fact that, in contradistinction to the Millais portrait, this Ophelia does not – will not – drown (the body in the water is an illusion only, a product of the camera's self-conscious playfulness). The moment, in fact, recalls *Tardid*'s opening scene (where the camera pans in the reverse direction from toe to head to suggest the drowned body of Hemmatollah/Old Hamlet) and points up how Mahtab/Ophelia reserves the right to change the course of her Shakespearean destiny.

In the closing stages of *İntikam Meleği*, the emphasis of the film is firmly upon Girik's Hamlet and the successful execution of her father's injunctions. In the lead-up not to a formal duel but to an indiscriminate gun battle in the forest, Hamlet is pictured, wearing a sun-hat and poncho, practising on a target range and firing at a *papier-mâché* construction featuring figures and a rifle. Not a soldier, she appears here as a type of cowboy, the change of costume bringing back into the interpretive frame the memory of Ahmet/Old Hamlet; his daughter, it is suggested, prepares for a fatal confrontation in the guise of the absent patriarch. The legacies of the father are referenced again when Hamlet tells Kasim/Claudius, 'Pick up your rifle: I won't shoot an unarmed man' – the scene brings the opening image of Ahmet/Old Hamlet full circle via the codes of the Western. In the wake of the deaths of all the major players – Gönül/Gertrude, accidentally shot in the chaos, and Orhan/Laertes and Kasim/Claudius, both dispatched by the protagonist in heroic retaliation – the stress once more falls on the significances of Hamlet's performance. Wounded, she staggers back to the firing-range, the white of her jumpsuit graphically registering the spread of blood and the fact of her injured female form. The slow-motion photography deployed here, as Hamlet smashes the targets to the ground with the butt of her rifle, invites us to think about her actions within a larger scheme. Several critics have maintained that Hamlet's destructiveness constitutes an argument for pacifism in a war-torn national context, but it might also be suggested that the film's culminating montage bespeaks the protagonist's final internal drama, as she consigns to oblivion the accoutrements of her theatrical endeavour.[60] Attacking the surrealist *papier-mâché* properties with which she honed herself as a revenger, Hamlet, her education completed and her quest fulfilled, renounces the art that enabled and sustained her enterprise. The freeze-frame on her body, racked with pain, leaves unresolved the issue of her fate, demonstrating how both *İntikam Meleği* and *Tardid* find valences in Hamlet figures caught in transitional states, whether of country and culture or of life and death.

Conclusions

As this chapter has argued, so as to address their fraught experiences, the protagonists of *İntikam Meleği* and *Tardid* turn to the arts, with both films casting glances back in time and reflecting on social and cultural icons or practices that more recent events have occluded. With *Tardid*, the lost signifier is cinema, an institution in Iran that, as the film discloses, has been a casualty but later a beneficiary of the revolutionary impulse. For *İntikam Meleği*, surrealist forms of representation offer equivalent resources of meaning, and, indeed, it is in part the dissident tendencies of the surrealist movement that grant the film its critical edge. Drawing upon the arts in such a fashion, *İntikam Meleği* and *Tardid* make an aesthetic virtue from their own internal dramas. Performance insets in *İntikam Meleği* attest to that film's multi-layered theatricality, but the shadowy presence of *Hamlet* in *Tardid* also suggests a play within, an *ur*-text located inside the filmic action. In this sense, the films demonstrate how historical rootedness has a contemporary purchase, illuminating the ways in which art might mould and refigure political debate in the here and now: theatre and cinema have the potential to work in reformative capacities and shape a better future. Inflected thus, *İntikam Meleği* and *Tardid* reanimate Hamlet's maxim of the 'mirror up to Nature' (3.2.22) even as they also suggest that the arts – in older and newer technological forms – are not simply mimetic but also interventionist.

As adaptations of *Hamlet*, it is important that *İntikam Meleği* and *Tardid* are appreciated, and not least because of their concern with the artist's responsibilities and the responsibilities of art. In their fields of circulation, *İntikam Meleği* and *Tardid* showcase the extent to which they pitch themselves, via the mediation of the Shakespearean word, to various audiences and interpretive contexts. Winner of the Crystal Simorgh Award at the Fajr Film Festival, Iran, one of the highest film honours in the country, *Tardid* was also shown at the Yerevan International Film Festival, Armenia, although it has not been distributed internationally. With a marginally greater international visibility is *İntikam Meleği*, which was screened at the Los Angeles and Moscow film festivals, an index, it may be argued, both of Erksan's desire to prove how *Yeşilçam* might produce a work to rival the products of Hollywood and his use of the Hamlet name (*Kadın Hamlet*) to pique wider interest. But the fact remains that neither film made much of a name for itself beyond its own national borders and, as a result, *İntikam Meleği* and *Tardid*'s salutary reflections on, and anticipations of, the costs of instability and governmental malfeasance have been confined to particular reception networks. Responsive to the political, this pairing of Shakespearean appropriations contemplates how solutions might emerge – from a sense of personal conviction (the suggestion of *İntikam Meleği*) or from within a country's own institutional interstices (as *Tardid* demonstrates). In particular, *İntikam Meleği* and *Tardid* bear witness to discussion about what forms of organization replace the structures challenged by the films' Hamletian figures. For *Tardid*, hope resides with youth (Siavash/Hamlet, Garo/Horatio and Mahtab/Ophelia embody a youthful group sharply differentiated from the other players), and, more significantly, with women: in Mahtab/Ophelia is inscribed a gendered agitation for a louder voice and a demand for a more self-evident representation. Despite its distance in time from

Tardid, İntikam Meleği might also be said to look forward to the later film's construction of women and implication in Iran's wider world. For *İntikam Meleği* anticipates the 'real-life' political career of its star, Fatma Girik, who, from 1989 to 1994, served as mayor of Şişli, Istanbul, in which capacity she campaigned for women's improved access to education and employment. Interestingly, an editorial describing Girik's election brings the gendered complexions of her Hamlet to mind in the same moment as it recalls *İntikam Meleği*'s performance-oriented thematic: 'A leading actress has broken one barrier for women on Turkey's political stage', it is stated.[61] Gesturing, on the one hand, to a secular movement that was emancipating women and, on the other hand, to an Islamic system in which women's emancipation is still being fought for, *İntikam Meleği* and *Tardid* negotiate different manifestations of Middle Eastern modernity.

While there is no sense of direct imitation (Varuzh Karim-Masihi makes no obvious reference in *Tardid* to Metin Erksan's *İntikam Meleği*), both films share an accidental contiguity that is mutually enriching. These are works to speak to each other in illuminating ways, and there are benefits to reading them together: the one appears the more intriguing in the light of the other, and, accessed in combination, *İntikam Meleği* and *Tardid* are greater than the sum of their individual parts. As previous parts of this chapter have suggested, a thread binding both films is the concern with the Hamlet figure as a type estranged from her/his point of origin. The US education of Girik's Hamlet places her at several removes from her compatriots; by the same token, having been elsewhere, Siavash/Hamlet is ill-equipped to understand both his family and its affairs. Similarly conceptualized, these Hamlets raise questions about where the Shakespearean Hamlet might best be located, and it is no small step to seeing in their dilemmas of place national preoccupations with issues of image and identity. *İntikam Meleği* and *Tardid* launch conversations about Middle Eastern countries themselves undergoing processes of change, with Hamlet being deployed to mediate strains of individual and popular feeling and arguments about self-definition. Of course, neither Girik's Hamlet nor Siavash/Hamlet is a transparent cipher; nevertheless, they are distinctive for precipitating enquiries (doubts, as *Tardid* has it) and expressing aspirations. *İntikam Meleği* and *Tardid* use art to address matters of 'conscience' (3.1.82), to negotiate how to act and how 'To be' (3.1.55). They demonstrate the extent to which *Hamlet* can be rewritten to address specific national and cultural requirements and, in so doing, point up both the pertinence of the adaptive process and the vitality of local instantiations of Shakespearean authority.

Notes

1. See Metin And, 'Shakespeare in Turkey', *Theatre Research*, 6.2 (1964), pp. 75–84; Narguess Farzad, 'The Essay: Shakespeare Around the Globe', BBC Radio 3, 15 May 2012, www.bbc.co.uk/programmes/b01hjprs (accessed 7 September 2018); Willem Floor, *The History of Theatre in Iran* (Washington DC: Mage Publishers, 2005), p. 215; Stephen Landrigan and Qais Akbar Omar, *Shakespeare in Kabul* (London: Haus Publishing, 2012), p. 38; Saliha Paker, '*Hamlet* in Turkey', *New Comparison*, 2 (1986), pp. 89–105.

2. In the tenth-century Persian epic, *Shahnameh*, Kaveh, a blacksmith, rises up against the evil tyrant, Ẓaḥḥak, while according to late second-/eighth-century sources, the iman, al-Husayn, achieved martyrdom in being defeated in battle by the Umayyad Caliph, Yazid. See Abolqasem Ferdowsi, *Shahnameh: The Persian Book of Kings*, tr. Dick Davis (London and New York: Penguin Books, 2006), pp. 18–21; David Waines, *An Introduction to Islam*, 2nd ed. (Cambridge: Cambridge University Press, 2003), pp. 159–62.

3. Savaş Arslan, 'Turkish Hamlets', *Shakespeare*, 4.2 (2008), p. 158. For an alternative reading, which suggests that feminist and postcolonial readings may be fruitful, see Inci Bilgin, '*Hamlet* in Contemporary Turkey: Towards Postcolonial Feminist Rewrites?', *Multicultural Shakespeare*, 12.27 (2015), pp. 65–74.

4. Tony Howard, *Women as Hamlet: Performance and Interpretation in Theatre, Film and Fiction* (Cambridge: Cambridge University Press, 2007), p. 210.

5. Monika Seidl, '*Hamlet*, the Sponge and *Hamlet, the Angel of Vengeance*: About a Turkish Version of Hamlet', *Shakespeare Yearbook*, 13 (2002), p. 405. On the film's Turkish reception, see Savaş Arslan, *Cinema in Turkey: A New Critical History* (Oxford: Oxford University Press, 2011), p. 65; Atilla Dorsay, 'An Overview of Turkish Cinema from its Origins to the Present Day', in Günsel Renda and C. Max Kortepeter, eds, *The Transformation of Turkish Culture: The Atatürk Legacy* (Princeton: Kingston Press, 1986), p. 124.

6. Siavash (or Seyavash) is the hero-martyr-prince in the epic, *Shahnameh*. See Ferdowsi, *Shahnameh*, pp. 215–80.

7. Interview between Varuzh Karim-Masihi and Mark Thornton Burnett (15 October 2014). Unless otherwise stated, all Karim-Masihi quotations are from this interview and appear in the text.

8. Feroz Ahmad, *The Making of Modern Turkey* (London and New York: Routledge, 1993), pp. 13, 150, 152, 163, 165, 167; Carter Vaughn Findley, *Turkey, Islam, Nationalism, and Modernity: A History, 1789–2007* (New Haven: Yale University Press, 2010), p. 320; Nicole Pope and Hugh Pope, *Turkey Unveiled: A History of Modern Turkey* (London and New York: Overlook Duckworth, 2011), pp. 131–32; Norman Stone, *Turkey: A Short History* (London: Thames & Hudson, 2011), p. 161.

9. Kevin Robins and Asu Aksoy, 'Deep Nation: The National Question and Turkish Cinema Culture', in Mette Hjort and Scott Mackenzie, eds, *Cinema and Nation* (London and New York: Routledge, 2000), p. 215; Stone, *Turkey*, p. 163.

10. Farideh Farhi, 'The Tenth Presidential Elections and Their Aftermath', in Negin Nabavi, ed., *Iran: From Theocracy to the Green Movement* (New York: Palgrave, 2012), p. 14.

11. See Farhany Erfani, *Iranian Cinema and Philosophy: Shooting Truth* (New York: Palgrave, 2012), p. 188; Fatemeh Sadeghi, 'The Green Movement: A Struggle against Islamist Patriarchy?', in Nabavi, ed., *Iran*, p. 125.

12. Hamid Naficy, *A Social History of Iranian Cinema: The Globalizing Era, 1984–2010* (Durham and London: Duke University Press, 2012), p. 192.

13. Michael Axworthy, *Iran: Empire of the Mind, a History from Zoroaster to the Present Day* (Harmondsworth: Penguin, 2008), p. 263; Hamid Naficy, 'Iranian Cinema', in Geoffrey Nowell-Smith, ed., *The Oxford History of World Cinema* (Oxford: Oxford University Press, 1996), p. 675; Hamid Naficy, 'Islamizing Film Culture in Iran: A Post-Khatami Update', in Richard Tapper, ed., *New Iranian Cinema: Politics, Representation and Identity* (London and New York: I. B. Taurus, 2002), pp. 27, 30.

14. Agnès Devictor, 'Classic Tools, Original Goals: Cinema and Public Policy in the Islamic Republic of Iran', in Tapper, ed., *New Iranian*, p. 67.

15. Shohini Chaudhuri, *Contemporary World Cinema: Europe, the Middle East, East Asia and South Asia* (Edinburgh: Edinburgh University Press, 2005), p. 73; Shahab Esfandiary, *Iranian Cinema and Globalization: National, Transnational and Islamic Dimensions* (Bristol and Chicago: Intellect, 2012), p. 70; Naficy, 'Islamizing Film Culture', p. 29; Asghar Seyed-Gohrab and Kamran Talattof, 'Politics and Persistence: The Development of Iranian Film', in Asghar Seyed-Gohrab and Kamran Talattof, eds, *Conflict and Development in Iranian Film* (Leiden: Leiden University Press, 2013), p. 11; Richard Tapper, 'Introduction', in Tapper, ed., *New Iranian*, pp. 4, 6, 8.

16. See Chaudhuri, *Contemporary*, p. 67.

17. *Yeşilçam*, which translates as 'Green Pine', is a synonym for the Turkish Hollywood.

18. Eylem Atakav, *Women and Turkish Cinema: Gender Politics, Cultural Identity and Representation* (London and New York: Routledge, 2013), p. 47; Ahmet Gürata, 'Translating Modernity: Remakes in Turkish Cinema', in Dimitris Eleftheriotis and Gary Needham, eds, *Asian Cinemas: A Reader and Guide* (Edinburgh: Edinburgh University Press, 2006), p. 247.

19. Gönül Dönmez-Colin, *The Routledge Dictionary of Turkish Cinema* (London and New York: Routledge, 2014), p. 1.

20. Dimitris Eleftheriotis, 'Turkish National Cinema', in Eleftheriotis and Needham, eds, *Asian Cinemas*, p. 223.

21. Dönmez-Colin, *Dictionary*, p. 121. See also Gönül Dönmez-Colin, *Turkish Cinema: Identity, Distance and Belonging* (London: Reaktion, 2008), pp. 36, 49; Richard Peña, Doğa Kayalar Polat, Sean M. Dixon and Alexandra N. Sprano, *The Space Between: A Panorama of Cinema in Turkey* (New York: The Film Society of Lincoln Centre, 2012), p. 4.

22. In this period-set murder mystery, the actor hires a troupe of itinerant performers to put on a fatal drama of his own devising.

23. For a discussion of Mahtab/Ophelia in terms of 'the emergence of the New Woman', see Shekufeh Owlia, 'The New Woman and the Oriental Tropes as Portrayed in the Iranian Film *Tardid* Based on *Hamlet*', in Maryam Beyad and Ali Salami, eds, *Culture-Blind Shakespeare: Multiculturalism and Diversity* (Newcastle-upon-Tyne: Cambridge Scholars, 2016), pp. 107–18.

24. Metin And, *A History of Theatre and Popular Entertainment in Turkey* (Ankara: Forum Yayinlari, 1963–64), plate LXVII; And, 'Shakespeare in Turkey', pp. 78, 82.

25. Dönmez-Colin, *Turkish Cinema*, p. 143.

26. Dönmez-Colin, *Turkish Cinema*, p. 30.

27. See 'Metin Erksan Comments', a 2007 interview with the director accompanying the DVD release of *İntikam Meleği/Kadin Hamlet* for the domestic market.

28. James W. Stone, *Crossing Gender in Shakespeare: Feminist Psychoanalysis and the Difference Within* (New York and London: Routledge, 2010), pp. 61. 62.

29. Howard, *Women as Hamlet*, p. 212.

30. The tracks, 'Fly Robin Fly' and 'Get up and Boogie', by the group, Silver Convention, are used to identify his duplicitous actions and those of his cronies.

31. Ann K. S. Lambton, *Persian Vocabulary* (Cambridge: Cambridge University Press, 1953), p. 40.

32. Marjorie Garber, *Dream in Shakespeare: From Metaphor to Metamorphosis* (New Haven and London: Yale University Press, 2013), pp. 95, 218.

33. On *zār* rituals, see Pedran Khosronejad, 'The People of the Air: Healing and Spirit Possession in South Iran', in Thierry Zarcone and Angela Hobart, eds, *Shamanism and Islam: Sufism, Healing Rituals and Spirits in the Muslim World* (London and New York: I. B. Taurus, 2013), pp. 131–67. *Zar* is a term with multiple meanings, including 'crying', a 'bad situation', 'mourning' and 'visitation'. In as much as the ritual in *Tardid* centres on Calif/Marcellus' condition, it also illuminates Siavash/Hamlet's despair over his father's death. See Khosronejad, 'People', pp. 139, 140; Taghi Modarressi, 'The Zar Cult in South Iran', in Raymond Prince, ed., *Trance and Possession States* (Montreal: R. M. Bucke Memorial Society, 1968), p. 151.

34. The play discovers by report an Old Hamlet who is foolish enough to endanger his kingdom by engaging in personal 'combat' (1.1.83) with Old Fortinbras, 'pricked on by a most emulate pride' (1.1.82).

35. Oleg Grabar, *The Formation of Islamic Art*, 2nd ed. (New Haven and London: Yale University Press, 1987), p. 98.

36. Rhodri Lewis, 'Hamlet, Metaphor, and Memory', *Studies in Philology*, 109.5 (2012), p. 614.

37. Margaret Litvin, 'Arab Near East', in Peter W. Marx, ed., *Hamlet-Handbuch: Stoffe, Aneignungen, Deutungen* (Stuttgart and Weimar: Verlag J. B. Meltzler, 2014), p. 324.

38. Ahmad, *Making of Modern Turkey*, pp. 13, 151, 156; Douglas A. Howard, *The History of Turkey* (Westport: Greenwood, 2001), pp. 147–48.

39. Howard, *Women*, p. 216.
40. Meredith Anne Skura, *Shakespeare the Actor and the Purposes of Playing* (Chicago and London: University of Chicago Press, 1993), p. 149.
41. Andrew Rippin, *Muslims: Their Religious Beliefs and Practices*, 3rd ed. (London and New York: Routledge, 2005), p. 137.
42. Waines, *Introduction*, pp. 138, 141.
43. Gülşen Sayin, 'Shakespeare's Turkish Drama: A Cultural Transfer from *Hamlet* to *The Angel of Vengeance* (1976)', *Journal of Adaptation in Film and Performance*, 4.1 (2011), pp. 18, 33; And, *History*, p. 28.
44. Dönmez-Colin, *Dictionary*, p. 121.
45. Peña, Polat, Dixon and Sprano, *Space Between*, p. 4.
46. By contrast, Kasim/Claudius has only criminal links with the USA, as revealed in his letter to 'Mr Ragazza Stampanato', a New York mafia don, requesting Hamlet's murder.
47. In 1928, as part of his republican reforms, Atatürk replaced the Ottoman Arabo-Persian alphabet with an adapted Latin alphabet (M. Şükrü Hanioğlu, *Atatürk: An Intellectual Biography* [Princeton and Oxford: Princeton University Press, 2011], p. 214).
48. Minoo Moallem, *Between Warrior Brother and Veiled Sister: Islamic Fundamentalism and the Politics of Patriarchy in Iran* (Berkeley, Los Angeles and London: University of California Press, 2005), p. 74.
49. Christopher Gow, *From Iran to Hollywood and Some Places In-Between: Reframing Post-Revolutionary Iranian Cinema* (London and New York: I. B. Taurus, 2011), p. 55.
50. The archivist, whose basement room is housed in the depths of the company, suggests the gravedigger because of his association with past history. At the same time, a Yorick identification is hinted at in Siavash's fondness for the archivist and his recollection (echoing Hamlet's line, 'He hath bore me on his back a thousand times' [5.1.175–76]), 'I broke my toy . . . You put me on your back, carried me around the house'.
51. See Naficy, 'Islamizing Film Culture in Iran', p. 47; Naficy, *Social History*, pp. 95–96; Arzoo Osanloo, *The Politics of Women's Rights in Iran* (Princeton: Princeton University Press, 2009), p. 39; Robin Pomeroy, 'Ahmadinejad Aide Urges More Women's Rights', *The Guardian*, 30 September (2010), p. 23.
52. Parviz Jahed notes that recent Iranian cinema customarily represents women by avoiding 'transparency and directness', instead resorting to 'metaphorical, allegorical and symbolic meaning' ('Introduction', in Parviz Jahed, ed., *Directory of World Cinema: Iran* [Bristol and Chicago: Intellect, 2012], p. 9).
53. Naficy, *History*, p. 96; Waines, *Islam*, p. 254.
54. Saeed Zeydabadi-Nejad, 'Madness, Resistance and Iranian Cinema', in Karima Laachir and Saeed Talajooy, eds, *Resistance in Contemporary Middle Eastern Cultures: Literature, Cinema and Music* (London and New York: Routledge, 2013), p. 198.

55. Joanna Levin, 'Lady Macbeth and the Daemonologie of Hysteria', *English Literary History*, 69.1 (2002), p. 38.
56. Naficy, *History*, pp. 109, 110.
57. Naficy, *History*, p. 124.
58. Roland Mushat Frye, *The Renaissance Hamlet: Issues and Responses in 1600* (Princeton: Princeton University Press, 1984), pp. 182, 200, 204.
59. Tapper, 'Introduction', p. 20.
60. Howard, *Women*, p. 221; Sayin, 'Shakespeare's Turkish Drama', p. 35.
61. Emel Anil, 'Actress Breaks Male Barrier in Turkey by Becoming a Mayor', www.apnewsarchive.com (accessed 1 April 2014).

CHAPTER SEVEN

Materializing Hamlet *in the Cinemas of Russia, Central and Eastern Europe*

Both at and since its release, *Gamlet* (dir. Grigori Kozintsev, 1964) has established itself as one of the leading world cinema adaptations of *Hamlet*. The critical consensus is that *Gamlet* represents an apogee of achievement and authority, a remarkable summation of an extended history of Russian engagements with Shakespeare in literature, film and on stage.[1] Critics have approached the film broadly – as a product of Kozintsev's background in *avant-garde* theatre, as a harmonious interaction between the Boris Pasternak translation and the Dmitri Shostakovich score, as a concerted attempt to resurrect a play vilified by Stalin, as an anti-psychological treatise and, most often, as a retrospective 'Aesopian' political fable about Russia in the Soviet era.[2] This chapter takes a different tack. It contends that *Gamlet* is important not so much as an end-point than as a beginning. The film, I argue, establishes a template for interpretation that has deter-mined the thinking of subsequent Russian, Central and East European filmmakers. Notably, when Kozintsev was asked about his imaginative construction of Elsinore, he drew attention to materials and elements: 'Stone', connoting 'the firmly built government prison', 'Iron', as indicated in 'weaponry', 'Fire', signifying 'anxiety, revolt, movement', 'Sea', sugges-tive of 'chaos' and 'change', and 'Earth', the 'world beyond'.[3] *Gamlet* makes these reflections apparent: it mobilizes the material and elemental in such a way as to foreground a positive and dynamic Hamlet, at the same time creating points of contact between characters and episodes to suggest a cautiously affirmative reading of the protagonist's death. Key to this reading is the film's conjuration of space. Writing on the 'Thaw', the more liberated period of de-Stalinization from 1953 to 1964 overseen by Premier Nikita Khrushchev, Lida Oukaderova notes how Russian cinema came to be distinguished by 'an urge to interrogate and reanimate spatial experi-ence, and through this project to raise questions of ideology, social progress and subjectivity that were particularly pressing for post-Stalinist culture'.[4] *Gamlet* typifies this urge. As this chapter also argues, the film shows Hamlet defined by, and able to transcend, the limitations of his physical environment, the result being an understanding of a heroic prince that breaks the mould.

Plotting the fortunes of *Gamlet*, this chapter identifies a demythologization of *Hamlet* running concurrently with the erosion of ideologies, and social and economic challenges, that distinguish Russia in the post-'Thaw' era. Following Krushchev's ousting from power in 1964 and his replacement by Leonid Brezhnev as General Secretary of the Communist Party, a period of cultural retrenchment and stagnation ensued. Nationalism and separatism developed apace under President Mikhail Gorbachev, with shortages, deficits and inflation combining to exacerbate conditions of malaise that, in 1991, contributed to the collapse of the Soviet Union. 'The fragmentation that the empire has undergone and the thematics of that fragmentation [are] paradoxically constitutive of collective identity', Nancy Condee argues, going on to note how the 'cultural imaginary' works as 'as a field of ironic subversion ... a register ... of serotine play'.[5] The tendency, this chapter posits, has been particularly marked in cinema, not least as it is reflected in what has been termed 'a ludic preoccupation with the previous cultural canon in all of its multiplicity', and in the extent to which Russian film culture, as Martha P. Nochimson writes, 'is now full of rage, despair and sorrow at the betrayed utopian hopes raised by Soviet communism, which never produced the promised workers' paradise'.[6]

Despite – perhaps because of – the continuing visibility of the play on contemporary stages, the comic citation of *Hamlet* in Soviet and post-Soviet cultures has become so prevalent as to prompt critic Aleksey Bartoshevich to identify a 'history of attempts to convert the tragedy into mocking tragi-farce'.[7] In the late twentieth and early twenty-first centuries, this distinctive Russian *Hamlet* has crossed into other media, too (including novels and translations), cementing the ways in which the play is caught up in a process of *ostranenie* (defamiliarization) and increasingly regarded through the lens of intertextuality, quotation and bathos.[8] Even during the period in which the political ideals of *glasnost* and *perestroika* were being promoted, *Hamlet* was losing its Kozintsevian capacity to transmit an affirmative message. Developing the point, this chapter looks to a number of parodic iterations of the play in Russian cinema before offering an extended discussion of acerbic black comedy *Hamlet* adaptation, *Playing the Victim* (dir. Kirill Serebrennikov, 2006). Like Kozintsev, Serebrennikov has his origins in radical theatre. For *Playing the Victim*, Serebrennikov reimagined the play of the same name by the Presnyakov brothers, a work that had attracted to itself considerable notoriety since its Ekaterinburg premiere and, in translation, British tour sponsored by the Royal Court Theatre.[9] With President Vladimir Putin's rise to power, as Paul Bushkovitch writes, Moscow and other major Russian cities enjoyed a 'new prosperity', a result of oil revenues, the development of an internal market and increasing trade with global neighbours.[10] None of this is registered in *Playing the Victim* where the focus, instead, is on the Shakespearean resonances of Valya/Hamlet's situation in a straitened domestic *milieu*. The implication is that whatever material progress has been made in the Russia of modernity is glancing and superficial. Accordingly, *Playing the Victim* is coloured by a toxic, *chernukha* ('black' and 'pessimistic') aesthetic: its attachment to gutter vocabulary and urban discontent, as well as its gestures to Shakespeare, makes it a fit climax to the Russian *Hamlet* trajectory this chapter traces.[11] Winner of the main award at *Kinotavr* (the Sochi Open Russian Film Festival), *Playing the Victim*, like *Gamlet* before it, clearly captured the *zeitgeist*.

The break-up of the Soviet Union was exacerbated by the collapse of communist systems throughout Central and Eastern Europe, with nations previously in thrall to – or in tension with – Soviet influence emerging into new forms. These developments have been accompanied by huge material challenges, themselves exacerbated by world debts and budgetary imbalances, and it is against such an unstable backdrop that two recent Central and Eastern European films, *Hamlet, Ciganski Princ* (dir. Aleksandar Rajković, 2007) and *Cigán/Gypsy* (dir. Martin Šulík, 2011), respectively Serbian and Slovakian adaptations, must be initially understood. In 1989, the so-called 'Velvet Revolution' in Czechoslovakia hastened the move to the creation, in 1993, of the Czech Republic and Slovakia and the shift to democracy. By contrast, in the wake of the Balkan crisis, a conflict marked, in Roger D. Petersen's words, by a violent and virulent 'brand of ethno-religious nationalism', Montenegro announced its independence in 2006 and Serbia established itself as a separate entity, marking the dismantlement of the former Yugoslavia.[12] Both *Hamlet, Ciganski Princ* and *Gypsy* elect through *Hamlet* to represent the plight of the Roma peoples at a time of rapid political and social change. According to Rajković, Shakespeare's play answers to a will to privilege in film a character defined by an uncontrolled power who thinks alternatively but is unable to realize his ambitions, while, for Šulík, who began with the aim of raising knowledge about 'the culture and life of the Romanis', *Hamlet* provided a 'key' or 'prism', an 'archetypal story' that could mesh with the 'current present' to stimulate spectators 'to think over the forms of society'.[13] Although the directors' motivations may be different, both films bear comparison in the extent to which, in part reacting against the high cultural status of previous cinematic adaptations of *Hamlet* such as *Gamlet*, they depict abject worlds, prioritizing motifs of displacement and modes of existence that function at extremes of poverty.

Of course, Shakespeare has long been a cultural reference-point in Central and Eastern Europe. As historians have argued, English travelling players first came to Austria, Bohemia and Poland in the sixteenth century, inaugurating what was to become a long-lasting history of Shakespearean performance.[14] Filtered through traditions of romanticism and translation, *Hamlet* in the twentieth century, and particularly under communism, proved, as Krystyna Kujawińska Courtney and Katarzyna Kwapisz Williams write, a 'weapon against Soviet hegemony', allowing for 'subversive commentary' from the stage: Bulgaria, Hungary, Poland and Romania can all lay claim to interwoven narratives in which the play has been used for politically oppositional ends.[15] Complementary, but lesser known, cinematic shorts and animations from Hungary and Poland have adapted *Hamlet* to cast an unfavourable light on the socialist initiative.[16] What brings *Hamlet, Ciganski Princ* and *Gypsy* together is their subscription to what might be termed 'gypsy' Shakespearean cinema, an identification borne out by Romani dialect dialogues, casts made up of mostly Roma actors, and the use of gypsy camps or shantytowns as settings.[17] Most obviously linking the two productions are the ways in which the *dramatis personae* of *Hamlet* are translated into a class of beggar kings. This chapter argues that comparing *Hamlet, Ciganski Princ* and *Gypsy* reveals the films' investment in scenes of desperation, an interrogation of contexts of disentitlement and the critical purchase of cultural particularity. Pursuing an inventive application of Shakespearean plotlines and characters, such as the Denmark-Norway conflict and the travelling players, the films uncover systems of racism that are shadowed in expressions of emasculation and processes of economic humiliation. Looming large as a shared thematic is the fate overtaking traditional communities and practices in the late twentieth and early twenty-first centuries, with both films charting the residues and remainders of a post-communist moment and identifying material need as the agent that shapes the lives of the most marginalized of Central and East European populations. In this way, *Hamlet, Ciganski Princ* and *Gypsy* are the distant inheritors of Kozintsev's sense of *Hamlet*, continuing in the vein of interpreting the play in a materialist fashion but simultaneously problematizing the Russian film's radical portrayal of the protagonist. For, as this chapter concludes, *Hamlet, Ciganski Princ* and

Gypsy – and in this they consort with the gloomy prognosis of *Playing the Victim* – offer irredeemably bleak visions that admit of no different prospects for their subjects. This chapter thus moves across a period of almost fifty years to contend that the resonances of Kozintsev's *Gamlet* are still being felt and debated.

Kozintsev's *Gamlet*

In Kozintsev's *Gamlet*, the material and the symbolic are closely allied. Even though, as Roger Manvell has identified, a ruined 'real castle' in Tallinn, Estonia, was used for some exterior shots, the 'monstrous mosaic', in Courtney Lehmann's words, of Hamlet's world 'never materializes as a whole'.[18] Rather, the film is far more interested in the castle's metaphorical functions, in the ways in which its constituent parts function to inhibit, incarcerate and inculcate a state of mind. The balustrade separating Hamlet (Innokenty Smoktunovsky) and Ophelia (Anastasiya Vertinskaya) in the 'nunnery scene' is one example of an architectural detail working suggestively; another is the canine-toothed portcullis that, resembling bars, lowers to stigmatize the castle's occupants as inmates. Such imprisoning structures are also enshrined in gesture and dress: Polonius (Yuri Tolubeev) jangles the keys of the trunks on which Ophelia perches herself, cementing his role as gaoler, while shots of her stifling black ruff, and of a parrot in a cage, point up the idea that, throughout, she is hemmed in by custom and convention. Hamlet is no less constrained. The walls of the castle are embossed with family crests and forbidding faces implying variously eavesdropping, the onus of ancestral history and ossified traditions – frequently lensed against them, the protagonist is seen in relation to the iconic expressions of his past. Objects reinforce state power in Elsinore, as intimated in a domestic interior adorned with tapestries of military victories and portraits of Claudius (Mikhail Nazvanov) on horseback: the slow unveiling of the castle's *décor* consorts with the film's evocation of increasing attempts to tighten authority. The royal bed is raised on a stage, as if in the capacity of a throne, and behind Gertrude (Elza Radzina) in her closet is ranged a collection of mannikins bearing her dresses, mute servants to her vanity. Concentrating on these inanimate figures, the camera, in the same way that it picks out increasing numbers of sentries and armoured knights, conjures an Elsinore in which a surrogate female army complements the militaristic expressions of male rule.

The stationary condition of the mannikins suggests that Kozintsev's castle inculcates a system that is routinized and mechanistic. Commands

Figure 22: Carved expressions of ancestral history dominate in *Gamlet* (dir. Grigori Kozintsev, 1964). Courtesy of Sputnik.

are automatically acted upon, as when a sentry motions for a flag to be unfurled, and human labour supports a well-oiled political engine. The upper angle shot of serfs circularly toiling to raise the castle drawbridge equates them with just so many cogs in a machine of state. The idea is more forcefully returned to in the castle clock sequences in which symbolic figures – a Bishop, King, Queen, Knight and Death – parade on the hour. Their regular motions are multiply resonant, establishing points of contact between scenes, anticipating the tragic conclusion and reinforcing a sense that time is not so much 'out of joint' (1.5.186) as despotically organized. 'Elsinore chains [Ophelia] to a lifeless ceremonial', notes Kozintsev, and this is made manifest in the scene in which, to twanging music played on a lute by a black-robed crone, she dances a formulaic measure.[19] On the one hand, the interlude references the first quarto's stage direction, '*Enter Ofelia playing on a Lute*'; on the other hand, it undergirds a character who is discovered as an object of instruction, as explicitly still in tutelage.[20] In the later mad scenes, when the physical movements Ophelia traces evoke the dance steps she was earlier rehearsing, a sad parody of her education is intimated. The injunctions she launches at the court during these sequences, including 'You must sing "a-down a-down"' (4.5.165), sound, therefore, as pathetic echoes of requirements for performance. The operations of Elsinore have correspondingly damaging effects, twisting its subjects into contorted postures and parodic versions of themselves.

Stultifying effects notwithstanding, Kozintsev's aim, critics have argued, is to privilege a Hamlet defined by passion, activity, virility and 'a sense of hope'.[21] *Gamlet*'s realization of 1.2 illustrates the method. The business of state concluded, Hamlet traverses the reception hall, his 'How weary, stale, flat and unprofitable' (1.2.133) soliloquy sounding as voiceover. At once, the idea is that Hamlet must 'hold [his] tongue' (1.2.159), but the richer suggestion is that, moving in the opposite direction, the protagonist walks against the tide. As the soliloquy concludes, Hamlet is represented leaving the hall, moving to a space outside; in this moment, at least, the 'door' (3.2.329) is not barred on his 'liberty' (3.2.330). At other points, Hamlet opens doors, navigating a route through architectural interstices, even sometimes casting an alternative shadow over the castle's corridors (the shadow image is most often indicative of Elsinore's totalitarian influence).

Typically, in a *Hamlet* that confronts 'Hamletism' – the idea of a hero tarred with 'pessimism' and insufficient 'strength and will-power' – the shift in orientation is communicated via material things.[22] Ophelia's bedroom is draped with tapestries showing a unicorn, a firebird, deer and doves. Culled from Russian fairy tales, these fantastical creatures belong with a folk tradition in which impoverished young women are liberated from spells and drudgery or changed into alternative forms; for Ophelia, then, there are possibilities for release and the prospect of an alteration in her circumstances.[23] Engineering alignment, *Gamlet* ties this representation of Ophelia to Hamlet, not least through the tapestries that hang in his own chambers; these depict the Ovidian myth in which Phoebus embraces Daphne as she is being transformed into a laurel tree, and hence illustrate a moment of metamorphosis, a union that can and only ever will be symbolic.[24] At other points, the conditions of Hamlet and Ophelia are poetically allied through parallel montage. When Hamlet, for example, appears in long shot within an arch, he is made minuscule by the foregrounded image of the gargantuan Ghost (Grigori Gaj), and this procedure is repeated in the scenes (3.1 and 4.5) where Ophelia is comparably reduced by an arch and stained-glass window. As *Gamlet* progresses, indeed, Hamlet and Ophelia's fates follow arrestingly similar paths.

Such a figuration of Ophelia – and Hamlet – is made possible in part because the film strips or remodels so many of the play's soliloquies. The 'O all you host of heaven' (1.5.92–112) soliloquy is cut, as are ''Tis now the very witching time of night' (3.2.378) and 'How all occasions do inform against me' (4.4.31), the effect of which is to moderate Hamlet's introspection. When soliloquies remain, they are delivered as voiceover, thereby minimizing stage conventions via the deployment of cinematic technique, or are accompanied by props. 'O, what a rogue and peasant slave am I!' (2.2.485), for instance, is rendered as Hamlet beats on a drum, the thrumming of his fingers picking out the iambic rhythms of his speech and accelerating the narrative. The drum has a counterpoint in Ophelia's embroidery work and cradling of Hamlet's 'tenders / Of . . . affection' (1.3. 98–99). In an interpolated scene, Ophelia in her bedroom reads aloud the poem, '*Doubt thou the stars are fire, / Doubt that the sun doth move*' (2.2. 114–15), the effect of which is to allow her an imaginative engagement with Hamlet through the material objects that characterize their romantic exchange. In the play, of course, the words are not hers, yet, in Kozintsev's adaptation, the transposition of the lines to Ophelia hint at additional dimensions to her sensibility, at other realms of inwardness and at a voice.

The most striking example of soliloquy as voiceover is in the realization of 'To be, or not to be'. In thinking about how to film the soliloquy, Kozintsev entertained several possible scenarios to deliver on his theory that 'monologues . . . are . . . currents of thought'.[25] For example, Hamlet bumps into walls as he wanders through Elsinore, or he squeezes himself into a narrow alley in pursuit of a single ray of sunshine, the common denominator here being a matching of movement to thought and an intellectual progression that involves the mobility of the body and inanimate objects.[26] The idea is fully elaborated in the film proper. On a rocky beach, Hamlet turns one way and then another, passing the boulders that lie in his way. His movement precisely addresses the soliloquy's allusions to 'troubles' (3.1.58), a 'rub' (3.1.64), an 'oppressor' (3.1.70) and 'fardels' (3.1.75), to the extent that, with each physical hindrance overcome, psychic development takes place. This is ratified when, at the soliloquy's conclusion, Hamlet climbs a vast flight of steps at the references to 'resolution' (3.1.83) and 'enterprises' (3.1.85), although not without an attendant realization that all must be kept secret (the injunction, 'Soft you now' [3.1.87], is delivered as an instruction to himself rather than as a recognition of Ophelia's arrival). Space has been encountered and confronted in the soliloquy; key stages in thinking are given visual equivalents; and Hamlet is prioritized in terms of how he negotiates and overcomes an impasse that is realized in the complexions of his material landscape.

Most obviously, the 'troubles' (3.1.58) of 'To be, or not to be' are itemized against a background of 'sea' (3.1.58), the sea being continually returned to as a natural entity with which Hamlet feels a particular affinity. Images of the sea mark the film rhythmically (e.g. at the arrival of the players and then at their departure), and the sea also takes on different emotional contours, but primarily it works as a connective medium. When Hamlet returns to Elsinore, he is pictured on a clifftop ('the dreadful summit . . . That beetles o'er his base into the sea' [1.4.70–1]) overlooking the ocean; from this vantage-point, he watches a seagull flying from left to right, right to left and finally again from left to right. The bird's swooping towards Hamlet and away from him into the skies, directly before Ophelia's funeral, suggests her departing spirit: the winged creatures of the tapestries, it seems, have come to life. In this intimation of 'augury' (5.2.197) we find realized, in Bernice W. Kliman's words, a sense of 'exaltation' – a coming together of energies, a journey that court expectations prohibit, a force rising inexorably upwards.[27] An affirmatively imagined journey also characterizes Hamlet's end. With the duel having run its course, the protagonist walks out of the hall, and through its doors and passageways, to the castle's outermost defences. His body seemingly magnified, contrasting with the diminishment of before, he dies in a natural niche in the rocks – it is as if he assumes his rightful throne. The living Hamlet is assisted to his 'rest' (5.2.344) by Horatio, but, in a second movement, the body is taken by Fortinbras' soldiers to a point beyond the castle walls, the forces of Denmark and Norway uniting to honour the prince. This closing tableau thus brings the protagonist into contact with stone, iron, earth and sea, suggesting a final accommodation with the elements and materials that have defined Elsinore in its inner and outer manifestations. In a draft ending for the film, Kozintsev imagined the Ghost heading the funeral march, and, although this idea was eventually dropped, a schema of multiple narrative parts – generational, political and locational – coalescing still obtains: Hamlet, spectated upon by the people, is now seen in a full relation to environment and world.[28] The resolved relation of Hamlet with his locations has, in fact, already been prepared for. Because the pithy expression, 'Let be' (5.2.201–202), is delivered shortly before the duel on the very same steps that Hamlet ascends after the 'To be, or not to be' soliloquy, a sense of completion is implied, of questions that have found an answer. As it has done before, *Gamlet* turns to the material to understand a now unshackled hero and to underline a departure from pre-existing Soviet era interpretations.

After *Gamlet*

The mourning notes of the ending of *Gamlet* typify its consistently serious and stately tone, and, as Hamlet, Smoktunovsky delivers a performance stamped by its sobriety. Cuts honour the orientation: Hamlet's opening witticisms are removed (1.2.65, 67), and much of the banter with the gravedigger is excised. In view of the film's emphases, later Russian cinematic engagements with *Hamlet*, in their attention to humour and satire, work to cast a wry eye over, or even gently to mock, Kozintsev's landmark reading. Released just two years after *Gamlet*, *Beware of the Car* (dir. Èl'dar Riazanov, 1966) is a typical instance. The film centres on endearing righter-of-wrongs, Detochkin, who sells the stolen cars of corrupt officials to support orphanages (he steals from the rich to help the poor) and who, via a series of bizarre events, finds himself playing the lead in an amateur production of *Hamlet* alongside the state investigator who has been on his tail. Casting suggests a purposeful dismantling of the status of *Gamlet* (Smoktunovsky plays Detochkin), while the discordantly portentous music that plays during the production parodies the earlier film's classic Shostakovich score. A *protégé* of Kozintsev, Riazanov, it seems, was drawn to *Hamlet* for the opportunity it offered to ridicule his testy mentor.[29] *Three Stories* (dir. Kira Muratova, 1997) develops the idea of an ironically imagined vigilante in pursuit of injustice in an equally comedic but more acidic dialogue with Kozintsev, with female director Muratova extracting the Ophelia figure to intimate *Gamlet*'s representational shortcomings. In the inset story, 'Ophelia', the eponymous 'Ofa' (Renata Litvinova), a nurse and *aficionado* of the Shakespearean heroine, tracks down her mother (who has given her up for adoption) in order to drown her in a narrative that subjects themes of suicide and revenge to a gendered critique.[30] Spiralling outwards from *Gamlet*, several Russian films are intertextually informed by their cinematic predecessor. Thus, *Fat Stupid Rabbit* (dir. Slava Ross, 2006) finds diversion in the *fabliau* of a children's performer who, to stave off the monotony of playing a rabbit in a run-down theatre, experiments with 'To be, or not to be'. The stage becomes a parodic site within which Hamlet's famous dilemma can be inverted and unsettled in a process that recalls Kozintsev's reflections on how to animate the Shakespearean soliloquy and points up the shrunken circumstances in which the play of *Hamlet* has come to operate. So do allusions to, and constructions of, *Hamlet* and minor Hamlets evoke memories of an illustrious Russian cinematic forbear.

The most sustained recent Russian engagement with *Hamlet* is the black comedy, *Playing the Victim* (dir. Kirill Serebrennikov, 2006), a film that takes to an extreme the situating of the play in reduced and straitened settings. Because the film prefers a stylized narrative mode, the city of Ekaterinburg, in which the action takes place, becomes an 'everywhere', and Valya/Hamlet (Yuri Chursin), the protagonist, a corresponding 'everyman'.[31] Crucially, Valya/Hamlet, a thirty-year-old former student never without his trusty baseball cap and casual wear that has seen better days (his *South Park* T-shirt aligns him with surreal humour and antagonistic energies), works for the police, standing in for the 'victim' in filmed crime scene re-enactments which are then used as legal 'evidence' (he signifies, then, as play, proxy and absent material body). Continually admonished and treated only in terms of his physical instrumentality, he is more broadly represented as infantilized, as his dingy bedroom stuffed with plastic toy animals confirms; in this alone, *Playing the Victim* demonstrates its distance from Kozintsev and partnership with a subsequent parodic *Hamlet* trajectory. In a nondescript apartment, which Valya/Hamlet shares with his family (the Shakespearean royal family is pointedly debunked), a petty bourgeois *Hamlet* plot unravels: Old Valya/the Ghost is poisoned (during a 'usual dinner') by Valya/Hamlet's mother, Galya/Gertrude (Marina Golub), and uncle, Petya/Claudius, bringing to a head the protagonist's acerbically realized angst. Old Valya/the Ghost and Petya/Claudius are

Figure 23: Valya/Hamlet (Yuri Chursin) typifies domestic angst in *Playing the Victim* (dir. Kirill Serebrennikov, 2006) Courtesy of Novye Lyudi/New People.

played by the same actor (Fyodor Dobronravov), suggesting the repetition of, and currents running between, domestic abuse narratives. When Valya/Hamlet is woken at night by Old Valya/the Ghost, a sea-captain in a peaked cap and epaulets, and made aware of the suspicious circumstances surrounding the death, the spectral father simultaneously reprimands him for wasting electricity. Underpinning the conceit of *Playing the Victim* is an envisioning of Valya/Hamlet as a source of paternal disappointment, a son incapable of living up to the image and institutional respectability of his seafaring father.

Playing the Victim affirms its investment in summoning and deflating *Hamlet* through domestic detail. Glimpses of empty bottles, bare floorboards and unfinished walls evoke the cheerlessness of the shared space, while unforgiving lighting and an off-kilter shooting style (the camera captures family squabbles from inside fridges and wardrobes) accentuate the sense of a run-down high-rise habitat. The layout of the apartment lends itself to performative hyperbole, as when Valya/Hamlet (in a scene that replays Polonius' invitation to 'walk out of the air' [2.2.203]) unwillingly accepts Petya/Claudius' request that he step out onto the balcony, only to end up in a tussle with his overbearing uncle. Similarly, around the tiny apartment dinner table, Valya/Hamlet (using chopsticks) and Petya/Claudius (wielding a spoon) argue over how best to eat, taking up diagrammatically opposed views about, on the one hand, the dissolution of

'East . . . West . . . borders' and, on the other, 'our Russia': the generational conflict suggests competing notions of cultural-national integrity. In this *Hamlet* adaptation, warring implements of sword and rapier are bathetically reimagined as common household utensils.

Hamlet is adumbrated in *Playing the Victim* in citation, echo and inference. For example, when Karas (Marat Basharov), the first of the accused, is asked about the mutilated body of his girlfriend ('Where did you put the pieces?'), lines from the play filter to the surface ('you must tell us where the body is' [4.2.23–4]), the effect of which is to underscore a grotesque comic consanguinity. Hamlet stores Polonius in the 'lobby' in contrast to Karas who disposes of his victim in a public eco-toilet. Similarly, the scene in which a naked Valya asks Olya (Yelena Morozova) to 'scarf' (asphyxiate) him smacks of the scene in which Hamlet appears before Ophelia with 'his doublet all unbraced' (2.1.75): the parallel pushes at the sexual charge of the Shakespearean encounter to spotlight a relationship comically premised on erotic extremity. Poison in *Playing the Victim*, as in *Hamlet*, is the means of getting rid of Old Valya/ the Ghost, although the film is more extensively concerned with toxicity, the theme erupting in Valya/Hamlet's warning not to buy 'poisoned' Armenian and Turkish *lavash* flatbread (as opposed to the Russian *Moscovsky* or Moscow 'long loaf'); here, he sends up ethnocentric attitudes even as he arraigns the contaminating and contaminated forces of his world. Foodstuffs in the film, indeed, form a bridge between its various re-enactments. In a later scene in a Japanese restaurant, a drunken and elderly Russian hostess (Liya Akhedzhakova), wearing a *kimono* and flowers, sings to a *karaoke* machine a sentimental folk song in which a 'beautiful Japanese girl', impregnated and abandoned by an 'English . . . sailor', answers her son's questions about his paternity. In that the hostess' performance indexes Ophelia's song about 'Saint Valentine's Day' (4.5.48), the frame of reference is Shakespearean, only *Playing the Victim* plays a variation on the theme, identifying parody in the disappointments of an older woman and seeing in her a sad reminder of her much younger dramatic equivalent. Aleksei Semenenko writes that 'allusions to *Hamlet*' in *Playing the Victim* 'have no direct function and serve as an empty signifier, emphasizing the absurdity of the action and life as a whole'.[32] But his observation is only partially true. Severed yet suggestive, meaningful yet misplaced, bits and pieces of *Hamlet* in *Playing the Victim* emblematize what is left – after Kozintsev, after the fascination with *Hamlet* as an inviolable text had faltered, after the break-up of the Soviet Union. What remains are referents whose power inheres precisely in their fragmentary appearances.

If *Hamlet* is pervasive in *Playing the Victim*, so, too, is 'To be, or not to be'. Its either/or sentiments are everywhere – in the 'scarfing' episode, in the general cultivation of suicide chic and in the major exposition of the soliloquy, the scene in which Valya/Hamlet imagines throwing himself off a grimy stairwell, murmuring to himself not Hamlet's words but 'I live . . . I don't live', a satirically realized first-person balancing-act between different destinies. Writing on the 'mental health . . . crisis' of the Putin era and the rising incidence of 'psychoses . . . schizophrenia . . . and mental disorders as a whole', David E. Powell notes that 'treatment facilities and . . . government support' have proved 'grossly inadequate', and it is within these contexts that Valya/Hamlet's condition takes on a peculiar urgency.[33] Psychic imbalance in the film is a constant, with blue-filtered lighting in the bedroom scenes suggesting an altered state of mind. At one point, in an echo of Hamlet's putting on of an 'antic disposition' (1.5.170), Valya dons a rabbit mask, becoming one with the toys that litter the floor. On other occasions, he imitates Christ ('They pierced his ribs') and mimes, in the same outburst, interrogation procedures ('Second Infantry, please don't!'), an imam's prayers, sounds of explosions, presidential announcements and the public response to 9/11: 'Oh no, why Mr President?' Taking their cue from Hamlet's 'confusion' (3.1.2) and 'wildness' (3.1.39), these episodes help to construct Valya/Hamlet in terms of an excess that shows itself in media saturation and disorientation. At the same time, references to martyrs past and present speak to the ways in which Valya/Hamlet sees himself in terms of victimhood, as fighting his own war on domestic terror.

Black-and-white animation sequences inter-spliced with the apartment scenes emphasize the idea of a pent-up protagonist: combining cinematic surrealism, painterly symbolism and Shakespearean allusion, they feature drilled skulls as motifs of disturbance. In the final animation sequence, a shot of a skull, subsequently superimposed on Valya/Hamlet's face, bobbing in the ocean hints at his demise, while, in an earlier bedroom scene, the camera's lingering on a television *manga* cartoon inset of a pig being cut up and fried in a pan suggests how he is divided from himself. Via imagery of chopsticks as weapons, these sequences are particularly suggestive of Valya/Hamlet's fantasies of revenge. A lover of retro Japanese pop music, and a fan of US popular culture, Valya/Hamlet is represented (at a time when Russia is 'looking westward for . . . welcome, yet . . . [keeping] . . . its options to the East wide open') as continually in search of points of identification.[34] Invariably ignited by domestic crises, animation in *Playing the Victim* conveys an inability to express, and an underlying rage, of nightmarish proportions (Valya and Hamlet alike suffer from 'bad dreams' [F, 2.2.18]). 'To be, or not to be' is everywhere not least in part because its themes of *ressentiment* and extinction are also rehearsed in the animations that are so integral a part of Valya/Hamlet's afflicted imagination.

Picking up on the Hamletian mindset, Valya is cynical, berating to camera how 'Russian cinema is fucked'. 'Fyodor Bondarchuk is the only one who rocks', he states, adding, 'his father won an Oscar: he'll win one as well'. Instancing the success of the Bondarchuk-directed war film, *The 9th Company* (2005), but taking an adversarial attitude towards the resurgence of nationalism in the Russian 'blockbuster' genre, Valya/Hamlet emphasizes the cronyism and nepotism informing the industry and subscribes to a fatalism that illuminates the ways in which, in *Playing the Victim*, the metatheatrical is envisaged in metacinematic terms.[35] 'The purpose of art', he reflects, 'is self-sacrifice', a pronouncement that references Hamlet's observation that 'the purpose of playing . . . is to hold . . . the Mirror up to Nature' (3.2.20–22) and that establishes Valya/Hamlet as a stymied creative practitioner. Indeed, the melodramatic relish with which he takes on the role of victim points up how Valya/Hamlet conceives of himself as a type of free-wheeling, postmodern performer. The 'crimes' investigated through re-enactment in *Playing the Victim* are familial-domestic revenge tragedies explained as accidents (they are 'casual slaughters . . . for no cause' [5.2.366, 367]). So, Karas stabs his girlfriend in the park, Sysoev (Andrei Fomin) pushes his wife out of a window, Zakirov (Igor Gasparian) drowns his lover in a swimming pool, and Verkhushkin (Maksim Konovalov) shoots his college friend in a restaurant, and it is as the 'accidental' victim that Valya/Hamlet comes into his own, his police work indicating a sense of self defined through the rehearsal of other fractured identities. In a conflictual relation with his family, Valya/Hamlet connects only with the victims whose deaths he enacts for the legal record and is animated only through ironically realized impersonations.

Prioritizing re-enactments, *Playing the Victim*, in fact, structures itself around the conceit of the 'dumb show', the premise being that, by making manifest the victims' experiences, the material 'truths' of the circumstances of their deaths will emerge (each 'play' ideally works to 'catch . . . conscience' [2.2.539–540]). In *Hamlet*, of course, *The Mousetrap* is also the reconstruction of a crime, with *Playing the Victim* taking that central idea and elaborating it several times over to suit the film's narrative logic. However, as in the play, in which Horatio is distinctly non-committal about the success of *The Mousetrap* as a force of exposure ('I did very well note him' [3.2.282]), what is enacted in *Playing the Victim* introduces more doubt than it does clarification. Key claims in the testimony are never precisely established, meaning that the findings of the multiple investigations remain inconclusive. Commenting on Russia in the late twentieth and early twenty-first centuries, Steven Rosefielde and Stefan Hedlund note how 'gains' have been 'offset . . . by eviscerated democracy . . . ordinary people . . . remain disenfranchised . . . and have partly or wholly lost many former constitutional . . . protections', and, in this light, the filmic representation of the accused – Zakirov, whose diminutive stature and Middle Eastern accent mark him out as 'other', or Verkhushkin, whose anxieties about his manhood and the economy impel him to violence – takes on a sharp suggestiveness.[36] All are locked in destructive and self-destructive behaviours. Failing and unfulfilled in a bleakly comic vein, the accused analogize the diminished and uncertain subjects of the eclipsed Russian proletopia.

Playing the Victim invites an empathetic response to the accused in part because it represents the investigating force as incompetent and corrupt. Inadequacies are comically highlighted in Lyuda/Horatio (Anna Mikhalkova), the distracted officer who records the re-enactments on her camera: she allows her focus to wander, or concentrates on the wrong object, an instance of Shakespearean delay. But they are more critically identified in the ways in which the police operate coercively. Unlike the typical Russian television crime series in which, as Birgit Beumers states, the morally upright 'policeman . . . is the winner', Stasik (Vitali Khayev), the police captain in *Playing the Victim*, is uninterested in the truth, bullies other officers and subjects the accused to violence.[37] He functions as a satirical incarnation of the ways in which recent 'police re-empowerment' in Russia, together with 'increased economic, political, social and civic repression directed against selected individuals and groups', have exacerbated 'corruption . . . brutality [and] judicial malpractice'.[38] Stasik implodes in the Japanese restaurant, purposefully eating the 'poison' fish, *fuga*, to tempt disaster ('It's a global fuck-up!'), indulging in homophobic rant ('fucking faggots!') and excoriating the Russian football team ('every championship goes to shit!'). A flawed Fortinbras, strong-armed but ineffectual, he resonates as a fundamentally damaged authority, every bit as troubled as those whose fates he oversees. In this sense, *Playing the Victim* purposefully demythologizes any expectation of hierarchical integrity.

It is in a netherworld of compromised categories and overlapping classifications that *Playing the Victim* makes its most corrosive statement. At the close, Valya/Hamlet poisons his family at his engagement party, and Olya/Ophelia, Galya/Gertrude and Petya/Claudius die at his hands.[39] Crucially, in a reversal of the film's dynamic, Valya/Hamlet here leaves behind him his substitute designation and joins the ranks of the accused; he is the 'thing … itself' (1.4.67) as opposed to body double. Tracing the *Hamlet* plot from victim to revenger, *Playing the Victim* puts Valya/Hamlet at the centre of a 'real-life' crime and its re-enactment, suggesting how he graduates from frustrated creative to scripting auteur. As such, he plays the starring role and, briefly, is given a new lease of energy, as indicated in the recharged battery icon showing on the camcorder. And, suiting the film's hyperbolic ethos, the Shakespearean plotline is affirmed if not exceeded: Valya/Hamlet executes a revenge never required of him in Old Valya/the Ghost's revelations. Even though, as Birgit Beumers and Mark Lipovetsky argue, Valya/Hamlet's revenge signals 'an attempt[ed] departure beyond the limits of ambiguous norms', he remains in a muddled and limbo-like state.[40] First, in the same way that *Hamlet* ends with a synopsis of 'accidental judgements' (5.2.366), *Playing the Victim* closes with a statement that foregrounds the contingent and unpredictable. 'I didn't know for sure whether they'd be poisoned or not', Valya/Hamlet explains, situating his crime in a Russian roulette universe in which nothing is definite. Second, rather than confessing to motive, Valya/Hamlet is represented as still storytelling, worried about how material deaths will be realized on film: 'I was … observing, trying to remember [how] … to re-enact it … [I knew that] you'd need to know exactly how all this happened', he tells his police colleagues now captors. Complicating things still further, *Playing the Victim* suggests that Valya/Hamlet's actions precipitate both his own death (imprisonment by the state) and a symbolic death thanks to his father's ghostly return (Old Valya/the Ghost is represented first as judge and then as executioner). In a black-and-white epilogue to *Playing the Victim*, Valya/Hamlet, roused from sleep, finds himself in a boat with his seafaring father, only to be cast into the sea and sink beneath the waves. The episode brings to a head the film's discovery of Valya/Hamlet as haunted by memories of traumatic childhood swimming lessons (in this sense, the maritime memorabilia on the apartment walls betoken a history of paternal-filial tensions) and as crushed by familial and institutional praxes. As Valya/Hamlet disappears, the camera, specked with droplets, is the only witness. Horatio's perspective may be intimated, but, with the water engulfing a darkening scene, it is in fact no more than a disembodied point of view that remains. In this post-Soviet *Hamlet*, the protagonist, as at the end of Kozintsev's *Gamlet*, is aligned with the natural element of the sea, but with no attendant hint of social or political recovery.

Margins and Minorities

Independently conceived, *Hamlet, Ciganski Princ* (dir. Aleksandar Rajković, 2007) and *Gypsy* (dir. Martin Šulík, 2011) share the uncompromising outlook of Serebrennikov's *Playing the Victim*. Both match their characters to inhospitable terrains and highlight via minority narratives the travails of Romani experience. Concerned with a displacement that has pushed existence onto the margins of the cityscape, *Hamlet, Ciganski Princ* unfolds on a landfill site (Deponija) on the outskirts of Belgrade. The film makes a symbolic virtue of piles of *débris*: mountains of waste approximate Elsinore's battlements; stacked tyres suggest a graveyard. This is a soulless and monstrously impoverished world where acts of surveillance serve to accentuate living conditions grimly lacking in privacy. Such a melancholic situation is also registered in the film's tense, irreverent atmosphere. The oscillating light thrown by guttering fires, combined with the flicker of shadows, impart an eerie glow to the proceedings, while encroaching darkness hints at undiscovered black deeds. Daytime shots of swarms of gulls flocking about the dump operate as apt expressions of the Shakespearean Hamlet's cynical references to the 'kites' of the 'region . . . fatted' with 'offal' (2.2.514–15) even as they also communicate the merciless codes of a universe in which one either scavenges or is scavenged in turn.[41] The setting, in fact, references the situation of some 100,000 Romani families who live in Belgrade recycling plastic and metal *and* brings to mind Hamletian metaphors and interests, as reflected in details of the 'unweeded garden' possessed by what is 'rank and gross' (1.2.135–6) and 'something [that] is rotten in the state' (1.4.90).[42] It is, then, in unremittingly hostile landscapes that *Hamlet, Ciganski Princ* most powerfully articulates, to use the director's own formulation, a signature strain of hopelessness. Inside such an environment, when Hamlet (Igor Đorđević) is reduced to defecating in the grass or breaking the ice on his pail of washing water, his question, 'Is there any place worse than this?', a rendering of the Shakespearean idea of a 'stale, flat, and unprofitable . . . world' (1.2.133–34), takes on an awful appositeness. In addition, frozen ground and a weary colour-scape suggest a dystopian revision to a 'gypsy' film aesthetic centred on, as Caterina Pasqualino puts it, 'an unadulterated community living in delightful harmony with nature'.[43] Fired by the currency of Shakespeare's language and imagery, *Hamlet, Ciganski Princ* dismisses the paradigm as unequal to the task of representing late twentieth- and early twenty-first-century Romani realities.

Gypsy similarly concentrates on the marginal – up to 320,000 Romanies inhabit Slovakia – although the locus of attention in this adaptation is a shantytown in Richnava, Eastern Slovakia.[44] The opening romantic images of Adam/Hamlet (Jan Mizigar) bounding through a lush forest with his dog, running down through the trees to a gently undulating river, quickly shift: once the gaze transmogrifies and alights on the shantytown, perched precariously on a scarred hillside, the urgent exigencies of his life become the focus. Attempts to alleviate monotony – the camera picks out a makeshift game of table tennis – can do little to detract from more pressing material requirements, as instanced in shots of roofs being repaired, a sheep being skinned, wood being hewn and tatty furniture being laboriously moved up a precipitous pathway. Clustered tightly together, the shantytown's flimsy dwellings are a patchwork of shapes and colours, but there is little sense of security or comfort. As in *Hamlet, Ciganski Princ*, repeated establishing shots of an unwelcome scene have an oppressive effect. For example, the *mise-en-scène* picks out open sewers traversing cratered, half-finished roads and chimneys belching smoke into otherwise clear skies – even as vestiges of the pastoral intrude, the impression is of desperate environmental conditions. The shantytown is additionally bisected by a train-track, but the train speeds through without stopping: the implication, in Frantz Fanon's phrase, is that Adam/Hamlet's world is a 'zone of non-being' which has been edged to the sidelines of the Central European imaginary.[45] In Shakespearean terms, the 'goodly frame the earth', then, appears as an isolated 'promontory' (2.2. 264–65), unforgiving and inimical. *Hamlet, Ciganski Princ* – in which steaming methane vapours point up a sense of stagnation and aftermath and in which metaphysical questions are posed amidst dirt and detritus – again invites comparison. The equivalent view in *Gypsy* is realized in rhythms and visuals. After a spring start, the film moves to winter, and it is this season that dominates the second half. The camera now identifies snow falling, a woman struggling with a bundle of sticks and youths pushing a car that has stalled in the cold, while the sonic scene is pierced by dogs barking with increasing frenzy – 'The air bites shrewdly' (1.4.1). Dividing up the action in this way, the film deploys natural processes to underline the escalating dominion of want.

The kinds of deprivation explored in *Hamlet, Ciganski Princ* and *Gypsy* are congruent with the effects of the collapse of state socialism

Figure 24: Elsinore as Slovakian shantytown in *Cigán/Gypsy* (dir. Martin Šulík,
2011). Courtesy of In Film Praha.

and an 'unfavourable starting-point' for the Roma 'at the outset of the
transition from planned to market economies'.[46] *Hamlet, Ciganski
Princ* indexes the 'problem' of the Roma peoples via rubbish – working
with rubbish, and becoming indistinguishable from it, illuminate the
material ramifications of state policies towards minorities and the
divisive consequences of the Balkan crisis. As the fool figure,
a cinematic chorus, announces to camera at the start in an exclamation
that equates demographics and dross: 'Goddam gypsies! You're
scumbags!'[47] Beyond this, and certainly in the former Czechoslovakia,
laws restricting itineracy, the liquidation of settlements, efforts to
assimilate Romanies as part of the socialist initiative, interment and
even genocide are the constituent components of a traumatic memory.
After 1989, for Roma in Slovakia, as Will Guy argues, the 'break-up of
the federal Republic led to an immediate deterioration of their
position'.[48] Most recently, in the winter of 2003/2004, there was
a wave of protests in Roma communities, resulting in the mobilization
of the army, against cuts in social benefit introduced by the neoliberal
government.[49] Across Central and Eastern Europe, Romanis have fared
poorly as newly constituted nation-states pursue intersecting agendas of
identity formation and capitalist enterprise.

The situation is expressed with heightened eloquence in *Gypsy*'s representation of male-on-male and father-son relations. Within contexts of enforcing peripheries, the film's figuration of Emil/the Ghost and Žigo/Claudius (Miroslav Gulyas) as embittered and disappointed serves a key purpose. Wearing a shabby outdoor coat, Emil/the Ghost visits Adam/Hamlet to lament how monetary needs, and family disputes, got in the way of knowing his son properly. Emil/the Ghost itemizes a series of crises – prison, the death of a daughter, an alcoholic father – that robbed him of masculine agency and visibility. As *Gypsy* makes clear, Emil/the Ghost is also deceived by the 'white' community he embraced as a Christian convert. His admission – 'They tricked us: heaven doesn't exist, God only has a small office up there, and there's a long queue in front of it' – works less as a précis of purgatory than as an example of how in life as in death he is denied a better dispensation. In this outlining of his experience established religion plays a prominent part. The church, it is implied, keeps Romanis submissive, and the critique extends even to the priest (Attila Mokos), who, standing in for Horatio, is represented as attentive to Adam/Hamlet's 'story' (5.2.333), and keen to transform his lot via the boxing club, but ultimately powerless. Repeated shots of Catholic icons are indicative here, suggesting, as they do, that the church's overseeing functions exist only at the level of the image.

Both the priest and Žigo/Claudius, whose tattered T-shirt with a crown motif proclaims him king or, in the film's terms, community fixer and 'loan-shark', attempt to exercise in their relations with Adam/Hamlet paternal responsibilities. In confessional vein, Žigo/Claudius seeks to find accommodation with Adam/Hamlet through advice and discourses of gypsydom and commonality – 'the whites . . . beat the crap out of them . . . I have nothing in common with those bastards . . . be a gypsy', he urges. The instructive tenor of his words reveals how keenly Žigo/Claudius agitates to win Adam/Hamlet over and create a bond, and it is by mobilizing binaries between gypsies and 'whites' (rather than between Adam/Hamlet and his biological father) that he argues his case. His elevation of ethnicity is accentuated when, in the hospital, and in the same way that Claudius declares 'the most immediate to our throne' (1.2.109), he announces the arrival of his child with group rather than national pride: 'another Gypsy has been born', he exclaims. And it is arguably against histories of persecution that we need to read *Gypsy*'s elaboration of the wake, the wedding between Žigo/Claudius and Jolana/Gertrude, Emil/the Ghost (presented in terms of cinematic realism) and the song (a type of 'dumb show') about escaping 'poverty'.[50]

Countering the romantic or magic realist gypsy screen visions of auteurs such as Dušan Hanák and Emir Kusturica, these elements make visible Romani cultures in integral and assertive, and resistant and rehabilitative, ways.[51]

A will to enshrine if not protect Roma traditions is shared across both films. *Hamlet, Ciganski Princ*, for example, is notably responsive to the occluded cultures of an older Yugoslavia, as in its representation of the chief bear-tamer (the film's substitute for the travelling player), whose tambourine, tinkling bells and incantatory snatches of folk song bring to mind a disappearing mode of representation.[52] At a deeper level, the fact that the bear-tamers are travelling evokes the kinds of displacement often forced upon the Roma, making them emblematic of the mobile existence dictated to by the pressures of inhabiting societies in flux. Gane/Guildenstern (Zdravko Ranković) notes of the bear-tamers' incongruous winter visit to the dump, 'Everything changes, no one is interested in bears, and television has ruined everything', his comment registering the extent to which a global media industry has swamped localism and homogenized cultural diversity. The point is stridently made in *Gypsy* in which the camera repeatedly pauses for several beats on satellite dishes adorning the fronts of the shantytown dwellings. A disconnect between technology and a primitive backdrop is underscored, while the multiplication of dishes suggests an invading force, a militaristic onslaught that threatens to ruin Roma distinctiveness.

The surfaces of technology mask underlying privations and lack, a state of being which both films understand primarily in economic terms. In *Hamlet, Ciganski Princ*, the aberrancies of the system have made Jova/Claudius (Petar Božović) viciously acquisitive. As he discloses in confession, he murdered Djura/Old Hamlet (Dragoljub Topalović) 'because of the money', the equation between cash and crime being reflected in shots of wads of notes concealed in a makeshift outside toilet. That this is dirty money the toilet analogy makes explicit, but there is also the suggestion of the desperate lengths to which the inhabitants of the dump are prepared to go to ensure survival. The absence of money provokes correspondingly anxious actions which are best illustrated in the scene in which Jova/Claudius, sitting behind a glass door and counting his ill-gotten gains, argues with one of his young henchmen: 'That's all?', he demands, his question pointing up the fact that he requires more but that there is no more to give. More broadly, the dump is discovered as a place where rubbish figures as a commodity around which the film's substitutes for political powers conduct a deadly trade. The backstory to *Hamlet, Ciganski*

Princ centres on the conflict between rival orthodox Roma and local Muslim gangs who wish to control the rubbish empire: the dump, then, is both domain and kingdom. (For its part, *Gypsy*'s equivalent contest is between the Roma, representing Denmark, and the 'whiteys', representing Norway.) Notably, Jova/Claudius is represented as adulterating commodities when dealing with Murat/Old Norway, selling paper that is dampened to increase its weight and worth: in this environment, the fraudulent and the economic pervasively interpenetrate.

People, too, in Jova/Claudius' estimation, are commodities to be managed via his own brand of backhanders. 'How much did he give you?', Hamlet demands of Gane/Guildenstern and Mija/Rosencrantz (Jovan Fetouski), his immediate suspicion being that Jova/Claudius pays people off and that the fawning pair are motivated by a common venality (the play's euphemistic reference to 'thanks / As fits a king's remembrance' [2.2.26] is here baldly translated). But the needs of the economy in *Hamlet, Ciganski Princ* do not level in a unifying fashion. Zoran/Laertes refuses Jova/Claudius' offer of money in the wake of Dusko/Polonius' death, his angry exclamation testifying to his integrity and to something more important than mere financial gain. Even more removed is Hamlet. There is only one occasion on which he handles cash; Hamlet asks the bear-tamer, 'Listen: do you know how to perform?', and afterwards discreetly passes him some notes, an act that is justified in that it supports the traditional moral efficacy of the 'artist'. If the protagonist is revealed as indifferent to the 'business' being transacted around him, then he also apprehends rubbish less as a commodity than as a collection of aesthetically arresting objects, such as in the scene where, in a reworking of the play's sexual concern with 'treasure open' (1.3.30) and 'memory locked' (1.3.84), he picks up a key, remarking to Zorica/Ophelia (Mirjana Šišić), 'They never think about using the old stuff'. This and similar exchanges mark out Hamlet's difference – his equitable relationship with Zorica/Ophelia, his eco-instincts, his alternative notions of value. Hamlet is characterized by self-denial: his is not the realm of expenditure. A not dissimilar imagining of Hamlet undergirds *Gypsy*, for, in this adaptation, Adam/Hamlet is represented as resisting the pressure to steal, attracting to himself in the process a 'faggot' designation: masculinity and crime are inseparable.

In both films, indeed, the Hamlet character stands out from the rest. *Gypsy* takes the idea to an extreme in its rendition of Adam/Hamlet, fifteen years old, lustrous-eyed and tousle-headed, struggling with his place in the community. Janet Adelman notes how Gertrude is imagined as a 'contaminating material body . . . the object of moral revulsion', but, in

Gypsy, her oppressed – and pregnant – condition necessitates Adam/ Hamlet's assumption of the bread-winner role: it is to alleviate her circumstances that he tries to 'make money' and gives up his education.[53] Throughout, he is impelled to take on a responsibility beyond his years (a princely burden is placed on his shoulders). Pregnancy, as *Gypsy* and *Hamlet, Ciganski Princ* establish, makes women vulnerable, the latter film illustrating the point with Shakespearean specificity. When Jova/Claudius forces himself on Yelena/Gertrude (Suzana Petrović), for example, she fears another pregnancy as a result (the reference to the 'enseamed bed' [3.4.90] is graphically realized). By contrast, in *Gypsy*, Shakespearean echoes cluster mainly around Adam/Hamlet who, in a series of insets, is represented looking directly to camera (interestingly in weather that is increasingly harsh and adversarial). The device both pushes the viewer, in director Martin Šulík's words, to 'start thinking about the boy's difficult life situation' and meets the requirement of the soliloquy, silently communicative moments standing in for the verbal richness of 'To be, or not to be'.

Yet, as the film simultaneously establishes, Adam/Hamlet from the perspective of the wider world is far from individuated, and his characteristic sports-top 'hoodie', stamped with an '86', suggests how Romanis are invariably seen in anonymous, statistical terms. Underlying each of Adam/Hamlet's encounters in *Gypsy* is the systemic and structurally engrained racism that works, in Aidan McGarry's words, as a 'legally sanctioned form of discrimination', a synthesis of 'anti-Roma prejudice'.[54] A loose reworking of the 'closet scene', the episode in which Jolana/Gertrude is kept in hospital after the birth of her child is a salient instance. Visited by her family on the ward, and interrupted by the nurse (a type of Polonius), she is generally demeaned ('This place is driving me nuts … They said they'd put the baby in an orphanage'), to the extent that the hospital appears more incarcerating than recuperative. Similarly, when Adam/Hamlet and his brother, Marian, are gaoled after being caught as part of a gang stealing diesel, the brutality to which they are subjected by the police confirms the anti-pathetic mentalities of social institutions. At a more general level, when Adam/Hamlet is ostracized from casual employment ('Don't come tomorrow: no work') or chased through the woods by the police, the film exposes praxes of dehumanization which understand him as quarry and blur animal and human taxonomies.

Whether imagined or 'real', animals in both films are thematically purposeful. A traditional aspect of gypsy culture serves narrative priorities.[55] For example, in *Hamlet, Ciganski Princ*, different attitudes towards animals bring differences between Jova/Claudius and Hamlet to light. The white rabbit that the protagonist cradles hints at his solicitude while, in the same moment, suggesting an Alice-in-wonderland type of distraction and an alliance with his white-suited ghostly father. In contradistinction, the pig that Jova/Claudius fondly scratches pejoratively resembles, in its fleshy proportions, the form of its master, for not only does the creature tar the king with its significances, reinforcing the brute notion and explicit imagery of 'making love / Over the nasty sty' (3.4. 91–2), it also reveals the workings of a regime in which humanity itself is treated in animal-like ways. Thus, in the scene where the pig is disembowelled, the suggestion is that Hamlet, recently exiled to Vienna and death, is a further sacrifice: he will be dispatched at the hands of those fawning followers who will 'pluck out the heart of [his] mystery' (3.2.357–58). Crucially, the pig is killed because it is deemed valuable (it is roasted and eaten), whereas the white rabbit, glimpsed later dead in its cage, is appreciated simply for its own sake. However, in a violent extension to the animal analogy, the film reveals how it is Gane/Guildenstern and Mija/ Rosencrantz who will suffer a fate that makes them the objects of sacrifice. Trussed up like pigs for slaughter, the roped pair are burned alive in a car which then ends up, with its conflagrated contents, as another piece of trash. Their deaths are at one with the animal economies of the dump that proves their undoing.

Gypsy is without obvious Rosencrantz and Guildenstern figures, although some of their treacherous functions are picked up in the scenes devoted to the three ethnomusicologists who visit the shantytown to record Roma music. They bring in their wake happy memories of earlier times (photographs or a 'presentment' [3.4.52] of Emil/Old Hamlet), a sense of previous connections and a more positive reading of gypsy life. The lead female ethnomusicologist, standing in for the Player Queen and the otherwise preoccupied and absent Jolana/Gertrude, fires Adam/ Hamlet with tales of 'scholarships [at] engineering school'. Yet, during the final meeting, the Lucianus figure, the most unsympathetic of the ethnomusicologists, tells an anti-Roma joke, prompting Adam/Hamlet to leave in disgust. The film's 'players', then, merge into Rosencrantz and Guildenstern types: they expose their own prejudice and eventually embody forces of repression rather than release. (This portrayal reflects a development in the director's thinking: Šulík mentions in interview initially organizing 'the script according to the schema of the players' but changing the emphases 'when we started to visit the Roma settlements'.)

Figure 25: Julka/Ophelia (Martina Kotlarova) gathers berries in *Cigán*/*Gypsy* (dir. Martin Šulík, 2011). Courtesy of In Film Praha.

Over the course of *Gypsy*, Adam/Hamlet's hopes and projections are consistently deflated. Associated with berries and fertility, Julka/Ophelia (Martina Kotlarova) is bartered for in such a way that she blights his romantic aspirations. Her status as sexual commodity is settled when she is sold off to a 'Czech guy', the transformation being highlighted in the sequence where, inexpertly made-up, and stumbling on high heels, she informs Adam/Hamlet of her departure. The widescreen shot of her leaving the shantytown in a glimmering Mercedes replays the nunnery scene in a different key, echoing Shakespearean accusations ('I have heard of your paintings . . . You jig and amble' [3.1.141, 143]) inside an unpalatable 'deal . . . the family needs the money'.[56] The Shakespearean plotline of madness and drowning cedes place to a concentration on Julka/Ophelia's utility as an object of exchange.

What might be entailed in leaving a familiar environment is a question asked by *Hamlet, Ciganski Princ* and *Gypsy* alike. Each film ends by steering a course between the pressures of moving on or staying put. Typical is *Hamlet, Ciganski Princ* in which, captured in a widescreen shot that encompasses a comprehensive point of view, the fool abandons the dump in the company of the travelling bear-tamers, the implication being that they are embarking on a journey. The fool and the bear-tamers find, in their association, a common purpose. The departure comes hard upon the knife fight between Hamlet and Zoki/Laertes which, echoing a playful fight between children at the start, shows the rival combatants participating, as in the play-within-the-play, in a dreadful entertainment. And, while the order that Hamlet represents passes (his body is laid out on a pyre, and gulls congregate to try the remains), the rubbish empire continues. Thanks to an earlier deal Hamlet has done with Mesa/Fortinbras ('Mesa will get what's his, and he'll start over again: it's only fair', the protagonist states), the rival Muslim Roma gang now takes charge. Mesa/Fortinbras enters the frame to claim his dues; he is rubbish-as-commodity's elected heir. *Hamlet, Ciganski Princ*, then, ends poised between scenarios: one concerned with movement, the other concerned with the perpetuation of a degraded and degrading economy. Crucially, neither scenario represents an alternative; rather, marshalling all too recognizable tropes of travel and penury, the film highlights the impossibility of meaningful change, the lack of solutions, and ongoing confrontations with material imperatives. A comparable state of affairs is represented in *Gypsy*, although the stress in this adaptation is less with the situation of the community than with the plight of the individual. The knife fight approximation of the Shakespearean duel is again enlisted, with Adam/Hamlet, having pieced together the facts and realized that Emil/the Ghost did not die in a 'car accident', stabbing Žigo/Claudius to death during a break in their journey to the hospital, only to find himself stranded at an out-of-the-way bus-stop. Enacting gypsy law, however, as the ending clarifies, has no ameliorative effect, for Adam/Hamlet is still locked in the either/or dichotomy that has defined him, divided between the shantytown and 'white' society beyond.[57] Echoing an earlier scene in which the bus had failed to stop, *Gypsy* spotlights the crisis of a Hamlet who is at one and same time bound for nowhere and caught in stasis. The only moving property is an ostrich, an *émigré* from a group of ostriches stolen by the shantytown Romanis in lieu of withheld payments. This isolated bird, like Adam/Hamlet, is, as the director argues, a 'stranger in the settlement', yet, as surrogate, the ostrich also suggests symbolic money, a fragile economy, evaporating opportunities and the ceaseless struggle for resources. Most importantly, as his metaphorical equivalent moves outside the filmic frame, Adam/Hamlet remains confined within it. Key Hamletian questions about how to be and how to act, and key contemporary issues touching on disenfranchisement and dispossession, find no reply or remedy in an evocative but despairingly open-ended tableau.

Conclusions

Films like *Hamlet, Ciganski Princ* and *Gypsy* take us from high cultural Shakespeare to independent/unfamiliar Shakespeare, from established film directors to lesser known auteurs, from the artistic centre to the touchline of representation. In this process, *Hamlet* occupies a singular place as a resource through which the damaged constituencies and impoverished conditions of some parts of Russia, Central and Eastern Europe are lent creative expression. Marshalled for interrogative purposes, the play gives the lie to the notion that material growth and improvement are the defining features of the communist and post-communist worlds; rather, presenting anti-visions of the Soviet Union and after, *Playing the Victim*, *Hamlet, Ciganski Princ* and *Gypsy* puncture the narrative of progress, concentrating on separation and separateness, neglect and stigmatization – the peoples and societies that economic and political transformation leaves out. In this sense, at the same time as the distance travelled between *Gamlet* and its cinematic descendants signals far-reaching changes in terms of the organization of society and the role and definition of nation-states, it also confirms a shrinkage in the capacities of the subject, a diminution in the individual's world-view, and a decline in an idea of human dignity.

Playing the Victim, Hamlet, Ciganski Princ and *Gypsy* gravitate towards each other in the extent to which they dispassionately reflect upon the implications and failures of political systems past and present, whether this shows itself in imagined projections of post-Soviet lives or in conceptually attuned stories of Romani existences that have slipped through the net of institutions such as the EU, which, as Aidan McGarry writes, 'maintains Romaphobia through its commitment to neoliberalism', bolstering 'economic marginalization' and 'social inequities'.[58] This is not to suggest that, as a symptom of contemporary developments, *Hamlet* is vitiated or exhausted. Demythologizing *Hamlet* instead only ratifies the play's timeliness. Whatever generic choice is made for the play cinematically (and, as we have seen, at least in Russia, the tendency is to insert *Hamlet* into a parodic register), its utility persists: travesty and tragedy mutually reinforce each other. And, even if the styles of films such as *Playing the Victim*, *Hamlet, Ciganski Princ* and *Gypsy* differ, the onus of representation is still focused on uncompromising systems with no ameliorative prospects and isolated selves at odds with, or cast adrift from, national membership structures and initiatives. The films explored in this chapter engage with the spirit of *Gamlet*, but sculpt their own agendas for specific ends. Space, once signifying hopes for agency or emancipation, becomes, in the hands of later filmmakers, a physical phenomenon that cannot be overcome, unless in situations of wish-fulfilment, make-believe and mediatized replay. *Hamlet* in its Russian, Central and Eastern European guises on film is fundamentally inflected by the political scene; it also intervenes in it in echoing and enervating conjurations of possible and ultimately impossible performances and economies.

Notes

1. See Laurie E. Osborne, 'Filming Shakespeare in a Cultural Thaw: Soviet Appropriations of Shakespearean Treacheries in 1955–6', *Textual Practice*, 9.2 (1995), pp. 325–47; Eleanor Rowe, *Hamlet: A Window on Russia* (New York: New York University Press, 1976), *passim*; Mark Sokolyansky, 'Russia', in Peter W. Marx, ed., *Hamlet-Handbuch: Stoffe, Aneignungen, Deutungen* (Stuttgart and Weimar: Verlag J. B. Meltzler, 2014), pp. 312–16.
2. Patrick Burke, '"Hidden Games, Cunning Traps, Ambushes": The Russian *Hamlet*', *Shakespeare Yearbook*, 8 (1997), p. 172; John Collick, *Shakespeare, Cinema and Society* (Manchester and New York: Manchester University Press, 1989), pp. 129, 135, 137, 139, 141; Barbara Leaming, *Grigori Kozintsev* (Boston: Twayne, 1980), pp. 1, 14, 17, 25, 34, 95; Irena R. Makaryk, 'Wartime *Hamlet*', in Irena R. Makaryk and Joseph G. Price, eds, *Shakespeare in the Worlds of Communism and Socialism* (Toronto, Buffalo and London: University of Toronto Press, 2006), p. 120; Mark Sokolyansky, 'Grigori Kozintsev's *Hamlet* and *King Lear*', in Russell Jackson, ed., *The Cambridge Companion to Shakespeare on Film*, 2nd ed. (Cambridge: Cambridge University Press, 2007), p. 205; Alfred Thomas, *Shakespeare, Dissent and the Cold War* (Basingstoke and New York: Palgrave, 2014), pp. 58–96.
3. Grigori Kozintsev, *Shakespeare: Time and Conscience*, tr. Joyce Vining (London: Dennis Dobson, 1967), p. 266.
4. Lida Oukaderova, *The Cinema of the Soviet Thaw: Space, Materiality, Movement* (Bloomington: Indiana University Press, 2017), p. 2.
5. Nancy Condee, *The Imperial Trace: Recent Russian Cinema* (Oxford: Oxford University Press, 2009), pp. 47, 239.
6. Vlad Strukov, *Contemporary Russian Cinema: Symbols of a New Era* (Edinburgh: Edinburgh University Press, 2016), p. 255; Martha P. Nochimson, *World on Film: An Introduction* (Oxford: Wiley-Blackwell, 2010), p. 106.
7. Aleksey Bartoshevich, *Gamlety nashih dnej. Shekspirovskie chtenija* (Moscow: Izdaltel'stvo Moskcovskogo gumanitararnogo universiteta, 2010), p. 210; John Givens, 'Shakespearean Tragedy in Russia: In Equal Scale Weighing Delight and Dole', in Michael Neill and David Schalkwyk, eds, *The Oxford Handbook of Shakespearean Tragedy* (Oxford: Oxford University Press, 2016), p. 775.
8. Aleksei Semenenko, '"Adieu, Remember Me": The *Hamlet* Canon in Post-Soviet Russia', in Brian James Baer and Susanna Witt, eds, *Translation in Russian Contexts: Culture, Politics, Identity* (London and New York: Routledge, 2018), p. 287.

9. Birgit Beumers, *A History of Russian Cinema* (Oxford and New York: Berg, 2009), p. 253; Oleg and Vladimir Presnyakov, *Playing the Victim*, tr. Sasha Dugdale (London: Nick Hern Books, 2003), n.p.; Laurence Senelick, 'Theatre', in Nicholas Rzhevsky, ed., *The Cambridge Companion to Modern Russian Culture*, 2nd ed. (Cambridge: Cambridge University Press, 2012), p. 314.

10. Paul Bushkovitch, *A Concise History of Russia* (Cambridge: Cambridge University Press, 2012), p. 457.

11. On the *chernukha* aesthetic, see Eliot Borenstein, *Overkill: Sex and Violence in Contemporary Russian Culture* (Ithaca and London: Cornell University Press, 2008), pp. 11–23.

12. Roger D. Petersen, *Understanding Ethnic Violence: Fear, Hatred, and Resentment in Twentieth-Century Eastern Europe* (Cambridge: Cambridge University Press, 2002), pp. 212–13.

13. Interview between Mark Thornton Burnett and Aleksandar Rajković (24 April 2013); interview between Mark Thornton Burnett and Martin Šulík (20 October 2017). Unless otherwise stated, all Rajković and Šulík quotations are from these interviews and appear in the text or notes.

14. Zdeněk Stříbrný, *Shakespeare and Eastern Europe* (Oxford: Oxford University Press, 2000), pp. 6, 10.

15. See Nicoleta Cinpoeş, '*Hamlet* or the Skeletons in the Cupboard', in Keith Gregor, ed., *Shakespeare and Tyranny: Regimes of Reading in Europe and Beyond* (Newcastle-upon-Tyne: Cambridge Scholars, 2014), p. 223; Krystyna Kujawińska Courtney and Katarzyna Kwapisz Williams, 'Central Eastern Europe', in Marx, ed., *Hamlet-Handbuch*, pp. 304, 308; Veronika Schandl, 'History Interrupted: *Hamlet* and 1956 in Hungary', in Ruth J. Owen, ed., *The Hamlet Zone: Reworking 'Hamlet' for European Cultures* (Newcastle-upon-Tyne: Cambridge Scholars, 2012), p. 105; Alexander Shurbanov and Boika Sokolova, 'From the Unlove of *Romeo and Juliet* to *Hamlet* without the Prince: A Shakespearean Mirror Held up to the Fortunes of the New Bulgaria', in Michael Hattaway, Boika Sokolova and Derek Roper, eds, *Shakespeare in the New Europe* (Sheffield: Sheffield Academic Press, 1994), p. 42.

16. See *Hamlet* (dir. György Kovásznai, 1967) and *Hamles/Little Hamlet* (dir. Jerzy Skolimowski, 1960). For discussion, see Brigitta Iványi-Bitter, *Kovásznai, a Cold War Artist: Animation, Painting, Freedom*, tr. Andrea Ágnes Szekeres (Budapest: Kovásznai Research Centre Foundation, 2016), p. 124; Ewa Mazierska, *Jerzy Skolimowski: The Cinema of a Non-Conformist* (New York and Oxford: Berghahn, 2010), pp. 149–50, 178.

17. The genre of 'gypsy' Shakespearean cinema is relatively unexplored, but examples, in addition to those explored here, may include, at temporal removes, *Los Tarantos* (dir. Francisco Rovira Beleta, 1963), a Spanish adaptation of *Romeo and Juliet*, and *Romani Kris* (dir. Bence Gyöngyössy, 1997), a Hungarian adaptation of *King Lear*. Despite its negative connotations, 'Gypsy', as Paloma Gay y Blasco notes, 'remains a preferred mode of self-ascription for

many individuals and communities across Europe' and may thus tentatively be deployed 'to refer to exoticising and orientalising representations'. See her 'Picturing "Gypsies": Interdisciplinary Approaches to Roma Representation', *Third Text*, 22.3 (2008), pp. 297–98.

18. Roger Manvell, *Shakespeare and the Film* (London: Dent, 1971), p. 80; Mark Thornton Burnett, Courtney Lehmann, Marguerite H. Rippy and Ramona Wray, *Great Shakespeareans: Welles, Kurosawa, Kozintsev, Zeffirelli* (London and New York: Bloomsbury, 2013), p. 103.

19. Kozintsev, *Shakespeare*, p. 216.

20. See *Hamlet*, ed. Ann Thompson and Neil Taylor, revised ed. (London and New York: Bloomsbury, 2016), 16.1 t.n.

21. See Anthony B. Dawson, *Shakespeare in Performance: 'Hamlet'* (Manchester: Manchester University Press, 1995), p. 188; Tiffany Ann Conroy Moore, *Kozintsev's Shakespeare Films: Russian Political Protest in 'Hamlet' and 'King Lear'* (Jefferson and London: McFarland, 2012), p. 26; Kenneth S. Rothwell, *A History of Shakespeare on Screen: A Century of Film and Television*, 2nd ed. (Cambridge: Cambridge University Press, 2004), p. 175.

22. Mikhail M. Morozov, *Shakespeare on the Soviet Stage*, tr. David Magarshack (London: Soviet News, 1947), pp. 42, 43.

23. Alexander Afanasyev, *Russian Fairy Tales* (New York: Planet, 2013), pp. 5–21; Suzanne Massie, *Land of the Firebird: The Beauty of Old Russia* (New York: Simon and Schuster, 1980), pp. 17–19.

24. Ovid, *The Metamorphoses*, tr. Mary M. Innes (Harmondsworth: Penguin, 1955), pp. 44–47.

25. Kozintsev, *Shakespeare*, p. 230.

26. Grigori Kozintsev, *'King Lear': The Space of Tragedy*, tr. Mary Mackintosh (London: Heinemann, 1977), pp. 114–15; Kozintsev, *Shakespeare*, pp. 230, 271.

27. Bernice W. Kliman, *'Hamlet': Film, Television, and Audio Performance* (Madison and Teaneck: Fairleigh Dickinson University Press, 1988), p. 101.

28. Grigori Kozintsev, *Vremia tragedii* (Moscow: Vagrius, 2004), p. 327.

29. Grigori Kozintsev, *Vash Grigorii Kozintsev*, ed. Iakov Butovskii and Valentina Kozintseva (Moscow: Artist, Rezhisser, Teatr, 1996), p. 62. For discussion of the film, see Alexander Etkind, 'Mourning the Soviet Victims in a Cosmopolitan Way: *Hamlet* from Kozintsev to Riazanov', *Studies in Russian and Soviet Cinema*, 5.3 (2011), pp. 403–06; David MacFadyen, *The Sad Comedy of Èl'dar Riazanov: An Introduction* (Montreal and Kingston: McGill-Queen's University Press, 2003), pp. 112, 117, 121.

30. Condee, *Imperial*, p. 126.

31. 'Moscow' is referenced as the 'nunnery' to which Olya/Ophelia is to be banished, and Ekaterinburg is identifiable only via the 'Malyshev' street name.

32. Aleksei Semenenko, '"No text is an Island": Translating *Hamlet* in Twenty-First Century Russia', in Brian James Baer, ed., *Contexts, Subtexts and Pretexts: Literary Translation in Eastern Europe and Russia* (Amsterdam and Philadelphia: John Benjamins, 2011), p. 253.

33. David E. Powell, 'Putin, Demography, Health, and the Environment', in Dale R. Herspring, ed., *Putin's Russia: Past Imperfect, Future Uncertain*, 2nd ed. (Lanham and New York: Rowman and Littlefield, 2005), p. 113.

34. J. Larry Black, *Vladimir Putin and the New World Order: Looking East, Looking West?* (Lanham and New York: Rowman and Littlefield, 2004), p. 348.

35. See Steven N. Norris, *Blockbuster History in the New Russia: Movies, Memory, and Patriotism* (Bloomington and Indianapolis: Indiana University Press, 2012), pp. 111–12, 143–154.

36. Steven Rosefielde and Stefan Hedlund, *Russia Since 1980: Wrestling with Westernization* (Cambridge: Cambridge University Press, 2009), p. 206.

37. Beumers, *History*, p. 242.

38. Rosefielde and Hedlund, *Russia*, pp. 206, 208.

39. Valya/Hamlet resents the pregnancy that necessitates his marriage: Olya/Ophelia will not be a 'breeder of sinners' (3.1.120–21).

40. Birgit Beumers and Mark Lipovetsky, *Performing Violence: Literary and Theatrical Experiments of New Russian Drama* (Bristol and Chicago: Intellect, 2009), p. 298.

41. In gypsy folklore, birds are coloured with ominous associations, and it is in keeping with this idea that a crow features in the film at fraught emotional moments, particularly during episodes in which Jova/Claudius plots his next move, emphasizing the extent to which this creature signals not only the waning of power but also future misfortune. See Raymond Buckland, *Gypsy Dream Dictionary*, 2nd ed. (St Paul: Llewellyn Publications, 1998), p. 89.

42. For the Roma and Belgrade, see 'Severed Lives', *The Sunday Times Magazine*, 25 July (2010), pp. 42–43.

43. Caterina Pasqualino, 'The Gypsies, Poor but Happy', *Third Text*, 22.3 (2008), p. 343.

44. Richard Filčák, *Living Beyond the Pale: Environmental Justice and the Roma Minority* (Budapest and New York: Central European Press, 2012), p. 45.

45. Frantz Fanon, *Black Skin, White Masks*, tr. Charles Lam Markmann (London: Pluto Press, 1986), p. 2.

46. Dena Ringold, Mitchell A. Orenstein and Erika Wilkens, *Roma in an Expanding Europe: Breaking the Poverty Cycle* (Washington, D.C.: The World Bank, 2005), p. xiv.

47. The director states that the fool talks about racial prejudices openly; the type is not unbalanced as such but a part of Serbian tradition where the mentally challenged are respected as God's people (interview between Mark Thornton Burnett and Aleksandar Rajković [24 April 2013]).

48. Will Guy, 'The Czech Lands and Slovakia: Another False Dawn?', in Will Guy, ed., *Between Past and Future: The Roma of Central and Eastern Europe* (Hatfield: University of Hertfordshire Press, 2001), p. 299.

49. Martin Marušak and Leo Singer, 'Social Unrest in Slovakia 2004: Romani Reaction to Neoliberal "Reforms"', in Nando Sigona and Nidhi Trehan, eds,

Romani Politics in Contemporary Europe: Poverty, Ethnic Mobilization, and the Neoliberal Order (Basingstoke: Palgrave, 2009), p. 186.

50. See Josef Kaldova, 'The Gypsies of Czechoslovakia', in David Crowe and John Kolsti, eds, *The Gypsies of Eastern Europe* (Armonk and London: M. E. Sharpe, 1991), p. 105; Yaron Matras, *The Romani Gypsies* (Cambridge, Mass.: Harvard University Press, 2015), pp. 93, 98, 100, 101. In interview, Martin Šulík notes that 'the magical and mystical are, in Roma cultures, continually present . . . when a dead father appears, it is not in a dream (as in Shakespeare) but in the real here-and-now' (interview between Mark Thornton Burnett and Martin Šulík [20 October 2017]).

51. See Pavle Levi, *Disintegration in Flames: Aesthetics and Ideology in the Yugoslav and Post-Yugoslav Cinema* (Stanford: Stanford University Press, 2007), p. 86; Martin Votruba, '*Rosy Dreams*', in Adam Bingham, ed., *Directory of World Cinema: East Europe* (Bristol and Chicago: Intellect, 2011), pp. 78, 79.

52. Other than indexing the extra-theatrical sports of Shakespeare's London, the bear-tamers are arresting in other ways. Thus, when the bear performs for the tamer – 'With her left hand she puts on powder', he explains – Hamlet is stimulated to suspect Zorica/Ophelia immediately afterwards. In this way, the juxtaposition of the two episodes both points up the ubiquity of a world of false appearances (a transposition of the Shakespearean idea of painting 'an inch thick' [5.1.183]) and the situation of Zorica/Ophelia, forced to act and dissimulate for others' benefit. Significantly, the bear is called Cassandra, a name which evokes the classical heroine of Greek mythology, a figure associated, appropriately enough, with tragic genres, madness and the ability to see into the future.

53. Janet Adelman, *Suffocating Mothers: Fantasies of Material Origin in Shakespeare's Plays, 'Hamlet' to 'The Tempest'* (London and New York: Routledge, 1992), pp. 14, 15.

54. Aidan McGarry, *Romaphobia: The Last Acceptable Form of Racism* (London: Zed Books, 2017), p. 2.

55. For gypsies' traditional involvement in animal dealing and/or displaying, see Angus Fraser, *The Gypsies* (Oxford: Blackwell, 1995), pp. 46–8, 124–25.

56. 'The plot involving Shakespeare's Ophelia', states Martin Šulík, 'changed because of our encounter with an eighteen-year-old young woman whose parents had sold her in marriage several times over' (interview between Mark Thornton Burnett and Martin Šulík [20 October 2017]).

57. The division is also suggested in dialogue: depending on the situation, Adam/Hamlet speaks either Slovak or the Roma language (the Spišská dialect).

58. McGarry, *Romaphobia*, p. 9.

Filmography

The filmography provides details of the thirty world cinema adaptations of *Hamlet* explored in this book. It identifies title, director, language, the country of origin and date. Where there is a significant co-production element, this has been noted.

Title	Director	Date	Language	Country
A Herança/The Inheritance	Ozualdo Candeias	1971	Brazilian Portuguese	Brazil
The Bad Sleep Well	Akira Kurosawa	1960	Japanese	Japan
The Banquet	Xiaogang Feng	2006	Mandarin	China
Castle of Flames	Katô Tai	1960	Japanese	Japan
Cigán/Gypsy	Martin Šulík	2011	Romani and Slovak	Slovakia
Dans la Poussière de la Soleil/In the Dust of the Sun	Richard Balducci	1971	French	France and Spain
Der Rest ist Schweigen/ The Rest Is Silence	Helmut Käutner	1959	German	Germany
El Triunfo/The Triumph	Mireia Ros	2006	Spanish	Spain
Elf Onkel/Eleven Uncles	Herbert Fritsch	2010	German	Germany
Festen/Celebration	Thomas Vinterberg	1998	Danish	Denmark
Gamlet	Grigori Kozintsev	1964	Russian	Russia
Haider	Vishal Bhardwaj	2014	Hindi and Urdu	India
Hamlet	Hugues Serge Limbvani	2007	French, *Baoulé, Dyula, Kikongo* and *Wolof*	Republic of Congo and France
Hamlet	Kishore Sahu	1954	Hindi and Urdu	India
Hamlet, Ciganski Princ	Aleksandar Rajković	2007	Romani	Serbia
Hamlet liikemaailmassa/ Hamlet Goes Business	Aki Kaurismäki	1987	Finnish	Finland
Hamile: The Tongo 'Hamlet'	Terry Bishop	1965	English and *Twi*	Ghana
Hemanta	Anjan Dutt	2016	Bengali	India

(cont.)

Title	Director	Date	Language	Country
İntikam Meleği/Kadin Hamlet	Metin Erksan	1976	Turkish	Turkey
Io, Amleto/I, Hamlet	Georgio Simonelli	1952	Italian	Italy
Ithele Na Ginei Vasilias/ He Wanted to Become King	Angelos Theodoropoulos	1967	Greek	Greece
Karmayogi	V. K. Prakash	2012	Malayalam	India
Khoon-ka-Khoon	Sohrab Modi	1935	Hindi and Urdu	India
O Jogo da Vida e da Morte/A Game of Life and Death	Mário Kuperman	1971	Brazilian Portuguese	Brazil
Ophélia	Claude Chabrol	1963	French	France
Playing the Victim	Kirill Serebrennikov	2006	Russian	Russia
Prince of the Himalayas	Sherwood Hu	2006	Tibetan	China
Quella Sporca Storia nel West/Johnny Hamlet	Enzo G. Castellari	1968	Italian	Italy
Tardid/Doubt	Varuzh Karim-Masihi	2009	Farsi	Iran
Un Amleto di Meno/One Hamlet Less	Carmelo Bene	1973	Italian	Italy

Other Films, Documentaries and 'Shorts'

The Alexandria Trilogy (dir. Youssef Chahine, 1979, 1982, 1989)

A Margem/The Margin (dir. Ozualdo Candeias, 1967)

A Opção/The Option (dir. Ozualdo Candeias, 1981)

Amleto . . . Frammenti (dir. Bruno Bignoni, 1997)

Barrière (dir. Andreas Kleinert, 2010)

Beware of the Car (dir. Èl'dar Riazanov, 1966)

Brave Records of the Sanada Clan (dir. Katô Tai, 1963)

Broken Lance (dir. Edward Dmytryk, 1954)

Cabaret (dir. Bob Fosse, 1972)

Cabeças Cortadas/Severed Heads (dir. Glauber Rocha, 1970)

Chicken Rice War (dir. Chee King Cheah, 2000)

Come Persi La Guerra/How I Lost the War (dir. Carlo Borghesio, 1947)

Crouching Tiger, Hidden Dragon (dir. Ang Lee, 2000)

Deus e o Diabo na Terra do Sol/Black God, White Devil (dir. Glauber Rocha, 1964)

Dezdemona (dir. Manyazewai Endeshaw, 2010)

A Dry Summer (dir. Metin Erksan, 1963)

Fat Stupid Rabbit (dir. Slava Ross, 2006)
Faustão/Faust (dir. Eduardo Coutinho, 1971)
Femmes Aux Yeux Ouverts (dir. Anne Laure Folly, 1993)
A Full Life (dir. Hani Susumu, 1962)
The Great Mêlée (dir. Eiichi Kudo, 1964)
Guns and Talks (dir. Jang Jin, 2001)
Hamlet (dir. Michael Almereyda, 2000)
Hamlet (dir. Kenneth Branagh, 1996)
Hamlet (dir. Stephen Cavanagh, 2005)
Hamlet (dir. Alexander Fodor, 2007)
Hamlet (dir. György Kovásznai, 1967)
Hamlet (dir. Laurence Olivier, 1948)
Hamlet (dir. Franco Zeffirelli, 1990)
The Hamlet Adventure (dir. Greg Roach and Ivaylo Dikanski, 2008)
Hamlet en Palestine (dir. Nicolas Klotz and Thomas Ostermeier, 2017)
Hamles/Little Hamlet (dir. Jerzy Skolimowski, 1960)
Hero (dir. Yimou Zhang, 2002)
Hitler, Ein Film aus Deutschland (dir. Hans Jürgen Syberberg, 1978)
The Horse Thief (dir. Tian Zhuangzhuang, 1986)
House of Flying Daggers (dir. Yimou Zhang, 2004)
Il Était Une Fois Hamlet et Ophélie à Shanghai (dir. Ellénore Loehr, 2016)
In Nome del Popolo Italiano (dir. Dino Risi, 1971)
Jubal (dir. Delmer Daves, 1956)
Julie et Roméo (dir. Boubakar Diallo, 2011)
Kundun (dir. Martin Scorsese, 1997)
La Nube/The Cloud (dir. Fernando E. Solanas, 1998)
Le Champignon des Carpathes (dir. Jean-Claude Biette, 1990)
Les Lutteurs/The Wrestlers (dir. Jean-Michel Tchissoukou, 1982)
LOC: Kargil (dir. J. P. Dutta, 2003)
Los Tarantos (dir. Francisco Rovira Beleta, 1963)
Maine Pyar Kiya (dir. Sooraj Barjatya, 1989)
Mossane (dir. Safi Faye, 1996)
The 9th Company (dir. Fyodor Bondarchuk, 2005)
Nu är du Hamlet (dir. Ulrika Bengts, 2002)
O Cangaceiro/The Bandit (dir. Lima Barreto, 1953)
O Vigilante/The Vigilante (dir. Ozualdo Candeias, 1992)
Ofelia's Bloomster (dir. Jørgen Leth, 1968)
Opération Shakespeare à la Vallée de Joux (dir. Anne Cuneo, 2006)
Orfeu do Carnaval/Black Orpheus (dir. Marcel Camus, 1959)
Orphée (dir. Jean Cocteau, 1950)

Parde-ye Akhar/The Last Act (dir. Varuzh Karim-Masihi, 1991)
Persepolis (dir. Vincent Paronnaud and Marjane Satrapi, 2007)
The Phantom Lover (dir. Ronnie Yu, 1995)
Plangent Rain (dir. Kenneth Scicluna, 2010)
Pola X (dir. Leos Carax, 1999)
Rashomon (dir. Akira Kurosawa, 1950)
Revenge of the Snakes (dir. Metin Erksan, 1962)
Rio 40°/Rio, 40 Degrees (dir. Nelson Pereira dos Santos, 1955)
Roja (dir. Mani Ratnam, 1992)
Romani Kris (dir. Bence Gyöngyössy, 1997)
Romeo and Juliet (dir. Franco Zeffirelli, 1968)
Sangdil Sanam (dir. Shomu Mukherjee, 1994)
Seven Years in Tibet (dir. Jean-Jacques Annaud, 1997)
The Seventh Seal (dir. Ingmar Bergman, 1957)
Three Stories (dir. Kira Muratova, 1997)
Throne of Blood (dir. Akira Kurosawa, 1957)
Thunderbolt (dir. Tunde Kelani, 2000)
A Time to Love (dir. Jianqi Huo, 2005)
To Be or Not to Be (dir. Peter Woditsch, 1999)
uGugu no Andile (dir. Minky Schlesinger, 2008)
Vidas Secas/Barren Lives (dir. Nelson Pereira dos Santos, 1963)
Viramundo (dir. Geraldo Sarno, 1965)
West Side Story (dir. Jerome Robbins and Robert Wise, 1961)
Yabure Daiko/The Broken Drum (dir. Keisuke Kinoshita, 1949)
Youth in Fury (dir. Shinoda Masahiro, 1960)

Bibliography

Printed Sources

Adelman, Janet, *Suffocating Mothers: Fantasies of Material Origin in Shakespeare's Plays, 'Hamlet' to 'The Tempest'*. London and New York: Routledge, 1992.

Adler, Peter, and Nicholas Barnard, *African Majesty: The Textile Art of the Ashanti and the Ewe*. London: Thames and Hudson, 1992.

Aebischer, Pascale, *Screening Early Modern Drama: Beyond Shakespeare*. Cambridge: Cambridge University Press, 2013.

Afanasyev, Alexander, *Russian Fairy Tales*. New York: Planet, 2013.

Agence Presse-France, 'Indian Forces in Kashmir Kill Top Commander of Militant Group', *The Guardian*, 27 December (2017), p. 21.

Agovi, Kofi Ermeleh, 'Joe de Graft', in Bernth Lindfors and Reinhard Sander, eds, *Twentieth-Century Caribbean and Black African Writers*. Detroit and London: Gale Research, 1992, pp. 134–41.

'The Origin of Literary Theatre in Colonial Ghana, 1920–1957', *Research Review (Lagon)*, 6.1 (1990), pp. 1–23.

Ahmad, Feroz, *The Making of Modern Turkey*. London and New York: Routledge, 1993.

Aima, Mohan Lal, 'Kashmiri Drama', in K. L. Kalla, ed., *The Literary Heritage of Kashmir*. Delhi: Mittal Publications, 1985, pp. 115–19.

Akomfrah, John, 'On the National in African Cinema/s: A Conversation', in Valentina Vitali and Paul Willemen, eds, *Theorising National Cinema*. London: BFI, 2006, pp. 274–92.

Albó, Xavier, 'Our Identity Starting from Pluralism Is the Base', in John Beverley, Michael Aronna and José Oviedo, eds, *The Postmodern Debate in Latin America*. Durham and London: Duke University Press, 1995, pp. 18–33.

Allatson, Paul, *Key Terms in Latino/a Cultural and Literary Studies*. Oxford: Blackwell, 2007.

Allinson, Gary D., *Japan's Postwar History*, 2nd ed. Ithaca and New York: Cornell University Press, 2004.

Allman, Jean, and John Parker, *Tongnaab: The History of a West African God*. Bloomington: Indiana University Press, 2005.

Amorim, Marcel Álvaro de, 'Shakespeare no Sertão: Uma Leitura Brasileira de *Hamlet*, por Ozualdo Candeias', *Cadernos do IL*, 53, January (2017), pp. 10–29.

'Shakespeare no Subúrbio: Uma Leitura Brasileira de *Hamlet*, por Mário Kuperman', *Scripta Uniandrade*, 14.2 (2016), pp. 86–122.

And, Metin, *A History of Theatre and Popular Entertainment in Turkey*. Ankara: Forum Yayinlari, 1963–64.

'Shakespeare in Turkey', *Theatre Research*, 6.2 (1964), pp. 75–84.

Andrew, Dudley, 'An Atlas of World Cinema', in Stephanie Dennison and Song Hwee Lim, eds, *Remapping World Cinema: Identity, Culture and Politics in Film*. London and New York: Wallflower Press, 2006, pp. 19–29.

Angelo, Vítor, '*A Herança*', in Eugênio Puppo, ed., *Cinema Marginal Brasileiro e Suas Fronteiras: Filmes Produzidos Nos Anos 60 e 70*. São Paulo: Heco Produções, Ltda., 2004, pp. 88–89.

Anyidoho, Kofi, 'Ghanaian *Kente*: Cloth and Song', in Lynn Gumpert, ed., *The Poetics of Cloth: African Textiles/Recent Art*. New York: Grey Art Gallery, 2008, pp. 33–47.

Anzai, Tetsuo, 'A Century of Shakespeare in Japan: A Brief Historical Survey', *Shakespeare Yearbook*, 9 (1999), pp. 3–12.

Appadurai, Arjun, *Modernity at Large: Cultural Dimensions of Globalization*. Minneapolis: University of Minnesota Press, 1996.

Araújo, Inácio, Gabriel Carneiro, Gabe Klinger, Felipe Furtado, Alfredo Sternheim and Matheus Trunk, 'An Abecedarium of the Boca do Lixo', in Gerwin Tamsma, ed., *The Mouth of Garbage/Boca do Lixo: Subculture and Sex in São Paulo, 1967–1987*. Rotterdam: International Film Festival, 2012, pp. 12–27.

Armes, Roy, *African Filmmaking North and South of the Sahara*. Edinburgh: Edinburgh University Press, 2006.

Third World Filmmaking and the West. Berkeley, Los Angeles and London: University of California Press, 1987.

Arslan, Savaş, *Cinema in Turkey: A New Critical History*. Oxford: Oxford University Press, 2011.

'Turkish Hamlets', *Shakespeare*, 4.2 (2008), pp. 157–68.

Atakav, Eylem, *Women and Turkish Cinema: Gender Politics, Cultural Identity and Representation*. London and New York: Routledge, 2013.

Aveh, Africanus, 'The Rise of the Video Film Industry & Its Projected Social Impact on Ghanaians', *African Literature Today*, 28 (2010), pp. 122–32.

Axworthy, Michael, *Iran: Empire of the Mind, a History from Zoroaster to the Present Day*. Harmondsworth: Penguin, 2008.

Ayers, P. K., 'Reading, Writing, and *Hamlet*', *Shakespeare Quarterly*, 44.4 (1993), pp. 423–39.

Bailey, Helen Phelps, *Hamlet in France: From Voltaire to Laforgue*. Geneva: Librairie Droz, 1964.

Bakari, Imruh, 'Introduction: African Cinema and the Emergent Africa', in June Givanni, ed., *Symbolic Narratives/African Cinema: Audiences, Theory, and the Moving Image*. London: BFI, 2000, pp. 3–24.

Bakewell, Peter, *A History of Latin America*, 2nd ed. Oxford: Blackwell, 2004.

Banham, Martin, and Eldred Durosimi Jones, '" . . . tinap aber we leck giant": African Celebrations of Shakespeare', in Shirley Chew and Alistair Stead, eds, *Translating Life: Studies in Transpositional Aesthetics*. Liverpool: Liverpool University Press, 1999, pp. 121–36.

Banham, Martin, Roshni Mooneram and Jane Plastow, 'Shakespeare and Africa', in Stanley Wells and Sarah Stanton, eds, *The Cambridge Companion to Shakespeare on Stage*. Cambridge: Cambridge University Press, 2002, pp. 284–99.

Bartoshevich, Aleksey, *Gamlety nashih dnej. Shekspirovskie chtenija*. Moscow: Izdaltel'stvo Moskcovskogo gumanitararnogo universiteta, 2010.

Barua, Bhaben, 'Shakespeare, Indian Renaissance in Bengal, and Assamese Literature', in D. A. Shankar, ed., *Shakespeare in Indian Languages*. Shimla: Institute of Advanced Study, 1999, pp. 85–111.

Basham, A. L., *The Wonder That Was India*, 3rd ed. London: Sidgwick and Jackson, 1988.

Bassi, Shaul, 'The Tragedies in Italy', in Michael Neill and David Schalkwyk, eds, *The Oxford Handbook of Shakespearean Tragedy*. Oxford: Oxford University Press, 2016, pp. 691–705.

Bayman, Louis, 'Neorealism', in Louis Bayman, ed., *Directory of World Cinema: Italy*. Bristol and Chicago: Intellect, 2011, pp. 54–57.

Beauregard, David, '"Great command o'ersways the order": Purgatory, Revenge, and Maimed Rites in *Hamlet*', *Religion and the Arts*, 11 (2007), pp. 45–73.

Behera, Navnita Chadha, *Demystifying Kashmir*. Washington, D.C.: Brookings Institution Press, 2006.

Ben-Ghiat, Ruth, 'Unmaking the Fascist Man: Masculinity, Film and the Transition from Dictatorship', *Journal of Modern Italian Studies*, 10.3 (2005), pp. 336–65.

Bene, Carmelo, *Opere: Con l'autographia di un ritratto*. Milan: Bompiani, 2008.

Bennett, Susan, and Christie Carson, eds, *Shakespeare Beyond English: A Global Experiment*. Cambridge: Cambridge University Press, 2013.

Bentes, Ivana, '*Deus E O Diablo Na Terra Do Sol/Black God, White Devil*', in Alberto Elena and Marina Díaz López, eds, *The Cinema of Latin America*. London and New York: Wallflower, 2003, pp. 89–97.

'The *Sertão* and the *Favela* in Contemporary Brazilian Film', in João Luiz Viera, ed., *Cinema Novo and Beyond*. West Haven, Conn.: Herlin Press, 1998, pp. 113–22.

Berensmeyer, Ingo, 'Cultural Ecology and Chinese *Hamlets*', *New Literary History*, 42.3 (2011), pp. 419–38.

Berry, Michael, 'Chinese Cinema with Hollywood Characteristics, or How *The Karate Kid* became a Chinese Film', in Carlos Rojas and Eileen Cheng-Yin Chow, eds, *The Oxford Handbook of Chinese Cinemas*. Oxford: Oxford University Press, 2013, pp. 170–89.

Bethe, Monica, 'Interlude: *Noh* and *Kyogen* Costumes and Masks', in Jonah Salz, ed., *A History of Japanese Theatre*. Cambridge: Cambridge University Press, 2016, pp. 62–67.

Betz, Mark, *Beyond the Subtitle: Remapping European Art Cinema*. Minneapolis and London: University of Minnesota Press, 2009.

Beumers, Birgit, *A History of Russian Cinema*. Oxford and New York: Berg, 2009.

Beumers, Birgit, and Mark Lipovetsky, *Performing Violence: Literary and Theatrical Experiments of New Russian Drama*. Bristol and Chicago: Intellect, 2009.

Bevington, David, *'Murder Most Foul': 'Hamlet' Through the Ages*. Oxford: Oxford University Press, 2011.

The Bhagavad Gita, ed. S. Radhakrishnan. London: George Allen and Unwin, 1948.

Bhardwaj, Vishal, with Basharat Peer, *'Haider': The Original Screenplay*. New Delhi: HarperCollins, 2014.

Bilgin, Inci, '*Hamlet* in Contemporary Turkey: Towards Postcolonial Feminist Rewrites?', *Multicultural Shakespeare*, 12.27 (2015), pp. 65–74.

Birrell, Anne, ed., *New Songs from a Jade Terrace: An Anthology of Early Chinese Love Poetry*. London, Boston and Sydney: George Allen and Unwin, 1982.

Black, J. Larry, *Vladimir Putin and the New World Order: Looking East, Looking West?*. Lanham and New York: Rowman and Littlefield, 2004.

Blier, Suzanne Preston, and James Morris, *Butabu: Adobe Architecture of West Africa*. New York: Princeton Architectural Press, 2004.

Boldt, Thea D., 'European Identities Made in Germany', in Atsuko Ichijo, ed., *Europe, Nations and Modernity*. Basingstoke: Palgrave, 2011, pp. 60–84.

Bolin, Michael, Erika Kraus and Felicie Read, *Benin*, 2nd ed. Milton Keynes: Other Places, 2014.

Bondanella, Peter, 'From Italian Neorealism to the Golden Age of Cinecittà', in Elizabeth Ezra, ed., *European Cinema*. Oxford: Oxford University Press, 2004, pp. 119–38.

Bonsaver, Guido, 'Mussolini's Fascism, Literary Censorship, and the Vatican', *Primerjalna Književnost*, 31 (2008), pp. 201–12.

Boone, Jon, and Michael Safi, 'India Strikes Back at Pakistan with Deadly Night Raids as Kashmir Dispute Escalates', *The Guardian*, 30 September (2016), p. 19.

Borenstein, Eliot, *Overkill: Sex and Violence in Contemporary Russian Culture*. Ithaca and London: Cornell University Press, 2008.

Bould, Mark, *Film Noir: From Berlin to Sin City*. London and New York: Wallflower, 2005.

Bradshaw, Graham, and Kaori Ashizu, 'Reading *Hamlet* in Japan', in Jonathan Bate, Jill L. Levenson and Dieter Mehl, eds, *Shakespeare and the Twentieth Century*. Newark: University of Delaware Press, 1998, pp. 350–63.

'British Films: *Hamile/Hamlet* (Ghana)', *Variety: Film Reviews 1907–1980*, 16 vols. New York and London: Garland, 1983, XI, n.p.

Brizio-Skov, Flavia, 'Spaghetti Westerns and Their Audiences', in Peter Bondanella, ed., *The Italian Cinema Book*. London: BFI, 2014, pp. 181–87.

Brown, Rebecca, and Judy Oder, 'The Protection of Women's Economic, Social and Cultural Rights in Africa', in Danwood Mzikenge Chirwa and Lilian Chenwi, eds, *The Protection of Economic, Social and Cultural Rights in Africa: International, Regional and National Perspectives*. Cambridge: Cambridge University Press, 2016, pp. 121–54.

Buchanan, Judith, *Shakespeare on Silent Film: An Excellent Dumb Discourse*. Cambridge: Cambridge University Press, 2009.

Buchanan, Tom, *Europe's Troubled Peace: 1945 to the Present*, 2nd ed. Oxford: Wiley-Blackwell, 2012.

Buckland, Raymond, *Gypsy Dream Dictionary*, 2nd ed. St Paul: Llewellyn Publications, 1998.

Buckley, Thea, 'Hero as Avatar: *Karmayogi*, Kerala's Kalarippayattu *Hamlet*', *The Shakespeare Institute Review*, 2, Spring (2013), pp. 41–46.

Burgen, Stephen, 'Court Remands Catalan Leader', *The Guardian*, 27 March (2018), p. 19.

Burke, Patrick, '"Hidden Games, Cunning Traps, Ambushes": The Russian *Hamlet*', *Shakespeare Yearbook*, 8 (1997), pp. 163–80.

Burnett, Mark Thornton, 'Global Shakespeare and the Censor: Adaptation, Context, and *Shakespeare Must Die*, a Thai Film Adaptation of *Macbeth*', *Shakespeare Survey*, 71 (2018), pp. 276–94.

Shakespeare and World Cinema. Cambridge: Cambridge University Press, 2013.

Burnett, Mark Thornton, Courtney Lehmann, Marguerite H. Rippy and Ramona Wray, *Great Shakespeareans: Welles, Kurosawa, Kozintsev, Zeffirelli*. London and New York: Bloomsbury, 2013.

Burt, Richard, *Unspeakable ShaXXXspeares: Queer Theory and American Kiddie Culture*. Basingstoke: Macmillan, 1998.

Burton, Julianne, 'Toward a History of Social Documentary in Latin America', in Julianne Burton, ed., *The Social Documentary in Latin America*. Pittsburgh: University of Pittsburgh Press, 1990, pp. 3–30.

Bushkovitch, Paul, *A Concise History of Russia*. Cambridge: Cambridge University Press, 2012.

Calbi, Maurizio, *Spectral Shakespeares: Media Adaptations in the Twenty-First Century*. New York: Palgrave, 2013.

Camí-Vela, María, 'Contemporary Barcelona Through the Female Eye', in Helio San Miguel and Lorenzo J. Torres Hortelano, eds, *World Film Locations: Barcelona*. Bristol and Chicago: Intellect, 2013, pp. 106–7.

Cardullo, Bert, ed., *Akira Kurosawa: Interviews*. Jackson: University Press of Mississippi, 2008.

Carlson, Marvin, *Performance: A Critical Introduction*. London and New York: Routledge, 1996.

Casavella, Francisco, *El Triunfo*. Barcelona: Editorial Anagrama, 2017.

Castro-Gómez, Santiago, '(Post)Coloniality for Dummies: Latin American Perspectives on Modernity, Coloniality, and the Geopolitics of Knowledge', in Mabel Moraña, Enrique Dussel and Carlos A. Jáuregui, eds, *Coloniality at Large: Latin America and the Postcolonial Debate*. Durham and London: Duke University Press, 2008, pp. 259–85.

Cetera, Anna, 'Translating Shakespeare for Performance', in Bruce R. Smith, ed., *The Cambridge Guide to the Worlds of Shakespeare*, 2 vols. Cambridge: Cambridge University Press, 2016, II, pp. 1375–80.

Chakravarti, Paromita, 'Theatre Reviews: *Haider*', *Shakespeare Bulletin*, 34.1 (2016), pp. 129–32.

'Urban Histories and Vernacular Shakespeare in Bengal: *Kolkatar Hamlet, Hemlet* and *Hamlet 2011*', in Shormishtha Panja and Babli Moitra Saraf, eds, *Performing Shakespeare in India: Exploring Indianness, Literatures and Cultures*. London and New Delhi: Sage, 2016, pp. 41–59.

Chanan, Michael, 'Latin American Cinema: From Underdevelopment to Postmodernism', in Stephanie Dennison and Song Hwee Lim, eds, *Remapping World Cinema: Identity, Culture and Politics in Film*. London: Wallflower, 2006, pp. 38–51.

Chandavarkar, Rajnarayam, *History, Culture and the Indian City*. Cambridge: Cambridge University Press, 2009.

Chandran, T. V., *Ritual as Ideology: Text and Context in Teyyam*. New Delhi: Indira Gandhi National Centre for the Arts, 2006.

Chapman, James, *Cinemas of the World*. London: Reaktion, 2003.

Charnes, Linda, *Hamlet's Heirs: Shakespeare and the Politics of a New Millennium*. New York and London: Routledge, 2006.

Chasteen, John Charles, 'Black Kings, Blackface Carnival, and Nineteenth-Century Origins of the Tango', in William H. Beezley and Linda A. Curcio-Nagy, eds, *Latin American Popular Culture: An Introduction*. Lanham: Scholarly Resources, 2004, pp. 43–60.

Born in Blood and Fire: A Concise History of Latin America, 2nd ed. New York: W. W. Norton, 2006.

National Rhythms, African Roots: The Deep History of Latin American Popular Dance. Albuquerque: University of New Mexico Press, 2004.

Chaudhuri, Shohini, *Contemporary World Cinema: Europe, the Middle East, East Asia and South Asia*. Edinburgh: Edinburgh University Press, 2005.

Chaudhuri, Supriya, 'Remembering Shakespeare in India: Colonial and Postcolonial Memory', in Clara Calvo and Coppélia Kahn, eds, *Celebrating Shakespeare: Commemoration and Cultural Memory*. Cambridge: Cambridge University Press, 2015, pp. 101–20.

Choudhury, Kushanava, *The Epic City: The World on the Streets of Calcutta*. London and New York: Bloomsbury, 2017.

Chen, Ya-Chen, *Women in Chinese Martial Arts Films of the New Millennium: Narrative Analyses and Gender Politics*. Lanham and Boulder: Lexington Books, 2012.

Chibnall, Steve, and Brian Macfarlane, *The British 'B' Film*. Basingstoke: Palgrave, 2009.

Chrisafis, Angelique, 'Myths of 68?', *The Guardian*, 15 January (2018), p. 37.

Ciecko, Anne, 'Contemporary Meta-Chinese Film Stardom and Transnational Transmedia Celebrity', in Song Hwee Lim and Julian Ward, eds, *The Chinese Cinema Book*. London: BFI, 2011, pp. 185–93.

Cinpoeş, Nicoleta, '*Hamlet* or the Skeletons in the Cupboard', in Keith Gregor, ed., *Shakespeare and Tyranny: Regimes of Reading in Europe and Beyond*. Newcastle-upon-Tyne: Cambridge Scholars, 2014, pp. 223–40.

Clark, Martin, *Modern Italy, 1871–1995*, 2nd ed. London and New York: Longman, 1996.

Clements, Jonathan, *Wu: The Chinese Empress who Schemed, Seduced, and Murdered her Way to Become a Living God*. Thrupp: Sutton Publishing, 2007.

Clogg, Richard, *A Concise History of Greece*, 3rd ed. Cambridge: Cambridge University Press, 2013.

Collick, John, *Shakespeare, Cinema and Society*. Manchester and New York: Manchester University Press, 1989.

Compan, Magali, 'Island Geography as Creole Biography: Shenaz Patel's Mauritian Literary Production', in Freida Ekoto and Kenneth Harrow, eds, *Rethinking African Cultural Production*. Bloomington and Indianapolis: Indiana University Press, 2015, pp. 177–96.

Condee, Nancy, *The Imperial Trace: Recent Russian Cinema*. Oxford: Oxford University Press, 2009.

Cook, Patrick J., *Cinematic 'Hamlet': The Films of Olivier, Zeffirelli, Branagh, and Almereyda*. Athens: Ohio University Press, 2011.

Corbridge, Stuart, John Harris and Craig Jeffrey, *India Today: Economy, Politics and Society*. Cambridge and Malden: Polity, 2013.

Courtney, Krystyna Kujawińska, and Katarzyna Kwapisz Williams, 'Central Eastern Europe', in Peter W. Marx, ed., *Hamlet-Handbuch: Stoffe, Aneignungen, Deutungen*. Stuttgart and Weimar: Verlag J. B. Meltzler, 2014, pp. 304–12.

Cowie, Peter, ed., *World Filmography 1967*. London: Tantivy, 1977.

Croteau, Melissa M., 'Aki Kaurismäki's *Hamlet Goes Business*: A Socialist Shakespearean Film Noir Comedy', in Richard Fotheringham, Christa Jansohn and R. S. White, eds, *Shakespeare's World/World Shakespeares*. Newark: University of Delaware Press, 2008, pp. 193–208.

Crowl, Samuel, *Screen Adaptations: Shakespeare's 'Hamlet'*. London and New York: Bloomsbury, 2014.

Curtin, Michael, *Playing to the World's Biggest Audience: The Globalization of Chinese Film and TV*. Berkeley, Los Angeles and London: University of California Press, 2007.

Cutler, Aaron, 'Marginal Revolutionary', *Sight & Sound*, 24.10, October (2014), pp. 50–51.

Cutrofello, Andrew, *All for Nothing: Hamlet's Negativity*. Cambridge, Mass.: MIT Press, 2014.

Daas, Manishita, 'The Cloud-Capped Star: Ritwik Ghatak on the Horizon of Global Art Cinema', in Rosalind Galt and Karl Schoonover, eds, *Global Art*

Cinema: New Theories and Histories. Oxford: Oxford University Press, 2010, pp. 238–51.

DaMatta, Roberto, *Carnivals, Rogues, and Heroes: An Interpretation of the Brazilian Dilemma*, tr. John Drury. Notre Dame and London: University of Notre Dame Press, 1991.

Daniélou, Alain, *The Myths and Gods of India: The Classic Work on Hindu Polytheism*. Rochester: Inner Traditions, 1991.

Dardanelli, Paolo, *Restructuring the European State: European Integration and State Reform*. Montreal and Kingston: McGill-Queen's University Press, 2017.

David, Ann R., 'King of Bollywood? The Construction of a Global Image in Shah Rukh Khan's Dance Choreography', in Rajinder Dudrah, Elke Mader and Bernhard Fuchs, eds, *SRK and Global Bollywood*. Oxford and New Delhi: Oxford University Press, 2015, pp. 279–307.

Dawson, Anthony B., *Shakespeare in Performance: 'Hamlet'*. Manchester: Manchester University Press, 1995.

De, Esha Niyogi, 'Modern Shakespeares in Popular Bombay Cinema: Translation, Subjection and Community', *Screen*, 43.1 (2002), pp. 19–40.

de Graft, Joe, 'Interview', in Bernth Lindfors, ed., *Africa Talks Back: Interviews with Anglophone African Writers*. Trenton and Asmara: Africa World Press, 2002, pp. 69–88.

de Grazia, Margreta, *'Hamlet' Without Hamlet*. Cambridge: Cambridge University Press, 2007.

Deleuze, Gilles, *The Deleuze Reader*, ed. Constantin V. Boundas. New York: Columbia University Press, 1993.

della Coletta, Cristina, *When Stories Travel: Cross-Cultural Encounters Between Fiction and Film*. Baltimore and London: Johns Hopkins University Press, 2012.

Dennison, Stephanie, 'The New Brazilian Bombshell: Sônia Braga, Race and Cinema in the 1970s', in Stephanie Dennison and Song Hwee Lim, eds, *Remapping World Cinema: Identity, Culture and Politics in Film*. London: Wallflower, 2006, pp. 135–43.

Deshpande, Shekhar, and Meta Mazaj, *World Cinema: A Critical Introduction*. London and New York: Routledge, 2018.

Desjardins, Chris, *Outlaw Masters of Japanese Film*. London and New York: I. B. Taurus, 2005.

Desser, David, *Eros Plus Massacre: An Introduction to the Japanese New Wave Cinema*. Bloomington and Indianapolis: Indiana University Press, 1988.

'Toward a Structural Analysis of the Postwar Samurai Film', in Arthur Nolletti and David Desser, eds, *Reframing Japanese Cinema: Authorship, Genre, History*. Bloomington and Indianapolis: Indiana University Press, 1992, pp. 145–64.

Devictor, Agnès, 'Classic Tools, Original Goals: Cinema and Public Policy in the Islamic Republic of Iran', in Richard Tapper, ed., *New Iranian Cinema: Politics, Representation and Identity*. London and New York: I. B. Taurus, 2002, pp. 66–76.

Devji, Faisal Fatehali, 'Subject to Translation: Shakespeare, Swahili, Socialism', *Postcolonial Studies*, 3.2 (2000), pp. 181–89.

Diawara, Manthia, *African Cinema: Politics and Culture*. Bloomington and Indianapolis: Indiana University Press, 1992.

Dickson, Andrew, *Worlds Elsewhere: Journeys around Shakespeare's Globe*. London: Bodley Head, 2015.

Dionne, Craig, and Parmita Kapadia, 'Shakespeare and Bollywood: The Difference a World Makes', in Craig Dionne and Parmita Kapadia, eds, *Bollywood Shakespeares*. New York and Basingstoke: Palgrave, 2014, pp. 1–18.

Diop, Birago, *Leurres et lueurs*. Paris: Présence Africaine, 1960.

D'Lugo, Marvin, 'Catalan Cinema: Historical Experience and Cinematic Practice', in Catherine Fowler, ed., *The European Cinema Reader*. London and New York: Routledge, 2002, pp. 163–73.

'Dogme 95 – The Vow of Chastity', in Catherine Fowler, ed., *The European Cinema Reader*. London and New York: Routledge, 2002, pp. 83–84.

Domenico, Roy Palmer, *Remaking Italy in the Twentieth Century*. Lanham and Boulder: Rowman and Littlefield, 2002.

Dönmez-Colin, Gönül, *The Routledge Dictionary of Turkish Cinema*. London and New York: Routledge, 2014.

   Turkish Cinema: Identity, Distance and Belonging. London: Reaktion, 2008.

Dorsay, Atilla, 'An Overview of Turkish Cinema from Its Origins to the Present Day', in Günsel Renda and C. Max Kortepeter, eds, *The Transformation of Turkish Culture: The Atatürk Legacy*. Princeton: Kingston Press, 1986, pp. 113–29.

Douglas, Michael, '*Jidai-geki*/Period Drama', in John Berra, ed., *Directory of World Cinema: Japan 2*. Bristol and Chicago: Intellect, 2012, pp. 225–27.

Dromgoole, Dominic, *Hamlet: Globe to Globe*. Edinburgh: Canongate, 2017.

Drouet, Pascale, and Nathalie Rivère de Carles, 'French Receptions of Shakespearean Tragedy: Between Liberty and Memory', in Michael Neill and David Schalkwyk, eds, *The Oxford Handbook of Shakespearean Tragedy*. Oxford: Oxford University Press, 2016, pp. 726–45.

Dutta, Krishna, *Calcutta: A Cultural and Literary History*. Oxford: Signal, 2003.

Dwyer, Rachel, and Divia Patel, *Cinema India: The Visual Culture of Hindi Film*. London: Reaktion, 2002.

Edmond, Rod, *Leprosy and Empire: A Medical and Cultural History*. Cambridge: Cambridge University Press, 2006.

Edmondson, Paul, Paul Prescott and Erin Sullivan, eds, *A Year of Shakespeare: Re-living the World Shakespeare Festival*. London and New York: Bloomsbury, 2013.

Eisenhofer, Stefan, *African Art*. Los Angeles and Cologne: Taschen, 2010.

Eleftheriotis, Dimitris, 'Turkish National Cinema', in Dimitris Eleftheriotis and Gary Needham, eds, *Asian Cinemas: A Reader and Guide*. Edinburgh: Edinburgh University Press, 2006, pp. 220–28.

Elsaesser, Thomas, *German Cinema – Terror and Trauma: Cultural Memory Since 1945*. London and New York: Routledge, 2014.

Emmerichs, Sharon, 'Shakespeare and the Landscape of Death: Crossing the Boundaries of Life and the Afterlife', *Shakespeare*, 8.2 (2012), pp. 171–94.

Erfani, Farhany, *Iranian Cinema and Philosophy: Shooting Truth*. New York: Palgrave, 2012.

Esfandiary, Shahab, *Iranian Cinema and Globalization: National, Transnational and Islamic Dimensions*. Bristol and Chicago: Intellect, 2012.

Eskola, Marjo, Tiina Räisä and Henrik Stenius, 'Identity Construction and Modernity in Finland: Borders, Ruptures and Significant Others', in Atsuko Ichijo, ed., *Europe, Nations and Modernity*. Basingstoke: Palgrave, 2011, pp. 183–207.

Espiritu, Talitha, 'Multiculturalism, Dictatorship, and Cinema Vanguards: Philippine and Brazilian Analogies', in Ella Shohat and Robert Stam, eds, *Multiculturalism, Postcoloniality, and Transnational Media*. New Brunswick: Rutgers University Press, 2003, pp. 279–98.

Etkind, Alexander, 'Mourning the Soviet Victims in a Cosmopolitan Way: *Hamlet* from Kozintsev to Riazanov', *Studies in Russian and Soviet Cinema*, 5.3 (2011), pp. 389–409.

Faiz, Ahmed Faiz, *The Rebel's Silhouette: Selected Poems*, tr. Agha Shahid Ali. Amherst: University of Massachusetts Press, 1995.

Fanon, Frantz, *Black Skin, White Masks*, tr. Charles Lam Markmann. London: Pluto Press, 1986.

Farhi, Farideh, 'The Tenth Presidential Elections and Their Aftermath', in Negin Nabavi, ed., *Iran: From Theocracy to the Green Movement*. New York: Palgrave, 2012, pp. 3–15.

Fayard, Nicole, 'France', in Peter W. Marx, ed., *Hamlet-Handbuch: Stoffe, Aneignungen, Deutungen*. Stuttgart and Weimar: Verlag J. B. Meltzler, 2014, pp. 284–88.

Ferdowsi, Abolqasem, *Shahnameh: The Persian Book of Kings*, tr. Dick Davis. London and New York: Penguin Books, 2006.

Ferguson, Alisa Grant, *Shakespeare, Cinema, Counter-Culture: Appropriation and Inversion*. London and New York: Routledge, 2016.

Filčák, Richard, *Living Beyond the Pale: Environmental Justice and the Roma Minority*. Budapest and New York: Central European Press, 2012.

Findley, Carter Vaughn, *Turkey, Islam, Nationalism, and Modernity: A History, 1789–2007*. New Haven: Yale University Press, 2010.

Fischlin, Daniel, 'Outerspeares: Shakespeare, Intermedia, and the Limits of Adaptation', in Daniel Fischlin, ed., *OuterSpeares: Shakespeare, Intermedia, and the Limits of Adaptation*. Toronto, Buffalo and London: University of Toronto Press, 2014, pp. 3–50.

Floor, Willem, *The History of Theatre in Iran*. Washington, D.C.: Mage Publishers, 2005.

Fraser, Angus, *The Gypsies*. Oxford: Blackwell, 1995.

Freud, Sigmund, *The Interpretation of Dreams*, tr. A. A. Brill. Ware: Wordsworth, 1997.

Fritsch, Herbert, and Sabrina Zwach, *Hamlet_X: Interpolierte Fressen*. Berlin: Theater der Zeit, 2006.

Frye, Roland Mushat, *The Renaissance Hamlet: Issues and Responses in 1600*. Princeton: Princeton University Press, 1984.

Fryer, Peter, *Rhythms of Resistance: African Musical Heritage in Brazil*. London: Pluto Press, 2000.

Gabriel, Theodore, *Playing God: Belief and Ritual in the Muttappan Cult of North Malabar*. London and Oakville: Equinox, 2010.

Galloway, Patrick, *Warring Clans, Fighting Blades: A Samurai Film Companion*. Berkeley: Stone Bridge, 2009.

Gandhi, Mahatma, *The Writings of Gandhi*, ed. Ronald Duncan. London: Fontana/Collins, 1983.

Garber, Marjorie, *Dream in Shakespeare: From Metaphor to Metamorphosis*. New Haven and London: Yale University Press, 2013.

Garritano, Carmela, *African Video Movies and Global Desires: A Ghanaian History*. Athens: Ohio University Press, 2013.

Gay y Blasco, Paloma, 'Picturing "Gypsies": Interdisciplinary Approaches to Roma Representation', *Third Text*, 22.3 (2008), pp. 297–303.

Ghālib, Mirza, *Love Sonnets of Ghālib*, ed. Sarfaraz K. Niazi. New Delhi: RUPA, 2011.

Gibbs, James, 'Joe de Graft: Theatrical Prophet with Strange Honours', in Martin Banham, James Gibbs and Femi Osofian, eds, *Playwrights and Politics*. Oxford: James Currey, 2001, pp. 72–83.

Gibbs, James, and Christine Matzke, '"accents yet unknown": Examples of Shakespeare from Ghana, Malawi and Eritrea', in Norbert Schaffeld, ed., *Shakespeare's Legacy: The Appropriation of the Plays in Post-Colonial Drama*. Trier: WVT, 2005, pp. 15–36.

Gillies, John, Minami Ryuta, Ruru Li and Poonam Trivedi, 'Shakespeare on the Stages of Asia', in Stanley Wells and Sarah Stanton, eds, *The Cambridge Companion to Shakespeare on Stage*. Cambridge: Cambridge University Press, 2002, pp. 259–81.

Givens, John, 'Shakespearean Tragedy in Russia: In Equal Scale Weighing Delight and Dole', in Michael Neill and David Schalkwyk, eds, *The Oxford Handbook of Shakespearean Tragedy*. Oxford: Oxford University Press, 2016, pp. 761–76.

Goodman, David G., 'Japan', in James R. Brandon, ed., *The Cambridge Guide to Asian Theatre*. Cambridge: Cambridge University Press, 1993, pp. 142–79.

Gooptu, Sharmistha, *Bengali Cinema: 'An Other Nation'*. New York and London: Routledge, 2011.

Gopal, Sangita, and Biswarup Sen, 'Inside and Out: Song and Dance in Bollywood Cinema', in Rajinder Dudrah and Jigna Desai, eds, *The Bollywood Reader*. Maidenhead and New York: Open University Press/ McGraw-Hill, 2008, pp. 147–57.

Gordon, Colette, '"Mind the Gap": Globalism, Postcolonialism and Making up Africa in the Cultural Olympiad', in Paul Prescott and Erin Sullivan, eds,

Shakespeare on the Global Stage: Performance and Festivity in the Olympic Year. London and New York: Bloomsbury, 2015, pp. 191–225.

Gow, Christopher, *From Iran to Hollywood and Some Places In-Between: Reframing Post- Revolutionary Iranian Cinema*. London and New York: I. B. Taurus, 2011.

Gozzano, Guido, *The Man I Pretend to Be*, tr. Michael Palma. Princeton: Princeton University Press, 1981.

Grabar, Oleg, *The Formation of Islamic Art*, 2nd ed. New Haven and London: Yale University Press, 1987.

Grammaticus, Saxo, *The History of the Danes*, ed. Hilda Ellis Davidson, 2 vols. Cambridge: D. S. Brewer, 1979.

Greenblatt, Stephen, *Hamlet in Purgatory*. Princeton and Oxford: Princeton University Press, 2001.

Gregor, Keith, *Shakespeare in the Spanish Theatre: 1772 to the Present*. London and New York: Continuum, 2010.

Griggs, Yvonne, 'Dogmatic Shakespeare: A "Recognition of Ghostly Presences" in Thomas Vinterberg's *Festen* and Kristian Levring's *The King Is Alive*', *Journal of Adaptation in Film and Performance*, 2.2 (2009), pp. 109–19.

Gugler, Joseph, *African Film: Re-Imagining a Continent*. Bloomington and Indianapolis: Indiana University Press, 2003.

Guneratne, Anthony, *Shakespeare, Film Studies, and the Visual Cultures of Modernity*. New York: Palgrave, 2008.

Gupt, Somnath, *The Parsi Theatre: Its Origins and Development*, tr. Kathryn Hansen. Calcutta and New Delhi: Seagull Books, 2005.

Gürata, Ahmet, 'Translating Modernity: Remakes in Turkish Cinema', in Dimitris Eleftheriotis and Gary Needham, eds, *Asian Cinemas: A Reader and Guide*. Edinburgh: Edinburgh University Press, 2006, pp. 242–54.

Guy, Will, 'The Czech Lands and Slovakia: Another False Dawn?', in Will Guy, ed., *Between Past and Future: The Roma of Central and Eastern Europe*. Hatfield: University of Hertfordshire Press, 2001, pp. 285–323.

Hake, Sabine, *German National Cinema*. London and New York: Routledge, 2002.

Hahner-Herzog, Iris, Maria Kecskési and Lászlo Vagda, *African Masks from the Barbier-Mueller Collection, Geneva*. Munich, London and New York: Prestel, 2004.

Hanchard, Michael, 'Black Cinderella? Race and the Public Sphere in Brazil', in Michael Hanchard, ed., *Racial Politics in Contemporary Brazil*. Durham and London: Duke University Press, 1999, pp. 59–81.

Hanioğlu, M. Şükrü, *Atatürk: An Intellectual Biography*. Princeton and Oxford: Princeton University Press, 2011.

Hashmi, Ali Madeeh, *Love and Revolution: Faiz Ahmed Faiz, the Authorized Biography*. New Delhi: Rupa, 2016.

The Way It Once Was: Faiz Ahmed Faiz – His Life, His Poems. New Delhi: HarperCollins, 2012.

Hatchuel, Sarah, 'Plays-within-the-Film', in Bruce R. Smith, ed., *The Cambridge Guide to the Worlds of Shakespeare*, 2 vols. Cambridge: Cambridge University Press, 2016, II, pp. 1946–53.

Hatchuel, Sarah, and Nathalie Vienne-Guerrin, eds, *Shakespeare on Screen: 'Hamlet'*. Mont-Saint-Aignan: Publications de l'Université de Rouen et du Havre, 2011.

Heldt, Gustav, ed., *The Kojiki: An Account of Ancient Matters*. New York: Columbia University Press, 2014.

Hirsch, Foster, *Film Noir: The Dark Side of the Screen*. New York: Da Capo, 1981.

Höfele, Andreas, *No Hamlets: German Shakespeare from Nietzsche to Carl Schmitt*. Oxford: Oxford University Press, 2016.

Hogan, Patrick Colm, *Imagining Kashmir: Emplotment and Colonialism*. Lincoln and London: University of Nebraska Press, 2016.

Hortmann, Wilhelm, *Shakespeare on the German Stage: The Twentieth Century*. Cambridge: Cambridge University Press, 1988.

Howard, Douglas A., *The History of Turkey*. Westport: Greenwood, 2001.

Howard, Tony, *Women as Hamlet: Performance and Interpretation in Theatre, Film and Fiction*. Cambridge: Cambridge University Press, 2007.

Hsieh, 'Camilla Chun-Pai, Using Sinicised Adaptations for Pedagogy in Taiwan: *The Banquet* and *Bond*', in Kate Flaherty, Penny Gay and L. E. Semler, eds, *Teaching Shakespeare Beyond the Centre: Australasian Perspectives*. Basingstoke: Palgrave, 2013, pp. 193–210.

Hutcheon, Linda, *A Theory of Parody: The Teachings of Twentieth-Century Art Forms*. Urbana and Chicago: University of Illinois Press, 2000.

Ichijo, Atsuko, 'Introduction: Europe as Modernity', in Atsuko Ichijo, ed., *Europe, Nations and Modernity*. Basingstoke: Palgrave, 2011, pp. 1–10.

Iezzi, Julie A., '*Kabuki*: Superheroes and *Femmes Fatales*', in Jonah Salz, ed., *A History of Japanese Theatre*. Cambridge: Cambridge University Press, 2016, pp. 102–40.

Invitation to Premiere: '*O Jogo da Vida e da Morte/A Game of Life and Death*', Accesso D996 (Miscellaneous), Cinemateca Brasileira, São Paulo.

Ippaso, Katia, *Amleto a Gerusalemme*. Roma: Editoria & Spettacolo, 2009.

Iványi-Bitter, Brigitta, *Kovásznai, a Cold War Artist: Animation, Painting, Freedom*, tr. Andrea Ágnes Szekeres. Budapest: Kovásznai Research Centre Foundation, 2016.

Jacoby, Alexander, *A Critical Handbook of Japanese Film Directors: From the Silent Era to the Present Day*. Berkeley: Stone Bridge, 2008.

Jahed, Parviz, 'Introduction', in Parviz Jahed, ed., *Directory of World Cinema: Iran*. Bristol and Chicago: Intellect, 2012, pp. 6–9.

Jameson, Fredric, 'Afterword: Adaptation as a Philosophical Problem', in Colin MacCabe, Kathleen Murray and Rick Warner, eds, *True to the Spirit: Film Adaptation and the Question of Fidelity*. Oxford: Oxford University Press, 2011, pp. 215–33.

The Geopolitical Aesthetic: Cinema and Space in the World System. Bloomington and Indianapolis: Indiana University Press, 1992.

Postmodernism, or, The Cultural Logic of Late Capitalism. London: Verso, 1991.

Jatoo, Sushma, and Sudhir Lall, 'Introduction', in Sushma Jatoo and Sudhir Lall, eds, *Bhand Pather: The Folk Theatre of Kashmir*. Delhi: B. R. Publishing, 2016, pp. 1–6.

Johnson, Randal, and Robert Stam, eds, *Brazilian Cinema*, 2nd ed. New York: Columbia University Press, 1995.

Jørgensen, Anne Mette, 'Sankofa and Modern Authenticity in Ghanaian Film and Television', in Mai Palmberg and Maria Eriksson Baaz, eds, *Same and Other: Negotiating African Identity in Cultural Production*. Stockholm: Nordiska Afrikainstitutet, 2001, pp. 119–41.

Josipovici, Gabriel, *Hamlet: Fold on Fold*. New Haven and London: Yale University Press, 2016.

Joubin, Alexa Alice, *Chinese Shakespeares: Two Centuries of Cultural Exchange*. New York: Columbia University Press, 2009.

'The Paradox of Female Agency: Ophelia and East Asian Sensibilities', in Kaara L. Peterson and Deanne Williams, eds, *The Afterlife of Ophelia*. New York: Palgrave, 2012, pp. 79–100.

Judt, Tony, *Postwar: A History of Europe Since 1945*. London: Vintage, 2010.

Jurkowski, Henryk, 'African Puppets and Masks: Links in a Historical Chain', in Don Rubin, Ousmane Diakhaté and Hansel Ndumbe Eyoh, eds, *The World Encyclopedia of Contemporary Theatre: Africa*. London and New York: Routledge, 1997, pp. 38–40.

Kääpä, Pietari, *The National and Beyond: The Globalization of Finnish Cinema in the Films of Aki and Mika Kaurismäki*. Oxford and Bern: Peter Lang, 2010.

Kabir, Ananya Jahanara, *Territory of Desire: Representing the Valley of Kashmir*. Minneapolis and London: University of Minnesota Press, 2009.

Kadono, Izumi, 'The Kabuki Version of *Hamlet*: *Hamlet Yamato No Nishikie*', *Shakespeare Yearbook*, 9 (1999), pp. 105–21.

Kagaya, Shinko, and Miura Hiroko, '*Noh* and *Muromachi* Culture', in Jonah Salz, ed., *A History of Japanese Theatre*. Cambridge: Cambridge University Press, 2016, pp. 24–61.

Kaldova, Josef, 'The Gypsies of Czechoslovakia', in David Crowe and John Kolsti, eds, *The Gypsies of Eastern Europe*. Armonk and London: M. E. Sharpe, 1991, pp. 93–115.

Kalsang, Ladrang, *The Guardian Deities of Tibet*, tr. Pema Thinley. Laxmi Nagar: Winsome Books, 1996.

Kanda, K. C., ed., *Urdu Ghazals: An Anthology from 16th to 20th Century*. New Delhi: Sterling, 1995.

'Kashmir Clashes Kill 7', *The Guardian*, 10 July (2017), p. 32.

Kennedy, Dennis, 'Found in Translation', *Around the Globe*, 50, Spring (2012), pp. 2–4.

Khilnani, Sunil, *The Idea of India*. London and New York: Penguin, 2012.

Khosronejad, Pedran, 'The People of the Air: Healing and Spirit Possession in South Iran', in Thierry Zarcone and Angela Hobart, eds, *Shamanism and*

Islam: Sufism, Healing Rituals and Spirits in the Muslim World. London and New York: I. B. Taurus, 2013, pp. 131–67.

King, Richard, *Indian Philosophy: An Introduction to Hindu and Buddhist Thought.* Edinburgh: Edinburgh University Press, 1999.

Kiséry, András, *Hamlet's Moment: Drama and Political Knowledge in Early Modern England.* Oxford: Oxford University Press, 2016.

Kliman, Bernice W., *'Hamlet': Film, Television, and Audio Performance.* Madison and Teaneck: Fairleigh Dickinson University Press, 1988.

Koechlin, Kalki, *A Document in Madness: Do Indian Women Mirror Ophelia?.* London: British Council, 2016.

Koliodimos, Dimitris, *The Greek Filmography, 1914 Through 1996.* Jefferson and London: McFarland, 1999.

Kopytoff, Igor, 'Ancestors as Elders in Africa', in Roy Richard Grinker and Christopher B. Steiner, eds, *Perspectives on Africa: A Reader in Culture, History, and Representation.* Oxford: Blackwell, 1997, pp. 412–21.

Kozintsev, Grigori, *'King Lear': The Space of Tragedy,* tr. Mary Mackintosh. London: Heinemann, 1977.
    Shakespeare: Time and Conscience, tr. Joyce Vining. London: Dennis Dobson, 1967.
    Vash Grigorii Kozintsev, ed. Iakov Butovskii and Valentina Kozintseva. Moscow: Artist, Rezhisser, Teatr, 1996.
    Vremia tragedii. Moscow: Vagrius, 2004.

Kurlansky, Mark, *1968: The Year That Rocked the World.* New York: Random House, 2004.

Kurup, K. K. N., *Poorakkali and Maruthukali: A Performance of Male Dancers in the Bhagavati Temples of Malabar.* New Delhi: National Mission for Manuscripts, 2017.

Laachir, Karima, and Saeed Talajooy, 'Introduction', in Karima Laachir and Saeed Talajooy, eds, *Resistance in Contemporary Middle Eastern Cultures: Literature, Cinema and Music.* London and New York: Routledge, 2013, pp. 1–12.

Ladner, Lorne, 'Practice: Seeing with Eyes of Compassion', in Lorne Ladner, ed., *The Wheel of Great Compassion: The Practice of the Prayer Wheel in Tibetan Buddhism.* Boston: Wisdom Publications, 2000, pp. 3–14.

Laforgue, Jules, *Moral Tales,* tr. William Jay Smith. London: Picador, 1985.
    Poems of Jules Laforgue, ed. J. A. Hiddleston. Oxford: Blackwell, 1975.

LaGamma, Alisa, *Kongo: Power and Majesty.* New York: Metropolitan Museum of Art, 2015.

LaGamma, Alisa, and Christine Giuntini, *The Essential Art of African Textiles: Design Without End.* New Haven and London: Yale University Press, 2008.

Lambton, Ann K. S., *Persian Vocabulary.* Cambridge: Cambridge University Press, 1953.

Landrigan, Stephen, and Qais Akbar Omar, *Shakespeare in Kabul.* London: Haus Publishing, 2012.

Landy, Marcia, *Italian Film.* Cambridge: Cambridge University Press, 2000.

Lane, Jill, *Blackface Cuba, 1840–1895*. Philadelphia: University of Pennsylvania Press, 2005.

Lanier, Douglas M., 'Film Spin-Offs and Citations', in Richard Burt, ed., *Shakespeares After Shakespeare: An Encyclopedia of the Bard in Mass Media and Popular Culture*, 2 vols. Westport and London: Greenwood, 2007, I, pp. 132–365.

    '*Hamlet*: Tragedy and Film Adaptation', in Michael Neill and David Schalkwyk, eds, *The Oxford Handbook of Shakespearean Tragedy*. Oxford: Oxford University Press, 2016, pp. 572–87.

    '*Nouveau Noir*: Claude Chabrol's *Ophélia*, Shakespeare's *Hamlet*, and the *Nouvelle Vague*', in Sarah Hatchuel and Nathalie Vienne-Guerrin, eds, *Shakespeare on Screen: 'Hamlet'*. Mont-Saint-Aignan: Publications de l'Université de Rouen et du Havre, 2011, pp. 235–55.

    'Shakescorp *Noir*', *Shakespeare Quarterly*, 53.2 (2002), pp. 157–80.

Leaming, Barbara, *Grigori Kozintsev*. Boston: Twayne, 1980.

Lebdai, Benaouda, 'Traces of Shakespeare's Tragedies in Africa', in Eric C. Brown and Estelle Rivier, eds, *Shakespeare in Performance*. Newcastle-upon-Tyne: Cambridge Scholars, 2013, pp. 182–93.

Leggatt, Alexander, *Shakespeare's Tragedies: Violation and Identity*. Cambridge: Cambridge University Press, 2005.

Lentz, Carola, *Ethnicity and the Making of History in Northern Ghana*. Edinburgh: Edinburgh University Press, 2006.

Levenson, Jill L., and Robert Ormsby, eds, *The Shakespearean World*. London and New York: Routledge, 2017.

Levi, Pavle, *Disintegration in Flames: Aesthetics and Ideology in the Yugoslav and Post-Yugoslav Cinema*. Stanford: Stanford University Press, 2007.

Levin, Joanna, 'Lady Macbeth and the Daemonologie of Hysteria', *English Literary History*, 69.1 (2002), pp. 21–55.

Lewis, Rhodri, *Hamlet and the Vision of Darkness*. Princeton and Oxford: Princeton University Press, 2017.

    'Hamlet, Metaphor, and Memory', *Studies in Philology*, 109.5 (2012), pp. 609–41.

Li, Ruru, 'Millennium Shashibiya: Shakespeare in the Chinese-Speaking World', in Dennis Kennedy and Yong Li Lan, eds, *Shakespeare in Asia: Contemporary Performance*. Cambridge: Cambridge University Press, 2010, pp. 170–87.

    Shashibiya: Staging Shakespeare in China. Hong Kong: Hong Kong University Press, 2003.

Lieblein, Leanore, 'Nuancing Diversity: The Boyokani Company *Hamlet*', *alt. theatre*, 4.2–3 (2006), pp. 22–24, 31.

Liew, Maria Van, 'Immigration Films: Communicating Conventions of (In)visibility in Contemporary Spain', in Jay Beck and Vicente Rodríguez Ortega, eds, *Contemporary Spanish Cinema and Genre*. Manchester and New York: Manchester University Press, 2008, pp. 259–78.

Litvin, Margaret, 'Arab Near East', in Peter W. Marx, ed., *Hamlet-Handbuch: Stoffe, Aneignungen, Deutungen*. Stuttgart and Weimar: Verlag J. B. Melzler, 2014, pp. 321–29.

Loder, Conny, 'Siting *Hamlet* for the Online Generation: The *Hamlet_X* Project', in Ruth J. Owen, ed., *The Hamlet Zone: Reworking 'Hamlet' for European Cultures*. Newcastle-upon-Tyne: Cambridge Scholars, 2012, pp. 85–90.

Loftis, Sonya Freeman, Allison Kellar and Lisa Ulevich, 'Introduction: Post-*Hamlet*', in Sonya Freeman Loftis, Allison Kellar and Lisa Ulevich, eds, *Shakespeare's 'Hamlet' in an Era of Textual Exhaustion*. London and New York: Routledge, 2018, pp. 1–25.

Luna, Francisco Vidal, and Herbert S. Klein, *Brazil Since 1980*. Cambridge: Cambridge University Press, 2006.

Ma, Sheng-Mei, *East-West Montage: Reflections on Asian Bodies in Diaspora*. Honolulu: University of Hawai'i Press, 2007.

Macaulay, Thomas Babington, *Prose and Poetry*, ed. G. M. Young. Cambridge, Mass.: Harvard University Press, 1957.

MacCabe, Colin, 'Introduction: Bazinian Adaptation', in Colin MacCabe, Kathleen Murray and Rick Warner, eds, *True to the Spirit: Film Adaptation and the Question of Fidelity*. Oxford: Oxford University Press, 2011, pp. 3–25.

McClean, James L., *Japan: A Modern History*. New York and London; Norton, 2002.

MacFadyen, David, *The Sad Comedy of Èl'dar Riazanov: An Introduction*. Montreal and Kingston: McGill-Queen's University Press, 2003.

McGarry, Aidan, *Romaphobia: The Last Acceptable Form of Racism*. London: Zed Books, 2017.

McLuskie, Kate, '*Macbeth/uMabatha*: Global Shakespeare in a Post-Colonial Market', *Shakespeare Survey*, 52 (1999), pp. 154–65.

Maduakor, Obi, 'Joe de Graft & the Ghana Cultural Revival', in Martin Banham, James Gibbs and Femi Osofian, eds, *Playwrights and Politics*. Oxford: James Currey, 2001, pp. 65–71.

The Mahābhārata, ed. John D. Smith. London and New York: Penguin, 2009.

Maher, Mary Z., *Modern Hamlets and Their Soliloquies*. Iowa City: University of Iowa Press, 2003.

Makaryk, Irena R., 'Wartime *Hamlet*', in Irena R. Makaryk and Joseph G. Price, eds, *Shakespeare in the Worlds of Communism and Socialism*. Toronto, Buffalo and London: University of Toronto Press, 2006, pp. 119–35.

Malère, Kaf, 'Un *Hamlet* africain', *Horizons Maghrébins: Le Droit à la Mémoire*, 53 (2005), pp. 163–71.

Manchester, William, *The Arms of Krupp, 1587–1968: The Rise and Fall of the Industrial Dynasty that Armed Germany at War*. New York and Boston: Little Brown, 2003.

Manning, Patrick, *Francophone Sub-Sarahan Africa, 1880–1995*, 2nd ed. Cambridge: Cambridge University Press, 1998.

Manvell, Roger, *Shakespeare and the Film*. London: Dent, 1971.

Martin-Jones, David, *Deleuze, Cinema and National Identity: Narrative Time in National Contexts*. Edinburgh: Edinburgh University Press, 2006.

Marušak, Martin, and Leo Singer, 'Social Unrest in Slovakia 2004: Romani Reaction to Neoliberal "Reforms"', in Nando Sigona and Nidhi Trehan, eds, *Romani Politics in Contemporary Europe: Poverty, Ethnic Mobilization, and the Neoliberal Order*. Basingstoke: Palgrave, 2009, pp. 186–208.

Marx, Peter W., ed., *Hamlet-Handbuch: Stoffe, Aneignungen, Deutungen*. Stuttgart and Weimar: Verlag J. B. Meltzler, 2014.

Massai, Sonia, '"The Wide World": Shakespeare Across the Globe', in Gordon McMullan and Zoë Wilcox, eds, *Shakespeare in Ten Acts*. London: The British Library, 2016, pp. 63–79.

Massie, Suzanne, *Land of the Firebird: The Beauty of Old Russia*. New York: Simon and Schuster, 1980.

Matras, Yaron, *The Romani Gypsies*. Cambridge, Mass.: Harvard University Press, 2015.

Matzke, Christine, 'Afrika', in Peter W. Marx, ed., *Hamlet-Handbuch: Stoffe, Aneiguungen, Deutungen*. Stuttgart and Weimar: Verlag J. B. Meltzler, 2014, pp. 330–42.

Mazierska, Ewa, *European Cinema and Intertextuality: History, Memory and Politics*. Basingstoke: Palgrave, 2011.

Jerzy Skolimowski: The Cinema of a Non-Conformist. New York and Oxford: Berghahn, 2010.

Meade, Teresa E., *A Modern History of Latin America*. Oxford: Blackwell, 2010.

Mensah, Atta Annan, 'The Great Ode of History: Music and Dance in Africa', in Don Rubin, Ousmane Diakhaté and Hansel Ndumbe Eyoh, eds, *The World Encyclopedia of Contemporary Theatre: Africa*. London and New York: Routledge, 1997, pp. 30–37.

Mikedakis, Emmi, 'Manipulating Language: Metaphors in the Political Discourse of Georgios Papadoulos (1967–1973)', in Elizabeth Close, Michael Tsianikas and George Frazis, eds, *Greek Studies in Australia: Research Perspectives*. Adelaide: Flinders University Press, 2003, pp. 76–86.

Milton, John, 'Severino in English', *Cadernos de Literatura em Tradução*, 2 (1998), pp. 107–17.

Moallem, Minoo, *Between Warrior Brother and Veiled Sister: Islamic Fundamentalism and the Politics of Patriarchy in Iran*. Berkeley, Los Angeles and London: University of California Press, 2005.

Mock, Stephen J., *Symbols of Defeat in the Construction of National Identity*. Cambridge: Cambridge University Press, 2002.

Modarressi, Taghi, 'The Zar Cult in South Iran', in Raymond Prince, ed., *Trance and Possession States*. Montreal: R. M. Bucke Memorial Society, 1968, pp. 149–55.

Modenessi, Alfredo Michel, 'Meaning by Shakespeare South of the Border', in Sonia Massai, ed., *World-Wide Shakespeares: Local Appropriations in Film and Performance*. London and New York: Routledge, 2005, pp. 104–11.

'Of Shadows and Stones: Revering and Translating "The Word" Shakespeare in Mexico', *Shakespeare Survey*, 54 (2001), pp. 152–64.

Modenessi, Alfredo Michel, and Margarida Gandara Rauen, 'Latin America', in Peter W. Marx, ed., *Hamlet-Handbuch: Stoffe, Aneignungen, Deutungen*. Stuttgart and Weimar: Verlag J. B. Meltzler, 2014, pp. 366–73.

Montero, Alfred P., *Brazilian Politics: Reframing a Democratic State in a Changing World*. Cambridge: Polity, 2005.

Moore, Tiffany Ann Conroy, *Kozintsev's Shakespeare Films: Russian Political Protest in 'Hamlet' and 'King Lear'*. Jefferson and London: McFarland, 2012.

Morozov, Mikhail M., *Shakespeare on the Soviet Stage*, tr. David Magarshack. London: Soviet News, 1947.

Mosteghanemi, Ahlem, *When Shakespeare Thought I Was Cleopatra*. London: British Council, 2016.

Murphy, David, and Patrick Williams, *Postcolonial African Cinema: Ten Directors*. Manchester and New York: Manchester University Press, 2007.

Naden, A. J., and R. L. Schaefer, 'The Meaning of "Fra-Fra"', *Institute of African Studies Research Review*, 9.2 (1973), pp. 7–12.

Naficy, Hamid, 'Iranian Cinema', in Geoffrey Nowell-Smith, ed., *The Oxford History of World Cinema*. Oxford: Oxford University Press, 1996, pp. 672–78.

'Islamizing Film Culture in Iran: A Post-Khatami Update', in Richard Tapper, ed., *New Iranian Cinema: Politics, Representation and Identity*. London and New York: I. B. Taurus, 2002, pp. 26–65.

A Social History of Iranian Cinema: The Globalizing Era, 1984–2010. Durham and London: Duke University Press, 2012.

Nagib, Lúcia, *Brazil on Screen: Cinema Novo, New Cinema, Utopia*. London and New York: I. B. Taurus, 2007.

Neill, Michael, *Issues of Death: Mortality and Identity in English Renaissance Tragedy*. Oxford: Clarendon, 1997.

Neto, João Cabral de Melo, *Selected Poetry, 1937–1990*, ed. Djelal Kadir. Hanover and London: Wesleyan University Press, 1994.

Newman, Karen, *Essaying Shakespeare*. Minneapolis and London: University of Minnesota Press, 2009.

Nkrumah, Kwame, *I Speak of Freedom*. London: Heinemann, 1961.

Nochimson, Martha P., *World on Film: An Introduction*. Oxford: Wiley-Blackwell, 2010.

Norris, Steven N., *Blockbuster History in the New Russia: Movies, Memory, and Patriotism*. Bloomington and Indianapolis: Indiana University Press, 2012.

'Obituaries: Berthold Beitz', *The Times*, 2 August (2013), p. 49.

O'Leary, Niamh J., 'Ambition and Desire: Gertrude as Tragic Hero in Feng Xiaogang's *The Banquet*', *The Upstart Crow*, 31 (2012), pp. 63–80.

Osanloo, Arzoo, *The Politics of Women's Rights in Iran*. Princeton: Princeton University Press, 2009.

Osborne, Laurie E., 'Filming Shakespeare in a Cultural Thaw: Soviet Appropriations of Shakespearean Treacheries in 1955–6', *Textual Practice*, 9.2 (1995), pp. 325–47.

Ottenberg, Simon, 'Artistic and Sex Roles in a Limba Chiefdom', in Christine Oppong, ed., *Female and Male in West Africa*. London, Boston and Sydney: George Allen and Unwin, 1983, pp. 76–90.

Oukaderova, Lida, *The Cinema of the Soviet Thaw: Space, Materiality, Movement*. Bloomington: Indiana University Press, 2017.

Ovid, *The Metamorphoses*, tr. Mary M. Innes. Harmondsworth: Penguin, 1955.

Owen, Ruth J., ed., *The Hamlet Zone: Reworking 'Hamlet' for European Cultures*. Newcastle-upon-Tyne: Cambridge Scholars, 2012.

Owlia, Shekufeh, 'The New Woman and the Oriental Tropes as Portrayed in the Iranian Film *Tardid* Based on *Hamlet*', in Maryam Beyad and Ali Salami, eds, *Culture-Blind Shakespeare: Multiculturalism and Diversity*. Newcastle-upon-Tyne: Cambridge Scholars, 2016, pp. 107–18.

Owusu, Heike, *African Symbols*. New York and London: Sterling, 2000.

Owusu-Addo, J., 'Traditional Forms of Architecture in Ghana', *International Social Science Journal*, 30.3 (1978), pp. 449–76.

Page, Ben, '"And the Oscar Goes to . . . *Daybreak in Udi*": Understanding Late Colonial Community Development and Its Legacy Through Film', *Development and Change*, 45.5 (2014), pp. 838–68.

Paker, Saliha, '*Hamlet* in Turkey', *New Comparison*, 2 (1986), pp. 89–105.

Papadimitriou, Lydia, 'Music, Dance and Cultural Identity in the Greek Film Musical', in Lydia Papadimitriou and Yannis Tzioumakis, eds, *Greek Cinema: Texts, Histories, Ideologies*. Bristol and Chicago: Intellect, 2012, pp. 147–66.

Pasqualino, Caterina, 'The Gypsies, Poor but Happy', *Third Text*, 22.3 (2008), pp. 337–45.

Pavlović, Tatjana, Inmaculada Álvarez, Rosana Blanco-Cano, Anitra Grisales, Alejandra Osorio and Alejandra Sánchez, *100 Years of Spanish Cinema*. Oxford: Wiley-Blackwell, 2009.

Peer, Basharat, *Curfewed Night: A Memoir of War in Kashmir*. London: HarperCollins, 2011.

Peña, Richard, Doğa Kayalar Polat, Sean M. Dixon and Alexandra N. Sprano, *The Space Between: A Panorama of Cinema in Turkey*. New York: The Film Society of Lincoln Centre, 2012.

Petersen, Roger D., *Understanding Ethnic Violence: Fear, Hatred, and Resentment in Twentieth-Century Eastern Europe*. Cambridge: Cambridge University Press, 2002.

Petrini, Armando, '*Amleto' da Shakespeare a Laforgue per Carmelo Bene*. Pisa: Edizioni ETS, 2004.

Pieke, Frank N., *Knowing China: A Twenty-First Century Guide*. Cambridge: Cambridge University Press, 2016.

Plastow, Jane, 'Introduction', in Jane Plastow, ed., *Shakespeare in and out of Africa*. London: James Currey, 2013, pp. x–xiv.

Polsgrove, Carol, *Ending British Rule in Africa: Writers in a Common Cause*. Manchester and New York: Manchester University Press, 2009.

Pomeroy, Robin, 'Ahmadinejad Aide Urges More Women's Rights', *The Guardian*, 30 September (2010), p. 23.

Pope, Nicole, and Hugh Pope, *Turkey Unveiled: A History of Modern Turkey*. London and New York: Overlook Duckworth, 2011.

Powell, David E., 'Putin, Demography, Health, and the Environment', in Dale R. Herspring, ed., *Putin's Russia: Past Imperfect, Future Uncertain*, 2nd ed. Lanham and New York: Rowman and Littlefield, 2005, pp. 89–118.

Prescott, Paul, and Erin Sullivan, eds, *Shakespeare and the Global Stage: Performance and Festivity in the Olympic Year*. London and New York: Bloomsbury, 2015.

Presnyakov, Oleg and Vladimir, *Playing the Victim*, tr. Sasha Dugdale. London: Nick Hern Books, 2003.

'Prince of the Himalayas': A Sherwood Hu Film, publicity book. Los Angeles and Shanghai: Hus Entertainment/CineHyte Films, 2006.

Prince, Stephen, *The Warrior's Camera: The Cinema of Akira Kurosawa*. Princeton: Princeton University Press, 1999.

Quigly, Isabel, 'Drums Over Elsinore', *The Spectator*, 7162, 1 October (1965), pp. 410, 412.

Rajadhyaksha, Ashish, and Paul Willemen, *Encyclopaedia of Indian Cinema*, rev. ed. New Delhi: Oxford University Press, 1999.

Rauen, Margarida Gandara, 'Brazil', in Michael Dobson and Stanley Wells, eds, *The Oxford Companion to Shakespeare*. Oxford: Oxford University Press, 2001, p. 54.

Reis, João José, *Death Is a Festival: Funeral Rites and Rebellion in Nineteenth-Century Brazil*, tr. H. Sabrina Gledhill. Chapel Hill and London: University of North Carolina Press, 2003.

Reis, Moura, *Ozualdo Candeias: Pedrase Sonhos no Cineboca*. São Paulo: Coleção Aplauso, 2010.

Rena, *'Ithele Na Ginei Vasilias/He Wanted to Become King'*, *Variety*, 25 October (1967), n.p.

Resende, Aimara da Cunha, 'Introduction: Brazilian Appropriations of Shakespeare', in Aimara da Cunha Resende, ed., *Foreign Accents: Brazilian Readings of Shakespeare*. Newark: University of Delaware Press, 2002, pp. 11–41.

  'Shakespeare on the Screen: Brazilian Cinema and TV', *Actes des Congrès de la Société Française Shakespeare*, 33 (2015), pp. 2–13.

Richie, Donald, *The Inland Sea*. Berkeley: Stone Bridge, 2002.

Ringold, Dena, Mitchell A. Orenstein and Erika Wilkens, *Roma in an Expanding Europe: Breaking the Poverty Cycle*. Washington, D.C.: The World Bank, 2005.

Rinpoche, Sogyal, *The Tibetan Book of Living and Dying*, ed. Patrick Gaffney and Andrew Harvey. London and Sydney: Rider, 2008.

Rippin, Andrew, *Muslims: Their Religious Beliefs and Practices*, 3rd ed. London and New York: Routledge, 2005.

Robins, Kevin, and Asu Aksoy, 'Deep Nation: The National Question and Turkish Cinema Culture', in Mette Hjort and Scott Mackenzie, eds, *Cinema and Nation*. London and New York: Routledge, 2000, pp. 203–21.

Rohter, Larry, *Brazil on the Rise: The Story of a Country Transformed*. New York: Palgrave Macmillan, 2010.

Rollet, Brigitte, 'French Funding and Francophone Cinema', in Blandine Stefanson and Sheila Petty, eds, *Directory of World Cinema: Africa*. Bristol and Chicago: Intellect, 2014, pp. 36–38.

Rosefielde, Steven, and Stefan Hedlund, *Russia Since 1980: Wrestling with Westernization*. Cambridge: Cambridge University Press, 2009.

Rothschild, N. Harry, *Wu Zhao: China's Only Woman Emperor*. New York and London: Pearson/Longman, 2008.

Rothwell, Kenneth S., *A History of Shakespeare on Screen: A Century of Film and Television*, 2nd ed. Cambridge: Cambridge University Press, 2004.

Rowe, Eleanor, *Hamlet: A Window on Russia*. New York: New York University Press, 1976.

Royal Shakespeare Company: William Shakespeare, 'Hamlet', RSC Programme. Stratford-upon-Avon: RSC, 2016.

Russell, Ralph, *The Pursuit of Urdu Literature: A Select History*. London and New Jersey: Zed Books, 1992.

Sá, Daniel Serravalle de, 'Cinema Marginal', in Nátalia Pinazza and Louis Bayman, eds, *World Film Locations: São Paulo*. Bristol: Intellect, 2013, pp. 46–47.

Sadeghi, Fatemeh, 'The Green Movement: A Struggle against Islamist Patriarchy?', in Negin Nabavi, ed., *Iran: From Theocracy to the Green Movement*. New York: Palgrave, 2012, pp. 123–36.

Sadlier, Darlene J., *Brazil Imagined: 1500 to the Present*. Austin: University of Texas Press, 2008.

Safi, Michael, '"A Great First Step": Elation in India after Gay Sex Is Legalised', *The Guardian*, 7 September (2018), p. 27.

Salm, Steven J., and Toyin Falola, *Culture and Customs of Ghana*. Westport and London: Greenwood Press, 2002.

Sama, Emmanuel, 'African Films Are Foreigners in Their Own Countries', in Imruh Bakari and Mbye B. Cham, eds, *African Experiences of Cinema*. London: BFI, 1996, pp. 148–56.

Sanders, Julie, *Adaptation and Appropriation*, 2nd ed. London and New York: Routledge, 2016.

Sandon, Emma, Tom Rice and Peter Bloom, 'Changing the World: Sean Graham', *Journal of British Cinema and Television*, 10.3 (2013), pp. 524–36.

Sangharakshita, *Tibetan Buddhism: An Introduction*. Birmingham: Windhorse, 1999.

Sanura, Nives, *Immer Wieder 'Hamlet': Shakespeares Tragödie im Film – Immer Wieder Anders*. Trier: WVT, 2004.

Sarpong, Peter, *The Sacred Stools of the Akan*. Accra-Tema: Ghana Publishing Corporation, 1971.

Sayin, Gülşen, 'Shakespeare's Turkish Drama: A Cultural Transfer from *Hamlet* to *The Angel of Vengeance* (1976)', *Journal of Adaptation in Film and Performance*, 4.1 (2011), pp. 17–37.

Schandl, Veronika, 'History Interrupted: *Hamlet* and 1956 in Hungary', in Ruth J. Owen, ed., *The Hamlet Zone: Reworking 'Hamlet' for European Cultures*. Newcastle-upon-Tyne: Cambridge Scholars, 2012, pp. 105–14.

Schauert, Paul, *Staging Ghana: Artistry and Nationalism in State Dance Ensembles*. Bloomington and Indianapolis: Indiana University Press, 2015.

Schelling, Vivian, 'Popular Culture in Latin America', in John King, ed., *The Cambridge Companion to Modern Latin American Culture*. Cambridge: Cambridge University Press, 2004, pp. 171–201.

Seddon, Deborah, 'The Colonial Encounter and *The Comedy of Errors*: Solomon Plaatje's *Diphosho-phosho*', *The Shakespeare International Yearbook*, 9 (2009), pp. 66–86.

Seidl, Monika, '*Hamlet, the Sponge* and *Hamlet, the Angel of Vengeance*: About a Turkish Version of Hamlet', *Shakespeare Yearbook*, 13 (2002), pp. 401–18.

Semenenko, Aleksei, '"Adieu, Remember Me": The *Hamlet* Canon in Post-Soviet Russia', in Brian James Baer and Susanna Witt, eds, *Translation in Russian Contexts: Culture, Politics, Identity*. London and New York: Routledge, 2018, pp. 276–91.

'"No Text Is an Island": Translating *Hamlet* in Twenty-First Century Russia', in Brian James Baer, ed., *Contexts, Subtexts and Pretexts: Literary Translation in Eastern Europe and Russia*. Amsterdam and Philadelphia: John Benjamins, 2011, pp. 249–63.

Semenza, Greg Colón, 'Introduction', *Shakespeare Studies*, 38 (2010), pp. 19–25.

Senelick, Laurence, 'Theatre', in Nicholas Rzhevsky, ed., *The Cambridge Companion to Modern Russian Culture*, 2nd ed. Cambridge: Cambridge University Press, 2012, pp. 279–315.

'Severed Lives', *The Sunday Times Magazine*, 25 July (2010), pp. 42–3.

Seyed-Gohrab, Asghar, and Kamran Talattof, 'Politics and Persistence: The Development of Iranian Film', in Asghar Seyed-Gohrab and Kamran Talattof, eds, *Conflict and Development in Iranian Film*. Leiden: Leiden University Press, 2013, pp. 9–18.

Shakespeare, William, *Hamlet*, tr. Jean-Michel Déprats. Paris: Éditions Gallimard, 2002.

Hamlet, ed. Ann Thompson and Neil Taylor, revised edition. London and New York: Bloomsbury, 2016.

Sheppard, Philippa, *Devouring Time: Nostalgia in Contemporary Shakespearean Screen Adaptations*. Montreal and Kingston: McGill-Queen's University Press, 2017.

Shigetoshi, Kawatake, Yoshikawa Yoshio and Takekosi Kazuo, *Theatre in Japan*. Tokyo: Japanese National Commission for UNESCO, 1963.

Shingehiko, Hasumi, 'Samurai Loyalty: A Film Geneaology of Katô Tai', in Sadao Yamane and Hasumi Shingehiko, eds, *Midnight Surprise: Katô Tai*. Tokyo: The Japan Foundation, *c.* 1997, pp. 19–30.

Shillington, Kevin, *History of Africa*, 3rd ed. Basingstoke and New York: Palgrave, 2012.

Shurbanov, Alexander, and Boika Sokolova, 'From the Unlove of *Romeo and Juliet* to *Hamlet* without the Prince: A Shakespearean Mirror Held Up to the Fortunes of the New Bulgaria', in Michael Hattaway, Boika Sokolova and

Derek Roper, eds, *Shakespeare in the New Europe*. Sheffield: Sheffield Academic Press, 1994, pp. 24–53.

Silva, Marcel Vieira Barreto, *Adaptação Intercultural: O Caso de Shakespeare no Cinema Brasileiro*. Salvador: Edufba Compós, 2013.

Singh, Jyotsna G., *Colonial Narratives/Cultural Dialogues: 'Discoveries' of India in the Language of Colonialism*. London and New York: Routledge, 1996.

'Introduction', in Jyotsna G. Singh and David D. Kim, eds, *The Postcolonial World*. London and New York: Routledge, 2017, pp. 1–31.

Shakespeare and Postcolonial Theory. London and New York: Bloomsbury, 2019.

Skidmore, Thomas E., *Brazil: Five Centuries of Change*. New York and Oxford: Oxford University Press, 1999.

Skidmore, Thomas E., and Peter H. Smith, *Modern Latin America*, 6th ed. New York and Oxford: Oxford University Press, 2005.

Skura, Meredith Anne, *Shakespeare the Actor and the Purposes of Playing*. Chicago and London: University of Chicago Press, 1993.

Smidt, Kristian, 'The Discovery of Shakespeare in Scandinavia', in Dirk Delabastita and Lieven D'Hulst, eds, *European Shakespeares: Translating Shakespeare in the Romantic Age*. Amsterdam and Philadelphia: John Benjamins, 1993, pp. 91–104.

Smith, Bruce R., ed., *The Cambridge Guide to the Worlds of Shakespeare*, 2 vols. Cambridge: Cambridge University Press, 2016.

Smith, Ian, 'We Are Othello: Speaking of Race in Early Modern Studies', *Shakespeare Quarterly*, 67.1 (2016), pp. 104–24.

Smyth, Rosaleen, 'Images of Empire on Shifting Sands: The Colonial Film Unit in West Africa in the Post-War Period', in Lee Grieveson and Colin MacCabe, eds, *Film and the End of Empire*. London: BFI, 2011, pp. 155–76.

Sokolyansky, Mark, 'Grigori Kozintsev's *Hamlet* and *King Lear*', in Russell Jackson, ed., *The Cambridge Companion to Shakespeare on Film*, 2nd ed. Cambridge: Cambridge University Press, 2007, pp. 203–15.

'Russia', in Peter W. Marx, ed., *Hamlet-Handbuch: Stoffe, Aneignungen, Deutungen*. Stuttgart and Weimar: Verlag J. B. Meltzler, 2014, pp. 312–16.

Sorlin, Pierre, *Italian National Cinema*. London and New York: Routledge, 1996.

Stam, Robert, *Tropical Multiculturalism: A Comparative History of Race in Brazilian Cinema and Culture*. Durham and London: Duke University Press, 1997.

Stepan, Peter, *Spirits Speak: A Celebration of African Masks*. Munich, London and New York: Prestel, 2005.

Stone, James W., *Crossing Gender in Shakespeare: Feminist Psychoanalysis and the Difference Within*. New York and London: Routledge, 2010.

Stone, Norman, *Turkey: A Short History*. London: Thames & Hudson, 2011.

Stone, Rob, Paul Cooke, Stephanie Dennison and Alex Marlow-Mann, 'Introduction: The Longitude and Latitude of World Cinema', in Rob Stone, Paul Cooke, Stephanie Dennison and Alex Marlow-Mann, eds, *The Routledge Companion to World Cinema*. London and New York: Routledge, 2018, pp. 1–20.

Storm, Rachel, *Myths and Legends of India, Egypt, China and Japan*. Wigston: Anness, 2011.

Strangways, A. H. Fox, *The Music of Hindostan*. Oxford: Clarendon, 1914.

Stříbrný, Zdeněk, *Shakespeare and Eastern Europe*. Oxford: Oxford University Press, 2000.

Strukov, Vlad, *Contemporary Russian Cinema: Symbols of a New Era*. Edinburgh: Edinburgh University Press, 2016.

Sutherland-Addy, Esi, 'The Funeral as a Site for Choreographing Modern Identities in Contemporary Ghana', in Kwasi Konadu and Clifford C. Campbell, eds, *The Ghana Reader: History, Culture, Politics*. Durham and London: Duke University Press, 2016, pp. 428–33.

Tai, Katô, 'The Fundamentals of My Filmmaking', in Sadao Yamane and Hasumi Shingehiko, eds, *Midnight Surprise: Katô Tai*. Tokyo: The Japan Foundation, *c*. 1997, pp. 5–18.

Tai, Katô, Sadao Yamane and Yoshio Yasui, *Katô Tai, eiga o kataru*. Tokyo: Chikuma Shobo, 1994.

Tan, Tian Yuan, Paul Edmondson and Shih Pe Wang, eds, *1616: Shakespeare and Tang Xianzu's China*. London and New York: Bloomsbury, 2016.

Tapper, Richard, 'Introduction', in Richard Tapper, ed., *New Iranian Cinema: Politics, Representation and Identity*. London and New York: I. B. Taurus, 2002, pp. 1–25.

Tempera, Mariangela, '"Not to Be": Referencing the Rest of *Hamlet* on Screen', in Sarah Hatchuel and Nathalie Vienne-Guerrin, eds, *Shakespeare on Screen: 'Hamlet'*. Mont-Saint-Aignan: Publications de l'Université de Rouen et du Havre, 2011, pp. 345–68.

Ternavasio, Maurizio, *Macario: Vita di un Comico*. Turin: Lindau, 1998.

Thackway, Melissa, *Africa Shoots Back: Alternative Perspectives in Sub-Saharan Francophone African Film*. Bloomington and Indianapolis: Indiana University Press, 2003.

Thakur, Vikram Singh, 'Parsi Shakespeare: The Precursor to "Bollywood" Shakespeare', in Craig Dionne and Parmita Kapadia, eds, *Bollywood Shakespeares*. New York and Basingstoke: Palgrave, 2014, pp. 21–44.

Thomas, Alfred, *Shakespeare, Dissent and the Cold War*. Basingstoke and New York: Palgrave, 2014.

Thomas, Rosie, *Bombay Before Bollywood: Film City Fantasies*. New York: SUNY Press, 2013.

Thomson, C. Claire, *Thomas Vinterberg's 'Festen' ('The Celebration')*. Seattle: University of Washington Press, 2013.

Tipton, Elise K., *Modern Japan: A Social and Political History*, 2nd ed. London and New York: Routledge, 2008.

Trivedi, Poonam, 'Introduction', in Poonam Trivedi and Dennis Bartholomeusz, eds, *India's Shakespeare: Translation, Interpretation, and Performance*. Newark: University of Delaware Press, 2005, pp. 13–46.

Trivedi, Poonam, and Paromita Chakravarti, 'Shakespeare and Indian Cinemas: "Local Habitations"', in Poonam Trivedi and Paromita Chakravarti, eds,

Shakespeare and Indian Cinemas: 'Local Habitations'. London and New York: Routledge, 2018, pp. 1–19.

Ukadike, Nwachukwu Frank, *Black African Cinema*. Berkeley, Los Angeles and London: University of California Press, 1994.

Vakhlu, S. N., 'The Nightingale of Kashmir (Habba Khatoon: Her Life and Work)', in K. L. Kalla, ed., *The Literary Heritage of Kashmir*. Delhi: Mittal Publications, 1985, pp. 198–208.

Vālmīki, *The Rāmāyana*, ed. Arshia Sattar. New Delhi: Penguin, 1996.

Van Cutsen, Anne, and Mauro Magliani, *Powerful Headdresses: Africa/Asia*. Milan: 5 Continents Editions, 2010.

Vaughan, Virginia Mason, *Performing Blackness on English Stages, 1500–1800*. Cambridge: Cambridge University Press, 2005.

Venkiteswaran, C. S., 'Shakespeare in Malayalam Cinema: Cultural and Mythic Interface, Narrative Negotiations', in Poonam Trivedi and Paromita Chakravarti, eds, *Shakespeare and Indian Cinemas: 'Local Habitations'*. London and New York: Routledge, 2018, pp. 75–92.

Verma, Rajiva, '*Hamlet* on the Hindi Screen', *Hamlet Studies*, 24 (2002), pp. 81–93.

Viejo, Breixo, '*O Cangaceiro*', in Alberto Elena and Marina Díaz López, eds, *The Cinema of Latin America*. London and New York: Wallflower, 2003, pp. 63–69.

Votruba, Martin, '*Rosy Dreams*', in Adam Bingham, ed., *Directory of World Cinema: East Europe*. Bristol and Chicago: Intellect, 2011, pp. 77–79.

Waines, David, *An Introduction to Islam*, 2nd ed. Cambridge: Cambridge University Press, 2003.

Walsh, Brian, 'Resisting Hamlet: Revenge and Nonviolent Struggle in Vishal Bhardwaj's *Haider*', *Literature/Film Quarterly*, 46.2 (2018), pp. 1–8.

Warren, Nathan W., *Racial Revolutions: Antiracism and Indian Resurgence in Brazil*. Durham and London: Duke University Press, 2001.

Waugh, Thomas, '"I Sleep Behind You": Male Homosociality and Homoeroticism in Indian Parallel Cinema', in Ruth Vanita, ed., *Queering India: Same-Sex Love and Eroticism in Indian Culture and Society*. London and New York: Routledge, 2002, pp. 193–206.

Wells, Miriam, 'Brazil Persecutes Slave-era Cults', *The Sunday Times*, 7 September (2014), p. 28.

Wells, Stanley, 'Hamlet the Hoop', *Times Literary Supplement*, 7 February (2014), p. 6.

White, R. S., *Avant-Garde Hamlet: Text, Stage, Screen*. Madison and Teaneck: Fairleigh Dickinson University Press, 2015.

Wiens, Birgit, 'Hamlet and the Virtual Stage: Herbert Fritsch's Project, *hamlet_x*', in Freda Chapple and Chiel Kattenbelt, eds, *Intermediality in Theatre and Performance*. Amsterdam and New York: Rodopi, 2006, pp. 223–36.

Williams, Linda, *Playing the Race Card: Melodramas of Black and White from Uncle Tom to O. J. Simpson*. Princeton and Oxford: Princeton University Press, 2001.

Wilson-Lee, Edward, *Shakespeare in Swahililand*. London: HarperCollins, 2016.

Wright, Gordon, *France in Modern Times*, 5th ed. New York and London: Norton, 1995.

Wu, Hui, 'Three Hamlets, Two Gentlemen and One Time to Love: Shakespeare on the Chinese Screen', in Lawrence Raw, ed., *The Silk Road of Adaptation: Transformations from Across Disciplines and Cultures*. Newcastle-upon-Tyne: Cambridge Scholars, 2013, pp. 110–21.

Xavier, Ismail, *Allegories of Underdevelopment: Aesthetics and Politics in Modern Brazilian Cinema*. Minneapolis: University of Minnesota Press, 1997.

Xiangua, Wang, 'Shakespeare in China', in Jacob Sutton, ed., *Shakespeare and Friends*. London: Claude & Co., 2012, pp. 80–83.

Yamane, Sadao, 'Filmography of Katô Tai', in Sadao Yamane and Hasumi Shingehiko, eds, *Midnight Surprise: Katô Tai*. Tokyo: The Japan Foundation, *c.* 1997, pp. 58–79.

    'A Profile of Katô Tai', in Sadao Yamane and Hasumi Shingehiko, eds, *Midnight Surprise: Katô Tai*. Tokyo: The Japan Foundation, *c.* 1997, pp. 1–4.

Yang, Lingui, 'Shakespeare's Cultural Capital Made in China: From Pre-modern to Post-modern', *Shakespeare Yearbook*, 17 (2010), pp. 79–100.

Yang, Mayfair Mei-hui, 'From Gender Erasure to Gender Difference: State Feminism, Consumer Society, and Women's Public Sphere in China', in Mayfair Mei-hui Yang, ed., *Spaces of Their Own: Women's Public Sphere in Transnational China*. Minneapolis and London: University of Minnesota Press, 1999, pp. 35–67.

Yoshimoto, Mitsuhiro, *Kurosawa: Film Studies and Japanese Cinema*. Durham: Duke University Press, 2000.

Younge, Paschal Yao, *Music and Dance Traditions of Ghana: History, Performance and Teaching*. Jefferson and London: McFarland, 2011.

Yunhun, Luo, 'Queen Xiaowu', in Barbara Bennett Peterson, ed., *Notable Women of China: Shang Dynasty to the Early Twentieth Century*. London and New York: Routledge, 2000, pp. 63–65.

'Zafar', Bahadur Shah, *Selected Poems*, ed. Khwaja Tariq Mahmood. New Delhi: Star Publications, 2003.

Zak, William F., *Hamlet's Problematic Revenge: Forging a Royal Mandate*. Lanham and Boulder: Lexington Books, 2015.

Zarrilli, Phillip B., *When the Body Becomes All Eyes: Paradigms, Discourses and Practices of Power in Kalarippayattu, a South Indian Martial Art*. New Delhi: Oxford University Press, 1998.

Zaslavsky, Claudia, *Africa Counts: Number and Pattern in African Cultures*, 3rd ed. Chicago: Lawrence Hill Books, 1999.

Zeydabadi-Nejad, Saeed, 'Madness, Resistance and Iranian Cinema', in Karima Laachir and Saeed Talajooy, eds, *Resistance in Contemporary Middle Eastern Cultures: Literature, Cinema and Music*. London and New York: Routledge, 2013, pp. 184–203.

Zimmermann, Heiner O., 'Is Hamlet Germany? On the Political Reception of *Hamlet*', in Mark Thornton Burnett and John Manning, eds, *New Essays on 'Hamlet'*. New York: AMS, 1994, pp. 293–318.

Web Sources

Anil, Emel, 'Actress Breaks Male Barrier in Turkey by Becoming a Mayor', www.apnewsarchive.com (accessed 1 April 2014).

'*The Banquet*: About the Production', www.metrodomereleasing.com/films/banquet (accessed 12 May 2009).

Chandran, Suba, 'The First Suicide Bomb in Kashmir', *IPCS: Institute of Peace and Conflict Studies*, 11 May 2000, www.ipcs.org/focusthemsel (accessed 27 July 2018).

Dulai, Shaminder, 'Back in the Shadows: The Perils of Being LGBT in India', *Newsweek*, 29 December 2014, www.newsweek.com/india-gay-lgbt (accessed 20 July 2018).

Farzad, Narguess, 'The Essay: Shakespeare Around the Globe', BBC Radio 3, 15 May 2012, www.bbc.co.uk/programmes/b01hjprs (accessed 7 September 2018).

'Global Shakespeares', globalshakespeares.mit.edu (accessed 8 August 2018).

'Leprosy Elimination: World Health Organization Regional Office for Africa', www.afro.who.int (accessed 4 January 2017).

Rice, Tom, 'Gold Coast Film Unit', www.colonialfilm.org.uk (accessed 15 January 2017).

Index